Being Saved

Explorations in Human Salvation

Edited by
Marc Cortez
Joshua R. Farris
S. Mark Hamilton

scm press

© Marc Cortez, Joshua R. Farris and S. Mark Hamilton 2018

Published in 2018 by SCM Press
Editorial office
3rd Floor, Invicta House,
108–114 Golden Lane,
London EC1Y 0TG, UK
www.scmpress.co.uk

SCM Press is an imprint of Hymns Ancient & Modern Ltd
(a registered charity)

Hymns Ancient & Modern® is a registered trademark of
Hymns Ancient & Modern Ltd
13A Hellesdon Park Road, Norwich,
Norfolk NR6 5DR, UK

All rights reserved. No part of this publication may be reproduced,
stored in a retrieval system, or transmitted,
in any form or by any means, electronic, mechanical,
photocopying or otherwise, without the prior permission of
the publisher, SCM Press.

The Authors have asserted their right under the Copyright,
Designs and Patents Act 1988 to be identified as the Authors of this Work

British Library Cataloguing in Publication data

A catalogue record for this book is available
from the British Library

978 0 334 05495 5

Typeset by Manila Typesetting Company
Printed and bound by
CPI Group (UK) Ltd

From Marc Cortez to Jerome Wernow
From Joshua R. Farris to Gene Longo
From S. Mark Hamilton to Paul Helm

Contents

List of Contributors vii
Acknowledgements ix
Foreword by Michael Horton xi
Introduction: Being Saved – Explorations in Human Salvation xiii
    Marc Cortez, Joshua R. Farris and S. Mark Hamilton

Part 1 Sin, Evil and Salvation   1

1. Identity Through Time and Personal Salvation
   R. T. Mullins   3
2. Divine Hiddenness, the Soteriological Problem of Evil, and Berkeleyan Idealism
   Gregory E. Trickett and Tyler Taber   24
3. Retributivism Rejected: A Restorative Hope for Justice in the Age to Come
   Jonathan Rutledge   40
4. Original Sin in Abelard's Commentary on Romans
   Daniel W. Houck   54
5. Reparative Substitution and the 'Efficacy Objection': Toward a Modified Satisfaction Theory of Atonement
   Joshua R. Farris and S. Mark Hamilton   68

Part 2 The Nature of Salvation   83

6. Theosis and Participation
   Oliver D. Crisp   85
7. Ascension and Pentecost: A View from the Divine Missions
   Adonis Vidu   102
8. Saved by Degrees? Augustine's Ontological Pluralism
   Kate Kirkpatrick   124

9 Spirit, Selfhood and Salvation
   Myk Habets   143
10 Christian Doctrines of Humanity and Salvation Provide
   Theological Foundations for Virtue Epistemology
   Benjamin H. Arbour   157

Part 3 The Process of Salvation   173

11 The Doctrine of Predestination and a Modified Hylomorphic
   Theory of Human Souls
   Andrew Loke   175
12 The Priority of Justification to Sanctification
   John V. Fesko   185
13 Barth and Boethius on *Stellvertretung* and Personhood
   Adam Johnson   201
14 Being Christ: Salvation and Bonhoeffer's
   Christo-Ecclesiology
   W. Madison Grace II   218
15 Redeeming the Eucharist: Transignification
   and Justification
   James M. Arcadi   233
16 Regeneration and the Spirit
   Paul Helm   246

Part 4 The Body, the Mind and Salvation   263

17 Two Visions of Being Saved as Deiform Perfectibility
   Carl Mosser   265
18 Theological Musings on Mental Illness: Between Sin
   and Sanctification
   Hans Madueme   281
19 Saving Panpsychism: A Panpsychist Ontology
   and Christian Soteriology
   Joanna Leidenhag   303
20 The Body and the Beatific Vision
   Marc Cortez   326

Index of Names   344
Index of Subjects   353

Contributors

Benjamin H. Arbour is the executive director of the Institute for Philosophical and Theological Research.

James M. Arcadi is Assistant Professor of Biblical and Systematic Theology at Trinity Evangelical Divinity School in Deerfield, Illinois. Formerly he was a Postdoctoral Research Fellow (2015–18) in the Analytic Theology Project at Fuller Theological Seminary in Pasadena, California.

Marc Cortez is Professor of Theology at Wheaton College and Graduate School.

Oliver D. Crisp is Professor of Systematic Theology in the School of Theology, Fuller Theological Seminary in Pasadena, California, and professorial fellow of the Institute for Analytic and Exegetical Theology, University of St Andrews, Scotland.

Joshua R. Farris is Assistant Professor of Theology at Houston Baptist University.

John V. Fesko is Academic Dean and Professor of Systematic and Historical Theology at Westminster Seminary California.

W. Madison Grace II is Associate Professor of Baptist History and Theology at Southwestern Baptist Theological Seminary in Fort Worth, Texas.

Myk Habets is Professor of Theology, Director of Research, Dean of Faculty, and Head of Carey Graduate School, at Carey Baptist College, New Zealand.

CONTRIBUTORS

S. Mark Hamilton is PhD candidate, Dogmatic Theology, Free University of Amsterdam.

Paul Helm is Professor Emeritus of the History and Philosophy of Religion, King's College, London.

Michael Horton is the J. Gresham Machen Professor of Systematic Theology and Apologetics, Westminster Seminary California.

Daniel W. Houck is a Research Fellow at the Henry Center of Trinity International University.

Adam Johnson is Assistant Professor of Theology at Biola University.

Kate Kirkpatrick is Lecturer in Philosophy at the University of Hertfordshire and Lecturer in Theology at St Peter's College, University of Oxford.

Joanna Leidenhag is a PhD candidate at the University of Edinburgh.

Andrew Loke is Assistant Professor at Hong Kong Baptist University.

Hans Madueme is Associate Professor of Theological Studies at Covenant College in Lookout Mountain, Georgia.

Carl Mosser is Professor of Theology at Gateway Seminary.

R. T. Mullins is a postdoctoral fellow at the University of St. Andrews.

Jonathan Rutledge is a research postgraduate in St Mary's College of Divinity at the University of St Andrews.

Tyler Taber earned his PhD in Systematic Theology at the Free University of Amsterdam.

Gregory E. Trickett is Associate Professor of Philosophy at Weatherford College in Weatherford, TX.

Adonis Vidu is Professor of Theology at Gordon-Conwell Theological Seminary in South Hamilton, Massachusetts.

Acknowledgements

Hammering out the idea for this book in Mark Hamilton's family room, this project met with some early support from a variety of friends and colleagues to whom we owe a debt of gratitude, several of whom immediately and eagerly volunteered contributions. A similar debt of gratitude is owed to David Shervington and all those at SCM Press for their wholehearted support for this project. We also want to offer a special thanks to Michael Horton who kindly agreed to compose the Foreword to this volume, and to both Justin Zahraee and Joshua Steele for preparing the indices and carefully reading many of the contributions. Our families were, as ever, a wonderful source of support from the very start of this project to its consummation. Finally, thank you to all the contributors for giving us your latest and best work. It is our hope that this volume will add fuel to the fires of future systematic theological inquiry, and it is to such individuals that we dedicate this volume.

Marc Cortez, Joshua R. Farris and S. Mark Hamilton
Ad maiorem dei gloriam.
New Year 2018

Foreword

MICHAEL HORTON

'Are you saved?' Among the contributors to this volume, I am not alone in my childhood experience of hearing adults ask that question. The verb itself gets us off on the right foot in this collection: in spite of considerable diversity of theological conviction, everyone seems to agree that what is involved is the *redeeming* and *saving* of creation by the Creator. As far as I can tell, no one harbours Gnostic sympathies, cherishing flights of fancy from the world of space and time in order to be deposited like a drop of water in the great ocean of being. 'Being saved' is just that: God's mission of recovering what was lost and bringing the work of the Father, in the Son and by the Spirit, into the consummated kingdom of Sabbath joy.

From this common conviction, paths diverge. Indeed, I expected there to be a closer kinship of perspective in this volume. Yet, it turns out, the diversity is one of this volume's strengths.

First, rather than follow a tight script from the editor's hands, authors were selected based on their expertise and significant contributions on the point that they defend here. Consequently, readers are rewarded by not having to wade through first thoughts, but are introduced to intriguing proposals by specialists who have given considerable thought to their subject matter. Each chapter offers a window into the very best of contemporary discussions in the various fields represented. Once upon a time, theologians were also mathematicians, natural philosophers (i.e. scientists), philologists and often even astronomers. In contrast, academic fields of all kinds are split up into myriad guilds. Rather than hope to return to a period of well-informed generalists, perhaps the best approach for us now is the interdisciplinary conversation typified in this volume.

Second, the diversity allows *readers* to catch up to speed on areas of particular interest that lie outside the scope of our own expertise. If, unfortunately, the guilds of systematic theology and biblical studies are often ships passing in the night, philosophy of religion is more like a space shuttle orbiting miles above the rest of us. So people like me are tutored in the intersection of time and theodicy as well as discussions of panpsychism in relation to theosis. Meanwhile, Christian philosophers are drawn outside their comfort zone to encounter terms like *ordo salutis* whose time-honoured use by philosophically adept thinkers demands more than a shrug. If the authors get a lot out of this interdisciplinary conversation, then readers should as well.

Third, *Being Saved* is distinguished by its international diversity. In recent decades there have been illuminating treatments of doctrine from non-Western perspectives. Yet, it seems to me, attempts at 'An African Theology of X' or 'Asian Theology of Y' typically fail on several counts. Often, 'global theologies' are driven by Western (even Anglo-American) interests and theological trends. Even 'theologies of liberation', tailored to specific contexts, betray their dependence on Western theologians. Further, it is as difficult to imagine a Korean theologian representing 'Asian' theology any more than I, despite my fondest dreams, could represent 'North American' theology. Perhaps most importantly, such an approach risks substituting syncretistic religious studies for a genuinely catholic (global Christian) theological enterprise.

There are decent surveys of contemporary theology covering particular loci, as well as technical and highly specialized monographs and chapters on the relevant issues. But what distinguishes this volume is its diverse forays into questions that cut across the various loci of soteriology from an equally diverse set of concerns and specializations.

The chapters here are too diverse to allow agreement with everything. At the same time, every chapter provokes serious reflection on a familiar theme from various angles. Whatever one's conclusions, the reader will come away with a greater appreciation for the significance and complexity of what Christians mean by 'being saved'.

Introduction:

Being Saved – Explorations in Human Salvation

MARC CORTEZ, JOSHUA R. FARRIS
AND S. MARK HAMILTON

There is a growing interest in theological anthropology at the intersection of philosophy and systematic theology. Many recent works have offered theologically thoughtful treatments of the human person from a philosophical perspective, some ranging broadly over the entirety of theological anthropology, and others focusing more specifically on particular anthropological issues. To date, though, few works have tried to marry the findings of these theological and philosophical discussions with the doctrine of salvation. *Being Saved: Explorations in Human Salvation* attempts to fill the lacuna between human ontology and soteriology in a way that reflects the fruits of these philosophical and theological developments. This collection of chapters facilitates an increased interdisciplinary dialogue that brings various dogmatic subcategories in the doctrine of Salvation – e.g. Divine Decrees, Regeneration, Faith, Justification, Sanctification, Union with Christ, Resurrection, Satisfaction, and Glorification – into conversation with contemporary philosophical discussions of the nature of human persons.

On the one hand, these chapters emphasize the importance of maintaining the link between theological anthropology and soteriology. Historically speaking, theologians have always maintained that we can only understand who and what human persons are in light of how they are saved in and through the work of the triune God. On the other hand, we cannot comprehend the nature of salvation independently of our beliefs about the nature of those creatures God seeks to save. The relationship between anthropology and soteriology has been so tightly joined historically that earlier theological works often did not treat theological anthropology as a discrete doctrine. With the modern era, however, we see an increased emphasis on anthropology as its own field of study, leading to an increased tendency, even among Christian theologians, to study human persons in relative independence from soteriological considerations. Although the chapters in this volume often evidence a desire to understand the human person in dialogue with modern philosophical developments, they actually bear witness to an older theological intuition that insists on the inseparability of anthropology and soteriology in systematic theology.

That we understand our anthropology in this way seems particularly important in light of our contemporary cultural climate, characterized as it is by intellectual disintegration and growing fragmentation. Clear, cogent, holistic, and synthetic thinking is needed for communicating the Christian message. The task of theologians is an important part of the task of communicating Divine truth in every age. In our opinion, theological thinking is not complete until we have, at a minimum, forged a link between the doctrinal location of the topic at hand to a wider doctrinal frame of reference. The success of the systematician's task is reflected in the ongoing attempt to clarify doctrine and organize it in our cultural context and historical period, in order that we might effectively carry on the message of what we believe as a message of hope for modern times. And it is along two conversational or dialogical axes that this message unfolds.

The first axis of the dialogue represented by these chapters is an intramural conversation between the various loci of systematic theology, specifically those focused more on anthropological and soteriological issues. The second axis of the conversation operates in a more interdisciplinary mode, utilizing various philosophical resources for engaging theological issues. Here again we are confronted with the intuitive link between the who and what of anthropology and the how of salvation, this time drawing more intentionally on the many ways that philosophical discussions might shed light on all three of these questions. For example, philosophical discussions regarding the nature of human constitution (e.g. the issues surrounding the relationship of body and soul) affect our understanding of the role the body might play in salvation both now and in the eschaton. Similarly, discussions of divine and human action as they relate to the process of salvation are inevitably shaped by philosophical considerations regarding things like agency, action, causality and freedom. Or we might consider the many issues involved in the doctrine of sin, including debates about personal identity, corporate liability, the transferability of guilt, and so on. All of these are areas that have received considerable attention in the philosophical literature, generating areas of potentially fruitful dialogue for systematic theologians today.

In what follows, we have attempted to exemplify both axes of this dialogue in a set of chapters that address a range of soteriological and anthropological issues through engagement with a variety of philosophical resources.

Although united in their commitment to explore both the intramural and interdisciplinary axes described above, the chapters in this volume represent a diverse group of thinkers. Perhaps the most obvious manifestation of this diversity lies in the methodological differences represented by each chapter.

Some leverage more philosophy than theology; others, more theology than philosophy. Although each offers some kind of constructive engagement with its source material, some chapters prioritize the expository work of retrieval through extended dialogue with some aspect of the Christian tradition. Others offer a more systematic approach to a particular set of issues. Some chapters deal in large part with the Christian Scriptures; others focus more on dogmatics. A number of these chapters manifest the attributes commonly associated with the analytic philosophical tradition, particularly the emphasis on logical argumentation and terminological precision. Others operate with a clear commitment to clarity but without any obvious dependence on such analytic modes of discourse.

Avoiding a homogenous approach to this multi-levelled discussion is a conscious editorial choice; one that we think provides readers with a critical resource that will undoubtedly invigorate some much-needed discussion about the intersection of Christian theology and philosophy. Organized according to a traditional, dogmatic theological categorization of Christian soteriology, *Being Saved: Explorations in Human Salvation* examines key structures of the doctrine of salvation in light of diverse metaphysical commitments about human persons for the purpose of theological exploration and dogmatic construction.

Sin, Evil and Salvation

The first set of chapters in the volume focuses on questions related to sin and evil. Christian theologians have long reflected on the nature of salvation in light of the fundamental problems from which the world needs to be saved. Consequently, the four chapters in this part delve into some of the challenging issues that arise from any attempt to understand salvation in the context of a world shaped so pervasively by sin and evil.

Ryan Mullins begins this discussion by arguing that we should understand salvation in the context of the defeat of evil and the hope of resurrection, both of which require us to reflect on the ontological status of past events – often shaped by sin, evil and suffering – in the eschatological state. Mullins thus makes a soteriological argument in favour of a presentist account of temporal persistence. On his so-called 'minimalist criterion' for what the work of Christ's actually amounts to and accomplishes for the believer – deliverance from evil, alleviation of suffering and full (physical and spiritual) healing – Mullins recommends that Christians adopt an understanding of the nature of time and their place in it which says that the only things that exist are those that exist right now, in the present (hence, presentism). While arguing in favour of this, Mullins also argues against the so-called eternalist position, (roughly) according to which all moments of time (past, present and future moments) exist in some real sense.

Greg Trickett and Tyler Taber take on the difficult questions raised by God's apparent 'hiddenness' in the midst of pain and suffering, focusing more specifically on a soteriological form of that argument: the fact that divine hiddenness seems to be a contributing factor in why so many fail to respond to the gospel. If God was more obvious, it would seem reasonable to think that more might be saved. To respond to this worry, Trickett and Taber provocatively draw on the idealist ontology of George Berkeley to contend that the metaphysical assumption that all physical things are Divine communications to human minds eliminates the problem of Divine hiddenness.

Moving away from questions focused primarily on evil and suffering, Jonathan Rutledge engages the question of the relationship between retribution and salvation. According to Rutledge, we should reject any strong version of retributive logic in which God must punish all sin. Arguing against both philosophical and biblical arguments for strong retributivism, Rutledge contends that we have no good reasons for thinking that retribution is the primary motivation behind divine acts of judgement, suggesting instead that we focus more on the restoration motifs he finds in the biblical texts.

Continuing this discussion of the relationship between sin and punishment, Daniel Houck's chapter focuses more specifically on original sin as a key problem that must be addressed by any adequate account of salvation. Noting the increasing popularity of accounts that seek to differentiate sin as 'punishment' (or maybe consequence) from sin as 'guilt' in their understanding of original sin, Houck contends that such accounts would benefit from examining the resources offered and challenges faced by an early form of that argument, one offered by Peter Abelard. After summarizing Abelard's argument in its historical context, Houck traces three key worries raised by such an approach, noting some of the difficult challenges that continue to face any such account of original sin and guilt.

Joshua Farris and Mark Hamilton touch on the issues of sin, evil and salvation in their chapter on Reparative Substitution and the efficacy objection, which they argue is a modified and updated version of Anselmian satisfaction. The penal substitution model of atonement in particular has precipitated a great deal of recent interest, being held up by many Protestants as 'the' doctrine of atonement. In this chapter, the authors make a defence against a common objection to the Anselmian model of atonement that is often levelled against it by exponents of the penal substitution model, namely that Christ's work does not accomplish anything for those whom it appears he undertakes his atoning work, but merely makes provision for salvation.

INTRODUCTION

The Nature of Salvation

With the second set of chapters, we turn our attention to understanding the nature of salvation itself. The chapters in this part focus on discussing larger questions about how we should understand salvation and/or providing theological frameworks within which we should think about the relationship between ontology and salvation.

Oliver Crisp begins this discussion by peeling back several layers of the debate surrounding the doctrine of theosis and its relationship to that ever illusive and presently popular notion of human participation in the divine nature. Taking up one version of the doctrine – one that he reckons to be synonymous with Eastern depictions of divinization that stop short of effacing the humanity of individual persons and thereby retaining the creator/creature distinction – Crisp's chapter issues some much-needed clarity about several developments to the doctrine of theosis in contemporary theological literature. Taking a cue from Thomas Flint and thereby a constructive step toward a more detailed model that reflects this clarity, Crisp offers several thought-provoking insights into Flint's suggestion that humanity is somehow taken up or absorbed into the divine nature via the hypostatic union of the God-man.

Adonis Vidu argues that the events of Ascension and Pentecost provide a necessary theological framework within which we must understand the nature of salvation. Vidu explores the logical relationship of Christ's ascension with the Spirit's appearance at Pentecost in light of the divine missions. Working from the Apostolic record of Christ's declaration that 'if I do not go away, the Helper will not come to you' (John 16.7), Vidu sets up the constructive segment of his argument in two parts. He offers up an exposition of Augustine and Aquinas' account of divine processions and relations of origin, which he then puts into conversation with the findings of contemporary Catholic (Dominican) theologian, Edward Schillebeeckx, and Protestant theologian, Kathryn Tanner. He closes with a medley of thought-provoking soteriological reflections that are keyed to matters related to human participation.

Kate Kirkpatrick's chapter takes up the question of whether we should understand salvation as the kind of thing that can happen by degrees, an idea that has long been viewed with suspicion by Protestant theologians. To explore this idea, Kirkpatrick takes us into the soteriological implications of Augustine's notion of being and non-being. Offering a close reading and exposition of several key primary texts, Kirkpatrick contends that Augustine's theology offers important resources for understanding a degreed account of salvation today.

Continuing the emphasis on the importance of pneumatology for understanding soteriology, the chapter by Myk Habets explores the resources that a 'Third Article Theology' offers for thinking about the nature of salvation. Habets argues for the necessity of reading Scripture as a coherent story that moves from *protos* to *telos*, with the Spirit playing a pivotal role in the outworking of this story. This then provides the framework for understanding salvation as the 'theopoetic transformation' of human persons that must be viewed as comprising a holistic duality of body and soul.

Working within the virtue ethics and epistemology literature, Benjamin Arbour presents a case for moving beyond several standard treatments. He argues that, within a weak foundationalism, thereby rejecting Cartesianism, we can and ought to ground our understanding of virtue epistemology in theology. For Arbour, it is the *imago Dei* that provides fertile soil enough to root and fruitfully extend the discussion on virtue epistemology. In this way, the present chapter touches on that aspect of salvation that consists of our ongoing salvation. Theologians call this the doctrine of sanctification, which is a process of transformation from corruption to holiness.

The Process of Salvation

The heading of the third part of this volume is intended to capture the sense that these chapters shift from thinking broadly about the nature of salvation as a whole to considering specific aspects of the outworking of salvation. These chapters thus involve discussions of the atonement, predestination, justification, regeneration and sanctification, among others.

With Andrew Loke's chapter, we turn our attention to the relationship between predestination and human freedom in our view of salvation. According to Loke, we face two significant difficulties when trying to affirm both predestination and human freedom. First, Loke addresses whether it is even possible to maintain the compatibility of two such apparently contrary ideas, drawing on the Middle Knowledge account developed by Luis de Molina to demonstrate one way in which we might maintain the coherence of affirming both ideas. Second, Loke deals with the classic debate regarding the origin of the soul, focusing on the worry that both Traducianism and Creationism view the person's destiny as determined by events that are 'external' to the person and consequently undermine that person's freedom. Instead, Loke argues for a modified hylomorphic view that, when combined with the molinism of the prior section, offers a way of resolving this difficulty. John Fesko's chapter turns our attention to the relationship between justification and sanctification. Fesko defends the idea that the holiness of the saints requires the corporate accomplishment and individual application of Christ's judicial work. With one eye on the doctrine of union with Christ and by the lights of such Reformation symbols as the Westminster Shorter

Catechism, Fesko makes a strong biblical case for his assertion that 'justification is the determining condition for sanctification'.

Since the atonement unquestionably stands as a central element of most Christian views of salvation, this part includes Adam Johnson's discussion of the atonement in dialogue with Karl Barth and Boethius on the nature of human personhood. Moving from Barth's understanding of Christ's saving work – particularly the implications of both the substitutionary and representative motifs – to the implications that this account of soteriology has for how we view the human person, Johnson contends that we must understand humanity teleologically as having its true identity 'in Christ'.

Arguably the most historical chapter in this collection, Madison Grace's 'Being Christ: Salvation and Bonhoeffer's Christo-Ecclesiology' resources Bonhoeffer's social ontology and brings Bonhoeffer into the contemporary discussions in constructive systematic theology. Like Bonhoeffer's contemporary, Karl Barth, Bonhoeffer's works are a trove of philosophical and theological ideas. Unlike Barth, whose works have been the source of much debate, much of Bonhoeffer's work remains untouched by contemporary theologians. Grace recommends Bonhoeffer's ecclesiology as a vehicle into other doctrinal topics, namely questions about union with Christ, the nature of the Church, society and the sacraments. Being an unlikely candidate, systematic theologians would be wise to engage more carefully and consciously with Bonhoeffer.

Staying on theme of justification, James Arcadi explores the connection between a particular way of understanding the Eucharist and the event of justification. Drawing on the theology of Edward Schillebeeckx and recent analytic discussions, Arcadi argues for a 'social ontology' in which the ontology of an object is shaped by what humans deem them to be. Applied to the Eucharist, this means that the elements actually become the body and blood of Christ because that is what they have been deemed to be by the minister through the power of the Spirit. Arcadi then contends that we can similarly view justification as an event in which God deems a human person to be righteous, explaining the implications that such an account would have for both Catholic and Protestant views.

Paul Helm examines the nature of the Spirit's activity in the soteriological work of Regeneration. Canvassing the Reformed scholastic development of this doctrine – with the Thomistically seasoned theology of Stephen Charnock as his principal interlocutor – Helm launches into a constructive exposition of Jonathan Edwards' Lockean-influenced account of regeneration. According to Helm, Charnock's account of the Spirit's work in regeneration sets Edwards' account in relief at a variety of formal and material points from the scholastic tradition. Aside from a clarification of Edwards' doctrine of regeneration, the result of Helm's work, among other things, is in it distinguishing Edwards from the more well-worn paths trodden by his scholastic forebears and its provoking a variety of questions for which readers will pause to consider their own doctrine.

The Body, the Mind and Salvation

Carl Mosser extends the discussion on the nature of salvation by applying it specifically to the perfectibility of human nature. What does it mean for a human to be 'perfect' and to what extent should we utilize technological resources to transform human persons? Mosser thus enters into a conversation with two perspectives on the perfectibility of humanity: transhumanism and deification, raising significant questions about the viability of the former for offering an adequate framework within which we can develop a theologically satisfying account of personal transformation.

No account of sanctification can ignore the difficult questions raised by mental disorders and the extent to which we should understand such disorders under the label 'sin'. Hans Madueme's chapter tackles this difficult topic, addressing the polarity represented by 'mental illness maximizers' who view mental illnesses primarily as expressions of underlying biological or physical disorders and 'sin maximizers', who view mental illnesses primarily through the categories of agency and disobedience. Behind both perspectives lie certain assumptions about the mind–body relationship and the extent to which this shapes personal agency and responsibility. Working within this tension, Madueme argues for a mediating approach in which we must affirm the insights of both psychology and theology, recognizing the interdependence of mind and body without undermining the reality of sin and personal agency.

Theologians have long recognized the import of the mind–body debate for understanding salvation. Yet this debate typically revolves around physicalist and dualist perspectives, with various forms of idealism making the occasional appearance. Without rejecting these as options, Joanna Leidenhag's chapter invites us to consider panpsychism as a viable alternative. Panpsychism is (roughly) the idea that mentality is a fundamental property of the universe such that all particular, even non-human particulars, possess some degree of consciousness. After summarizing the basic elements of panpsychism, Leidenhag discusses the implications such a view would have for soteriology, contending that panpsychism offers a viable way of understanding salvation that should be explored more thoroughly today.

In our final chapter, Marc Cortez discusses the significance of embodiment for the beatific vision, often viewed as the ultimate end of human salvation.

INTRODUCTION

Cortez addresses the argument that traditional views of the beatific vision, commonly represented by Thomas Aquinas, undermine the significance of the human body and that we should instead affirm the more embodied account of the beatific vision presented by Jonathan Edwards. After summarizing both accounts, Cortez argues instead that both views struggle to explain the eschatological significance of the human body and that we need to explore other avenues for conceiving the relationship between beatific vision and physical resurrection.

PART I

Sin, Evil and Salvation

I

Identity Through Time and Personal Salvation

R. T. MULLINS

After reading other chapters in this book, one will naturally come to the opinion that the Christian understanding of salvation is complex and multifaceted. In this chapter I shall narrow my focus to two facets of Christian salvation: the defeat of evil and the proleptic hope of resurrection. The first facet is with regards to a future salvation that awaits fulfilment. The second facet focuses on the present salvific and life-transforming work of the Holy Spirit that comes with the hope of this future salvation.

It is my contention that human persons need salvation from evil and death. Part of the Christian story of salvation is that God shall ultimately defeat evil and bring about eschatological healing. Christianity claims that one day redeemed human persons will be saved from death by being resurrected to everlasting life. These individuals shall be healed by God and placed in everlasting community with God and the rest of the redeemed. These facets of Christian salvation are intended to fill believers with hope towards the future and shape the way that believers conduct their daily lives. However, this hope might be unfounded if certain theories of time are true.

In this chapter, I shall introduce readers to basic issues with regards to personal identity through time, and its relevance for understanding our future salvation from evil, and the hope that is supposed to spring from this. Section 1 of this chapter will introduce readers to basic theories in the ontology of time, and the corresponding theories of persistence through time. Section 2 will briefly note some reasons why Christians adopt certain theories on time called four-dimensionalism and eternalism. In section 3, I will then lay out my own theological and philosophical beliefs on the nature of time. Sections 4 and 5 will examine the problems that arise when four-dimensional eternalism is combined with Christian belief. Ultimately, I will argue that Christians ought not to be four-dimensional eternalists because it undermines Christian hope in salvation from evil.

R. T. MULLINS

1 The Ontology of Time and Persistence Through Time

Presentism and *eternalism* are theories about the ontology of time, or about what moments of time exist. Each is typically linked with a theory of change and persistence through time. Presentism is usually held alongside *endurantism*, whereas eternalism typically holds some version of *four-dimensionalism*. Allow me to elaborate.

Presentism is the thesis that only the present, the now, exists. The past no longer exists and the future does not yet exist.[1] Time involves temporal becoming, or absolute generation, as well as real passage from one moment to the next. New things that did not formerly exist come into existence, and other things pass out of existence or cease to exist.[2] For the presentist, it simply is the case that the only objects that exist are the ones that presently exist. As Trenton Merricks says of presentism, 'an object has only those properties it has at the present time. The difference between past, present and future is metaphysical, not perspectival.'[3]

On presentism, an object *endures* through time. To say that an object endures through time is to say that an object is wholly present at each moment of its existence. Numerically one and the same object exists at each time that it exists, and it does not have parts at other times. On presentism and endurantism, objects undergo change by gaining and losing accidental properties over time. Let us say that some object O begins to exist at time t_1 and persists all the way through to time t_3. On this account, O exists entirely at each instant of time. Given presentism, as t_2 comes into existence t_1 ceases to exist and t_3 does not yet exist. So O exists entirely at each instant only when that instant is the present. As O endures through time it will gain and lose various accidental, or non-essential, properties. Let us say that O is an armchair. At t_1 the armchair is blue, and then at t_2 someone paints the armchair such that at t_3 the armchair is red. The armchair has retained all of its essential properties, but it has lost one accidental property – that of being blue – and gained a new accidental property – that of being red.

Eternalism will disagree with the presentist in several respects. On eternalism, all moments of time have equal ontological existence. To put it roughly, the past, present and future all exist – they are all equally real. To put it more technically, there is no real distinction between past, present and future. There is just the four-dimensional space-time manifold with no privileged moment that marks the present.[4] On this account there is no real passage of time, or temporal becoming, because all moments of time exist. Nothing ever comes into existence nor ceases to exist because everything simply does exist in the space-time manifold. As such, the experience of temporal passage is illusory.

On eternalism, the world is composed of time slices. Time slices are merely instants of time that can stand in earlier than and later than relations to other instants. The eternalist holds that all time slices simply exist in the space-time manifold. None ever come into nor pass out of existence. They are much like points on a map. In fact, most eternalists see a close connection between being located in space and being located at a time, whereas presentists reject the similarity between being located in space and located at a time.[5]

Recall that presentists hold that objects endure through time. On endurantism, objects persist over time by being wholly present at every moment at which they exist. There is numerically one object that persists from moment to moment. Eternalists typically disagree with presentists on how objects persist by rejecting endurantism. Thinkers who hold to eternalism typically hold to four-dimensionalism, which is the doctrine of temporal parts.[6] Instead of numerically one object persisting through time, four-dimensionalism says that objects are spread out over time by having different temporal parts located at each time. Four-dimensionalists will often invoke a spatial analogy to help people understand the claim that is being made here. Objects have spatial parts that are extended throughout the three dimensions of space. For instance, my body is currently spread throughout a particular region of space. I have parts at different points in this spatial region. My feet are on the ground, my hands are on my desk, and so on. In a similar way, the four-dimensionalist says that objects have temporal parts that are extended throughout time, or the fourth dimension.[7]

On four-dimensionalism the entire world is a collection of numerically distinct temporal parts that exist at each instant of time.[8] When thinking about how reality hangs together, four-dimensionalists commonly affirm two important metaphysical commitments that are worthy of our attention. These are metaphysical commitments that presentists and endurantists typically reject. The first four-dimensional commitment is *metaphysical universalism*. The metaphysical doctrine of universalism is the view that any collection of objects whatsoever has a sum, an object they compose. This is sometimes called an unrestricted mereology. 'Any combination of temporal parts of any objects from any times, no matter how scattered and disparate, composes an object.'[9] It could be possible for a four-dimensionalist to reject this metaphysical doctrine, though that will depend on other metaphysical and theological commitments she holds. For instance, she might adopt metaphysical universalism because she takes objects like bicycles and persons to be mere conventions.[10] However, being a conventionalist about persons sounds much closer to Buddhist metaphysics than Christian metaphysics.[11]

Another metaphysical commitment that four-dimensionalists typically hold, and that presentists typically reject, is *Humean supervenience*. Katherine

Hawley describes this as the view that 'facts about which intrinsic properties are instantiated at which points determine all the facts there are. There are no irreducibly holistic facts. In conjunction with four-dimensionalism, this entails that all the facts about a given persisting object supervene upon intrinsic facts about its briefest temporal parts.'[12] Again, a four-dimensionalist may reject this depending on her other metaphysical and theological commitments. What Christian thinkers must do, however, is make it clear which aspects of four-dimensionalism they wish to accept or reject if they wish to use four-dimensionalism in the defence and development of Christian doctrine. So far, this task has not been thoroughly undertaken.

Personal Persistence Through Time

In this chapter, I am not merely concerned with how objects persist over time. I am concerned with how persons persist over time. So I need to clear up a few issues with regards to personal persistence through time. In considering the matter of personal persistence, one needs to know how to answer the following question: what makes a person at one time the same person as an individual at some later time?

To illustrate this point, imagine that we ask Tony Bennett to sing 'I Left My Heart in San Francisco'. If you are unfamiliar with this song, I suggest that you go and listen to it now. It is alright, I can wait. The song lasts for 2 minutes and 46 seconds. This book will still be here once you are done listening. Now that you are back, ask yourself this: What makes the Tony Bennett at the beginning of the song the same person as the Tony Bennett at the end of the song?

There are several ways to answer this question. The endurantist will say that Tony Bennett is entirely present throughout the 2 minutes and 46 seconds of his performance. There is numerically only one thing, Tony Bennett, who endures through the song. One might find this unsatisfying, and continue to ask what *makes* the Tony at the beginning of the song the same Tony as the one at the end of the song. The endurantist will say that nothing makes them the same Tony. This is because the endurantist affirms something called the simple theory of personal identity. On the simple view, there are no non-trivial or non-circular conditions for personal identity over time. This is because personal identity is a primitive notion that is not subject to a deeper analysis.[13] The numerically one person that is Tony Bennett simply is identical to himself.

The four-dimensionalist will see things differently. For each second of the song there is a temporal part, or person stage, called Tony Bennett. The four-dimensionalist will say that each person stage is a Tony Bennett. There is the Tony Bennett that exists at t_1 and another Tony Bennett that exists at t_2, and so on. Yet one will ask how these Tony stages are the same person. The four-dimensionalist has a complicated story to tell here in order to answer this question. This is because the four-dimensionalist rejects the simple view of personal identity because she rejects numerical identity over time. Instead, she must adopt some version of the complex view of personal identity over time. On the complex view, there are substantive conditions for personal identity over time. The complex view says that personal identity can be explained in non-personal or sub-personal terms. What the complex theorist says is 'that a person persists over time is nothing more than some other facts which are generally spelled out in either biological or psychological terms, or both'.[14]

Recall that the four-dimensionalist holds to metaphysical universalism – any temporal parts whatsoever can compose an object. This creates a very large number of bizarre objects, but that need not concern us at this time. Since the four-dimensionalist has rejected numerical identity over time, she will try to identify a continuity relation that connects certain temporal parts together in order to talk about personal persistence through time. This is sometimes referred to as the gen-identity relation in order to emphasize the fact that this is not numerical identity.[15] As alluded to earlier, two sorts of continuity relations that a four-dimensionalist might appeal to are either biological or psychological. I shall focus on the psychological approach since it is the most popular.

On the psychological approach, what makes one person stage continuous with his later temporal counterpart is the fact that he is psychologically continuous with his later temporal counterpart. In other words, the two numerically distinct person stages share enough of the same psychology (memory, character traits, etc.) to count as the same person. Not just any kind of psychological continuity will do the trick. There has to be what is called an immanent causal relation that connects the person stages. An immanent causal relation obtains when one person stage causes a temporal counterpart at the next instant in time to have the relevant psychological states.[16] This immanent causal relation rejects any sort of gap in time between distinct person stages in order to secure a tight personal continuity relation. The Tony stage at the beginning of 'I Left My Heart in San Francisco' is the same person as the Tony stage at the end of the song because they are psychologically continuous with one another. Further, there is an immanent causal relation between the different Tony stages. The Tony stage at the beginning of the song passes on his psychological states to the Tony stage at the next instant. This Tony stage passes on his psychological states to the Tony stage at the instant after that, who in turn passes on his psychological stages to the next Tony stage, and so on until we reach the Tony stage at the end of the song. Thus, according to the four-dimensionalist, making the Tony temporal counterparts the same Tony.

2 Why Might a Christian Hold Four-Dimensionalism and Eternalism?

Contemporary Christian philosophers and theologians have adopted four-dimensionalism and eternalism for various reasons. In this section I shall briefly note several of the most prominent reasons offered in favour of four-dimensional eternalism.

First, some are motived by scientific concerns. Four-dimensionalism and eternalism are often said to be derived from certain interpretations of the special theory of relativity. Why? One reason for thinking this is because there is nothing within the special theory of relativity that allows us to pick out a preferred reference frame for the cosmic present.[17] In other words, nothing within the standard interpretations of the special theory of relativity helps us identify the present moment of time. Presentists disagree that the special theory of relativity entails four-dimensional eternalism.[18] I shall not bore readers with the details of this debate here. I shall simply note that it is a matter of contemporary dispute as to what, if any, particular ontology of time is entailed by contemporary science.[19]

I should also note that I find it somewhat implausible that one should deny the existence of a preferred reference frame simply because current relativity theory cannot pick it out. On the older Galilean understanding of space-time, one could pick out a preferred temporal reference frame. However, one could not determine if two events happened at the same spatial location.[20] I strongly doubt that the older generations of scientists and philosophers denied that there is a fact of the matter as to whether or not two events happened at the same spatial location, even though they could not determine it scientifically using the best available understanding of space-time. Myself, and other scientists and philosophers, feel a similar doubt should be in order with regards to contemporary interpretations of relativity theory and its inability to pick out a preferred temporal reference frame. This is because there are other interpretations that allow one to pick out a preferred temporal reference frame.[21]

Second, some philosophers and theologians are philosophically motivated to hold to eternalism and four-dimensionalism because these theories are said to comport well with truth-maker theory. On one version of truth-maker theory, it is said that every true proposition has something that makes the proposition true.[22] Consider the proposition 'Theresa May is the prime minister of the UK'. What makes this proposition true? There is an individual named 'Theresa May' who currently has the property *being the prime minister*. Theresa May, along with the properties she currently possesses, serves as the truth-maker for the proposition in question. Now consider another proposition: 'Abraham Lincoln is the sixteenth president of the USA'. What makes this proposition true? Eternalists will argue that presentism cannot offer a satisfactory answer to this question because, on presentism, the past no longer exists. The eternalist will complain that, on presentism, Lincoln no longer exists, so Lincoln can no longer serve as the truth-maker for the proposition in question. The eternalist goes on to point out that she can easily solve this problem. On four-dimensional eternalism, the past does exist. So temporal parts, or person stages, of Lincoln do exist at the relevant times, and they can serve as the truth-makers for the proposition Abraham Lincoln is the sixteenth president of the USA. Presentists have responded in various ways to this problem.[23] For instance, I for one believe that Lincoln currently exists in the intermediate state awaiting resurrection. Lincoln currently possesses the relevant properties needed to make this proposition true. As such, he can serve as the truth-maker for the proposition in question. Again, I shall not bore readers with details of the debate. I shall simply note that there is a debate to be had here.

Third, in recent literature one can find Christians adopting four-dimensional eternalism for explicitly theological reasons. For instance, Katherin Rogers and T. J. Mawson have used it to defend the classical doctrines of divine omniscience and timelessness against open theism. Oliver Crisp has used it to articulate the doctrine of atonement. Michael Rea has deployed it to make sense of original sin. Paul J. Griffiths thinks it is useful for developing Christian eschatology.[24] It might seem, then, that four-dimensional eternalism is a fruitful metaphysical doctrine.

But should Christians be four-dimensional eternalists? It seems to me that there are various areas of Christian thought that conflict with four-dimensional eternalism, and these conflicts have not been fully considered. Further, some of the salvific and eschatological proposals show a deficient understanding of the basic issues in the ontology of time and persistence through time. Below, I shall argue that Christians should not be four-dimensional eternalists since adopting this theory exacerbates the problem of evil and wreaks havoc on our eschatological hope of salvation.

3 Laying My Cards on the Table

Before moving forward, I should like to lay my own beliefs on the table. Perhaps this will help the reader better understand what I hold and what I am arguing against. It will also help the reader understand what I think a good option is for Christians to take instead of four-dimensional eternalism.

First, I am an unrepentant substance dualist.[25] To be sure, there are many other views within philosophical anthropology such as hylomorphism, physicalism and material constitution.²⁶ I believe, however, that a human person is a soul with a body. A person is identical to an immaterial substance (a mind) that has the capacity to think, feel and act. A person is a centre of consciousness that is capable of being self-aware – i.e. a thing with a first-person perspective. A *human* person is an immaterial substance that is appropriately related to a human organism or body. This appropriate relationship is to be understood in terms of satisfying various conditions for being embodied.²⁷

Second, I am an unrepentant endurantist and presentist. I believe that there is numerically one thing that is me that persists through time. This one thing that is me is wholly located at the present moment. There are not temporal parts of me laying about at other times, and there are no other times besides the present that are actual. Classical Christian theologians have long held to presentism and endurantism.²⁸ Though I disagree with various things about classical Christian theology, this is not one of them.²⁹ I believe that presentism and endurantism are the best ways to satisfy certain desiderata for personal salvation and identity through time. I shall now articulate some of these desiderata.

Third, I look forward to the resurrection of the dead. As noted above, there are many dimensions, or aspects, of the doctrine of salvation. As much contemporary work in soteriology will make clear, there is no such thing as *the* Christian doctrine of atonement. There are many different theories about the nature of salvation such as penal substitution, satisfaction theory, ransom theory, Christus victor, and so on. However, what I think is essential to any Christian doctrine of salvation is the claim that God is saving us from evil and death. God saves us from death through the resurrection of our bodies. God saves us from evil by placing us in a new/resurrected creation that is no longer subject to sin and suffering.³⁰

I believe that any theory of identity through time that entails that I will not be resurrected is an unsatisfactory theory for a Christian to hold. Of course, I am assuming here the security of my own salvation. If you are uncertain as to the security of my personal salvation, feel free to insert a person you feel confident is saved. Perhaps you could restate my claim as follows: 'Any theory of persistence through time that entails that my God-fearing grandmother will not be resurrected is an unsatisfactory theory for a Christian to hold.'

Fourth, I believe in the healing power of Jesus and the defeat of evil. I believe that there are many aspects to the doctrine of the resurrection and salvation, but I wish to focus on a particular issue here – eschatological healing and the defeat of evil. As many New Testament scholars will point out, the New Testament often speaks in terms of the present age and the age to come. The present age is marked by evil, sin, sickness and death.

Jesus is establishing a kingdom in the age to come that will be characterized by healing, life, righteousness and the presence of the Holy Spirit. This is something that Christ's earthly ministry has begun, and it is something that awaits eschatological fulfilment for its completion. There are many things that we suffer in this life, and Jesus has promised us healing and restoration in his future kingdom.

In Matthew 5, we see Jesus proclaim several things pertinent to our present discussion. Jesus makes various statements about the way things are now, and how they will be when his kingdom is fully established. In particular, Jesus makes the following claims: (1) those who presently mourn will be comforted; (2) those who are weak will inherit the earth; and (3) the righteous who are persecuted will receive rewards in heaven.

Here is the claim that I want to make in light of Jesus' promises of salvation from the present evil age. I believe that Jesus' promises require that the numerically same mind who suffers in this life, will be the numerically same mind who shall receive eschatological healing. I am the one who is currently suffering, and who is in need of comfort. I want to be the numerically same person who receives eschatological healing. I want to inhabit the renewed creation, and all of the heavenly rewards that come along with it. Perhaps I am being greedy here, but a boy can dream.

Fifth, I believe that all those who seek to be virtuous will be fully established in virtue in the eschaton.[31] I believe that God has created us for a life of virtue.[32] God has created a world where we can grow in virtue, and become more like God through the daily renewal of our minds (Rom. 12.2). In Matthew 5.6, Jesus promises that those who currently hunger and thirst for righteousness will be satisfied. Through the power of the Holy Spirit, and a life of devotion, those who presently seek righteousness will be firmly established in righteousness. God will ensure that those who seek to cultivate a virtuous character will in fact form a virtuous character in the eschaton. Once again, I believe that endurantism is needed in order to make sense of this promise. The people who presently seek virtue must be numerically identical to the people who will be established in virtue. Otherwise, I can make no sense of the moral order of the universe. As I shall argue below, four-dimensional eternalism undermines the Christian claims about developing a virtuous character.

With these commitments in mind, I now turn to my reasons for rejecting four-dimensional eternalism. The arguments I offer below assume four-dimensionalism and eternalism. One could easily modify my arguments to attack views that combine four-dimensionalism with presentism. I focus on the combination of four-dimensionalism and eternalism because that is the most commonly held combination among contemporary philosophers and theologians.

4 Four-Dimensional Eternalism and Salvation from Evil

Most four-dimensionalists reject substance dualism and opt for some form of physicalism. It is possible to be a substance dualist and affirm four-dimensionalism, but it is rare. Substance dualists who are endurantists often affirm the simple theory of personal identity through time. Again, on the simple view, there are no non-trivial or non-circular conditions for personal identity over time. This is because personal identity is a primitive notion that is not subject to a deeper analysis.[33] The dualist says that a person is identical to a simple, immaterial substance that persists through time.[34] There is no deeper analysis to give for personal identity over time.

On four-dimensionalism, personal persistence is typically understood in terms of causal and psychological continuity relations between numerically distinct temporal parts or person stages. Again, this is so because the four-dimensionalist explicitly denies numerical identity over time. The person stage that exists at time t_1 persists by being causally related to a temporal counterpart at some later time t_2. This later temporal counterpart will exemplify a psychological continuity to the earlier temporal counterpart in that each will have many of the same beliefs, memories, desires, and so on.[35]

Four-dimensionalists also typically hold that personal survival of death does not really matter to us because numerical personal identity through time does not really matter to us.[36] As the four-dimensionalist Eric Steinhart proclaims: 'Personal identity is *not* retained in the resurrection. It is *sacrificed*.'[37] According to Steinhart, and others, what really matters to us is that we have later resurrected temporal counterparts that are continuous with us in some interesting causal relationship. Apparently, human persons do not really concern themselves with personal survival, but only care about having later temporal counterparts. I should think that this will be quite shocking news to most human persons to hear that personal survival is not what matters to them. I, for one, hold that personal identity through time matters. I should think that our personal survival of death matters deeply to us.

It is at this point that I think one can begin to see the failure of four-dimensionalism for Christianity. On standard Christian defences and theodicies, the problem of evil is in part assuaged by the soteriological promises of personal eschatological healing, resurrected bodies, reconciliation with other persons (both human and divine), and an eternal and blissful union with God. The Christian claim is that God could not create a world where evil has the ultimate say, nor could he create a world where there is a perfect balance of good and evil. The Christian God is an evil defeater, not an evil balancer. God will bring about a state of affairs where goodness will outweigh any past evils.[38] One way to capture this is to say that God will ensure that human persons who participate in horrors will have their horrors defeated. God will ensure that these human persons will have a life that, on the whole, is one worth living. One day their suffering will cease, and they shall receive resurrected bodies and enter into God's everlasting kingdom.[39]

A presentist and endurantist has no problem making sense of these claims since past horrors no longer exist. The numerically same endurant person who participated in horrors will be the numerically same person who will be resurrected in the future. Those tragic moments of her past no longer exist, and she has an eternity of future healing and bliss to look forward to. I shall argue that a four-dimensional eternalist cannot make good on these claims. In particular, a four-dimensional eternalist cannot make good on the claim that the participant of horrors will cease to participate in those horrors, nor that God will ultimately defeat evil.

Blessed are Those Who Suffer, for They Shall be Comforted

On four-dimensional eternalism, persons persist by having temporal parts, or stages, that are psychologically continuous with earlier temporal parts. On four-dimensional eternalism the entire space-time manifold exists and contains all events. The temporal parts of each object exist only at the times at which they exist, and the temporal locations of those times are eternally fixed.[40] From God's perspective, it simply is the case that each temporal part exists at the times at which they do from all eternity. It is always the case that a temporal part of O exists at time t_x. Further, the entire four-dimensional universe is co-eternal with God in the sense that there is never a state of affairs where God exists without the universe.[41]

Imagine if you will that Sally is enjoying an absolutely delectable cheeseburger. Perhaps it is the best cheeseburger in town. On four-dimensional eternalism it is always the case that there is a temporal counterpart, or person stage if you prefer, of Sally enjoying this delectable cheeseburger. From all eternity this temporal counterpart of Sally is enjoying this cheeseburger. Not a bad situation to be in if you ask me.

Imagine a different scenario. There is another temporal counterpart, or person stage, of Sally that is experiencing an absolutely tragic evil. From all eternity that temporal counterpart of Sally is suffering this great evil. This temporal counterpart will never cease to suffer. Granted, other temporal counterparts of Sally are enjoying delectable cheeseburgers, or perhaps even enjoying the beatific vision. This would appear to offer no comfort to the temporal counterpart that is suffering. Her suffering will never cease. From all eternity God is sustaining this temporal counterpart in existence. This temporal counterpart of Sally is suffering an eternal torment with no chance of relief. This temporal counterpart will never be able to say: 'Thank goodness that is over.' This is a hard picture of reality to maintain. This seems to negate the promise of Jesus in Matthew 5 since it cannot make good on the claim that the suffering will cease, and that the individual who suffers will be comforted.

It should be noted that the intensity of Sally's suffering is not somehow greater on four-dimensionalism than it would be on presentism. The level of intensity is the same on either account. A stubbed toe is a stubbed toe on four-dimensional eternalism and presentism. The difference is that on presentism and endurantism Sally will eventually cease to suffer, and eventually be comforted. On four-dimensional eternalism, the person stage that exists at the time of the suffering will never cease to exist at the time of the suffering. Granted, Sally has later temporal counterparts that are not suffering, but that does not relieve the suffering of the earlier Sally stage. The suffering person stage is co-eternal with God. It is difficult to see how God can save people from evil on four-dimensional eternalism, and offer any comfort or healing to those who suffer.

This, so say I, undermines any plausible story of Christian salvation. Jesus' message of hope becomes: 'Blessed are those who mourn, for their temporal counterparts will be comforted in heaven.' There is no comfort for those earlier person stages to be found on four-dimensional eternalism.

Blessed are Those Who are Persecuted, for Theirs is the Kingdom of Heaven

Christians are committed to the claim that one day God will ultimately triumph over evil and renew creation (e.g. Rev. 20–22). It is hard to understand how, on this model, God can be said ultimately to triumph over evil and renew creation. As William Lane Craig points out: 'Creation is never really purged of evil on this view; at most it can be said that evil infects only those parts of creation that are earlier than' other events like Christ's return and the general resurrection of the dead.[42] It is difficult to understand how there will be no more tears when Christ comes again if other temporal parts of the saints are eternally experiencing great evil. The temporal parts of the martyrs from Nero's day are – tenselessly – serving as torches for his parties. Granted, other temporal parts of the martyrs are enjoying the new creation, but the flames of the previous temporal parts will never be extinguished. From all eternity the flames are lit at the times at which they exist.

Recall that, in Matthew 5, Jesus promises that the righteous who are persecuted will receive rewards in heaven. Several things are needed for God to defeat the horrors of these martyrs. First, God must make it the case that their suffering comes to an end. Second, God must take them out of the environment where they are vulnerable to horrors. Third, God must heal them.[43] Four-dimensional eternalism cannot make good on these claims. The suffering temporal parts eternally suffer. Their suffering cannot come to an end, nor can they be taken out of the environment in which they are vulnerable to horrors. This is because their temporal and spatial locations are eternally fixed. Their temporal and spatial locations are co-eternal with God. As such, these temporal parts will never be healed. Later temporal counterparts will be enjoying God's healing, but not the counterparts that are eternally suffering. It is awkward, to say the least, that the suffering counterparts do not receive any healing, but that the counterparts that never have and never will suffer do receive the healing.[44] This seriously calls into question the claim that God is saving humanity from evil.

5 Proleptic Hope

Eschatology becomes increasingly bizarre if four-dimensional eternalism is true. Eschatology has several themes, one of which is the already/not yet tension in the New Testament.[45] The central idea is that Jesus has begun the kingdom of God, or begun the 'age to come', such that in a sense we can say things like 'I am saved' or 'the kingdom of God is here'. However, the kingdom has not yet been fully realized, or fully consummated. This is why we can say things like 'I am being saved', 'I will be saved', or 'God, please bring about your kingdom'. The apostle Paul often speaks of the present experience of salvation and God's kingdom, but at the same time looks forward to the reappearing of Christ and his coming kingdom in which the general resurrection of the dead will take place and salvation will be complete.[46]

In light of this, theologians often emphasize that living in this already/not yet creates a prolepsis, or anticipation, towards God.[47] Because of the in-breaking kingdom of God as displayed through the work of Christ, we have certain promises from God about the future. These promises are about the general resurrection of the dead, the reconciliation of all things to God, the new creation, and the end of death and evil. Since we can currently experience these things to a limited degree through the work of the Holy Spirit, the life of Christ and the promises of God through Christ should call us to reorient the way we live our lives. Part of the idea of 'prolepsis' is to reorient our lives according to what God has done in the past, is doing in the present, and will do in the future when Christ reappears. In other words, believers are to cultivate virtue and righteousness in light of God's promises. The presentist and endurantist has no problem making sense of these claims, but the four-dimensional eternalist does.

If presentism and endurantism are true, human persons who currently exist can experience the proleptic work of the Holy Spirit in their lives. Since the future does not yet exist, a person can have hope for future resurrection. She can orient her life around the promises of God through Christ that have not yet been fulfilled. The numerically same person who orients her life around God's eschatological promises will be the numerically same person who will one day experience the fulfilment of those promises. When that day comes, and since the past no longer exists, she can finally heave a sigh of relief that evil is no more. Further, all of her thirsting towards righteousness will finally be satisfied.

If four-dimensional eternalism is true, I shall argue that these ideas within eschatology become perplexing to say the least. A number of questions arise at this point for the four-dimensional eternalist. How far should we proleptically reorient our lives given that Christ's reappearing is occurring at a particular time that tenselessly exists? Should we be concerned with the afterlife? Should we look forward to the new creation? Should we be concerned with hell? I shall take each question in turn.

Should We Proleptically Reorient Our Lives Towards the Reappearing of Christ?

One's own proleptic anticipation of Christ's future reappearing would seem rather odd on four-dimensional eternalism. Let us say that Christ comes again in the year 3000. For those of us who are temporal parts, or person stages, living at the time 2018, it seems as though we can look forward to Christ reappearing. However, it simply is the case that Christ is tenselessly reappearing at the year 3000. This is because both times and the temporal parts that exist at those times have equal ontological existence. This creates several problems.

In Romans 8.18–25, Paul writes:

> For I consider that the sufferings of this present time are not worth comparing with the glory that is to be revealed to us. For the creation waits with eager longing for the revealing of the sons of God. For the creation was subjected to futility, not willingly, but because of him who subjected it, in hope that the creation itself will be set free from its bondage to corruption and obtain the freedom of the glory of the children of God. For we know that the whole creation has been groaning together in the pains of childbirth until now. And not only the creation, but we ourselves, who have the firstfruits of the Spirit, groan inwardly as we wait eagerly for adoption as sons, the redemption of our bodies. For in this

hope we were saved. Now hope that is seen is not hope. For who hopes for what he sees? But if we hope for what we do not see, we wait for it with patience.

In this passage creation and humanity are eagerly awaiting the future redemption of all things. When Christ reappears he will bring about the resurrection of our bodies, and renew all of creation. Paul tells the Romans that they have hope for this future event. They have hope, because this event has not yet obtained – they haven't yet seen it or experienced it. If they had experienced it – if the event had obtained – they would have no hope. For no one continues to place her hope in something once that thing has obtained. If I have high hopes about eating a delectable cheeseburger, my hope comes to an end once I take my first bite of that cheeseburger. My hope gives way to the enjoyment, or disappointment, of what I had hoped for.

It would seem that, on four-dimensional eternalism, the groaning of creation in anticipation of the coming kingdom is futile. The kingdom has come at a particular time slice. Those who exist at earlier time slices who yearn for the coming kingdom will never experience the kingdom of God because they eternally exist at the times at which they do in fact exist. Whence then is their hope of salvation? These temporal counterparts have placed their hope in a future event that is eternally inaccessible to them. Perhaps one can say that these temporal counterparts do have genuine hope since the object of their hope is an event that is later than the time slice at which they exist. It is the case that they hope for what they do not see, but it would sound like a cruel joke to tell them to 'wait for it with patience' since no amount of patience will ever bring this event closer to them. Those patient temporal counterparts will never experience the eschatological glory and redemption that Paul speaks of. They may have genuine hope, but it seems that four-dimensional eternalism renders their hope futile. Their proleptic anticipation is in vain.

A related question is worth asking as well. What is Sally actually doing when she participates in the Lord's Supper? Supposedly she is celebrating Christ's death *until* he comes again (1 Cor. 11.26). However, on four-dimensional eternalism, Christ has come. Granted, he has not subjectively come from the perspective of those existing at earlier times, but objectively the event is actual.

Part of the idea of prolepsis is an excited, or celebratory, anticipation towards the future fulfilment of God's promises. When one comes to participate in the Eucharist she is celebrating what God has done in the past, what he is currently doing, and what he will do in the future. She celebrates Christ's life and his future return when all things will be put right. The body of Christ, the Church, is meant to come together to celebrate such things in the Lord's Supper, and as a body proleptically orient themselves towards this future return of Christ.

Yet it seems that four-dimensional eternalism cuts against the very idea of proleptic anticipation and celebration of the Lord's Supper. Consider Sally again. The Sally person stage that is participating in the Lord's Supper has little to celebrate for she will never experience the resurrected Lord. The stage that celebrates the Lord's Supper until Christ returns is celebrating something that is eternally inaccessible to her. What then is she celebrating? Perhaps she can celebrate the fact that her later temporal counterparts are enjoying the return of Christ, but it seems to me that it will be difficult to get into a celebratory mood over such things. It is hard to get excited about a party that you cannot possibly attend. How much more so, then, will it be difficult to get excited about the return of Christ when you know that you cannot possibly experience it? This has the potential to turn the celebration of the Lord's Supper into the mourning of a wake. At best, it has the potential to turn the body of Christ into a bunch of party poopers who come to take the bread and wine, but can only complain about the fact that they will never see the return of their Lord. Four-dimensional eternalism seems to wreak havoc on Christian hope and practice.

Should We be Concerned with the Afterlife?

Let us consider Sally again. Given four-dimensional eternalism there are Sally person stages that exist in the year 2018. Person stages are as fine-grained as instants and possible change. The number of person stages that exist in 2018 depends on whether time is continuous or discrete. Either way, there are a large number of Sally person stages that exist in 2018. It is the case that certain later temporal counterparts of Sally exist in either hell or the new earth. However, the Sally stage that exists at this time will never experience such things. The Sally stage that exists at this time will only exist at this time. She will never have the beatific vision or experience the torments of hell.

Consider first the new creation. Does Sally have anything to look forward to in regards to the new creation? The Sally that exists at this time has nothing to look forward to. She cannot possibly experience the joy of being reunited with loved ones in the new creation. She will never experience the eschatological healing of her body because a later temporal counterpart will be the one resurrected. No beatific vision awaits her for she eternally exists at the wrong time to experience such things. In moments of hardship, she might be tempted to take solace in the fact that one day she will fully experience the love and forgiveness of God. But upon reflecting on her ontological status within time, she will most likely lose whatever comfort such thoughts were intended to bring for she will eternally exist at that moment of hardship. So much for Jesus' promise to comfort those who mourn.

Perhaps things will not be so dire for certain Sally stages. Say there is a Sally stage that is not experiencing a moment of hardship, nor suffering a horrendous event. Say instead, there is a particular Sally stage that is experiencing a rather tantalizing sin. Should she be worried about the eternal consequences of this sin? Should she be worried about the eternal destiny of her soul? It seems she should not. She already knows that she will never experience new creation, but she can take solace in the fact that she has no worry of hell either. The stage that exists at this time will never have to experience hell. She eternally exists at the moment of enjoying this tantalizing sin. No need to worry about eternal consequences, for she will never have to experience them. For all eternity she will experience the pleasure of this tantalizing sin.

Perhaps the four-dimensionalist could argue that this particular Sally stage has a duty to seek the kingdom of God so that later temporal counterparts can enjoy the beatific vision and not experience the torments of hell. As such, this Sally stage should not take solace in the fact that she cannot possibly experience hell. Instead she should be concerned about the eternal destiny of her later temporal counterparts.[48] But surely her moral motivation is significantly undercut in the same way that her hope about the future is undercut. It eternally is the case that Sally's temporal counterparts exist at the times and places that they in fact exist. The destiny of Sally's temporal counterparts is eternally fixed for those times eternally obtain.

Concluding Remarks

I have argued that four-dimensionalism exacerbates the problem of evil for Christian theism, and that it eradicates the proleptic hope of the believer as well as wreaks havoc on eschatology. In other words, four-dimensional eternalism undermines several essential components of the Christian story of salvation. My suggestion is that Christian philosophers and theologians should reconsider their commitment to four-dimensional eternalism in light of these arguments. Ultimately, I would suggest that Christians should abandon four-dimensional eternalism and return to the loving arms of presentism and endurantism. Presentism served the Church well for over 1,800 years, and I say it could continue to do so again.[49] Without presentism and endurantism, I fail to see what hope the Christian story of salvation has to offer.[50]

Notes

1 Thomas M. Crisp, 'Presentism', in Michael J. Loux and Dean W. Zimmerman (eds), *The Oxford Handbook of Metaphysics* (New York: Oxford University Press, 2003), p. 212.

2 St Augustine, *Confessions* XI.20. Anselm, *Monologion* 21, 22, and 24. Also, *Proslogion* 13, 19 and 22.

3 Trenton Merricks, 'Goodbye Growing Block', in Dean W. Zimmerman (ed.), *Oxford Studies in Metaphysics*, Vol. 2 (New York: Oxford University Press, 2006), p. 103.

4 J. J. C. Smart, 'The Tenseless Theory of Time', in Theodore Sider, John Hawthorne and Dean W. Zimmerman (eds), *Contemporary Debates in Metaphysics* (Malden, MA: Blackwell, 2008), p. 227.

5 Trenton Merricks, *Truth and Ontology* (New York: Oxford University Press, 2007), pp. 121–5. Also, Theodore Sider, 'Four-Dimensionalism', in *Philosophical Review* 106, 2 (1997), pp. 197 and 204.

6 Michael Rea, 'Four-Dimensionalism', in Michael J. Loux and Dean W. Zimmerman (eds), *The Oxford Handbook of Metaphysics* (New York: Oxford University Press, 2003), p. 247.

7 Sally Haslanger, 'Persistence Through Time', in *The Oxford Handbook of Metaphysics*, p. 318.

8 Four-dimensionalism can actually come in two forms – perdurantism and stage theory. I focus on stage theory since it is the most popular version held today due to its precision and clarity. For a deeper discussion see Katherine Hawley, *How Things Persist* (Oxford: Oxford University Press, 2001). Also, Theodore Sider, *Four-Dimensionalism* (Oxford: Oxford University Press, 2001).

9 Katherine Hawley, 'Temporal Parts', *Stanford Encyclopedia of Philosophy*, <http://plato.stanford.edu/entries/temporal-parts/>. Also Sider, *Four-Dimensionalism*, p. 7. Hud Hudson, *The Metaphysics of Hyperspace* (Oxford: Oxford University Press, 2005), pp. 5–9.

10 Hawley, 'Temporal Parts'. Also Mark Heller, 'Temporal Parts of Four-Dimensional Objects', in Michael J. Loux (ed.), *Metaphysics: Contemporary Readings* (London: Routledge, 2001), pp. 343–8.

11 It is worth noting that debates over presentism, eternalism, endurantism and four-dimensionalism are not uniquely Christian debates. The same debates have taken place between Hindu and Buddhist philosophers. For instance, Buddhists traditionally reject the existence of any enduring substances, whereas various schools within Hinduism have explicitly affirmed the existence of enduring substances. Also, Buddhists have debated among themselves whether presentism or eternalism is true. See Bina Gupta, *An Introduction to Indian Philosophy: Perspectives on Reality, Knowledge, and Freedom* (New York: Routledge, 2012), ch. 12.

12 Hawley, 'Temporal Parts'.

13 Richard Swinburne, 'Personal Identity: The Dualist Theory', in Michael J. Loux (ed.), *Metaphysics: Contemporary Readings*, 2nd edn (New York: Routledge, 2008).

14 George Gasser and Matthias Stefan, 'Introduction', in George Gasser and Matthias Stefan (eds), *Personal Identity: Complex or Simple?* (Cambridge: Cambridge University Press, 2012), p. 3.

15 Peter van Inwagen, 'What Do We Refer to When We Say "I"?' in Richard M. Gale (ed.), *The Blackwell Guide to Metaphysics* (Oxford: Blackwell, 2002), p. 177.

16 David B. Hershenov, 'Four-Dimensional Animalism', in Stephan Blatti and Paul F. Snowdon (eds), *Animalism: New Essays on Persons, Animals, and Identity* (Oxford: Oxford University Press, 2016), pp. 211–12.

17 J. J. C. Smart, 'The Tenseless Theory of Time', in Theodore Sider, John Hawthorne and Dean W. Zimmerman (eds), *Contemporary Debates in Metaphysics* (Malden, MA: Blackwell, 2008), p. 232.

18 Dean Zimmerman, 'Presentism and the Space-Time Manifold', in Craig Callender (ed.), *The Oxford Handbook of Philosophy of Time* (Oxford: Oxford University Press, 2011). C. J. Isham and John Polkinghorne, 'The Debate Over the Block Universe', in Robert John Russell, Nancey Murphy and C. J. Isham (eds), *Quantum Cosmology and the Laws of Nature: Scientific Perspectives on Divine Action*, 2nd edn (Notre Dame, IN: University of Notre Dame Press, 1999). Craig Bourne, *A Future for Presentism* (Oxford: Oxford University Press, 2006), chapters 5–7. Robert John Russell, *Time in Eternity: Pannenberg, Physics, and Eschatology in Creative Mutual Interaction* (Notre Dame, IN: University of Notre Dame Press, 2012), chapter 5.

19 Bradley Monton, 'Prolegomena to Any Future Physics-Based Metaphysics', in Jonathan Kvanvig (ed.), *Oxford Studies in Philosophy of Religion Volume 3* (Oxford: Oxford University Press, 2011). John Polkinghorne, 'The Nature of Time', in Alain Comes, Michael Heller, Shahn Majid, Roger Penrose, John Polkinghorne and Andrew Taylor (eds), *On Space and Time* (New York: Cambridge University Press, 2008).

20 Cody Gilmore, 'Persistence and Location in Relativistic Spacetime', *Philosophy Compass* 3 (2008), 1226.

21 Roberto Mangabeira Unger and Lee Smolin, *The Singular Universe and the Reality of Time: A Proposal in Natural Philosophy* (Cambridge: Cambridge University Press, 2015).

22 D. M. Armstrong, *Truth and Truthmakers* (Cambridge: Cambridge University Press, 2004).

23 E.g. Trenton Merricks, *Truth and Ontology* (Oxford: Oxford University Press, 2007).

24 See T. J. Mawson, 'Divine Eternity', *International Journal for the Philosophy of Religion* 64 (2008). Katherin Rogers, 'Anselmian Eternalism: The Presence of a Timeless God', *Faith and Philosophy* 24 (2007). Oliver Crisp, 'Original Sin and Atonement', in Thomas Flint and Michael Rea (eds), *Oxford Handbook of Philosophical Theology* (New York: Oxford University Press, 2009). Michael Rea, 'The Metaphysics of Original Sin', in Peter van Inwagen and Dean Zimmerman (eds), *Persons: Human and Divine* (New York: Oxford University Press, 2007). Paul J. Griffiths, *Decreation: The Last Things of All Creatures* (Waco, TX: Baylor University Press, 2014), chapters 13 and 16.

25 For recent defences of substance dualism, see Richard Swinburne, *Mind, Brain, and Free Will* (New York: Oxford University Press, 2013). Stewart Goetz and Charles Taliaferro, *A Brief History of the Soul* (Oxford: Blackwell, 2011). Mark C. Baker and Stewart Goetz, *The Soul Hypothesis: Investigations into the Existence of the Soul* (London: Continuum International Publishing Group, 2011).

26 Eric T. Olson, *What Are We? A Study in Personal Ontology* (New York: Oxford University Press, 2007).

27 For details on the conditions for embodiment, see Robin Le Poidevin, 'The Incarnation: Divine Embodiment and the Divided Mind'. Richard Swinburne, *The Coherence of Theism* (Oxford: Oxford University Press, 1977), pp. 102–4.

28 See Robert Pasnau, 'On Existing All at Once', in Christian Tapp and Edmund Runggaldier (eds), *God, Eternity, and Time* (Surrey: Ashgate Publishing Limited, 2011). Also, Anselm, *Proslogion* 13 and 22. Gregory of Nyssa, *Against Eunomius*

I.42. Augustine, *City of God* XI.21 and *Confessions* XI. For a discussion of Augustine's puzzles over the present see Richard Sorabji, *Time, Creation and the Continuum: Theories in Antiquity and the Early Middle Ages* (London: Duckworth, 1983), pp. 29–32. J. R. Lucas, *A Treatise on Time and Space* (London: Methuen, 1973), chapter 4. Boethius, *Trinity is One God Not Three Gods*, IV. Thomas Aquinas, *Quaestiones Disputatae De Veritate* QII.12.

29 R. T. Mullins, *The End of the Timeless God* (Oxford: Oxford University Press, 2016).

30 N. T. Wright, *Evil and the Justice of God* (Downers Grove, IL: InterVarsity Press, 2006).

31 Kevin Timpe, *Free Will in Philosophical Theology* (London: Bloomsbury, 2014), chapter 6.

32 John Hick, *Evil and the Love of God* (New York: Palgrave Macmillan, 2010).

33 E. J. Lowe, 'The Probable Simplicity of Personal Identity', in *Personal Identity: Complex or Simple?*

34 Richard Swinburne, 'Personal Identity: The Dualist Theory', in *Metaphysics: Contemporary Readings*.

35 Tobias Hansson Wahlberg, 'Can I be an Instantaneous Stage and Yet Persist Through Time?', *Metaphysica* 9 (2008).

36 Derek Parfit, 'Personal Identity', in Loux, *Metaphysics*.

37 Eric Steinhart, 'The Revision Theory of Resurrection', *Religious Studies* 44 (2008), pp. 66–7.

38 Klaas J. Kraay, 'Theism, Possible Worlds, and the Multiverse', *Philosophical Studies* 147 (2010). Keith Yandell, 'Theology, Philosophy, and Evil', in James K. Beilby (ed.), *For Faith and Clarity: Philosophical Contributions to Christian Theology* (Grand Rapids, MI: Baker Academic, 2006). John S. Feinberg, *The Many Faces of Evil* (Wheaton, IL: Crossway Books, 2004).

39 Marilyn McCord Adams, *Christ and Horrors: The Coherence of Christology* (Cambridge: Cambridge University Press, 2006).

40 Two recent eschatological proposals try to deny that times and the objects that exist at them are completely fixed on the growing block. Robert John Russell, *Time in Eternity: Pannenberg, Physics, and Eschatology in Creative Mutual Interaction* (Notre Dame, IN: University of Notre Dame Press, 2012). Mark Ian Thomas Robson, 'Evolutionary Theodicy, Redemption and Time', *Zygon* 50 (2015), pp. 647–70. These proposals lack a detailed understanding of the ontology of time and persistence through time. In order to make sense of these proposals, they will need to abandon the growing block, and adopt something called the *morphing block*. Further, they must place this morphing block in *hypertime*. Russell and Robson both wish to reject hypertime, but I can see no way for them to avoid it. Such a discussion, however, is beyond the scope of this chapter. I shall simply refer readers to a recent defence of the morphing block and hypertime. Hud Hudson, *The Fall and Hypertime* (Oxford: Oxford University Press, 2014).

41 Katherin A. Rogers, 'Anselm on Eternity as the Fifth Dimension', *Saint Anselm Journal* 3 (2006).

42 William Lane Craig, 'Response to Paul Helm', in Gregory Ganssle (ed.), *God and Time: Four Views*, p. 66.

43 This is an unfortunately truncated modification of Adams' stages of horror defeat in *Christ and Horrors*. Space does not allow further discussion.

44 Steinhart's theory of the resurrection is quite explicit that only the resurrected counterparts receive healing while the suffering counterparts do not. See his 'Revision Theory of the Resurrection'.

45 For more on the already/not yet, see Craig C. Hill, *In God's Time: The Bible and the Future* (Grand Rapids, MI: Eerdmans, 2002).

46 Ben Witherington III, *The Paul Quest: The Renewed Search for the Jew of Tarsus* (Downers Grove, IL: InterVarsity Press, 1998), chapter 8.

47 Richard Bauckham, 'Eschatology', in John Webster, Kathryn Tanner and Ian Torrance (eds), *The Oxford Handbook of Systematic Theology* (New York: Oxford University Press, 2007), pp. 308–11.

48 See Taylor for an argument that four-dimensionalism is not compatible with satisfying obligations to persons with regard to the person's well-being. Taylor, 'The Frustrating Problem for Four-Dimensionalism'.

49 John Bigelow, 'Presentism and Properties', *Nous* 30 (1996), p. 35. See also Dean Zimmerman, 'The A-Theory of Time, Presentism, and Open Theism', in Melville Y. Stewart (ed.), *Science and Religion in Dialogue* (Malden, MA: Blackwell, 2010), p. 793.

50 I would like to thank my World Religions students at Northfield Mount Hermon for helpful comments on earlier drafts of this chapter. Earlier versions of this material are also published in R. T. Mullins, 'Four-Dimensionalism, Evil, and Christian Belief', *Philosophia Christi* 16 (2014).

2

Divine Hiddenness, the Soteriological Problem of Evil, and Berkeleyan Idealism

GREGORY E. TRICKETT AND TYLER TABER

Why if God exists is his existence not more obvious or evident or apparent? Call this the 'main question'. The main question represents, or points to, a much-discussed theme in contemporary analytic philosophy of religion entitled the problem of divine hiddenness (PDH hereafter).[1] Suppose that *from* PDH flows what may be termed the soteriological problem of evil (SPE hereafter). SPE, at least from a Christian perspective, is the problem that God has provided salvation for humanity but that there are some persons who never hear and accept the gospel of Jesus Christ, and so are lost.[2] For if God was more obvious, as one might postulate, then more persons could respond to the gospel and be saved; SPE, it could be argued, emerges from PDH. Perhaps by examining PDH – specifically the main question – one can in turn shed light on SPE. This chapter seeks to answer the main question from a Christian perspective informed by the Anglican bishop and philosopher George Berkeley (1685–1753), whose metaphysical commitments to idealism – the thesis, stated roughly, 'that minds are most real and the physical world is mind-dependent'[3] – may be advantageous in analysing PDH and thus SPE; in short, we believe that Berkeleyan idealism has the resources to address the main question. First, we *explain* the relationship between PDH and SPE with more specificity. Second, we *explain* Berkeleyan idealism with more precision. It is worth noting that our purpose is not to defend the success of Berkeleyan arguments but rather, assuming the success of such arguments, employ idealism to the issue of PDH and SPE. Thus, with both explanations in hand, we (third) *apply* Berkeleyan idealism to PDH and SPE. Fourth, we *consider* potential objections or worries to our application of Berkeleyan idealism to PDH and SPE. Finally, concluding remarks will be made.

Divine Hiddenness and the Soteriological Problem of Evil *Explained*

In this section, we explore similarities between PDH and the general problem of evil (POE), since many philosophers believe there to be a tight relationship between the two problems;[4] this exploration will demonstrate how SPE is relevant to POE and thus to PDH, and will in turn aid to elucidate SPE. We will then be positioned to describe Berkeleyan idealism.[5]

First, both PDH and POE can be taken as problems for theism. Evil and the 'hiddenness of God' are just what one might expect to find on, say, naturalism, but are problematic given a theistic position. Comparably, it is not difficult to see how SPE can be construed as a problem for theism; if God has made salvation available but there are some who are not saved then, prima facie, this is problematic, and hence becomes a soteriological worry. Second, POE and PDH can both take argumentative form, with premises, the conclusions of which state that there is no God, or that his existence is unlikely or improbable; such may include logical (deductive) or evidential (inductive) arguments. One could likewise develop the general SPE toward a specific argument, taking either logical or evidential form, against God's existence.[6]

Third, PDH can be construed as a *part* of the larger POE, or it may be the other way around, whereby POE is taken to be a *part* of the larger PDH. Concerning the former, J. L. Schellenberg, in his 1993 book *Divine Hiddenness and Human Reason*, claims that divine hiddenness – or, more specifically, reasonable non-belief – 'must be viewed as a special *instance* of the empirical problem of evil.'[7] Commenting on Eleonore Stump's work on suffering and evil, Evan Fales writes: 'Divine hiddenness is problematic because it seems to represent one *type* of gratuitous evil.'[8] Similarly, Paul Moser explains that 'God often seems hidden from some people at such times . . . and this fact of hiddenness emerges as a cognitive variation of the problem of evil.'[9] Consider now the latter, that POE can be conceived as part of the grander PDH. 'The entire problem of evil', explains Robert McKim, 'may be thought of *as a part of* the problem of the hiddenness of God, since the presence of evil in the world is a fact that makes for the hiddenness of God.'[10] Thomas V. Morris argues that 'the problem of evil can be seen *as a subcategory* of the problem of the hiddenness of God.'[11] Although James Keller does suggest that:

> the two problems are so closely related that either *can be construed as a part of the other*. Because some human suffering arises from a failure to have faith in God – or so theists usually allege – and from lack of knowledge of God's will, the hiddenness of God is part of the problem of evil; that is, if

God is as many theists have claimed, we might find it inexplicable that God remains hidden, since that hiddenness causes suffering . . . In this way, the evil in the world contributes to the hiddenness of God.[12]

If PDH is a part of the larger POE, then perhaps one will in turn take SPE to be a part of the larger POE; similarly, if POE is a part of the larger PDH, then perhaps one will take SPE to be a part of the larger PDH. We believe that SPE emerges from PDH, but do not pause here to determine if PDH is a part of the larger POE, or vice versa.

Fourth, there may be rapport between POE, PDH and the problem of religious diversity, which is the problem that there are competing religious claims about God, sin, salvation, and so on. SPE seems to fit at the intersection of these problems. Suppose one is an exclusivist, holding that there is only one uniquely true religion; suppose it is asked of the exclusivist why, on her position, God's particular path for salvation is not better known, or more apparent, which would in turn ensure that large swathes of alternative religious adherents are not led down the wrong salvific path. What precisely is being asked? Is it PDH, which asks why God is not more evident? Or is it POE, since the fact that some find themselves on the wrong salvific path amounts to an evil of sorts, what might be called SPE? It is not easy to say; but SPE does appear to surface.[13]

Fifth, defences and theodicies can be applied to PDH and POE. A defence is a *possible* account explaining why God might allow evil, whereas a theodicy is an *actual* account. There are different sorts of defences: free will defences, greater goods defences, and so forth; the same, too, with theodicies. Methodologically, defences and theodicies can also be applied to PDH. With respect to PDH, a *theodicy* is a theory which attempts to give actual reasons for why God's existence is not (more) obvious, whereas (as Michael Rea writes):

> a *defense* is simply a demonstration of consistency – an effort to show that there is no formal contradiction between the existence of God on the one hand and . . . the phenomenon of divine hiddenness on the other.[14]

Comparably, one can offer either a defence or a theodicy for SPE, either spelling out possible or actual responses for why some are not saved.

Sixth, sceptical theism can be applied to either POE or PDH; crudely stated, the sceptical theist, with respect to POE, is sceptical about one's ability to determine if so-called gratuitous evils truly are gratuitous.[15] Recently, sceptical theism has been applied to PDH,[16] and could be applied to SPE (discussed in the objection's section below). Seventh, both POE and PDH have existential repercussions. In addition to the logical and evidential arguments of evil, it is customary to speak also of the existential or pastoral problem of evil; one can speak of an existential or pastoral component to PDH,[17] and so, too, it seems with respect to SPE. For instance, in Romans 9, Paul has 'great sorrow' and 'unceasing anguish' (9.2) that some Israelites will not be saved, since merely being ethnically Jewish, he seems to reason, does not guarantee salvation (9.6ff.).

This section has analysed similarities between POE and PDH, using this analysis to clarify SPE. Space does not allow, but a more complete analysis would also consider *dissimilarities* between POE and PDH.[18]

Berkeleyan Idealism *Explained*

Idealism is the metaphysical view that there is no mind-independent reality. Christian idealism is the view that the mind on which reality ultimately depends is just the Christian God. Berkeleyan idealism is Christian idealism plus immaterialism, the view that there is no material substance. Thus, on Berkeleyan idealism, only minds and their ideas exist with all of reality depending ultimately on God for its existence. In what follows, we will assume a Berkeleyan approach to the issue of PDH.[19] Berkeley offers a host of arguments in favour of his idealism and there has been an explosion of analysis and exposition of these arguments in recent literature.[20] Since the bulk of our argument rests on what seems to be an implication of these arguments, we will only be concerned here to give a cursory summary of two of the most recognized arguments in favour of idealism and then focus on the related divine language argument that Berkeley gives as evidence of God before applying that argument to PDH.[21]

Berkeleyan Idealism (BI)

Although there are many recent ways that scholars parse Berkeley's arguments for idealism,[22] there are two main arguments that many Berkeley scholars recognize as integral to Berkeley's defence of his idealism: the argument against abstraction and the master argument.

Argument against abstraction. Berkeley's argument against abstraction rests on the notion that abstract ideas do not refer to anything. In his famous introduction to *The Principles of Human Knowledge*, he attempts to show that when one tries to think of an abstract idea, one finds it impossible. If abstraction is, as Berkeley states, 'the mind being able to consider each quality singly, or abstracted from those other qualities with which it is united, does by that means frame to itself abstract ideas' (*Introduction to Principles*, VII),[23] then what follows from abstraction is basically nothing.

This is because the activity of abstraction is, for example, the activity of the mind framing to itself 'the idea of colour exclusive of extension, and of motion exclusive of both colour and extension' (*Intro*, VII).[24] This, Berkeley states, is not easy to do.

Essentially, Berkeley is arguing that our ideas are constructed from the particulars that we experience. Furthermore, we can *only* have ideas of that which we experience. Any ideas we have are of particular things, and abstract ideas are by definition not particular; therefore, we can have no experience of abstract things. But then, if abstraction in this way is impossible, so too is it impossible to think of material substance. This is because material substance can only be arrived at by the process of abstraction if at all, since it lies beyond the realm of sensory experience.

The master argument. The master argument is a separate argument that Berkeley takes to be a kind of final argument for idealism. In the *Principles* Berkeley claims that so much argument in favour of idealism is really unnecessary, when his point could be made with a simple thought experiment:

> This easy trial may make you see, that what you contend for is a downright contradiction. Insomuch that I am content to put the whole upon this issue; if you can but *conceive* it possible for one extended moveable substance, or in general, for any one idea, or any thing like an idea, to exist otherwise than in a mind perceiving it, I shall readily give up the cause: and as for all that *compages* of external bodies which you contend for, I shall grant you its existence, though (1) *you cannot either give me any reason why you believe it exists, or* (2) *assign any use to it when it is supposed to exist.* I say, the bare possibility of your opinion's being true, shall pass for an argument that it is so (*Principles*, XXII).[25]

If one could but show him that it is possible to conceive of an idea that is unconceived, then he would give up the whole idealism project. Whether the master argument is successful or not turns on how one constructs Berkeley's argument from the *Principles* and *Dialogues*. While many such constructions render the master argument invalid,[26] others have shown that it could be constructed in such a way as to be a valid, if not sound, support of Berkeley's idealism.[27]

Although the degree to which these (and Berkeley's other) arguments are successful in showing idealism to be true is debatable, many scholars believe the bulk of them to be valid if not wholly persuasive. Yet it is not necessary to our argument that the arguments succeed to the degree of persuasion, rather merely that it is rational for one to hold to BI on the basis of these (or at least some of these) and other arguments. Therefore, since it is not our purpose to defend the success of these arguments, it is enough for us to assume their success for the purposes of applying the related divine language argument to PDH.

The Divine Language Argument (DLA). An interesting argument that seems to emerge from Berkeley's idealism is what has been referred to as the divine language argument (DLA).[28] This implication of Berkeley's views is well noted (though not often extensively discussed) in the literature. Dicker notes that, according to Berkeley, 'visible ideas are God's *language* for telling us what tangible ideas we would have if we acted in certain ways.'[29] The groundwork for the ensuing argument is laid out in Berkeley's previous work (most notably *Principles* and *New Theory of Vision*), in which Berkeley argues that vision constitutes a kind of system of signs and their relations to ideas. Dicker continues, '[Berkeley] argues in detail that (a) ideas of sight and ideas of touch are entirely heterogeneous, and (b) ideas of sight have features that suggest to us what ideas of touch we will have if we act or move in various ways.'[30] Essentially, vision constitutes a divine language by which God communicates, among other things, his own existence to us. Indeed, on Berkeley's view 'all of nature is really a divine language by whose means God communicates his intentions to us.'[31]

Roberts (rightly) notes that such an understanding of vision as a divine language indicates that the world around us is 'rendered intelligible to us by our ability to approach the natural world as an appropriate object of *interpretation*.'[32] Without this ability, the world around us will be quite unintelligible.

DLA itself is found in the fourth dialogue of Berkeley's *Alciphron*. Given the signification of vision, that the sensible ideas we perceive are arbitrary symbols of their meaning, we have reason to think of it as a kind of divine language.[33] Euphranor concludes:

> Since you cannot deny, that the great mover and author of nature constantly explaineth himself to the eyes of men by the sensible intervention of arbitrary signs, which have no similitude or connexion with the things signified; so as by compounding and disposing them, to suggest and exhibit an endless variety of objects differing in nature, time and place, thereby informing and directing men how to act with respect to things distant and future, as well as near and present. In consequence, I say, of your own sentiments and concessions, you have as much reason to think, the universal agent or God speaks to your eyes, as you can have for thinking any particular person speaks to your ears (*Alciphron*, 4.12).[34]

According to Keota Fields, this argument has been interpreted in the literature as a kind of inference to the best explanation. Fields observes: 'Just as other minds are posited as the best explanation of linguistic behaviour, a divine mind is posited as the best explanation of the visual language that Berkeley defends in *NTV*, and summarizes in *Alciphron*.'[35] Fields however disagrees that the argument amounts to such an inference, arguing instead that the argument constitutes part of a transcendental argument for God's existence. He argues that reading DLA as an inference to the best explanation rests on the mistaken assumption that such inferences were the general method of arguing from effects to causes, when it was actually transcendental arguments that were standard in such arguments.[36]

In contrast, Fields expresses the argument as a confluence of the passivity argument (that since my ideas are not caused by me, and since ideas must be the product of volition, my ideas must be caused by a different agent from me), the continuity argument (that things continue to exist when unperceived by finite minds because an infinite mind, that is God, continues to 'perceive' them), and DLA (that vision constitutes a language made by a divine agent) so that we are left with the valid argument:

1 If there were no God, then there could be no divine volitions.
2 If there were no divine volitions, then ideas of sense could not have representational content.
3 Ideas of sense have representational content.
4 Therefore, there are divine volitions.
5 Therefore, God exists.[37]

There is much more to this discussion about Berkeley's DLA; however, for our purposes, the interesting feature of Berkeley's argument is that it seems to hold a built-in defence against PDH.

A Berkeleyan Response to PDH and SPE *Applied*

Since PDH formally entered the wider consciousness of philosophers of religion with Schellenberg's original book on the topic, *Divine Hiddenness and Human Reason*,[38] there has been a wealth of responses to the problem. What we offer here is a deposit to the discussion. It must be acknowledged that it is a niche response, but as idealism has been gaining greater and greater respect as a tenable view to hold and not merely a curiosity to test one's sceptical muscles, an idealist response to PDH deserves a place at the table and a serious consideration.

Thus, given the preceding discussion, it may be possible to employ the intuitions behind Berkeleyan idealism, namely with respect to DLA, to PDH. Recall the main question of PDH: Why if God exists is his existence not more obvious or evident or apparent? As it turns out, *Alciphron* contains a version of the main question. In the fourth dialogue, Euphranor asks Alciphron, who has given a set of restrictions to the conversation about whether or not God exists, what proof he expects if he is to be persuaded that there is a God. Alciphron states that the proof he requires is:

in short, such proof as every man of sense requires of a matter of fact, or the existence of any other particular thing. For instance, should a man ask why I believe there is a king of Great Britain? I might answer, because I had seen him; or a king of Spain? because I had seen those who saw him. But as for this King of kings, I neither saw him myself, nor any one else that did ever see him. *Surely if there be such a thing as God, it is very strange that he should leave himself without a witness; that men should still dispute his being; and that there should be no one evident, sensible plain proof of it.* (Alciphron, 4.3, emphasis added)[39]

After some discussion in which Euphranor demonstrates to Alciphron that his evidence for other minds (reasonable motions, visible signs and tokens, effects and operations) could also constitute evidence for a divine mind (see *Alciphron*, 4.4–5), Alciphron clarifies what would count for evidence of God:

Upon second thoughts, therefore, and a minute examination of this point, I have found that nothing so much convinces me of the existence of another person as his speaking to me. It is my hearing you talk that, in strict and philosophical truth, is to me the best argument for your being. And this is a peculiar argument inapplicable to your purpose: for you will not, I suppose, pretend that God speaks to man in the same clear and sensible manner as one man doth to another. (*Alciphron*, 4.6)[40]

But of course this is precisely what Berkeley, through Euphranor, argues. So, one may ask, if God 'speaks to man in the same clear and sensible manner as one man doth to another', why are there those who do not believe? The answer lies in the notion that, as Roberts pointed out, language requires some interpretive ability in order to be intelligible. If one is linguistically illiterate with respect to a language, then that language will be unintelligible to that person, regardless of how strongly she desires to interpret it. It may be the case that one's illiteracy even prevents the simple recognition that a language is given.

Notice that in addressing the concern of PDH, this Berkeleyan approach also addresses SPE. The fact that one does not respond to the gospel could be seen as a problem of literacy, not divine hiddenness per se. It is worth noting as well that even with this response to SPE and PDH, there may persist a related soteriological problem of religious luck (the view that the particular circumstances, such as location and family, in which one hears about and responds to the gospel are not in that person's control),[41] but we understand that problem to be different from SPE, which merely claims that if God was more obvious, then more would be saved.[42]

Objections Considered

In this section we will identify some objections to the Berkeleyan response to PDH and SPE. By way of preface, we do not intend to answer these objections in detail, but offer lines of responses for additional consideration.

First, some may object to BI itself in advance of any solutions it may offer to PDH or SPE. To these objectors, we refer the recent works on Berkeleyan idealism previously mentioned. In light of particularly Christian concerns with idealism, a related objection to the orthodoxy of BI may be raised. This objection takes many forms, but usually rests at some point on an understanding of the Bible in which it is taken to endorse the existence of the material world. Here a distinction between that which is material (in the modern sense; i.e. mind independent substance) and that which is physical (a sensible object) can be made. As such, Scripture does not appear to endorse the existence of mind-independent substance, though certainly the existence of sensible objects is affirmed. Berkeley notes the objection first in *Principles*:

> Some there are who think, that though the arguments for the real existence of bodies which are drawn from reason, be allowed not to amount to demonstrations, yet the Holy Scriptures are so clear in the point, as will sufficiently convince every good Christian, that bodies do really exist, and are something more than mere ideas; there being in Holy Writ innumerable facts related, which evidently suppose the reality of timber, and stone, mountains, and rivers, and cities, and human bodies. (*Principles*, Part 1.82)[43]

And again in *Three Dialogues*, Hylas brings up this objection:

> The Scripture account of the Creation, is what appears to me utterly irreconcileable with your notions. Moses tells us of a Creation: a Creation of what? of ideas? No certainly, but of things, of real things, solid corporeal substances. (*Three Dialogues*, Third Dialogue)[44]

Again, the charge is that the Scriptures testify to the existence of matter, thus to reject the existence of material substance is to reject the veracity of Scripture and charge God with deception, a position not in keeping with concerns about Scripture's being inerrant or with concerns about the nature of God. If we are to take seriously (as did Berkeley) the view that Scripture is not in error about that to which it speaks, and if Scripture is rightly read to acknowledge the existence of material substance, then it is not in error about material substance's existence and BI is false. However, in the immediate contexts of the above quotes, we see Berkeley making the basic response that nowhere does Scripture affirm the existence of matter but rather the existence of 'immediate objects of the understanding, or sensible things which cannot exist unperceived, or out of a mind' (*Three Dialogues*, Third Dialogue).[45] Here the semantic distinction is unimportant:

> In common talk, the objects of our senses are not termed *ideas* but *things*. Call them so still: provided you do not attribute to them any absolute external existence . . . The Creation therefore I allow to have been the creation of things, of *real* things . . . But as for solid corporeal substances, I desire you to shew where Moses makes any mention of them. (*Three Dialogues*, Third Dialogue)[46]

After making similar points in *Principles*, Berkeley adds: 'I do not think, that either what philosophers call *matter*, or the existence of objects without the mind, is anywhere mentioned in Scripture' (*Principles*, Part 1.82).[47]

Read this way, Berkeleyan idealism is essentially consistent with Scripture because Scripture never makes any claim about material substance. Physical reality is certainly affirmed by Scripture and to deny physicality does seem to be against orthodoxy, but BI does no such thing.[48]

Second, an obvious objection, hinted at above, is that if God is not hidden on BI, then why are there those who claim not to be able to interpret the divine language? Why, in other words, are there those who do not perceive the clarity of God's existence? Now, according to Berkeley, via Euphranor, the Author of nature 'constantly explaineth himself to the eyes of men' (*Alciphron*, 4.12).[49] In *Principles*, Berkeley writes that 'we need only open our eyes to see the sovereign lord of all things with a more full and clear view' (*Principles*, Part 1.148).[50] He goes on, saying that 'to an unbiased and attentive mind, nothing can be more plainly legible, than the intimate presence of an *all-wise spirit*, who fashions, regulates, and sustains the whole system of being' (*Principles*, Part 1.151).[51] Some do not recognize God's existence, Berkeley notes, due to 'want of attention'. For 'what truth is there', he says, 'which shines so strongly on the mind, that by an aversion of thought, a willful shutting of the eyes, we may not escape seeing it?' (*Principles*, Part 1.154).[52]

While Berkeley never uses such terminology, he seems to argue that *sin* negatively affects the mind, what many in the Reformed tradition call the noetic effects of sin.[53] Sin, so we argue on BI, can impair one's ability to rightly interpret the divine language, which, as the Belgic Confession explains, communicates God's existence in creation before our eyes 'as a most elegant *book*' (Article 2).[54] It is not that God *himself* is hidden; it is rather that sin can distract us from God in his handiwork. Paul Helm notes that, because of sin's noetic effects, 'we *misinterpret* evidence, hide from evidence, are a prey to imagination, accept common opinion, and the like'.[55] Perhaps the advocate of BI can follow Alvin Plantinga; Plantinga argues that the most serious noetic effects have ultimately to do with our knowledge of God, writing that were 'it not for sin and its effects, God's presence and glory would be as obvious and uncontroversial to us all as the presence of other minds, physical objects, and the past'.[56]

Third, if God is not hidden on BI and if sin's noetic effects impair one's ability to rightly interpret the divine language, then why does God not give us *more* evidence of his existence to consider? Kevin Kinghorn, assessing Schellenberg's 1993 argument (in *Divine Hiddenness and Human Reason*), writes that:

> even if we grant that some sort of spiritual blindness is affecting the way in which a person assesses the [theistic] evidence available to her ... we will still want to know why God has not provided *more positive evidence* for her consideration.[57]

We argue from BI that this objection, though important, misses the point. The point is not that, due to sin, the evidence for God is lacking; it is rather, to follow Plantinga again, that:

> [w]ithout a change of heart *even a great deal of evidence* won't convince us human beings [of God's existence]. ('If they do not listen to Moses and the Prophets, they will not be convinced even if someone rises from the dead,' Luke 16.31.)[58]

William Wainwright, analysing PDH from the perspective of Jonathan Edwards,[59] reasons that one could answer the 'more evidence' objection by saying that:

> [c]ritics like Schellenberg consistently underestimate human corruption and sinfulness. Given our perversity, and tendency to idolatry, it is likely that even a fuller divine self-disclosure would be corrupted by us, and would thus not help us. What is needed isn't *more evidence* or a fuller revelation but a new heart to appreciate the evidence and revelation we have.[60]

Our argument here is that one can receive a new heart by receiving God's grace through faith in Jesus Christ (Eph. 2.8–9). Sin's effects are 'increasingly repaired in the process of faith ... and regeneration. The person of faith may be once more such that, at least on some occasions, the presence of God *is* completely evident to her.'[61]

Fourth, some may argue, in light of the previous objection's response, that BI intensifies both the problem of religious diversity as well as the soteriological problem of evil. BI claims, from a Christian standpoint, that God is not hidden but that sin can inhibit one's ability to read the divine language; yet for the person with faith in Jesus Christ, the effects of sin are mitigated, thus allowing one, at least on some occasions, to perceive God in his handiwork. What does a commitment to BI, a Christian position, mean for other non-Christian religions? Of course, putting the question this way seems to set Christianity up, on BI, as the exclusively true religion, Christ being the only way to be saved. The advocate of BI could push back, once again, by arguing that sin inclines the human race toward other religions outside of Christianity.

But then saying *that* now seems to put us in the realm of the soteriological problem of evil (SPE), since there are those who never hear about or accept God's 'salvific path' in Christ.[62] For if God's 'salvific path' by way of the gospel of Jesus Christ was more obvious or more evident, as one might postulate, then more persons could respond to the gospel and be saved, but *that* there are some who go unsaved might be considered evil. BI could offer a response to SPE once again by pointing to sin, arguing that the 'salvific path' is made known by God's divine language and any failure to understand the message of salvation God has for us in that language is ultimately because of unrepentant sin (Rom. 3.23; 6.23). Or perhaps the advocate of BI might respond by way of sceptical theism. Mentioned above, sceptical theism has been applied to PDH, and could be applied to SPE via BI. Perhaps here the sceptical theist proposes that God has reasons, reasons *unknown* to us but *known* by him, for why there are persons who are not saved.

Conclusion

Let us take stock. In this chapter, we have sought to answer the main question by way of BI. First, we explained the relationship between PDH and POE in an attempt to elucidate SPE. Second, we explained BI. Third, we applied BI to PDH and SPE. Fourth, objections or worries to our application were considered. The upshot is that if BI is true, then it affords us unique and adequate ways to respond to PDH and SPE. But even if not true, considering its application to these issues could lead some to think in positive ways toward other solutions to PDH and SPE. It is our hope that our contribution to the conversation will encourage and motivate further conversation about these issues.

Notes

1 The two most important edited volumes on PDH are Daniel Howard-Snyder and Paul K. Moser (eds), *Divine Hiddenness: New Essays* (Cambridge: Cambridge University Press, 2002); Eleonore Stump and Adam Green (eds), *Hidden Divinity and Religious Belief: New Perspectives* (Cambridge: Cambridge University Press, 2016). For a review of the latter work, see Tyler Taber, 'Review of Adam Green and Eleonore Stump (eds), *Hidden Divinity and Religious Belief: New Perspectives* (Cambridge: Cambridge University Press, 2016)', *European Journal for Philosophy of Religion* 9 (2017), pp. 240–3.

2 For discussion of the soteriological POE, see David P. Hunt, 'Middle Knowledge and the Soteriological Problem of Evil', *Religious Studies* 27 (1991), pp. 3–26; David Basinger, 'Divine Omniscience and the Soteriological Problem of Evil: Is the Type of Knowledge God Possesses Relevant?', *Religious Studies* 28 (1992), pp. 1–18.

3 Joshua R. Farris and S. Mark Hamilton, 'Introduction: Idealism and Christian Theology', in Joshua R. Farris and S. Mark Hamilton (eds), *Idealism and Christianity: Christian Theology*, vol. 1 (London: Bloomsbury, 2016), p. 1.

4 See Adam Green and Eleonore Stump, 'Introduction', in Adam Green and Eleonore Stump (eds), *Hidden Divinity and Religious Belief: New Perspectives* (Cambridge: Cambridge University Press, 2016), p. 1.

5 Some of what follows is summarized from Tyler Taber, 'Divine Hiddenness and the Problem of Evil', in Benjamin Arbour and John R. Gilhooly (eds), *Evil and a Selection of Its Theological Problems* (Newcastle upon Tyne: Cambridge Scholars Publishing, 2017), pp. 14–30.

6 See Rik Peels, 'Divine Foreknowledge and Eternal Damnation: The Theory of Middle Knowledge as a Solution to the Soteriological Problem of Evil', *Neue Zeitschrift für Systematische Theologie* 48 (2006), pp. 160–75.

7 J. L. Schellenberg, *Divine Hiddenness and Human Reason, With a New Preface* (Ithaca, NY: Cornell University Press, 2006), p. 9; emphasis added. See also Schellenberg, 'The Hiddenness Problem and the Problem of Evil', *Faith and Philosophy* 27 (2010), pp. 45–60. Schellenberg, since his 1993 argument in *Divine Hiddenness and Human Reason*, appears to have changed his position on the relationship between POE and PDH. 'Another less than serious attempt to deal with the hiddenness problem', he writes elsewhere, 'involves sweeping it under the rug of the problem of evil' so that 'the so-called problem of hiddenness may be safely ignored'. Schellenberg, *The Wisdom to Doubt: A Justification of Religious Skepticism* (Ithaca, NY: Cornell University Press, 2007), p. 207; see also his *The Hiddenness Argument: Philosophy's New Challenge to Belief in God* (Oxford: Oxford University Press, 2015), pp. 28–31, for discussion of PDH and POE.

8 Evan Fales, 'Journeying in perplexity', in Adam Green and Eleonore Stump (eds), *Hidden Divinity and Religious Belief: New Perspectives* (Cambridge: Cambridge University Press, 2016), p. 89; emphasis added. Eleonore Stump, *Wandering in Darkness: Narrative and the Problem of Suffering* (Oxford: Oxford University Press, 2010).

9 Paul K. Moser, *The Evidence for God: Religious Knowledge Reexamined* (Cambridge: Cambridge University Press, 2010), p. 261.

10 Robert McKim, 'The Hiddenness of God', *Religious Studies* 26 (1990), p. 141; emphasis added.

11 Thomas V. Morris, *Making Sense of it All: Pascal and the Meaning of Life* (Grand Rapids, MI: Eerdmans, 1991), p. 89; emphasis added.

12 James Keller, 'The Hiddenness of God and the Problem of Evil', *International Journal for Philosophy of Religion* 37 (1995), p. 14; emphasis added.

13 See further Robert McKim, *Religious Diversity and Religious Ambiguity* (Oxford: Oxford University Press, 2001).

14 Michael Rea, *Evil and the Hiddenness of God* (Stamford: Cengage, 2015), p. 2; emphasis added. See also Peter van Inwagen's discussion of defences and theodicies in van Inwagen, 'What is the Problem of the Hiddenness of God?', in Paul K. Moser and Daniel Howard-Snyder (eds), *Divine Hiddenness: New Essays* (Cambridge: Cambridge University Press, 2002), pp. 30ff.; van Inwagen, *Problem of Evil* (Oxford: Oxford University Press, 2006), pp. 7ff. For more on defences and theodicies, see Stewart Goetz, 'The Argument from Evil', in William Lane Craig and J. P. Moreland (eds), *The Blackwell Companion to Natural Theology* (Malden, MA: Blackwell, 2009), pp. 443ff.

15 See: Michael Bergmann, 'Skeptical Theism and the Problem of Evil', in Thomas P. Flint and Michael C. Rea (eds), *The Oxford Handbook of Philosophical Theology* (New York: Oxford University Press, 2009), pp. 374–402. Trent Dougherty and Justin P. McBrayer (eds), *Skeptical Theism: New Essays* (Oxford: Oxford University Press, 2014).

16 Justin P. McBrayer and Philip Swenson, 'Scepticism about the Argument from Divine Hiddenness', *Religious Studies* 48 (2012), pp. 129–50. John Greco, 'No-fault Atheism', in Adam Green and Eleonore Stump (eds), *Hidden Divinity and Religious Belief: New Perspectives* (Cambridge: Cambridge University Press, 2016), pp. 115–16.

17 See Ian Deweese-Boyd's essay, 'Lyric Theodicy: Gerard Manley Hopkins and the Problem of Existential Hiddenness', in Adam Green and Eleonore Stump (eds), *Hidden Divinity and Religious Belief: New Perspectives* (Cambridge: Cambridge University Press, 2016), pp. 260–77.

18 For dissimilarities, see Taber, 'Divine Hiddenness and the Problem of Evil', pp. 14–30.

19 While the argument that follows in the next section primarily relies on Berkeleyan idealism, it is likely that a version of the argument could be constructed on the more modest Christian idealism view.

20 See Keota Fields, *Berkeley: Ideas, Immaterialism, and Objective Presence* (Lanham, MD: Lexington Books, 2011); Samuel C. Rickless, *Berkeley's Argument for Idealism* (Oxford: Oxford University Press, 2013); Georges Dicker, *Berkeley's Idealism: A Critical Examination* (Oxford: Oxford University Press, 2011); and John Russell Roberts, *A Metaphysics for the Mob: The Philosophy of George Berkeley* (Oxford: Oxford University Press, 2007).

21 Other arguments discussed in the previously mentioned works include the semantic argument (Rickless, *Berkeley's Argument*, pp. 93–7; Dicker, *Berkeley's Idealism*, pp. 70–5), the argument from the likeness principle (Rickless, *Berkeley's Argument*, pp. 115–20; Dicker, *Berkeley's Idealism*, 149–69), and Rickless also discusses two 'simple arguments' that he ultimately judges as ineffective (Rickless, *Berkeley's Argument*, pp. 120–7).

22 Along with Dickers, Fields, Rickless and Roberts, see also George S. Pappas, *Berkeley's Thought* (Ithaca, NY: Cornell University Press, 2000) and Kenneth Winkler, *Berkeley: An Interpretation* (Oxford: Oxford University Press, 1989).

23 George Berkeley, *A Treatise Concerning the Principles of Human Knowledge*, in G. N. Wright (ed.), *The Works of George Berkeley*, vol. 1 (London: Thomas Tegg, 1843; reprint, Elibron Classics, 2005), p. 75. Note that parenthetical notations in

the text are general references to Berkeley's works while the endnote citations are to page numbers in the specific volume used.

24 Berkeley, *Principles*, p. 75.
25 Berkeley, *Principles*, p. 95.
26 See Dickers, *Berkeley's Idealism*, pp. 139–45.
27 See Rickless, *Berkeley's Argument*, pp. 127–37.
28 We focus on Keota Field's treatment of this argument in what follows, but other discussions of Berkeley's view of divine language include Dickers, *Berkeley's Idealism*, pp. 234–5 and Roberts, *Metaphysics*, pp. 84–6, 107–9.
29 Dickers, *Berkeley's Idealism*, p. 234.
30 Dickers, *Berkeley's Idealism*, p. 234.
31 Dickers, *Berkeley's Idealism*, p. 234.
32 Roberts, *Metaphysics*, p. 84.
33 Fields, *Berkeley*, 213. See also Dickers, *Berkeley's Idealism*, pp. 234–5 and Roberts, *Metaphysics*, pp. 75–6, 84–6.
34 George Berkeley, *Alciphron*, in *The Works of George Berkeley*, ed. G. N. Wright, vol. I (London: Thomas Tegg, 1843; reprint, Elibron Classics, 2005), pp. 393–4.
35 Fields, *Berkeley*, p. 209.
36 Fields, *Berkeley*, p. 212.
37 Fields, *Berkeley*, p. 224.
38 Schellenberg, *Divine Hiddenness and Human Reason*.
39 Berkeley, *Alciphron*, p. 385.
40 Berkeley, *Alciphron*, p. 388.
41 The problem of religious luck is related to the problem of moral luck (see Dana K. Nelkin, 'Moral Luck', *The Stanford Encyclopedia of Philosophy* (Winter 2013 Edition), Edward N. Zalta (ed.), <https://plato.stanford.edu/archives/win2013/entries/moral-luck/>) in which one can be held morally accountable 'only to the extent that what we are assessed for depends on factors under our control (call this the "Control Principle").' The problem arises because, 'at the same time, when it comes to countless particular cases, we morally assess agents for things that depend on factors that are not in their control'. The problem of religious luck with respect to SPE suggests that to come to a saving faith in Christ is a moral imperative. However, if for some, whether they come to Christ is a matter of religious luck (that is, their hearing about and responding to the gospel are a matter of circumstances beyond their control), then so too for many who don't hear about or respond to the gospel of Christ. See also Linda Zagzebski, 'Religious Luck', *Faith and Philosophy* 11 (1996), pp. 397–413 and Charlotte Katzoff, 'Religious Luck and Religious Virtue', *Religious Studies* 40 (March 2004), pp. 97–111.
42 This may be more significant than indicated here. BI may fail to address this properly on its own, but that doesn't mean the problem of religious luck can't be addressed by idealism. It may be that other, traditional responses to this problem would be perfectly compatible with BI or other forms of idealism.
43 Berkeley, *Principles*, p. 117.
44 George Berkeley, *Three Dialogues Between Hylas and Philonous*, in *The Works of George Berkeley*, vol. 1, ed. G. N. Wright (London: Thomas Tegg, 1843; reprint, Elibron Classics, 2005), p. 218.
45 Berkeley, *Three Dialogues*, p. 218.
46 Berkeley, *Three Dialogues*, p. 218.
47 Berkeley, *Principles*, p. 117.

48 See further James Spiegel, 'The Theological Orthodoxy of Berkeley's Immaterialism', *Faith and Philosophy* 13 (1996), pp. 216–35; Spiegel, 'Immaterialism as a Boon to Faith: Berkeley and Christian Theology', in Greg Ganssle and Benjamin Arbour (eds), *Christianity and the Modern Philosophers* (Grand Rapids, MI: Zondervan, forthcoming).

49 George Berkeley, *Alciphron*, in G. N. Wright (ed.), *The Works of George Berkeley*, vol. I (London: Thomas Tegg, 1843; reprint, Elibron Classics, 2005), p. 393.

50 Berkeley, *Principles*, p. 144.

51 Berkeley, *Principles*, p. 145.

52 Berkeley, *Principles*, p. 147.

53 See Stephen K. Moroney, *The Noetic Effects of Sin: A Historical and Contemporary Exploration of How Sin Affects Our Thinking* (Lanham: Lexington, 2000); Rik Peels, 'Sin and Human Cognition of God', *Scottish Journal of Theology* 64 (2011), pp. 390–409.

54 On which see Gijsbert van den Brink, 'A Most Elegant Book: The Natural World in Article 2 of the Belgic Confession', *Westminster Theological Journal* 73 (2011), pp. 273–92.

55 Paul Helm, 'John Calvin, the "Sensus Divinitatis", and the Noetic Effects of Sin', *International Journal for Philosophy of Religion* 43 (1998), p. 100; emphasis added.

56 Alvin Plantinga, *Warranted Christian Belief* (Oxford: Oxford University Press, 2000), p. 214.

57 Kevin Kinghorn, 'Why Doesn't God Make His Existence More Obvious?', *Asbury Theological Journal* 58 (2003), p. 190; emphasis added.

58 Alvin Plantinga, 'Internalism, Externalism, Defeaters, and Arguments for Christian Belief', *Philosophia Christi* 3 (2001), p. 382, n. 5; emphasis added.

59 For a comparison of Edwards and Berkeley on idealism, see William Wainwright, 'Berkeley, Edwards, Idealism, and the Knowledge of God', in Joshua R. Farris and S. Mark Hamilton (eds), *Idealism and Christianity: Christian Theology*, vol. 1 (London: Bloomsbury, 2016), pp. 35–53.

60 William Wainwright, 'Jonathan Edwards and the Hiddenness of God', in Daniel Howard-Snyder and Paul K. Moser (eds), *Divine Hiddenness: New Essays* (Cambridge: Cambridge University Press, 2002), p. 104; emphasis added.

61 Plantinga, *Warranted Christian Belief*, p. 487; emphasis added.

62 For discussion of SPE, see Rik Peels, 'Divine Foreknowledge and Eternal Damnation: The Theory of Middle Knowledge as a Solution to the Soteriological Problem of Evil', *Neue Zeitschrift für Systematische Theologie* 48 (2006), pp. 160–75.

3

Retributivism Rejected: A Restorative Hope for Justice in the Age to Come

JONATHAN RUTLEDGE

Retributivism is, roughly, the thesis that wrongdoers ought to be punished simply because they *deserve* to be punished. If asked *why* a wrongdoer *deserves* punishment, a strong retributivist of the sort I am considering in this chapter might respond by saying any number of things like the following: 'The world would be *morally objectionable* on the whole without punishing the wrongdoer.' Someone might baulk at this claim for often we do choose to refrain from punishing someone for wrongdoing. Children, for instance, are often forgiven by their parents and punishment is routinely forborne. Indeed, sometimes these very same children respond to this punishment-less forgiveness by becoming better people, presumably resulting in a world that has *more value* on the whole. But no, says the strong retributivist. Unless such wrongdoing, such sin, is met with punishment, the world is left in a sub-optimal moral state. It is this sort of claim to which I object.

In this chapter, I argue that strong retributivism of the sort described in the above paragraph ought to be rejected by Christian theologians.[1] Although there is not space to detail exhaustively why rejecting this strong retributivism matters in Christian theology, it plays a part in the development of a number of theological and practical doctrines, some of which are especially popular at the moment. These include traditional Reformed doctrines of penal substitution, atonement generally, advocation of the death penalty, biblical eschatology, the problem of sin, the permissibility of interpersonal and intergroup forgiveness, etc. In other words, if one is to engage with practical and systematic theology, whether or not strong retributivism characterizes the moral realm, i.e. whether it characterizes God's justice, really ought to be worked out.

I begin by defining retributivism[2] more carefully and follow with a brief foray into some philosophical considerations concerning retributivism. Then I discuss whether retributivism might plausibly be found in Scripture. The results fall against retributivism; that is, there are no positive philosophical or exegetical arguments *for* retributivism. But not *only* does Scripture provide reason to think that justice fails to demand punishment of the retributivist sort. It also characterizes punishment as concerned with *restoration* (e.g. new creation). Consequently, it is the latter rationale for punishment (i.e. restoration; not retribution) that ought to be championed by the Christian theologian.

Retributive Punishment – The Philosophical Case

The Definition of Retributivism

The proper definition of retributive punishment allows for several different construals of retributivism.[3] Despite the plethora of retributive positions, however, as a general rule retributivism can be said to affirm that wrongdoers *deserve* punishment for their wrongful actions. And when upon reflection one begins to explore the *grounding* of a wrongdoer's *just desert* of punishment, different retributivist theories begin to emerge.[4] In other words, retributivism is at bottom a theory about the *rationale* behind just punishment. That is, it offers a possible answer to the question, *when is punishment justified?*

Despite the different ways in which one might define retributivism, a strong definition of retributivism is primarily of interest here; that is, a definition that makes retribution an uncompromising feature of the moral realm. Thus, retributivism, for the purposes of this chapter, is essentially the claim that the punishment of wrongdoers is *required* because wrongdoers deserve to be punished.[5] Punishment of wrongdoers is good because morality demands it. If a wrongdoer were to go unpunished, then that would be a blight on the world. Indeed, it would reflect poorly on the governor of creation were sin left unaddressed by punishment. It is this understanding of retributivism with which I take issue.

Philosophical Considerations

There are, broadly speaking, two primary ways of philosophically motivating the acceptance of retributivism. First, retributivism has very strong intuitive support. Indeed, this intuitive support can be found in the form of an emotion that Jeffrie Murphy has dubbed 'retributive hatred'.[6] Only a moment's reflection on our immediate reactions and moral assessments of the perpetrators of great evils is necessary to reveal our deeply ingrained desire to see them 'brought to justice' via punishment. Thus, there is evidence from intuition that retributivism is true. Second, some theorists argue that retributivism is superior to consequentialist theories of punishment. For example, basic forms of utilitarianism suffer from the concern that they *in principle* might require innocents to be punished for society's benefit.[7] In this context, even if a consequentialist could persuasively argue that only the guilty can be rightly punished, they would still need to respond to the objection that *in principle* there is no limit to the amount of permissible punishment. But surely such a limit exists. Retributivist theories (e.g. *lex talionis*) have a much more plausible justification for preventing this sort of over-punishment. As a result, to the degree that a theory of punishment or justice addresses such concerns, it is superior to its alternatives.

Each of the above arguments for retributivism has its limits. In the case of intuitions, they undoubtedly provide *pro tanto* reasons to believe in retributivism for those that have them,[8] but they are hardly decisive. Such intuitions might be overridden by very strong moral intuitions to the contrary or by scriptural arguments to the contrary.

When countering the second sort of argument for retributive forms of punishment – i.e. those arguments that count the ability to explain why there should be *limits* on punishment as a positive feature – a plausible option available to the non-retributivist, one to which I incline, would be to endorse the following position composed of at least two claims:

Claim 1 – *punishments are justified in virtue of being reasonably thought to lead to certain ends (e.g. restoration, deterrence, societal protection, etc.), and they are not justified in virtue of being deserved in a retributive sense.*
Claim 2 – *there are limits to what punishments are permissible for bringing about the ends described in Claim 1.*

Now, endorsing Claim 2 is not the same thing as being a retributivist in my sense. Retributivism claims that we have a moral duty to punish wrongdoers to the degree to which their wrongdoing merits punishment. That is, retributivism tells us that some form of punishment is positively necessary in response to wrongdoing. A proponent of Claim 2 can straightforwardly deny this. Instead, all they claim is that *in the case that we do punish a wrongdoer, we must not over-punish them.* This is not to be a retributivist. It is merely to be sensible.

Despite the lack of a compelling philosophical case *for* retributive punishment, there is no knock-down case *against* it either. The reason for this is that a retributivist can admit of the goods posited by a non-retributivist. They merely deny that the sorts of consequential goods that non-retributivists have in mind fundamentally ground the reason for punishment.[9]

Thus, it seems that we must turn to Scripture if we are to have any strong case for or against retributive punishment and justice. In what follows,

I consider a few scriptural passages that, when taken alone, might seem to provide evidence for retributive justice underlying God's rationale for punishment. I will defend non-retributive readings of such passages against commonly affirmed retributive alternatives.

It would be best, however, to begin with some comments on what would *not* count as strong evidence of retributive justice in Scripture. First, to find that God's wrath is directed at humankind does not entail the presence of retributive justice. Non-retributivists often agree that wrath is an appropriate response to wrongdoing. What they disagree about is *the reason(s) punishment of the offence is morally justified.* Thus, finding wrath is not the same as finding retributivism. Second, finding claims that wrongdoers *deserve* punishment does not, by itself, entail retributivism. On the one hand, the idea that a wrongdoer got *what they had coming to them* entails neither the *proportionality aspect* of retributivism nor that the wrongdoer's alleged desert is punishment as opposed to the natural consequences of their action. On the other hand, even if the wrongdoer's desert is best characterized as punishment (i.e. instead of consequences), the question of *why* the wrongdoer deserves punishment must be answered prior to concluding that we have retributivism. For if the reason they deserve punishment is grounded in promoting a non-retributive good, then we have not found retributivism but justice of some other sort. Third, the retributivism we are concerned with is not *legal* retributivism. It is *moral* retributivism, meaning that it is the moral law, and not some human law, that requires the implementation of punishment. Let us, then, turn to some instances of possible scriptural evidence for retributivism.

The Scriptural Case Concerning Retributivism

It is clear that many scholars see *retributive justice* as part and parcel of Pauline theology.[10] Indeed, the entire letter to the Romans might be construed as an affirmation of retributivism. Consider what we read in Romans 2.3–11:

> [3] Do you imagine, whoever you are, that when you judge those who do such things and yet do them yourself, you will escape the judgment of God? [4] Or do you despise the riches of his kindness and forbearance and patience? Do you not realize that God's kindness is meant to lead you to repentance? [5] But by your hard and impenitent heart *you are storing up wrath for yourself* on the day of wrath, when God's *righteous judgment* will be revealed. [6] For *he will repay according to each one's deeds*: [7] to those who by patiently doing good seek for glory and honour and immortality, *he will give eternal life*; [8] while for those who are self-seeking and who

> obey not the truth but wickedness, there will be wrath and fury. ⁹ There will be anguish and distress for everyone who does evil, the Jew first and also the Greek, ¹⁰ but glory and honour and peace for everyone who does good, the Jew first and also the Greek. ¹¹ For God shows no partiality.[11]

This passage clearly teaches that God is a judge, and a righteous or just judge at that. Moreover, we see in verse 6 that God repays each person according to their deeds. Apart from any consideration of the context of Paul's argument or the Hebrew Scriptures echoing abundantly throughout the epistle,[12] one might indeed conclude that retributive justice simply *must* be included in the best explanation for various elements of the above passage (e.g. God's wrath, the calculation of repaying people for their deeds, etc.). However, if we reconsider the broad argument of the epistle to the Romans, it becomes starkly clear that retribution is *not* fundamental to God's *dikaiosune*.

First, it is imperative when reading Romans to realize what question Paul is attempting to answer. Contrary to common misperceptions, Paul is not trying to answer the question, *What must I do to be saved?* This question is not wholly orthogonal to Paul's project, but it is not what guides his discussion in Romans. Rather, as Richard Hays has aptly noted, Paul is engaging in the project of 'theodicy', seen especially in Romans 1.16–17, where Paul both echoes Isaiah 50.7–8 (i.e. 'I have not been disgraced . . . I know that I shall not be put to shame [LXX: αισχυνθώ]') and alludes to Habakkuk 2.4 (i.e. 'but the righteous [LXX: δίκαιος] live by my faith [LXX: πίστεως μου]').[13] That is, Paul is, with a slight deviation from the words of Milton, providing an account which justifies the ways of God to Jews and Gentiles.[14] Or put yet another way, Paul is defending the justice of God's decision to show 'no partiality' (Rom. 2.11).

But when Paul defends God's impartiality, we must ask *what* impartiality and *why* would Paul need to defend God's decision to be impartial? Indeed, insofar as Paul writes concerning God's *justice*, modern readers typically assume a just God simply *is* impartial. But we must remember that YHWH entered into a covenant with Israel in the Hebrew Scriptures, a covenant which was *not* impartial. And given the context of a covenant which was *partial to Israel*, the violation of which would amount to violating a promise (i.e. something which a morally perfect being would surely not do), God's breaking the covenant is indeed worrisome. Thus, the impartiality in need of defence is God's impartiality in extending salvation to both the Jews and the Gentiles. The reason this impartiality is in need of defence is because God's action is perceived by some in Israel as a violation of his promise to be their God. This is the topic of Romans.

But let us turn our attention directly to the text. It is ineluctably clear that Paul writes to explain the place of Gentiles in relationship to God. Consider the following characteristic passages of the text (all italics are my own):

For I am not ashamed of the gospel; it is the power of god for salvation to everyone who has faith, to *the Jew first and also to the Greek*. (Rom. 1.16)

There will be anguish and distress for everyone who does evil, *the Jew first and also the Greek*, but glory and honor and peace for everyone who does good, *the Jew first and also the Greek*. (Rom. 2.9–10)

What if God, desiring to show his wrath and to make known his power, has endured with much patience the objects of wrath that are made for destruction; and what if he has done so in order to make known the riches of his glory for the objects of mercy, which he has prepared beforehand for glory – including us whom he has called, *not from the Jews only but also from the Gentiles*? (Rom. 9.22–24)

For there is no distinction between Jew and Greek; the same Lord is Lord of all and is generous to all who call on him. (Rom. 10.12)

For I tell you that *Christ has become a servant of the circumcised* on behalf of the truth of God in order that he might confirm the promises given to the patriarchs, and in order *that the Gentiles might glorify God for his mercy*. As it is written,

'Therefore *I will confess you among the Gentiles*, and sing praises to your name.' (Rom. 15.8–9)

In all the above passages, we see the theme of theodicy (i.e. justifying God's decision to extend the benefits of salvation to both Jews and Gentiles) clearly. The theme of God's justice does not concern his justice in, say, punishing the wicked as one might expect were the author endorsing retributivism. Instead, the theme of justice concerns God's decision to extend *mercy* to all. And crucially, God does not extend mercy to morally perfect persons. He extends mercy to sinners (cf. Rom. 3.23). Thus, a mere discussion of God's justice found in Romans is not sufficient to conclude that Paul is a retributivist.

But let us not miss the brilliance of Paul's ability to weave enthymematic allusions into his dense texts, allusions which foreshadow his overall argument. Consider the most difficult part of his text for a non-retributivist in Romans 2, where we find this theme of the unrestricted scope of God's mercy in the veiled subtext: 'For *he will repay according to each one's deeds*' (v. 6). This line is almost a word-for-word lifting of Psalm 62.12 in the Septuagint, as well as Proverbs 24.12. In the latter case, the proverb emphasizes the appropriateness of *God* as judge, for he perfectly knows the heart of all. In the former case, the psalm emboldens its hearers to *hope*[15] in the Lord, for he provides deliverance and salvation to his people. Thus, as he develops his argument in Romans, Paul is subtly communicating to his readers that, despite the fact that Romans 2 and 3 include *everyone* in the class of people coming under condemnation, those who hope in the Lord for salvation may yet find mercy.[16] Indeed, in the preceding verse, Paul appears to echo Deuteronomy 9.27, the only Old Testament passage in which we find σκληρότητα (tr. 'stubbornness'). In that passage, Moses reminds the Israelites (cf. Num. 11.1–34) how he pleaded with YHWH to show mercy on Israel rather than to destroy them as a result of their grumbling in the wilderness. Thus, Paul is reminding his readers that even when we rightly fall under God's condemnation and serve as objects of God's wrath, God has mercy on those who truly repent.

What, then, is Paul communicating about God's justice by including both these echoes in Romans 2 and the letter's overarching theme of Gentile inclusion in the covenant? He reveals God's primary aim when it comes to punishing his people. God does *not* punish to restore the moral order as a retributivist might suggest. Were this the case, then God's decision to have mercy would itself be unjust, for wrongdoers would not receive the punishment due to them. Instead of a retributivist reading, then, Paul communicates that God desires the repentance of those at whom his wrath is directed. In other words, whatever punishment is implemented, it aims not at retribution but at restoration. And it is restoration that renders intelligible the justice of mercy, which is applied to those who repent.

Even on the reading of Romans just offered, however, a theologian might *insist* that retributive justice lies behind the text as a presupposition that best explains *why* God's mercy is just. For after all, little has yet been said about the role of Christ's death. But passages such as Romans 5 (i.e. with the Adam and Christ parallel) and Romans 6 (i.e. with the idea that we are buried and resurrected in Christ) require that we make sense of the need for Christ's death to attain God's mercy. The general thought process might be this:

> God desires to show us mercy, and he desired to show the Israelites mercy as well. However, because justice requires punishment, the only way in which God could show mercy to us was if the deserved punishment was actually implemented. This is why in Romans 5 Paul compares Adam and Christ with one another. For just as all humanity suffered as a result of Adam's sin, so too Christ represents all humanity in bearing the punishment for sin.

Despite the appeal of this line of thought, it is worth emphasizing that it is a theological gloss on Romans 5–6, which *imports* a particular mechanism of the atonement to explain the Adam and Christ parallel. If we look at the Romans text, however, we see suggestions of a different, though under-described, mechanism:

> all who believe are now justified by his grace as a gift, through the redemption that is in Christ Jesus, whom God put forward as a sacrifice of atonement [i.e. ἱλαστήριον[17]], by his blood, effective through faith. (Rom. 3.24–25a)

This brief nod to Christ's death as a part of a *sacrifice* might appear to support the theological objection to non-retributive readings of Romans that I suggested above, for after all (someone might think), what is a sacrifice but a substitutionary offering of punishment in place of the punishment one owes to God?

Such an understanding of sacrifices should not be maintained. First, even though we find the notion of Christ being a sin-offering here and elsewhere in Scripture (cf. Rom. 4.25; 8.3; 1 Cor. 15.3, 20, 23; 2 Cor. 5.21; Gal. 1.4), we must find a way to harmonize that understanding with the depiction of Christ as a *covenant* sacrifice (cf. 1 Cor. 11.25), a *yom kippur* sacrifice (Hebrews), a Passover sacrifice (1 Cor. 5.7–8), a first-fruits sacrifice (1 Cor. 15.20, 23), etc.[18] Second, whether or not the sacrifice is an *equivalent* punishment of the animal to the punishment deserved by a wrongdoer is highly dubious, as is the idea that the animal is truly punished in the first place. Thus, if we are to understand the sacrificial process as involving substitution at all, we must carefully explicate precisely *what* is substituted for *what* in the ritual. Let us set this problem of explaining the significance of sacrificial imagery aside, however, and turn to Isaiah 53.

Isaiah 53, one of several servant songs in Isaiah, has been called 'the most contested chapter in the Old Testament' due to its incredibly convoluted interpretive difficulties.[19] Even if we doubt that it is a cultic passage[20], it certainly deals with vicarious suffering (i.e. suffering that might count as punishment). Indeed, this is why it is a favourite atonement passage for many theologians. Thus, it is worth investigating whether Isaiah 53 presupposes retributivism.

> [4] Surely he has borne our infirmities
>   and carried our diseases;
> yet we accounted him stricken,
>   struck down by God, and afflicted.
> [5] But he was wounded for our transgressions,
>   crushed for our iniquities;
> upon him was the punishment that made us whole,
>   and by his bruises we are healed.

> ⁶ All we like sheep have gone astray;
>   we have all turned to our own way,
> and the LORD has laid on him
>   the iniquity of us all. (Isa. 53.4–6)

Before continuing on with the passage, let us pause here to see if we yet have textual support for retributivism. We have some textual evidence in verse 4 that the suffering servant (i.e. Jesus) *bears* suffering that is *in some sense* ours. The sense in which the suffering is ours, however, is not yet explained. One might say that Jesus bears *the same sorts* of suffering that we (i.e. either corporate humanity, the Church, or Israel) do. And such a suggestion might merely indicate the Incarnation – i.e. he was human in every way as we are (cf. Heb. 2.17–18) – or it might indicate something more. In verse 5 we see that Jesus was 'wounded *for* our transgressions' and 'crushed *for* our iniquities', but what is meant by the word 'for' here? Someone might think that the wounds *pay the price* due for our transgressions, but the only rationale given in this verse is this: these punishments *heal* us. How do they heal us? By paying the retributive price due? Nothing to this effect is said explicitly, and thus, this text can only be construed as endorsing such a retributivist element if there are good independent reasons to endorse retributivism. Finally in verse 6, however, we see that our sin was laid upon Jesus, the suffering servant. The language of 'laid upon' is again multiply ambiguous. It could be metaphysical or forensic imputation of sin to Christ, but also might be a shorthand way of saying that Jesus became a sin-offering. Indeed, this latter interpretation seems to be supported by what we find in verse 10:

> ¹⁰ Yet it was the will of the LORD to crush him with pain.
> *When you make his life an offering for sin,*
>   he shall see his offspring, and shall prolong his days;
> through him the will of the LORD shall prosper. (Isa. 53.10; italics mine)

In verse 10, we also find a theme of God *willing* the pain of the suffering servant towards the end of making a sin-offering. This, however, is not sufficient to demonstrate that the suffering servant was *retributively punished*, for no explanation is given for *why* the suffering was willed. Was it for retributive reasons? Or was it because *somehow* his suffering was essentially tied up with our redemption? These questions are left unanswered by the text.

There is much more that one might say concerning Isaiah 53, but this is sufficient to rule out the view that Christians are committed to retributivism by it. Let us turn, then, to a consideration of one further complication for non-retributivists; namely, the principle of *lex talionis*.

RETRIBUTIVISM REJECTED

We find the *lex talionis* presented explicitly in three different passages in the Pentateuch: Exodus 21.20–25, Leviticus 24.19–22, and Deuteronomy 19.18–21. For reference, consider just the Leviticus passage:

> Anyone who maims another shall suffer the same injury in return: fracture for fracture, eye for eye, tooth for tooth; the injury inflicted is the injury to be suffered. One who kills an animal shall make restitution for it; but one who kills a human being shall be put to death. You shall have one law for the alien and for the citizen: for I am the LORD your God.

Such passages bear witness to 'laws of retaliation' that we find in ANE law codes.[21] The comparative humaneness of the Hebrew *lex talionis* has been noted by many scholars,[22] and unlike other cultures, the class system seems to have played far less of a role in determining the punishment due for different crimes (hence, the command to 'have one law for the alien and for the citizen').

Moreover, the Hebrew *lex talionis* was applied as a limit on the punishment that could be administered for a particular offence (i.e. not as retributive *due* punishment). After all, there are obvious cases in which the literal *lex talionis* would not result in equivalent punishments being laid upon the wrongdoer. Suppose, for instance, that I go about knocking out teeth from 28 individuals and that I do so in such a way that I knock out a different type of tooth from each individual (e.g. never do I knock out the same molar-type in two different people). However many turps (i.e. badness points) I introduce into the world through this pernicious and calculated wrongdoing, that same number must be balanced out via the logic of retribution. But then, what should my punishment be? It might seem natural to assume that the proper punishment for me would be to remove all 28 of *my* teeth and call things even. But that would be absurd! For the number of turps introduced into the world conditional on my losing *all* my teeth would surely surpass the turps I introduced into the world when knocking out just *one* tooth in 28 other persons. So I should not be punished via the removal of all my teeth. But then what punishment would be apt? *Lex talionis*, if interpreted as literally requiring the very same punishment, gives the wrong answer in such a case.

This point is driven home again in Exodus 21.22–25 which, rather than sanction a true eye-for-an-eye penalty, opts for an eye-for-some-sufficient-value-of-an-eye penalty instead:[23]

> When people who are fighting injure a pregnant woman so that there is a miscarriage, and yet no further harm follows, the one responsible shall be fined what the woman's husband demands, paying as much as the judge determines. If any harm follows, then you shall give life for life, eye for eye, tooth for tooth. (Exod. 21.22–24a)

The literally equivalent punishment of the scenario here described would not be monetary, but rather would require the taking of an innocent life; namely, the life of the wrongdoer's next expected unborn child. Such a verdict would be morally horrendous, and so obviously requires straying from a strict *lex talionis* logic.[24] What then is the purpose of the *lex talionis* in the books of the law?

There are a number of plausible answers to this question, but whatever the rationale it excludes an affirmation of retributivism. Rather, it merely sets a *limit* to the punishment permissible for different offences. Thus, no affirmation of retributivism is to be found in the *lex talionis*.

From the Christian perspective on the *lex talionis*, however, even more can be said, for Christ calls Christians to an even greater standard. Matthew, for instance, represents Jesus as saying:

> You have heard that it was said, 'An eye for an eye and a tooth for a tooth'. But I say to you, do not resist an evildoer. But if anyone strikes you on the right cheek, turn the other also; and if anyone wants to sue you and take your coat, give your cloak as well; and if anyone forces you to go one mile, go also the second mile. Give to everyone who begs from you, and do not refuse anyone who wants to borrow from you. (Matt. 5.38–42)

Here we see Jesus citing directly the *lex talionis* measure and charging his listeners to demonstrate even greater love and mercy towards an offender. Someone might think Jesus is telling them to reject the *lex talionis*,[25] but this is to go beyond the teaching of the passage. Whether or not Jesus is teaching such rejection depends on the purpose of the *lex talionis* and the people over whom it has jurisdiction in his eyes. Perhaps, for instance, Jesus merely thinks *his followers* should follow such a demanding norm for action as turning the other cheek rather than all people. If so, then he is not rejecting the *lex talionis* so much as modifying (or clarifying) its scope.

Yet given that the *lex talionis*, as we have seen, is truly only prescribing a *maximum permissible* penalty for various offences, following Jesus' instructions is not a violation of that law. Suppose the appropriate *lex talionis* measure for a slap in the face is to *at most* slap one's offender in return. In that case, there are many ways to follow the *lex talionis* prescription. You could, of course, satisfy the *lex talionis* by slapping the offender, but you could equally well ignore the slap, pray over the offender, attempt to understand if something else is bothering the offender, buy them a drink, or as Jesus suggests, offer them your other cheek. So Jesus is not teaching anything in strict contradiction with the *lex talionis*; rather, he is simply teaching his followers to satisfy the *lex talionis* by way of a higher standard.

Conclusion

In the above section, we have seen that there are no compelling reasons to think retributivism is taught in the passages most likely to offer such reasons. Indeed, if any justification for the punishments referenced in Scripture is to be found, it is restorative in nature, for as Paul tells us in Romans, God's ultimate charitable motive is to bring sinners to repentance (i.e. a restorative rationale if there ever was one). However, we have also seen that there are not compelling philosophical arguments in favour of adopting retributivism as characterized in this chapter. Therefore, I suggest that strong retributive rationales for punishment in Christian theology be resisted in favour of adopting a more restorative tone; that is, one which follows the teleological cadence of the new heavens and earth.

Notes

1 It would be, to my mind, felicitous were all theologians to reject this sort of retributivism, but my argument will not be targeted at such a broad audience due to the different authorities with which I would have to engage.

2 For the remainder of this chapter, I will slip between using 'retributivism' and 'strong retributivism'. Context should highlight if a weaker form of retributivism is in play.

3 John Cottingham, 'Varieties of Retribution', *Philosophical Quarterly* 29 (1979), pp. 238–46 provides a taxonomy of nine different construals of *retributivism*. See also the supplementary paper on Cottingham's various construal of retributivism: Nigel Walker, 'Even More Varieties of Retributivism', *Philosophy* 74, 290 (1999), pp. 595–605.

4 E.g. Robert Nozick, *Philosophical Explanations* (Cambridge, MA: Harvard University Press, 1981), pp. 366–74 presents the view that desert can be calculated by taking account of the offender's degree of culpability and harm done.

5 Notice that on traditional penal substitution, this is affirmed. On such theories, sin is an offence against God, and it is punished (or at least, paid for) by Christ. Even if forgiveness is offered on such views, Christ's death was first required.

6 Jeffrie G. Murphy and Jean Hampton, *Forgiveness and Mercy* (Cambridge: Cambridge University Press, 1988), pp. 88–110.

7 J. J. C. Smart and Bernard Williams, *Utilitarianism: For and Against* (Cambridge: Cambridge University Press, 1973), pp. 92–3.

8 For discussions of this sort of common sense epistemology, see Michael Huemer, *Skepticism and the Veil of Perception* (New York: Rowman and Littlefield, 2001).

9 Indeed, I doubt a merely deontological construal of retributivism could sufficiently sift through alternative punishments whose value meets the demands of retributive justice but are differentiable with respect to consequences.

10 For a representative sample: (i) J. I. Packer, *What Did the Cross Achieve? The Logic of Penal Substitution* (Leicester: TSF Monograph, 1974); (ii) Leon Morris, *The Cross in the New Testament* (Exeter: Paternoster, 1966); (iii) Thomas R. Schreiner, 'Penal Substitution View', in James Beilby and Paul R. Eddy (eds), *The Nature of*

the Atonement (Downers Grove, IL: InterVarsity Press, 2006), pp. 67–116; and (iv) John R. W. Stott, *The Cross of Christ* (Downers Grove, IL: InterVarsity Press, 1986), p. 187.

11 NRSV. Italics mine.

12 Indeed, Paul implies that the Hebrew Scriptures contain the gospel he proclaims in Rom. 1.1–3a: 'Paul . . . set apart for the gospel of God, ²which he *promised beforehand through his prophets in the holy scriptures,* ³the gospel concerning his Son' (italics mine).

13 Richard B. Hays, *Echoes of Scripture in the Letters of Paul* (New Haven, CT: Yale University Press, 1989), pp. 38–40 and 53.

14 Cf. John Milton, *Paradise Lost* (New York: Penguin, 2000), Bk. 1.

15 Some translations (e.g. the NRSV) occlude the emphasis on *elpis* somewhat by translating it as some form of 'trust'. This is unfortunate given the context in which Paul quotes this text. Rather, the emphasis is on *hoping* in the Lord's salvation, despite being, oneself, a member of the condemned party in Romans 2.

16 Hays, *Echoes of Scripture in the Letters of Paul*, p. 42.

17 It is worth emphasizing that the Greek word (*h*)*ilasterion* is used to refer to the mercy seat or the altar of burnt offering (Ezek. 43.14, 17 and 20) in the LXX rather than to a type of *sacrifice* (cf. Christian Eberhart, *The Sacrifice of Jesus: Understanding Atonement Biblically*, Minneapolis, MN: Fortress Press, 2011, pp. 114–15), and the term is used similarly in Hebrews 9.5.

18 Christopher D. Marshall, *Beyond Retribution: A New Testament Vision for Justice, Crime, and Punishment* (Grand Rapids, MI: Eerdmans Publishing, 2001), p. 63.

19 Brevard Childs, *Isaiah* (OTL, Louisville, KY: Westminster John Knox, 2001), p. 410.

20 E.g. (i) Eberhart, *The Sacrifice of Jesus*, p. 119; (ii) Childs, *Isaiah*, p. 418. See J. Alan Groves, 2004, 'Atonement in Isaiah 53: "For He Bore the Sins of Many"', in Charles E. Hill and Frank A. James III (eds), *The Glory of the Atonement: Biblical, Historical and Practical Perspectives* (Downers Grove, IL: InterVarsity Press), p. 88, for discussion of appropriating Isaiah 53 as a non-cultic interpretation of one's suffering on humanity's (or Israel's) behalf (i.e. either vicariously or substitutionally).

21 Much of my discussion is indebted to the discussion found in Marshall, *Beyond Retribution*, pp. 79–84. See Denny J. Weaver, 'Transforming Nonresistance: From *Lex Talionis* to "Do Not Resist the Evil One"', in W. M. Swarley (ed.), *The Love of Enemy and Nonretaliation in the New Testament* (Louisville, KY: Westminster John Knox, 1992) pp. 32–71, for discussion of the relevance of such law codes.

22 Marshall, *Beyond Retribution*, pp. 79–80; G. J. Wenham, 1978, 'Law and the Legal System in the Old Testament', in B. N. Kaye and G. J. Wenham (eds), *Law, Morality, and the Bible: A Symposium* (Leicester: InterVarsity Press, 1978), pp. 24–52.

23 We see such a practice also in Josephus, *Ant.* 4.280.

24 There were, of course, scholars who may have thought otherwise, such as Philo, 1928–65, *The Special Laws*, tr. F. H. Colson, Vols 7–8 (Cambridge, MA: Harvard University Press, III), pp. 181–2. Yet clearly there were instances of rabbis who saw these sorts of difficulties in the Hebrew Scriptures: e.g. Babylonian Talmud, Tractate *Baba Qamma.* 83b–84a. For a discussion of the rabbinical interpretation of the

lex talionis, see Jacob Milgrom, 'Lex Talionis and the Rabbis', *Bible Review* 12.2 (1996), pp. 16–48.

25 Although see Dale C. Allison, *The Sermon on the Mount: Inspiring the Moral Imagination* (New York: Crossway Publishing, 1999), pp. 93–4, who claims that Christ is overturning *lex talionis* at the individual level while leaving it operative at the governmental level.

4

Original Sin in Abelard's Commentary on Romans

DANIEL W. HOUCK

One of the major objections to the doctrine of original sin is that it entails the doctrine of original guilt. The doctrine of original guilt affirms that infants are guilty from the beginning of their time in the womb. How could this be? According to Augustine – the most influential advocate of the doctrine of original sin – infants are guilty because they (in some sense) pre-existed their life in the womb and sinned in the Garden of Eden. 'We were all in that one [Adam], because we all were that one (*Omnes enim fuimus in illo uno, quando omnes fuimus ille unus*)'.[1]

The claim that infants are culpable for a sin they committed before they existed in utero is open to a number of objections. Perhaps the chief objection is that infants do not pre-exist their conception, and they can hardly be culpable for committing an action before they began to exist. There are other defences of original guilt. Some theologians have proposed that guilt is transmitted from Adam to his posterity through seminal transmission. Others have argued that God imputes guilt to infants, despite the fact that they have not done anything wrong. These proposals are also open to serious objections. As Oliver Crisp has argued, the conjunction of original sin and original guilt seems immoral and unjust: 'it is necessarily morally wrong to punish the innocent, and I am innocent of Adam's sin (I did not commit his sin or condone it). It is also immoral because the guilt of one person's sin does not transfer to another (I am not guilty of committing Adam's sin).'[2] Due at least in part to these difficulties, a growing number of theologians have attempted to separate original sin from original guilt.[3]

Whether contemporary theologians should defend original guilt is an important question. However, it not a question that I will attempt to answer here. Instead the aim of the present chapter is twofold. The first goal is to help frame the question historically by giving an account of the medieval theologian Peter Abelard's (1079–1142) view of original sin and guilt. Second, I will suggest that his account would be useful for contemporary theologians to consider. In general, the contemporary discussion of original sin in systematic theology would benefit from continued engagement with major figures in the Christian tradition. But why Abelard? He is one of the first major figures in the Western tradition – if not *the* first – to defend original sin while rejecting original guilt.[4] Yet his account is relatively neglected, and when mentioned it is often misconstrued. It is frequently asserted that he denied original sin outright. For example, Marcia Colish argues that Abelard 'dispenses with the need to explain the transmission of original sin by dropping the idea of original sin itself, in effect reducing original sin to actual sin'.[5] In his magisterial history of the dogma of original sin, Julius Gross likewise asserts that 'for Master Peter there is no original sin, only an original punishment, or better, a collective punishment'.[6] Others, such as Steven Cartwright, have suggested that Abelard was simply incoherent. '[Abelard] talks around original sin as guilt, denying it on the one hand but using similar terms to define it on the other. He also again speaks of the inherited nature of original sin and of the presence of humanity in Adam at the time of his sin.'[7] According to Paul Kemeny, for Abelard 'original sin is a misnomer'.[8]

Against these various claims, I will argue that Abelard clearly attempted to defend original sin without recourse to original guilt. A careful reading of his commentary on Romans 5 shows that he understands original sin to be the debt of damnation God imposes on the human race on account of Adam's first act of sin. Infants receive this same debt of punishment despite the fact that they are innocent. If they are not baptized, they will be condemned on account of it. However, Abelard argues, perhaps surprisingly, that this debt of damnation was imposed by God as an act of *mercy*. Both condemned infants and those who knew them – such as their parents – are better off than they would have been if such infants had not died prematurely. I will then discuss two criticisms of Abelard's account: it seems to imply that God is unjust, and the mode of sin's transmission is unclear. Though I do not endorse Abelard's account, it is worth considering, both because it helps us get a better handle on the history of the doctrine and because it provokes us to consider important questions we might have otherwise neglected. Especially given the increasing tendency of theologians to propose accounts of original sin which distinguish and separate it from original guilt, it should be helpful to see how this doctrinal experiment has gone in the past.

Original Sin in the Romans Commentary

Abelard's most in-depth treatment of the doctrine of original sin is found in his Romans commentary, probably written in Paris sometime during the 1130s.[9] A treatise on the doctrine is interpolated into the commentary after a brief gloss on Romans 5.12–19. Abelard comments in the gloss that Romans 5.12 – 'in whom all [Adam] sinned' (*IN QVO OMNES PECCAVERVNT*) – means that all human beings 'have incurred the penalty of sin'.[10] The discussion of original sin that follows is, in effect, an extended commentary on this verse. Abelard's gloss taken in itself is slightly misleading, however; as we shall see, he does not simply take original sin to be the divinely inflicted punishment for Adam's sin. He clarifies what he means in the treatise that follows.

The discussion of original sin begins with Abelard's observation that Paul's teaching on the subject has given rise to endless disputes.[11] We have difficulty grasping both what original sin is and how it comports with God's nature. Abelard, along with mainstream medieval theology in the West, accepted the teaching of Augustine – which had been adopted by the Council of Carthage in 418 – that unbaptized infants cannot enter the Kingdom of Heaven on account of their unforgiven original sin. But why would the God who proclaimed that the *regnum caelorum* belonged to little children bar them from entering (Matt. 19.14)? Prima facie, at least, the doctrine that infants are condemned on account of original sin seems to fly in the face of divine justice and mercy. Abelard is acutely aware of these sorts of objections and states them up front:

> By what justice does the most merciful judge hold the innocent son liable (*reus constituatur*) for his father's sin? This sentence would not be approved by civil jurists. Moreover, the one who committed this sin was forgiven, and it was removed from others through baptism. Why then is this sin punished in children who were unable to consent to it? Why are they, whose own sin does not condemn them, damned for the sin of another?[12]

There are at least two objections to original sin contained in this passage. The first pertains to divine justice. In civil law, children are not punished for the sins of their parents. How then could a just God punish Adam's children for his sin? The first objection, then, is that original sin implies that God is unjust because it is unjust to punish one for the sin of another. The objection is compounded by the Christian belief that God is paramountly merciful. If the exigencies of justice preclude punishing a child for his father's sin, how could mercy even consider it? There is another problem. The doctrine of original sin seems to require that Adam's children are condemned for the same numeric sin that he committed. But that sin was forgiven him.[13] If a sin is not held against the one who committed it, why is it held against those who neither committed nor approved of it? Original sin seems unjust and contrary to the biblical depiction of a merciful God.

Before responding to these objections, Abelard analyses the word 'sin' (*peccatum*). It is important to consider the word carefully, as 'sacred Scripture accepts the name of sin in multiple ways'.[14] First, and properly speaking, sin is said of the guilt of the soul and contempt for God.[15] For example, Adam's act of sin showed contempt for God's command and thereby brought guilt upon his soul. Whatever 'properly' (*proprie*) means here – and Abelard does not say – it does not mean that broader usages of the word sin are unimportant.[16] Another sense of the word is clearly central to the Christian faith: sin can mean 'sacrifice' (*hostia*), as Christ was called sin because he was a sacrifice for sin.[17] In what sense, however, could the word sin be predicated of infants? Original sin cannot be contempt for God because infants do not – like animals, the mentally disabled and the insane – have the use of free will or reason by which they could merit or demerit anything, let alone give homage or contempt to God.[18]

Abelard thus points out that the word sin can mean various things when used in the context of punishment: 'either the punishment we incur through sin itself, or the punishment for which we are liable on account of sin'.[19] The act of sin is its own punishment, insofar as the depraved will that follows from sinning is bad for the sinner. It also deserves further punishment from God. The fact that sin is often said with reference to punishment is the basis of, among other things, Christian language of forgiveness:

> According to this signification sins are said to be dismissed, that is, the penalties of sin are said to be forgiven. And the Lord is said to carry our sins because he bore the penalties of our sin. Moreover, when someone is said to have sin or be with sin who is not voluntarily sinning at that moment – such as when someone unjust is sleeping – it is as if she is acknowledged to be liable for the penalty of her own sin.[20]

We speak of sin's forgiveness when the penalty of sin is not exacted; we speak of Christ bearing our sin when he takes its penalty on himself.[21] And we speak of the sinner suffering the penalty of her own sin by virtue of her distorted will. Finally, punishment language is crucial for the doctrine of original sin:

> Because we are begotten and born with original sin and contract it from the first parent, it seems that original sin should be referred more to the penalty of sin, for which we are held liable to punishment, than to the guilt of the soul and contempt for God (*magis hoc ad poenam peccati, cui uidelicet poenae obnoxii tenentur, quam ad culpam animi et contemptum Dei referendum uidetur*).[22]

Human beings are born with original sin, which they contract ultimately from the first parent. This original sin should be understood as a punishment for Adam's sin – to be precise, as Abelard will clarify, the debt of punishment for Adam's sin – that Adam's offspring contract, rather than a culpable contempt of God.

We are thus born with original sin. It is the debt of damnation (*damnationis debitum*) with which we are bound, by which we are made liable to eternal punishment because of the guilt of our origin, that is of the prior parents from whom we take our origin. In him, as the Apostle said earlier, we have sinned. That is, we are assigned to eternal damnation on account of his sin, unless we are helped by the medicine of the divine sacraments, we are eternally condemned.[23]

Abelard has proposed an account of original sin with no reference to the pre-existence of infants in Adam (or anywhere else). Insofar as we consider the hypothesis of infant pre-existence implausible, this is a major advantage.

What led Abelard to deny original guilt? His arguments explicitly appeal to straightforward premises: infants do not have free will, and free will is required for culpability. That explains why he denied that guilt could be transmitted like a disease. Yet Abelard surely would have been familiar with the 'realist' idea that infants somehow pre-existed their life in the womb and freely sinned in Adam. In the text we have considered he does not directly say why he rejects this idea, but it is tempting to suspect that his philosophical views played an important role. For example, Abelard was committed to the view that there is nothing that is not a particular.[24] There is thus no universal human nature that brought it about that particular human beings are sinful. More work would be needed to establish this possible link between his metaphysics and hamartiology. We now turn to some objections to Abelard's account.

Objection 1: Abelard Implicitly Denies Original Sin

Given Abelard's trenchant criticism of original guilt, it is not surprising that Augustinian theologians forcefully rejected his proposal. During Abelard's own lifetime, Bernard of Clairvaux argued that he was Pelagian in all but name. In large part due to Bernard's campaign against him, Abelard's denial of original guilt was condemned at the Council of Sens, and Pope Innocent II approved the verdict.[25] Yet Abelard had powerful friends, including the abbot of the Benedictine abbey of Cluny, Peter the Venerable. Peter interceded to the Pope on Abelard's behalf, and Abelard was permitted to live out his days in peace in Cluny. It seems that many of Abelard's near contemporaries did not take the condemnation at Sens especially seriously. As Dom Lottin has pointed out, after a brief lull immediately following the Council, several prominent late twelfth-century theologians, such as Alain of Lille and Simon of Tournai (both professors at the University of Paris), openly advocated Abelard's account of original sin.[26] And during the thirteenth century, Abelard's critics (including Thomas Aquinas) tended not to identify his proposal with the heresy of Pelagianism; it was seen rather as a mistaken opinion about the nature of original sin.[27] We do not have space to discuss the specifics of Bernard's charge against Abelard. We can, however, ask how Abelard might have responded.

It strikes me that he could have argued that no good Pelagian would affirm that the word 'sin' should be predicated of infants; that this sin suffices to condemn unbaptized infants to an eternity of suffering; or that postlapsarian concupiscence is sinful. Abelard's account affirms all this. Where then is the Pelagianism? (It may also be worth pointing out that Abelard seems to have held that all human beings who reach the age of reason commit sin of their own volition.[28]) One might argue in response that original guilt is at the heart of Augustinian anthropology, and that Abelard's rejection of original guilt constitutes at least an implicit rejection of original sin. But what would the basis of this argument be? Does the fact that Abelard agrees with Pelagius and disagrees with Augustine on *one* important question (original guilt) make him a Pelagian? Surely not. For, if disagreement with Augustine over any substantive hamartiological question makes one a Pelagian, would not the vast majority of contemporary theologians *defending* original sin be Pelagians, by virtue of the fact that they reject Augustine's affirmation of infant damnation? Again, surely not. That said, we are not in a position to resolve this issue here. Abelard's account challenges us to reflect on the question of how much disagreement with Augustine's hamartiology is possible while maintaining original sin.

Objection 2: Abelard Implies that God is Unjust

The second objection is that it absurdly implies that God is unjust. We mentioned at the outset of this chapter that a number of theologians have raised objections to the doctrine of original guilt on the basis that it is unjust for God to punish the innocent. Strictly speaking, however, the objection that it is unjust to punish the innocent is more pertinent to theories of original sin like Abelard's, which *do* claim that God punishes the innocent. The doctrine of original guilt – at least in its historic Augustinian form – denies that God punishes the *innocent*. The objection that it is always wrong to punish the innocent would not dissuade a defender of original guilt from maintaining that God punishes infants, because *ex hypothesi* they are guilty. But Abelard's denial of original guilt does open his account up to objections related to God's justice. Here is a way such an objection could be formulated:

1 It is unjust to punish the wholly innocent.
2 God punishes infants who die unbaptized.

3 All infants who die unbaptized are wholly innocent.
Therefore
4 God unjustly punishes innocent infants.

While this argument is valid, Abelard rejects the conclusion as absurd. In order to argue that it is unsound, he needs to reject one of the premises. We know that in his medieval context (2) would have been non-negotiable and (3) is essential to his account. Consequently, Abelard needed to attack (1), and he did.

The first argument he gives against (1) begins with a distinction. We need to distinguish divine justice from human justice. Abelard implies that (1*) is true: normally, no human being can justly punish a wholly innocent human being. Yet (1**) is also true: God can justly punish a wholly innocent human being. Why should we accept (1**)? Before he explicitly defends this premise, Abelard draws our attention to several examples of divine law and exceptions thereto in Scripture. If we do not read Scripture carefully, we might be tempted to assume that the laws God imposes on us bind him as well. For example, he forbids theft, and this might lead us to believe that he cannot command anyone to seize another's property without permission. But God commanded the Israelites to plunder the Egyptians.[29] What is theft when committed without God's permission is 'morally appropriate plundering' when committed with God's permission. God can countermand his own commandments. This needn't give rise to any ethical dilemmas, because he would never command and forbid the same action simultaneously.

What applies to divine commands and human actions applies, *mutatis mutandis*, to the relation between divine commands and divine actions: God can do what he forbids us to do. We have come to the principle underlying Abelard's rejection of (1) and affirmation of (1**): God cannot do injustice to his creature, because *however* he treats his creature is just.[30] What is injustice when performed by a human being – throwing a man's son into a fire on account of his father's sin, for example – is just when decreed by God.[31] It can be just for God to punish the innocent because whatever God has chosen to do is just.[32] Indeed we have no way to define good or evil apart from the will of God.[33] We trust that all things are providentially ordered for the best, even if we cannot see how this could be the case.[34]

Abelard also offers what could be taken as a second reason for affirming that God can justly punish the innocent.[35] Abelard admits that acknowledging that God's will cannot be unjust will not lead us to praise his providence.[36] Upon further reflection, we can recognize the grace of God even in the punishment of innocent infants. The first grace, Abelard notes, citing Augustine, is that infants will suffer the lightest penalties in hell. 'We know this is the lightest punishment (*mitissimam poenam*), as the blessed Augustine attests in his *Enchiridion* . . . In my judgement, this punishment is nothing other than to suffer darkness, that is, to lack the vision of the divine majesty without any hope of ever gaining it.'[37] Abelard agrees with Augustine that condemned infants will be subjected to the lightest penalty in hell. But whereas Augustine had implied that even the lightest penalty involved material hellfire, Abelard opines that it will consist solely in the deprivation of the vision of God (with no hope of obtaining it).[38] This is a 'grace' presumably because Adam deserved severe punishment for his sin, and infants' debt of damnation renders them liable for the same punishment. This argument does not help us understand why God punished infants in the first place, however. Abelard addresses this next.

God chose to punish infants lightly because he foresaw that, if they had lived, they would have sinned grievously and eventually been subjected to severe punishment.[39] Consequently, the punishment that infants receive from Adam is actually God's gracious protection against an even more serious punishment. Moreover, Christians are motivated to avoid sin through consideration of its dire consequences.[40] If God is willing to damn Adam's children for the ordinary act of eating fruit, how much more should we flee sin? Abelard also suggests that God may have hidden reasons. Perhaps he uses the death of children to convert their parents, for example.[41] Toward the end of his discussion Abelard denies that other sins besides original sin are transmitted.[42] He concludes by humbly admitting that this account of original sin is only his opinion.[43]

In sum, Abelard argues that it is just for God to punish the innocent because (1) however God treats his creatures is just and (2) the punishment inflicted is mercifully lighter than what they would otherwise have received. What should we make of these arguments?

I am sceptical of Abelard's first argument for (1**). It is not clear from the fact that whatever God does is just, that it is just for God to punish the innocent. Of course, *if* God punishes the innocent, and whatever God does is just, then it is just for him to punish the innocent. But the question is precisely *whether* it is just for God to punish the innocent. It could be the case that it is impossible for God to punish the innocent because it is incompatible with his goodness and mercy. One might argue: whatever God does is just, but he cannot act contrary to his nature, and it is contrary to his nature to punish the innocent. To resolve this issue, though, we would need to investigate the concepts of debt and punishment further, as well as the relation between God's goodness and will. Someone sympathetic to Abelard's account could argue that God owes us nothing, except perhaps in the loose sense that if he is going to create a being of a certain kind, he 'owes' it what belongs to it essentially. But 'not being punished despite being innocent' is not essential to being human, and thus God could punish the innocent without violating any of his 'debts'. One way to respond to this counterargument would be to develop an account – as later medieval theologians did – of a 'debt of nature' (*debitum naturae*) that extends to God's wise direction of nature as a whole.[44]

Abelard's argument that the punishment of infants manifests divine mercy could function as an argument on behalf of the possibility of God punishing innocents as well. For example, perhaps God can punish the innocent if and only if the punishment is the only way to make the recipient of the punishment better off than she would have been without it. However, this argument seems to have problems as well. If *ex hypothesi* God decreases the punishment of damned infants by inflicting the *mitissima poena* on them, why didn't he allow them to grow up, damn them and *then* inflict the *mitissima poena*? In either case, they are punished lightly in hell for ever, but in the latter case they would have had the benefit of living a full human life, and they would not have been innocent during the duration of their eternal punishment. Another oddity of the punishment-as-mercy thesis is this: why didn't God arrange for the sinners who *are* punished severely in hell to die in infancy too?

Could the core of Abelard's account be maintained without reference to actual infant damnation? A modified Abelardian account might affirm with him that original sin is the debt of damnation imposed on all human beings as a result of the first sin and deny that water baptism is strictly necessary for salvation, such that all human beings who die in infancy are saved. An immediate problem with this proposal, however, is this objection: it is contradictory to assert that God imposes a debt of damnation on infants and that God wills the salvation of all infants. Given that the damnation is brought about by God's decision to hold Adam's sin against infants – that is, treat them as though they had committed Adam's sin – it would seem that God's will to save all infants would entail treating them as though they had not committed Adam's sin, in accordance with their innocence. That sounds more like a debt of salvation than a debt of damnation. It seems then that original sin cannot be rooted in God's will to damn if he in fact wills to save.

Objection 3: Abelard's Account of Original Sin's Transmission is Incoherent

Another objection is that Abelard did not offer a clear account of the transmission of original sin, that is, the connection between Adam's act of sin and his children's sin. At times he suggests that it is solely the divinely imposed debt of damnation for Adam's sin – this is his primary emphasis – but he also argues that original sin is contracted in conception via concupiscence.[45] He suggests that original sin is essentially linked to concupiscence in the context of explaining why original sin is passed on by Christian parents.

Abelard claims, 'nor should it be surprising if what is given to the parents is nevertheless withheld from the children, because the vicious generation of carnal concupiscence transfers sin and merits wrath (*uitiosa carnalis concupiscentiae generatio peccatum transfundat et iram mereatur*).'[46] Even though Christian parents have received forgiveness, they necessarily sin during sex on account of their concupiscence. And this *concupiscence* transfers sin to their children who in turn deserve the wrath of God. But this stands in tension with Abelard's view that God imposes the debt of punishment despite infants' innocence. That is, if the concupiscence of the parents brings original sin to the children, what need is there to claim, as Abelard did, that God assigns them the debt of damnation? The parents would be the only culprits, and Abelard would not have needed to respond to the problems his account creates for divine justice.

It is not clear, or at least not clear to me, why Abelard mentioned concupiscence in the context of sin's transmission. Perhaps he wanted to offset the radical character of his proposal of infant innocence with some Augustinian language. Or perhaps he implicitly had two original sins in mind, concupiscence from the parents and the debt of damnation assigned by God. In any case, I would submit that he could have maintained the core of his account without reference to the sexual transmission of sin. That is, he could have claimed that God imposes the debt of punishment on infants, regardless of whether the sex of their parents was tainted by lust or not. This should be clear from our discussion of divine justice in the previous section: God cannot do injustice to us, so it would be impossible for the presence of sinful sex to be a condition *sine qua non* of God imposing the debt of punishment.

Conclusion

Let's take stock. Abelard offered an original defence of the doctrine of original sin which did not appeal to original guilt. Infants are innocent. Their original sin is the divinely imposed debt of damnation for Adam's sin. It is remittable by baptism alone, and those who die without it are condemned. God condemns these infants for their sake and ours. For their sake, because they would have committed grievous sins if they had grown up and suffered horrible punishments in hell; for our sake, because their damnation is a stark reminder to fear God and avoid sin. All this comes through quite clearly. (Abelard also suggests, less clearly, that original sin is caused by carnal concupiscence.) Even if we reject all of the major arguments Abelard presents in his Romans commentary, he challenges us to consider a number of important questions. What distinguishes a creative reinterpretation of original sin from a Pelagian denial of the doctrine? What is the basis of the belief that God saves all children? Should it be understood in terms of a 'debt' or a 'gift', or both? Without original guilt, what could the word 'sin' mean when spoken of infants who are loved by God? Not all of these questions receive a great deal of attention in contemporary theology, but our reading (or rereading) of Abelard reminds us that they deserve more.

Notes

*Parts of this chapter derive from research I conducted as a Resident Fellow at the Carl F. H. Henry Center for Theological Understanding of Trinity International University, with a generous grant from the Templeton Religion Trust. I am deeply grateful both to Templeton and to Trinity.

1 *De civitate Dei contra paganos* XIII, c. 14, in *Corpus Christianorum Series Latina* XLVIII, 395. This and all translations are my own.

2 Oliver D. Crisp, 'On Original Sin', *International Journal of Systematic Theology* 17, no. 3 (2015), p. 6.

3 Crisp's article cited in n. 2 is an important recent example. He draws on Ulrich Zwingli (1484–1531) and proposes a 'moderate Reformed doctrine' of original sin without original guilt.

4 I do not have space to defend this opinion here. See Julius Gross's account of the medieval period, cited in n. 6, for an argument that Augustine's view of original sin was dominant in the West from the time of his death until the twelfth century. In the beginning of the twelfth century, debate over the doctrine began to intensify and views which had long been taken for granted – including original guilt – came to be disputed. My difference with Gross in this context is primarily over whether Abelard should be seen as a non-Augustinian advocate of original sin or a Pelagian who papered over his heresy with orthodox language.

5 Marcia L. Colish, *Peter Lombard*, vol. 1 (New York: E. J. Brill, 1994), p. 388.

6 '[F]ür Magister Petrus gibt es keine Erbsünde, sondern nur eine Erb-oder besser Kollektivstrafe'. Julius Gross, *Geschichte des Erbsündendogmas*, vol. 3, *Entwicklungsgeschichte des Erbsündendogmas im Zeitalter der Scholastik (12.–15. Jahhrh.)* (Munich: Ernst Reinhardt, 1971), p. 73.

7 Steven R. Cartwright, 'Introduction', in Peter Abelard, *Commentary on the Epistle to the Romans* (Washington, DC: The Catholic University of America Press, 2011), p. 54.

8 Paul C. Kemeny, 'Peter Abelard: An Examination of His Doctrine of Original Sin', *The Journal of Religious History* 16.4 (1991), p. 375.

9 John Marenbon, *Abelard in Four Dimensions: A Twelfth-Century Philosopher in His Context and Ours* (Notre Dame, IN: University of Notre Dame Press, 2013), p. 22.

10 *Commentaria in epistolam Pavli ad Romanos* II, cap. 5, in E. M. Buytaert (ed.), *Petri Abaelardi Opera Theologica* (Turnhout: CCCM XI, 1969), vol. 1 [=Buytaert], lines 125–6. For an English translation of the whole work, see Peter Abelard, *Commentary on the Epistle to the Romans*, trans. Steven R. Cartwright (Washington, DC: Catholic University of America Press, 2011). Nowadays the end of Romans 5.12 is usually translated 'because all have sinned' (NRSV). Though it is often claimed that the Vulgate's mistranslation of this verse was the foundation of the Western doctrine of original sin, the medievals would have disagreed. In addition to

the various theological arguments defending the doctrine they would have offered – that the denial of original sin absurdly implies that some human beings do not need Christ's salvation, for example – theologians like Abelard would have argued that original sin is clearly implied by Paul's point only a few verses later that the trespass of one man led to the sin, death, and condemnation of all (vv. 17–19) – not only those fortunate enough to reach the age of reason.

11 Original sin is the 'old quarrel and interminable question of the human race' (*Ad Romanos* II: *ueterem humani generis quaerelam et interminatam quaestionem* [Buytaert, p. 336; Cartwright, p. 215]).

12 *Ad Romanos* II (Buytaert, 341–8; Cartwright, p. 215).

13 Belief that Adam and Eve were both forgiven and ultimately saved was common in the Middle Ages.

14 *Ad Romanos* II: 'Pluribus autem modis peccati nomen Scriptura sacra accipit' (Buytaert, pp. 354–5; Cartwright, p. 215).

15 *Ad Romanos* II: 'Properly speaking, [sin is said] of the guilt of the soul and contempt for God, that is, our crooked will by which we are constituted [guilty] before God' (*[U]no quidem modo et proprie pro ipsa animi culpa et contemptu Dei, id est praua uoluntate nostra qua rei apud Deum statuimur* [Buytaert, pp. 355–7; Cartwright, p. 215]).

16 Consider Peter King's claim that for Abelard, 'the signification of a term is the informational content of the concept that is associated with the term upon hearing it, in the normal course of events.' Peter King, 'Peter Abelard', *The Stanford Encyclopedia of Philosophy* (Summer 2015 Edition), Edward N. Zalta (ed.), <https://plato.stanford.edu/archives/sum2015/entries/abelard/>. If using a word 'properly' is using it in accordance with its signification, we can see why Abelard would claim that sin, properly speaking, is the act of contempt for God. Contempt for God's law would have been strongly associated with the concept of sin, and Scripture says that sin is disobedience (1 John 3.4).

17 *Ad Romanos* II: 'In the third mode Christ himself is called "sin" by the Apostle, that is, a sacrifice for sin' (Buytaert, pp. 366–7; Cartwright, p. 216).

18 *Ad Romanos* II: 'It would be insane to deny that the insane, children, and those without the use of reason lack free will' (Buytaert, pp. 430–2; Cartwright, p. 218). *Ad Romanos* II: 'She who does not yet have free will, or any practice in reasoning – and who thus cannot merit the precept of obedience or recognize its author – no transgression or negligence is imputed to her, nor any merit by which she would deserve a reward or punishment. She deserves no more praise or blame than beasts do when they seem to help or hurt in something' (Buytaert, pp. 372–8; Cartwright, p. 216).

19 *Ad Romanos* II (Buytaert, pp. 357–9; Cartwright, p. 215).

20 *Ad Romanos* II (Buytaert, pp. 359–66; Cartwright, pp. 215–16).

21 See Thomas Williams, 'Sin, Grace, and Redemption in Abelard', in *The Cambridge Companion to Abelard*, ed. Jeffrey Brower and Kevin Guilfoy (Cambridge: Cambridge University Press, 2004), p. 266 *et passim*, for a discussion of the role of penal substitution in Abelard's theology.

22 *Ad Romanos* II (Buytaert, pp. 368–72; Cartwright, p. 216).

23 *Ad Romanos* II (Buytaert, pp. 594–601; Cartwright, p. 223).

24 For Abelard on nominalism and the problem of universals, see John Marenbon, *The Philosophy of Peter Abelard* (Cambridge: Cambridge University Press, 1997), pp. 117–19, 174–201.

25 For a classic discussion of the condemnation at Sens, see D. E. Luscombe, *The School of Peter Abelard: The Influence of Abelard's Thought in the Early Scholastic Period* (Cambridge: Cambridge University Press, 1969), pp. 103–42. The eighth condemned proposition is the following: 'That we do not contract guilt from Adam but punishment alone' (*Quod non contraximus culpam ex Adam, sed poenam tantum* [DH 728]). DH = Heinrich Denzinger, *Enchiridion Symbolorum: A Compendium of Creeds, Definitions, and Declarations of the Catholic Church*, 43rd edn, ed. Peter Hünermann (San Francisco, CA: Ignatius Press, 2012).

26 Dom Lottin, *Psychologie et morale aux XIIe et XIIIe Siècles*, tome IV, *Problèmes de morale, troisième partie*, vol. 1 (Louvain-Gembloux: 1954), pp. 166–7, see pp. 142–67 for discussion of Abelard's followers in the twelfth century.

27 Aquinas discusses Abelard's view (without naming him) in his commentary on Peter Lombard's *Sentences* II, d. 20, q. 1, a. 2, *corpus*. He distinguishes the *error Pelagii* from the error of those who deny infant culpability and claim that original sin is the debt of punishment. Only the former is explicitly identified as contrary to the truth of faith, that is, as a heresy.

28 'Although Abelard offers no discussion of inevitability and only occasional remarks on universality, he does affirm, without qualification, that all men commit actual sin, for which they alone are responsible and for which they need redemption through God's saving work in Jesus Christ. The universality of sin is a brute fact to be recognized rather than explained.' Richard E. Weingart, *The Logic of Divine Love: A Critical Analysis of the Soteriology of Peter Abailard* (Oxford: Oxford University Press, 1970), p. 49.

29 *Ad Romanos* II (Buytaert, pp. 510–11; Cartwright, p. 220).

30 *Ad Romanos* II: 'God does no injustice to his creature, however he may treat it' (Buytaert, pp. 491–3; Cartwright, p. 220).

31 *Ad Romanos* II: 'Even among human beings, would it not be judged most unjust if an innocent son were thrown into temporary flames on account of his father's sin (not to mention eternal flames)? I say it certainly would be unjust among human beings, for whom vengeance for one's own injuries is forbidden. But it is not forbidden to the God who says, *vengeance is mine, I will repay*' (Buytaert, pp. 486–91; Cartwright, p. 220). This was an odd example for Abelard to give because, as we are about to see, he denies that infants are burned with material hellfire.

32 This is not to say that God could have done anything that strikes us as logically possible. It seems that Abelard held that God cannot do anything other than what he has done. See William J. Courtenay, 'The Dialectic of Omnipotence in the High and Late Middle Ages', *Divine Omniscience and Omnipotence in Medieval Philosophy: Islamic, Jewish, and Christian Perspectives*, ed. Tamar Rudavsky (Boston, MA: D. Reidel, 1995), p. 246. Thus, Abelard presumably would not have been moved by counterfactual thought experiments designed to show the absurdity of suggesting that however God treats us is just.

33 *Ad Romanos* II: 'Nor can anything done by his will be called evil in any respect. We cannot distinguish good from evil, except in accordance with his will and good pleasure' (Buytaert, pp. 505–8; Cartwright, p. 220).

34 *Ad Romanos* II (Buytaert, p. 525; Cartwright, p. 221).

35 Technically Abelard only argues that the 'graces' of infant condemnation manifest God's goodness to us; he does not argue that they justify God's act of condemnation.

36 *Ad Romanos* II: 'Showing that God is just will not lead us to praise his providence in the damnation of children, unless we can also show some of his grace and goodness at work' (Buytaert, pp. 536–9; Cartwright, p. 221).

37 *Ad Romanos* II: *Scimus quippe hanc esse mitissimam poenam, beato in* Enchiridion *Augustino sic attestante ... Quam quidem poenam non aliam arbitror quam pati tenebras, id est carere uisione diuinae maiestatis sine omni spe recuperationis* (Buytaert, pp. 541–7; Cartwright, p. 221).

38 As far as I know, Abelard is the first prominent Western theologian after Augustine to clearly deny that infants will suffer the torment of hellfire.

39 *Ad Romanos* II: 'We believe, furthermore, that no children die and are assigned this lightest punishment unless God foresaw that if they had lived, they would have been evil and eventually suffered greater punishments. In this remission or alleviation of punishments these children are not unable to take the grace of divine goodness' (Buytaert, pp. 549–54; Cartwright, p. 222).

40 *Ad Romanos* II: 'God uses this lightest punishment of children well, for our correction, in order that we may be more cautious to avoid sin. For these innocents, to whom neither burials nor prayers of the faithful are given, are damned every day because of the sin of another. We should give thanks all the more because he graciously frees us from that perpetual fire after many crimes, and he does not save them. He wants to show clearly, through the first and even rather moderate transgression of the first parents, how much he hates iniquity and what punishments are reserved for greater and more frequent sins' (Buytaert, pp. 555–66; Cartwright, p. 222).

41 *Ad Romanos* II: 'There are particular causes for the damnation of certain children, although they are hidden to us, which are known to he who disposes nothing except for the best. And when these things happen frequently we can infer what these reasons are. It often happens that by divine grace, the death of such children makes a difference in the life of their parents. They grow concerned over their own damnation, damnation they brought to their children through their own concupiscence, and they ascribe the guilt wholly to themselves' (Buytaert, pp. 574–82; Cartwright, pp. 222–3).

42 After citing two famous texts in which Augustine affirmed it was probable that other sins were passed on in addition to Adam's, Abelard suggests that Augustine was only speaking of the opinion of others. *Ad Romanos* II: 'The blessed Augustine said this with reference to the probable opinion of others, as he himself implied, rather than to his own assertion' (Buytaert, pp. 709–11; Cartwright, p. 227).

43 *Ad Romanos* II: 'Suffice it to say that these things concerning original sin are put forward less as an assertion than as an opinion' (Buytaert, pp. 730–1; Cartwright, p. 227).

44 One such theologian was Thomas Aquinas. See Daniel W. Houck, '*Natura Humana Relicta est Christo*: Thomas Aquinas on the Effects of Original Sin', *Archa Verbi* 13 (2016), pp. 76–110, for a discussion of Aquinas' view of the relation between original sin and human nature.

45 The word 'concupiscence' is notoriously polysemous, but in this context it means, roughly, 'sinful sexual lust'. Many medievals followed Augustine in thinking that this sinful lust was present in every act of postlapsarian sex.

46 *Ad Romanos* II (Buytaert, pp. 664–7; Cartwright, p. 225).

5

Reparative Substitution and the 'Efficacy Objection': Toward a Modified Satisfaction Theory of Atonement[1]

JOSHUA R. FARRIS AND
S. MARK HAMILTON

Introduction

Compared one to another, some theories of the atonement simply 'do' more than others. What one thinks their theory of atonement 'does' has much to do with both the collective and individual voices of the theological tradition that inform what they believe, and these are in some sense negotiable, depending on the sort of tradition with which they ally themselves. In what follows, we take a look at an aspect of what we might think of as the logical deposit of what has become the dogmatic inheritance of the broader Reformed (i.e. Protestant), but particularly evangelical, tradition as it pertains to the (penal substitution theory of) atonement.

Generally speaking, when we talk about the atonement 'doing' this or that we are talking primarily about the interplay of two concepts: (1) the so-called mechanism of the atonement and (2) the effectual bearing that this mechanism has upon those for whom it was divinely purposed. For its supposed failure to achieve said effect, the Anselmian satisfaction theory of atonement is often criticized, mostly by penal substitution theorists. This is what we mean by the efficacy objection, namely, that the satisfaction theory simply does not do anything for humanity, but merely makes provision of the possibility of salvation. Before we describe the theories, we need to define some terms. Because we will be using several terms of art to make our case, for the sake of clarity consider our use of following terms:

1 'Mechanism' describes that thing which must necessarily obtain in order for some precise act or action to obtain.
2 'Sufficiency' is the capacity of doing something in a right manner (e.g. being in possession of enough of a smallpox vaccination to administer it to an entire village).

REPARATIVE SUBSTITUTION AND THE 'EFFICACY OBJECTION'

3 'Efficiency' is the thing done in a right manner (e.g. administering the smallpox vaccination to those in the village who need and want it).
4 'Efficacy' describes the thing done (e.g. those in the village to whom the smallpox vaccination was administered are insulated from the threat of contracting smallpox).

With these terms in mind, in what follows we offer up several arguments against the efficacy objection to the satisfaction theory, arguing in favour of what we have elsewhere referred to as Reparative substitution theory of atonement, which is our attempt at a sort of Protestantized version of Anselm's theory.[2] Do not be mistaken though. Reparative substitution is much more than that increasingly popular exercise of simply rebranding the atonement that appears so novel in contemporary constructive theology. Rather, it is more like a development of aspects of Anselm's theory that he left largely undeveloped; these developments being significant enough in our minds as constitutive of a theory separate unto itself. (Before we go any further, attention needs to be drawn to some confusion in contemporary theology when doctrines like the atonement are described in one context as a 'model' and in another context as a 'theory'. We too have fallen prey to this. For the sake of clarity, when we say 'model' we mean a broader category which is representative of how several theories of atonement function. When we say 'theory' we are referring to a more narrowly worked out, systematically detailed instance of a model. For example, both the satisfaction and moral government theories of atonement fall under what we have elsewhere described as belonging to 'restitution models of atonement', but we would now call these theories that fall under a restitution model.)

To this end, this chapter unfolds in two parts to a conclusion. In part one, we set up the problem by a brief discussion of the mechanism of the atonement, situating our discussion in the so-called sufficiency–efficiency debate.[3] In part two, we lay out some of the contours of the penal substitution, satisfaction and finally reparative substitution theories, paying particular attention to some of those contours of the latter which we take to be deliverances from the efficacy objection. By way of conclusion we offer up several reasons for thinking that, in point of fact, when compared to the reparative substitution theory, it is actually the penal substitution theory of atonement that we think has more for which to answer.

Mechanism, Sufficiency and Efficiency

What constitutes a legitimate theory of atonement? The answer to this is a bit tricky. For the sake of argument, a theory of atonement is legitimate according to the degree to which we can discover some mechanism that specifically describes the work that Christ accomplishes by his death. What this means, first of all, is that neither the incarnation nor the resurrection are the atonement, as some like to think (more in a moment). Following from this, it also means that there are several illegitimate theories of atonement. In this we agree with Kathryn Tanner who has recently and boldly asserted, for example, that 'Christus Victor is not a model of atonement at all in that it fails . . . to address the question of the mechanism of the atonement.'[4] Is this too strong? Perhaps not. For are those who would resist discerning a definitive mechanism for the atonement not by consequence resistant to an intelligible explanation of the significance of the death of Christ?

Our answer to this question limits our atonement options, to be sure. For not only is Aulén's Christus Victor thus undermined on this way of thinking, but so also is Abelard's Moral Exemplar theory and perhaps even (ironically) Tanner's Incarnation as Atonement theory. This is because these theories, save for some theologically constructive refashioning (something to which we are not at all opposed), are not really 'doing' anything – that is, doing anything as it pertains to the death of Christ – that is efficient for humanity.[5] Tanner endorses an incarnation theory of atonement that supposedly undoes any talk of legality where God is somehow bound to the law he has set in motion from the beginning of creation. What she highlights are the benefits humans receive from the incarnation. All that is required on her theory appears to be that God desires to be in union with humanity and God making his life available to humans exemplified to the greatest degree in the incarnation. The problem with this theory is that it does not sufficiently account for the Fall as an objective break between the divine and human relationship. Now, we say all this with less than complete confidence about Tanner's Incarnation theory. That said, by way of motivation we are not convinced that Scripture nor logic gives us reason to think that the incarnation itself accomplishes something like justification (i.e. making us right with God and/or his moral law). In fact, neither is this theory necessarily performing a work – again, as it pertains to the death of Christ – that ought to be regarded as sufficient for humanity. Such theories seem intent on leveraging a perceived measure of explanatory power afforded by other doctrines, like the incarnation, for example, in order to interpret the value of Christ's death.

Now, we will be the first to admit that such theological moves are not entirely out of order. The problem is when such moves are over-leveraged to such a degree that Christ's death is not able to be explained without them. Of course Christ could not die were he not incarnate. But the incarnation is not the atonement, no more than, say, creation is providence. Certainly, they bear a close conceptual relationship. But they are not numerically the same. For a theory to be considered a theory unto itself, the act of Christ's death must itself accomplish something. It must, that is, have some singular and definable efficacy.

For legitimate theories of atonement, particularly those that fall under the category of a restitution model, which is our interest here, the death of Christ has been traditionally regarded – at least since Lombard's proposal of the sufficiency–efficiency distinction – as accomplishing one of the following three redemptive goals:

1 Either the death of Christ is a work that makes atonement that is sufficient for all humanity but efficient for none (e.g. the satisfaction theory) or;
2 is sufficient for all humanity and efficient for some (e.g. the penal substitution theory) or;
3 is sufficient and efficient for all.[6]

It is within the constraints of this still important theological distinction that the question of most interest to us surfaces, namely, 'What does a given theory actually accomplish' (if anything), or more precisely, 'What does it accomplish for humanity' (if anything)? To answer this question, let us briefly take a closer look at the mechanism of atonement, first on penal substitution theory and then on the satisfaction theory, after which we will look more closely at the reparative substitution theory, which to our minds offers the most promise of doing something for humanity, and what is more, for God himself.

Mechanism, Efficacy and Penal Substitution

Penal substitution is (roughly) the theory according to which Christ assumes the legal responsibility for the sin(s) of human beings and by his substitutionary death pays their debt of punishment in order to satisfy God's retributive justice.[7] A development of the Protestant Reformation, penal substitution has since become the majority soteriological report among many contemporary Protestant evangelicals.[8] Unfortunately, this majority also thinks by and large that the doctrine of penal substitution has been a genetic and therefore dogmatic fixture of the Church going back as far as Irenaeus and Athanasius.[9] Such 'gross distortions' have of course been challenged.[10] According to Adonis Vidu's recent and thoroughgoing treatment of the historical development of the doctrine of the atonement, penal substitution makes its first full appearance with Calvin. Vidu carefully and helpfully exposits Berkhof's four points of departure from the Anselmian tradition that appear with Calvin, and here we quote him at length,

First, the satisfaction theory focuses on the honour and dignity of God rather than his justice. The context is that of private rather than public law. Second, there is no place in Anselm's thought for the biblical idea of Christ's bearing of our punishment on our behalf. Rather, Christ offers himself as a sacrifice acceptable in lieu of our being punished (Isa. 53.10). Third, Berkhof argues that there is no place for the active obedience of Christ. This might seem puzzling, yet it is not the death that effectively procures atonement for Anselm, but the infinitely valuable offer of Christ's life. Finally, the fourth weakness sensed by the Reformers is that the Latin satisfaction model turns on a purely external transfer of merits. The believer is left to his or her own devices to continue to earn the surplus merit of Christ. While, as we shall see, an economy of exchange will continue to characterize the Reformed understanding of the atonement, the satisfaction of God is construed in such a way that it can only be accomplished by the redeemer, and cannot be replicated by believers seeking to earn salvation. Christ's work is final (Heb. 7.27; 9.28; 1 Pet. 3.18) and unrepeatable.[11]

Vidu then launches into a more detailed treatment of the particulars of Calvin's thought, paying close attention to his account of divine love, law and wrath as they relate to the atonement, from which we are able to discern no less than five distinctive component parts of the penal substitution theory; components which appear common to its various expressions in the literature since. These include:

1 Christ's atonement is necessary to his redemptive work.
2 Christ's death is sufficient to assuage divine wrath for all humanity.
3 Christ dies as a penal substitute for individual persons.
4 Christ dies in order to absorb the retributive (penal) consequences of divine justice and wrath precipitated by human sin, being treated by God as if he were those individuals to whom the punishment were due (i.e. *the mechanism*).
5 Christ's death pays a debt of punishment.
6 Christ's death is a vicarious sacrifice.

The mechanism of the penal substitution theory is bound up in the act of Christ's death absorbing the cumulative force of divine retributive justice (i.e. wrath) against sins of particular human persons (some number of human persons less than the total number) whom Christ is said to represent. (It is worth some additional clarification at this point, that by absorbing wrath Christ is not hated by God, as some have recently and foolishly suggested. It appears that it is no longer enough to simply believe that Christ died as a penal substitute. In some evangelical quarters, it now seems necessary to believe that as a penal substitute, Christ's endurance of the wrath of his Father's justice makes him the object of God's hatred, albeit temporarily. Such thinking, when worked out with greater logical precision and rigour, seems to fall under the category of 'broken-Trinity theology'.[12]) In this act, Christ's death pays the debt of punishment owed by those over whom he is a so-called federal head. Paying the debt of punishment is what this theory does and absorbing this penalty for those whom he represents is what this theory does for humanity.

Now, the 'sufficiency–efficiency' distinction is often deployed by exponents of penal substitution to defend this mechanism. Generally, they seem to think that Christ's death is sufficient to absorb the wrath of God for all but is effectually restricted in application to only certain individuals, and that by divine decree. Interestingly, this is not the only way exponents of penal substitution defend this mechanism. Some argue for a definite atonement and think that God decrees that Christ dies as the legal representative (i.e. penal substitute) for particular individuals. This is quite different for those who believe in a limited atonement and think that God decrees that the benefits accruing from Christ's representative work be conferred only upon those whom he chooses. More interesting still is the fact that some penal substitution theorists have argued that Christ's work is both sufficient for all and efficient for all (e.g. Universalism or Salmurianism; it is of additional and interesting note, at this point, that the atonement theories proposed by those associated with the minority report within the Reformed tradition – hypothetical universalism – their own subtle differences notwithstanding, are likewise committed to this same mechanism, which ironically leads to what is often called the 'double payment of objection'). This is not a little problem, for which penal substitution theorists have yet to offer a strong rebuttal.[13] However this distinction is construed, the central question is still one of mechanism: did Christ's death pay a debt of punishment and did he do so (definitively) for particular individuals? Not according to Anselm.

Mechanism, Efficacy and Satisfaction

According to what we might think of as a classical Anselmian Satisfaction theory, Christ gives up his life in order to restore honour to God by paying a debt, one that satisfies the creditor; not a debt of punishment (as in the case of penal substitution), but a debt of honour. This again is something that Vidu carefully treats at length, and in concert with the broader articulation and later development of the satisfaction theory among Abelard, Aquinas and Duns Scotus.[14] Hitting on the major themes related to Anselm's satisfaction theory – his Platonic and realist philosophical assumptions, his theological approach to law, his emphasis on the private (rather than the public) offence of sin, his contrast of punishment versus satisfaction, the necessity of the incarnation, the sufficiency of Christ's meritorious work to pay humanities debt to God – Vidu shows with great precision and clarity why Anselm's theory became epoch-making for later medievals. We see the trace elements of Vidu's treatment of Anselm in such statements as those from *Cur Deus Homo*.

> [S]in is nothing other than not to give God what is owed him. Therefore, everyone who sins is under obligation to repay to God the honour which he has violently taken from him, and this is the satisfaction which every sinner is obliged to give to God (1.11). [I]f there is nothing greater and nothing better than God, then there is nothing, in the government of the universe, which the supreme justice, which is none other than God himself, preserves more justly than God's honour (1.13). To forgive sin in this way [that is, by mercy alone, without reparation] is nothing other than to refrain from inflicting punishment. And if no satisfaction is given, the way to regulate sin correctly is none other than to punish it (1.12). It is a necessary consequence, therefore, that either the honour which has been taken away should be repaid, or punishment should follow.[15]

Summarily speaking, Anselm's theory can be expressed (roughly) in the following set of numbered theses:

1 Christ's atonement (or a suitable equivalent) is necessary to his larger redemptive work.
2 Christ's death procures an infinite merit (i.e. *the mechanism*); the infinite merit of Christ's death pays a debt of honour to God.
3 Christ's death is a work of supererogation and therefore sufficient for all humanity.
4 Christ's death is efficient for those who by faith are united to Christ.

It should be clear from this that the mechanism of atonement on Anselm's theory is built around the idea that Christ's death somehow restores honour to the Father, namely, by virtue of the infinite merit of the sacrifice of his infinite self, thereby offsetting the infinite demerit of human sin. In this, Christ's act is one of equity to a debt; again, not a debt of punishment but a debt of honour.

It should also be clear that on Anselm's account of Christ's atoning work, his death is sufficient for all humanity but, interestingly, not efficient in the sense that some redemptive effect immediately obtains for humanity (or some part of humanity), as in the case of the penal substitution theory. Anselm's theory makes several other necessary conditions for salvation. In other words, Christ's atonement, according to Anselm, is not efficacious for humanity. For it to be so, there are conditions beyond those of the work that Christ's death achieves that must be met. This, we recall, is in contrast to the penal substitution theory, exponents of which often celebrate the positive benefits that belong to the elect (i.e. propitiation, expiation, justification, and imputation) as an immediate result of Christ's death on their behalf. It is important to note that the doctrine of penal substitution is the means of making one 'right' with God. In other words, the mechanism is that of Christ bearing our penalty for sins against God. Normally the nature of Christ's justifying act in the atonement is cashed out in terms of imputation, rather than as a version of realism or impartation. The doctrine of imputation is the view that God views us as if we were right or just, according to his moral law, because of Christ. However, Christ has not actually made us righteous nor has he imparted or infused righteousness into us. The problem with the doctrine of imputation is quite clear in much of the literature. Christ, as a result of assuming a debt (of punishment) he could not literally assume, becomes a fictional representative for us whom God accepts as a legally admissible stand-in, so to speak. This is what many have called the 'legal fiction' objection. Interestingly, it is the failure to claim these and other soteriological benefits as accomplished and therefore secured by Anselm's theory that is often promoted by penal substitution theorists as among the reasons to reject a straightforward satisfaction model. In other words, for penal substitution theorists, Anselm did not go far enough.[16]

Like the penal substitution theory, it seems charitable to take each theory on its own terms and to see how the theologian works out the logic of how it is that all the soteriological benefits are appropriated in the life of the believers. It seems overly simplistic to say that the atonement does all the work of salvation when we have so many other soteriological categories in Scripture. With respect to other theories, it is perhaps not enough to say that Anselm's theory is less than fully systematized. And it is at this particular point that we offer some additional theologically constructive specificity in the form of a new theory of atonement that we call reparative substitution.

Mechanism, Efficacy and Reparative Substitution

Summarily speaking, according to the reparative substitution theory, Christ dies in an act of divine love to pay a debt of divine honour owed by humanity to God by offering himself up in an act of supererogation that procures an infinite merit (of honour), offsetting the infinite demerit of human sin in order to satisfy the rectoral demands of divine justice, thereby restoring honour to God (and by consequence, his moral law). Consider the following nine constituent parts of reparative substitution:

1. Christ's atonement is necessary to his work.
2. Christ's death is an act of divine love.
3. Christ's death procures an infinite merit (i.e. *the mechanism*).
   (a) The infinite merit of Christ's death pays the full sum of humanity's debt of honour to God (Christ does this qua his divine nature).
   (b) The infinite merit of Christ's death pays the full sum of humanity's debt of honour [not a debt of punishment] to God's moral law (Christ does this qua his human nature).
4. Christ's death is sufficient for all humanity (what we might call a global substitute).
5. Christ's death efficiently defers divine wrath for all humanity until the consummation/Judgement.[17]
6. The incarnation establishes both a 'vital union' and 'legal union' between Christ and all humanity, without which Christ's work would not obtain for all humanity.
7. The resurrection generates a newly constituted humanity, whose 'members' include those who by faith (as the 'relative' union), at the Judgement will receive their remunerative benefit.
8. Christ's work is efficient for the 'elect' by settling all debts and eliminating eternal death.

Right away, the similarities with Anselm's satisfaction theory should be apparent, particularly those regarding Christ's payment of a debt of honour. It should also be readily apparent that unlike penal substitution, Christ bears or absorbs no penalty (perhaps not even the one demanded by the moral law, that is, unless he pays the penalty of death that the moral law demands for all humanity) on the reparative substitution theory. He remains a substitute, just not a penal one. This is because the intended mechanism of atonement is the restoration of divine honour, not the provision of opportunity for God to expend his wrath on Christ for sin or to satisfy the punitive demands of the moral law.

With reparative substitution, we are asserting that the love of Christ for his Father is the primary motive in his making atonement. Christ came to restore divine honour and he cannot do it only in part. By his death the honour of God's name – the thing for which he cares most – is publicly restored to him and not only that, but the honour of his irreproachable law is also restored (again, Christ is not penalized by the law, he is honouring the law with his active obedience; the active and passive obedience distinction is something we are in the process of developing). The demands of divine justice are universally met for all humanity. This follows from the incarnation but is achieved by Christ making reparations by his death.

By the Son assuming human nature as our covenantal representative, Christ enacts a new union with humanity. A union similar to the union found with Adam in the Creational covenant. In the new Creational covenant, Christ unites to our humanity. Christ enacts a vital and judicial union with humanity according to the moral law established by God for humanity. This new union establishes the ground for Christ paying our debt of honour to God and opens the door for newly transformed humanity at the resurrection.

What then of God's retributive justice? And what of those who ultimately reject God? In short, Christ's death defers the exercise of retributive justice until the consummation of all things, where both the retributive and remunerative aspects of rectoral justice will be meted out. This is not only where Christ's atoning work is sufficient for atonement in that his merit is available to all, but that it is efficient in staving off divine wrath for all until the consummation. God's honour is literally restored by Christ's act of giving himself up as a morally perfect sacrifice to the Father.

In so doing we are proposing both a soteriological and judicial shift in our understanding of the divine economy. Retribution is not exacted from the Son, but from those who in the end reject him. Christ is therefore not punished, for he is a morally perfect human (hence, a morally perfect sacrifice to God). The efficacy is found in Christ's setting aright the moral demands of divine justice. Christ pays off our debt to God. Christ effectively pays our debt of honour to God. God is thus honoured, and the moral law is satisfied in the death of Christ not by the absorption of a debt that no human can sufficiently satisfy, but by offering up a gift of honour of such a worth as to settle the due demands of the moral law.

By this, saints are truly pardoned. And with this we are in effect elevating the significance of faith – a move of which Anselm would likely approve – as well as faith's relationship to the nature of union with Christ. The result of all this, ironically, is the wholesale elimination of the need to even make the sufficiency–efficiency distinction or, at a minimum, a complex reworking of it. As we have seen, though, the distinction is not all that simple and has been worked out in numerous, albeit arguably consistent, ways. Christ's work on reparative substitution is sufficient and efficient for all. It appears that it is sufficient in that the work of Christ is of such a value that it can ultimately atone for demands of honour to God eternally. It is efficient, arguably, in the two senses listed above. It is efficient to settle the demands of the moral law and it is efficient for the elect who receive the full remunerative benefits by faith.

What does reparative substitution do? It restores to God the glory that was violently taken from him, who, as the apostle says, graciously 'passed over former sins', the result of which was his willingness to be dishonoured for a time. What does reparative substitution do for humanity? It defers divine retribution until all moral accounts will be settled. It fixes both the private and public problems that humanity faces for having transgressed God's rectoral justice. In this way, the reparative substitution theory is radically theo-centric, an idea we suppose few would want to publicly resist, and which is the principal reason for God's patient endurance of the reproach of sinners.

Conclusion

To this point we have tried to show that a developed version of Anselmian satisfaction – what we call reparative substitution – in no way succumbs to the penal substitution theorist's efficacy objection. Far from it. Reparative substitution actually does more, so we think, than penal substitution theorists think their theory does. For example, in what way does the penal substitution theory do anything positive or efficacious for God that is also efficacious for all humanity? Simply put, it does nothing positive. To put it rather bluntly, nothing is restored to God on the penal substitution theory. Neither are the benefits that follow from Christ's work beneficial for all humanity. Instead, and quite to the contrary of the apparent demands of God's retributive justice, penal substitution seems only to make provision for God to restore righteousness to some part of humanity, leaving God dishonoured and his Son crushed (as the prophet says) for this dishonour, and what is more, all of this being of no apparent benefit to himself, save perhaps for the opportunity to vent his just wrath. In other words, upon closer examination and a comparison of mechanism and efficacy with other theories of atonement, penal substitution seems rather anthropocentric. Not so for the reparative substitution theory, according to which Christ's sacrificial act actually achieves something for all humanity and for God, namely the restoration of divine honour.

With all that has been said, we realize that our suggesting a theory of the atonement against penal substitution is nothing short of anathema in some circles. Particularly, we have had in mind the evangelical community. We too identify with this community. Having been raised and nurtured in this environment, we are committed not only to the Protestant tradition with the *Solas*, but, more specifically, to the evangelical emphasis on the authority of Scripture, evangelism as the means for calling debtors to account, and the centrality of Christ's work as the sole means of salvation, among other commitments. What we have argued here and elsewhere seems to coherently and intimately grow out of these Protestant evangelical convictions. For this reason, it seems that evangelicals ought to reconsider the standard penal substitution theory of atonement and whether it can be justly regarded as *the* theory of atonement. Following from this, it seems that evangelicals ought to reconsider a more robust and systematized Anselmian theory of atonement, one that makes sense of the whole of divine justice and not just one part. The coherence of reparative substitution warrants such reconsideration.

In fact, this version of Anselm's atonement theory fares even better in terms of explanatory power (e.g. efficiency/efficacy), coherence (at least as it is compared to the standard/popular penal substitution theory), and appeal. While there is a need to develop the theory and its implications in other biblical and theological contexts, this should not detract from the merits the theory has in terms of efficiency and efficacy, as we have explained here. No doubt, advancing a theory of atonement requires additional reflection and application. Particularly, the theory deserves some reflection in the context of Christ's mission (e.g. missional theology), a common area of reflection in contemporary theology. The theory also deserves some more explicit grounding in the exposition and theological readings of various passages of Scripture, as is appropriate for any evangelical theory of atonement. Furthermore, there are several challenging (not impossible) texts that need to be reconciled, and integrated, with such a theory (e.g. Isaiah's suffering servant).

Again, it is worth noting that not all passages of Scripture nor all theological issues can be addressed in one chapter, let alone one book. What we have done here simply motivates the consideration of one novel theory in the Anselmian tradition taken in a Reformed/Protestant direction. By taking one of the most common theological objections to the Anselmian theory (as well as every theory of atonement other than penal substitution), we hope this, at a minimum, will gain a hearing from the evangelical community.

Notes

1 The present chapter is a modification of an article that was originally published in *Perichoresis*. See Joshua R. Farris and S. Mark Hamilton, 'Reparative Substitution and the "Efficacy Objection": Toward a Modified Satisfaction Theory of Atonement', *Perichoresis* 15, 3 (2017), pp. 97–110.

2 'The Logic of Reparation: Contemporary Restitution Models of Atonement, Divine Justice, and Somatic Death', co-authored with Joshua R. Farris, *Irish Theological Quarterly* (2017), <http://journals.sagepub.com/doi/10.1177/00211 40017742804>.

3 For more on this soteriological dictum, *Satisfactio Christi sufficienter pro omnibus, sed efficaciter tatum pro electis* (the atonement of Christ is sufficient for all but efficient only for the elect) and its controversial use in the Reformed theological tradition, see Henrich Heppe, *Reformed Dogmatics*, trans. G. T. Thomson (London: Collins, 1950), pp. 475–9; Herman Bavinck, *Reformed Dogmatics, Vol. 3, Sin and Salvation in Christ*, ed. John Bolt, trans. John Vriend (Grand Rapids, MI: Baker, 2006), pp. 455ff.

4 Kathryn Tanner, *Christ the Key* (Cambridge: Cambridge University Press, 2010), p. 253 (emphasis added). In chapter 6, Tanner endorses an incarnation model of atonement that supposedly undoes this talk of legality where God is somehow bound to the law he has set in motion from the beginning of creation. Instead, what she highlights are the benefits humans receive from the incarnation. Her theory makes no assumption of some sort of law-like necessity. All that is required is that God desires to be in union with us (see p. 256). There is a sense in which God has been making his life available to humans, but it is exemplified to a greater degree in the incarnation. The problem with the theory is that it does not take into account, significantly, the Fall as an objective break between the divine and human relationship.

5 This same sentiment is reflected in Ben Myers' excellent essay, 'The Patristic Atonement Model', in Oliver D. Crisp and Fred Sanders (eds), *Locating Atonement: Explorations in Constructive Dogmatics* (Grand Rapids, MI: Zondervan, 2015), pp. 71–88. Here, Myers offers just the sort of theologically constructive refashioning of Aulén's Christus Victor model that we have in mind.

6 Robert S. Franks, *A History of the Doctrine of the Work of Christ* (Eugene, OR: Wipf and Stock, 2001), p. 358. Interestingly, Franks describes the Salmurian theory as both sufficient and efficient for all, 'on the condition of faith' (358). This result is somewhat oddly similar to the satisfaction theory, faith being an integral part, though perhaps not the whole, of those conditions for salvation that Anselm had in mind.

7 For a more recent and helpful treatment of the development of the doctrine of atonement from a more judicial-development perspective, see Adonis Vidu, *Atonement, Law, and Justice: The Cross in Historical and Cultural Contexts* (Grand Rapids, MI: Baker Academic, 2014).

8 For more discussion on the history of the development of the penal substitution model of atonement in the Reformed tradition, see: William G. T. Shedd, *Dogmatic Theology*, ed. Alan W. Gomes, 3rd edn (Phillipsburg, NJ: Presbyterian and Reformed), pp. 451–5.

9 Steve Jeffery, Michael Ovey and Andrew Sach, *Pierced for Our Transgressions: Rediscovering the Glory of Penal Substitution* (Wheaton, IL: Crossway, 2007).

10 Vidu, *Atonement, Law, and Justice*, p. 1.

11 Vidu, *Atonement, Law, and Justice*, pp. 118–19.

12 Thomas H. McCall, *Forsaken: The Trinity and the Cross, and Why it Matters* (Downers Grove, IL: InterVarsity Press, 2012).

13 Oliver D. Crisp, *Deviant Calvinism: Broadening the Reformed Tradition* (Minneapolis, MN: Fortress Press), ch. 7.

14 Vidu, *Atonement, Law, and Justice*, pp. 45–88.

15 Anselm, *Why God became Man?* in *The Major Works*, ed. Brian Davies and G. R. Evans (Oxford: Oxford University Press, 1998), pp. 283, 286, 288, 349 (emphasis added).

16 One popular example of such thinking is partly reflected in Richard D. Philipps, *What is the Atonement?* (Phillipsburg, NJ: P&R Publishing, 2010), pp. 23–5.

17 Franks offers the following helpful and discriminating note, saying: 'The Remonstrants also all but abolish the satisfaction and merit of Christ, asserting that Christ died, in order that God the Father might have the right to contract with us anew, on what terms he pleased, concerning forgiveness and justification. But while Christ's obedience and death stand, there can be no other way of obtaining justification; and those, who are justified thereby, are not justified by any legal contract, but purely by grace; and being united to Christ by faith, are regenerated and purified in heart'; *The Work of Christ*, p. 440.

PART 2

The Nature of Salvation

6

Theosis and Participation

OLIVER D. CRISP

Once upon a time respectable academic theologians did not spend much energy thinking about the doctrine of theosis. It was regarded as a sort of Eastern affectation, a Byzantine curiosity that few Western thinkers took seriously. Today, there is a thriving cottage industry devoted to the exposition and application of the doctrine in Western as well as Eastern theological traditions.[1] In this chapter I shall outline one version of theosis, and then attempt to provide some conceptual framework for thinking about what I take to be the central concern of all doctrines of theosis, namely participation in the divine nature. The aim is a modest one: to make some progress towards a clearer picture of the two theologically interrelated notions of theosis and participation – notions that are often touted in the current theological literature but seldom analysed with the sort of care that they warrant.

We shall proceed as follows. In the first section, I set out one way of thinking about theosis. Then, in a second section, I consider the vexed matter of human participation in the divine life, which is integral to the doctrine of theosis. In a final section, I consider Thomas Flint's Theory of Final Assumptions as one way of thinking about human eschatological participation in the divine life. I conclude with some reflections on the upshot of the foregoing.

On Theosis

To begin with, we need to have some idea of the doctrine of theosis. For present purposes, I shall treat theosis as a synonym of theopoeisis (being made divine), deification and divinization. By my lights, the doctrine of theosis is the notion that somehow human beings become partakers of the divine nature by means of union with Christ via the power of the Holy Spirit.[2] Often, theosis is thought to be closely related to the process of sanctification in the Christian life, not as a change that radically alters the moral state of fallen human beings in an instant. The language used connotes some sort of transformation that occurs over time.

However, as it stands, this way of thinking about theosis is sufficiently conceptually fuzzy that it could be misunderstood or misconstrued in important respects. So let us attempt to clarify matters a little further. The 'clarifications' offered here may not be agreed upon by all parties. But I think that they reflect some of the important ways in which recent theological work in this area has sought to understand theosis for the purposes of constructive theology. Let me begin by ruling out two common misunderstandings of the doctrine before providing some content to the doctrine.

The first common misunderstanding is that becoming partakers of the divine nature means losing one's individual identity in the divine, as a drop of water is 'lost' in the ocean. This is a mistake that is still sometimes found in the literature, and that motivates some theologians to steer clear of the doctrine.[3] Yet theosis is not equivalent to some sort of merging with the divine. It is not that defenders of theosis expect human beings to eventually cease to be human, or to 'lose' their humanity in some experience of union with the divine. (We shall see that Thomas Flint thinks human beings could lose their personhood in the eschaton in order to be united to God, but that is not the same thing as being assimilated to the divine, or losing one's humanity or even ceasing to be human.)

A second common misunderstanding of theosis is that the doctrine implies that redeemed humans become divine as God is divine. Some of the remarks made by patristic authors and their modern interpreters may mislead the reader into thinking this is what is envisaged by these early theologians. For instance, Athanasius famously remarks that Christ 'assumed humanity that we might become God' (*On the Incarnation*, §. 54). And in recent times, Metropolitan Kallistos Ware has written: 'Such, according to the teaching of the Orthodox Church, is the final goal at which every Christian must aim: to become god, to attain theosis, "deification" or "divinization". For Orthodoxy, our salvation and redemption mean our deification.'[4] However, human beings are not transmuted into additional deities according to the doctrine of theosis, which would be a metaphysical bootstrapping of a monumental sort. Sometimes incautious remarks made by defenders of theosis might lead one to think that the doctrine implies the transmutation of human beings into divinities, but this is not in fact what it entails.[5] One traditional way of fending off this concern is to point out that theosis does not imply the claim that human beings are transformed so as to share the divine *essence*. Instead, they come to share the divine *nature*.[6] The idea seems to be this. The divine essence is what is shared between the divine persons of the Trinity, is essential to the triune persons, and is incommunicable to creatures. The divine nature is some quality or qualities that the divine persons possess that may or may not be essential to the divine persons, but that is communicable to creatures. For modern analytic metaphysicians, this may be less than clear. For on at least one way of carving these things up, 'essence' and 'nature' are synonyms, both referring to the properties or attributes God has necessarily, so that to 'participate' in a nature (whatever that means) is just to participate in an essence. In which case, this would be a distinction without a difference.[7]

But perhaps what is meant is something more like this. There are communicable attributes God possesses that he may share with creatures like humans. Humans may exemplify these attributes and may come to express those attributes in ways that reflect the divine in important respects. Here is an example. Perhaps human beings may exemplify, say, love in a fragmentary and imperfect manner. Yet through prolonged exposure to, and experience of, the divine nature, and through performing certain spiritual practices, human beings may come to exemplify love in a more complete manner – one that better approximates divine love (insofar as this is humanly possible), though it may never be identical to divine love. This is a matter to which we shall return presently.[8]

However one understands the nature/essence distinction, it should be clear from the foregoing that becoming 'partakers of the divine nature' (2 Pet. 1.4) does not necessarily imply becoming divine as God is divine. It does not imply the reduction or removal of the massive ontological gulf that exists between God as the creator of all things, and human beings as creatures. One might put it like this. Although the doctrine of theosis presumes that redeemed humans become partakers of the divine nature, the doctrine does not imply that this relation of participation is symmetrical. Nor does it necessarily presume that the sort of exalted existence enjoyed by the redeemed involves the transmutation of the redeemed into some metaphysically exalted state, making of them little deities.

With these two misunderstandings cleared away, let me say something by way of clarifying the conceptual content of theosis. As I have already mentioned, theosis is fundamentally concerned with participation in the divine life. The notion of participation, union with Christ, and other, related concepts, are very much in vogue in contemporary theology and biblical studies. But what does this amount to? What is meant by participation in the divine? According to the New Testament scholar and theologian Carl Mosser: 'It is this: what is presently true about the incarnate Son will be made true of the redeemed. Redemption in the fullest sense is simply for a human person to become everything Jesus presently is in his glorified, ascended, fully flourishing humanity enthroned at God's right hand.'[9] This is a strong claim that begs for further explication. Mosser seems to think that participation in the divine life for the redeemed means coming to exemplify the qualities and properties had by the human nature of Christ in his glorified state. Presumably, this includes some rather odd qualities such as the ability to appear in locked rooms, and physical immortality. But it does not mean that redeemed human beings are somehow made divine, thereby effacing the creator/creature distinction. On this view, participation in the divine involves exemplifying certain qualities had by the glorified human nature of Christ that are not currently enjoyed by fallen human beings. But it also involves a relation of intimate union with Christ, though one that (so it seems to me) stops short of hypostatic union. It is, I think, closer to the notion of a mathematical asymptote, where a curve is on a trajectory towards a line, though the two never finally intersect.

I like much of what Mosser says here. However, his claim that theosis 'is simply for a human person to become everything Jesus presently is in his glorified, ascended, fully flourishing humanity enthroned at God's right hand', while consistent with much patristic theology on this matter, may need some finessing. For it is not clear to me that the humanity of the glorified, ascended Christ is significantly different from his humanity during his earthly ministry. To my way of thinking, the difference between Christ's humanity in his earthly ministry and in a glorified, ascended state has more to do with the manifestation of the divine nature 'in' or 'through' his human nature than it does with some significant (perhaps, ontological) change to the human nature in question. For Christ's human nature is already without sin (Heb. 4.15), and is already capable of sustaining hypostatic union with a divine person (John 1.14). This rather different way of thinking about the humanity of the glorified, ascended Christ is consistent with a krypsis Christology, according to which Christ's divine nature is in a sense 'hidden' or 'concealed' in his incarnate state – a sort of weak functional kenoticism. On this way of thinking, the difference between Christ before his resurrection, and Christ in his glorified, ascended state after the resurrection, has much more to do with the way in which his divinity is no longer 'concealed' in the same way, so that it is made manifest 'in' his human nature.[10] So being conformed to the image of Christ, who is the image of God, in theosis is not (in my judgement) a matter of being conformed to the likeness of Christ's glorified humanity – as if that is significantly different from being conformed to the image of his pre-resurrection humanity. Rather, it is about coming to approximate the way in which the divine nature is manifest 'through' the human nature of Christ in his glorified, ascended state. Think of the difference between the coil of an electric light that shines dimly with a reduced electrical current running through it, and much more brightly when a stronger current is passed through it. The coil has not changed; the amount of electricity passing through it has. In a similar way, I am suggesting that the glorified, ascended humanity of Christ has not changed in any significant ontological sense. What has changed is not his humanity, but the way in which his divinity 'shines through' his human nature. So participation in the divine life in theosis does mean that (as Mosser has it) 'what is presently true about the incarnate Son will be made true of the redeemed.' Moreover, he may be right that redemption in the fullest sense on a theosis-compatible doctrine of participation means 'simply for a human person to become everything Jesus presently is in his glorified, ascended, fully flourishing humanity enthroned at God's right hand'. But in my view this does not mean that the human nature to which we are conformed is somehow significantly different from that of the pre-resurrection Christ.[11]

Let us take stock. We have seen that theosis does not mean losing one's individuality in the divine. Nor does it mean becoming divine as God is divine. Instead, it is about participation in the divine life, and about union with Christ by the power of the Holy Spirit. I presume that this participation is an ongoing thing, which will continue into the eschaton. It has a first moment but no last moment because, as Jonathan Edwards puts it in his dissertation *God's End in Creation*: 'God, in glorifying the saints in heaven with eternal felicity, aims to satisfy his infinite grace or benevolence, by the bestowment of a good infinitely valuable, because eternal: and yet there never will come the moment, when it can be said, that now this infinitely valuable good has been actually bestowed.'[12]

Participation in the Divine Life

The notion of participation is doing a lot of the conceptual heavy lifting for the doctrine of theosis. But as has already been intimated, what is meant by participation in the divine life in the context of doctrines of theosis is rather unclear. There is much gesturing in the direction of theosis in recent biblical studies and systematic theology. But there is much less by way of explanation of the notion of participation. Thus the Princeton theologian Bruce McCormack asks:

> What is finally meant by the well-worn phrase *participation in the life of God?* The phrase is ambiguous on the face of it. Does it mean 'participation in the life that is God's own, the life that is proper to him as God, that life that is his *essentially*?' If so, how is it possible to participate in it without participating in the divine essence? . . . To put a finer point on it: is the 'life of God' in which we are said to participate *uncreated* life or *created* life?[13]

These are important theological questions. But as we saw in the previous section, theosis doesn't imply reducing or removing the creator/creature distinction. Nor does it necessarily mean that the sort of participation redeemed creatures enjoy is tantamount to participation in uncreated life – for that would be to participate in divinity as God is divine, which would seem to be metaphysically impossible for creatures. Nor does it necessarily mean participation in that which is essential to the divine life. But then, as per McCormack's comment, some account of what is meant by participation in the divine life is still wanting.

However, before attempting to address that concern it is worth noting that some theologians may be wary of even embarking on such a project. One worry is that attempting to get a clearer picture of the notion of participation at work in the doctrine of theosis may be tantamount to attempting to plumb the depths of a mystery the resolution of which is beyond our ken. Similarly, one might worry about an attempt to provide an explanation of, say, the Trinity or the incarnation that such projects are in principle futile because the explanation of these doctrines is simply beyond our human cognitive abilities. Such concerns need not arise where what is being attempted is not an explanation as such, but a theological model or picture that may provide some insight into the matter in hand on analogy with scientific models of complex data. It is just such an approach that I favour. Explaining human participation in the divine life may be a rather tall order; providing a model or models for thinking about this is both conceptually less demanding, because more theologically modest, and, as a consequence, more likely to make some theological headway. Let us turn to provide some content for such a model by means of a kind of metaphysical just-so story about human reconciliation with, and participation in, the divine.

Suppose we begin by taking up Eleonore Stump's Thomist-inspired account of love, according to which a loving relation between two persons comprises the desire to see the beloved flourish, and the desire to be united with the beloved.[14] God has such love for his creatures. So God desires that we flourish and that he be united with us. To that end, God seeks union with his beloved creatures. We see this supremely in the case of Christ, where a divine person unites himself to a human nature in order to bring about human reconciliation with God. But, in addition to this, this union with human nature in Christ is the means by which other fallen human beings can be united to God as well. Christ is a kind of metaphysical bridge between divinity and humanity. As I have said in another place, he is a kind of hub, like a wireless hub, that connects us as fallen human beings to God.[15] Just as my personal computer is connected to the Internet by means of radio signals that are transmitted from the hub to my computer, and from my computer to the hub, which is hard-wired to a cable connection that links it to remote servers, so fallen human beings may be connected to the 'hub' that is Christ by the power of the Holy Spirit. This link connects fallen human beings with the divine via Christ's human nature, which is an interface between divinity and humanity.

However, although by means of a wireless connection my personal computer can be linked to the Internet, to connect with the vast amount of information on the digital superhighway, such 'participation' in the ethereal world of the world wide web seems to fall short of the sort of participation defenders of theosis envisage in the case of the union between Christ and the redeemed, having to do with 'participating in the divine nature' (2 Pet. 1.4) and becoming 'gods . . . sons of the Most High' (Ps. 82.6). The organic analogies in places like Ephesians 5, which present a relation between Christ and his body (the Church) more intimate and mysterious than that between spouses, indicate something of what it is that is still lacking. In short, we need an account of participation that is more intimate than the most intimate human relationships (according to Ephesians), that is unitive in nature (according to Peter), but that falls short of a loss of the human individual in the divine life. In his work on the indwelling of the Holy Spirit, William Alston points out that models for thinking about the intimate relationship between the Spirit and redeemed human beings need to pay attention to the need for shared reciprocity (that is, the kind of shared and reciprocal relationship that exists between creaturely agents, as well as between creaturely agents and divine agents).[16] This feature is also missing from the hub-computer analogy, which is not a union between agents.

A promising line of research on the relation of participation in this context can be found in the previously mentioned (and currently unpublished) paper by Carl Mosser.[17] In the course of this essay he suggests several possible models for thinking about participation in the divine life that pick up the biblical motifs as well as some of the most important post-biblical theological distinctions often found in discussion of the topic.[18]

One of these suggestions turns on understanding the notion of union with the divine in terms of powers-metaphysics.[19] I take it that powers are something like dispositional properties that may be actualized given the right circumstances. Normally, such dispositional powers have mutual manifestation partners, for example the power of solubility that a sugar cube has when it is placed in water (a common example that Mosser also uses). Sugar has the dispositional property of being soluble in water. When a sugar cube is placed in a glass of water the power of solubility that the cube has and the power of being an agent of solubility, which the water has, are mutually manifested with the result that the sugar cube is dissolved. Transpose this sort of thinking to the topic of participation in the divine life. Although human sin may inhibit human beings from manifesting the power of being united to God in Christ, the power of the Holy Spirit makes that possible, acting as a kind of manifestation partner, and bringing about union with God in Christ. This seems like one promising way of conceiving how the union relation at the heart of the doctrine of participation works, but it doesn't really do very much to explain the relation itself.

Perhaps the model of union on analogy with the notion of an instrumental union may address this concern. The paradigm of an instrumental union is between an agent and some artefact. A good example of this is chopping a carrot with a knife. The instrument (knife) is utilized to bring about a non-basic action that could not otherwise be brought about without the knife (chopping the carrot). We have such accidental instrumental unions all the time, from the use of kitchen implements to how we interact with our smartphones.[20]

Now, apply this to the question of participation in the divine life. Given our assumption that God desires union with his human creatures, one way of bringing that about might be to have Christ act as an interface between divinity and humanity in order that human beings can be united to God via the Holy Spirit. However, unlike the examples of the smartphone and the knife, in 'extending' himself to unite himself with human beings God does not reduce humans to mere instruments. That would be to fail in an important respect to treat us as created agents, and I suggest that it would be a significant shortcoming in God if he treated his creatures merely as instruments for the bringing about of his own purposes. Nevertheless, there may be a sense in which the unitive relation brought about by the Holy Spirit in the life of the redeemed individual does extend God's action into the life of that individual, bringing about a mutual awareness and reciprocity (such as William Alston suggests should characterize the indwelling of the Holy Spirit), as well as a unitive relation that is asymmetrical in important respects as the relation between the agent and the artefact (knife, smartphone) is asymmetrical. For here in the theological context it is God who takes the initiative, God who secures the means by which we may be united to him in Christ by the Spirit, and God who sustains and nourishes the relationship of participation as it develops. We might think of this theological application of instrumental union as a particular instance of a kind of asymmetrical accessing relation of the sort more familiar in discussion of Thomas Morris's two-minds Christology.[21] God has complete access to our minds and our desires; we have only partial access to the divine mind and desires. Yet, on this way of thinking, that access may grow and develop as the redeemed human continues to grow in her knowledge and understanding of this union with the divine. And, for all we know, this spiritual growth could be everlasting.

The Theory of Final Assumptions

Earlier, in attempting to clarify what the doctrine of theosis commits the theologian to, I said that one misunderstanding of the doctrine was that theosis means becoming divine as God is divine. Instead, as I have construed it, the doctrine is about being united to God in Christ by the Holy Spirit, and being conformed to the image of his glorified human nature; that is, a certain cluster of qualities his glorified human nature exemplifies. However, in the recent philosophical-theological literature Thomas Flint has argued that a 'consummation devoutly to be wished' is that redeemed human beings be assumed by Christ, so that they are hypostatically united to the divine nature. This, Flint maintains, is one plausible way to think about the existence enjoyed by the redeemed in the life to come. And although he doesn't put it this way, it may also provide a way of construing the metaphysics of the beatific vision.

His reasoning goes something like this. Suppose that incarnation involves the assumption of a concrete particular, a human nature, by a divine person. In assuming a human nature, a divine person 'uploads' himself into that nature, making it his own. Normally speaking, the concrete particular that is a human nature would be generated *in utero* forming a human person distinct from the divine persons of the Trinity. In the case of Christ, the formation of a normal human nature occurs *in utero*, but it does not become a human person distinct from a divine person although he has the complete natural endowment of human nature that would, under normal circumstances, simply form a human person. The difference in the case of the incarnation is that at the very moment at which a human person would normally begin to exist, the Second Person of the Trinity assumes the human nature in question. He makes it his own so that it never forms a person independent of the divine persons of the Godhead. In the language of medieval-school theology, Christ's human nature never forms a supposit or fundamental substance independent of the divine persons of the Godhead as would normally happen in the case of the biological development of a mere human. This is because the concrete particular of Christ's human nature is assumed before it can become a fundamental substance or supposit. It is personally united to a divine person instead, and it is the divine person 'in' Christ that forms the person of Christ – the fundamental substance that is at the root of Christ's being, so to speak.

So much for the metaphysics of the incarnation. Flint takes something like this model, a model that has a long theological history, and asks whether this could tell us something about the final goal of human beings. In particular, he asks whether God the Son could assume not just the human nature of Jesus of Nazareth, but also the human natures of all the redeemed in the eschaton. That is, could God the Son take possession of our human natures in addition to his own, bringing our human natures into personal union with his own nature? And could he do that in such a way that we would enjoy the intimate relation of participation with the divine that traditional doctrines of theosis presume, yet without effacing *us* in the process? Flint thinks that such a doctrine of multiple incarnations is metaphysically possible, and maybe even desirable. He calls this the Theory of Final Assumptions (hereinafter, TFA).[22]

93

According to Flint it is metaphysically possible for a divine person to bring multiple human natures into personal union with himself so that these redeemed concrete particulars cease to be persons. He writes: 'Why not think that the nature survives the assumption without any corruption of any sort, but that, because of its new state of union with the Son, it no longer qualifies as a person?'[23] This question motivates the central claim of the TFA, namely, that *the ultimate end of all human beings who attain salvation is to be assumed by the Son*. Although redeemed human beings do not become divine as such, they do come to be assumed by a divine person. They are hypostatically united to a divine person. This amounts to the claim that personhood is an accidental property of human beings. Flint speculates that human beings are either persons, or assumed by a divine person – that is, belong to a divine person as an assumed human nature.

Ryan Mullins has taken issue with Flint's account, Flint has replied, and Mullins has lodged a rejoinder.[24] In that debate Flint clarifies his position in several respects that are salient. First, he explains that the TFA means redeemed humans in the eschaton do cease to be human persons, but do not thereby cease to exist full stop. 'Rather', he says, 'they continue to exist, but now in an exalted position, as body/soul composites united with the Son in the unfathomably rich and complete way that CHN [Christ's Human Nature] was always united with him.'[25] The idea seems to be this. There is a group of entities that are all human beings. These human beings prior to their glorification are all human persons. However, at the moment of glorification they lose the property of personhood in virtue of being assumed by a divine person. They remain concrete particular individuals, but they cease to be 'independent substances of a rational nature', to appropriate the traditional Boethian account of personhood. They are now dependent substances of a rational nature because they belong to – that is, are the assumed human natures of – a divine person.

Now, Mullins has other concerns about Flint's position, including a concern about its theological orthodoxy. Although I do not propose to enter into those claims in detail here, some brief comment on Mullins' concerns seems appropriate.

First, Mullins thinks that, on Flint's view, kicking Crisp in the eschaton implies kicking Jesus because Crisp and Jesus are both assumed human natures that belong to one subject, namely, God the Son. He writes:

> at present, if you kick my body, you will have kicked me. You will not have kicked the Son. I bear the property *having been kicked*. When we reach the eschaton, however, things will be different. If you kick me, you will have kicked the Son. If the Son assumes my human nature, I cease to be a person. Through the *communicatio idiomatum* [that is, the

communication of attributes in Christ from one nature to the other, or from both natures to the person], the Son becomes the ultimate bearer of the properties of all the assumed human natures. So if you kick me in heaven, you will have ultimately kicked Christ. If I kick you in return, I will have kicked Christ. Given the *communicatio idiomatum*, Christ will have kicked Christ, and Christ will have responded to this kick by kicking Christ. That seems ludicrous.[26]

On the face of it this state of affairs does indeed seem odd, but it isn't clear to me that it is ludicrous. Consider the case of Eschatological Crisp and Jesus. These are two distinct human natures that are concrete particulars assumed by God the Son. However, given Flint's account of the metaphysics of the incarnation the two concrete particulars in question are clearly distinct; they are not identical to one another. True, they are both concrete particulars 'owned' by one divine person, and that is a very strange state of affairs – one in which a single divine subject 'owns' two (or more) human natures. But the compositional model of the incarnation favoured by Flint does not imply that God the Son is identical with Christ, only that God the Son is a part of Christ. Jesus is composed of his human nature and God the Son. Eschatological Crisp is composed of his human nature and God the Son. But if that is right, then clearly Jesus and Eschatological Crisp are not identical for they do not share all and only the same parts. True, one divine subject owns two human natures, on this way of thinking. Nevertheless, it is not incoherent to think that Eschatological Crisp may kick Jesus, although it is very strange to think he might do so for it does amount to a state of affairs in which one divine subject uses his Eschatological Crisp human nature to act upon his Jesus human nature. An exotic implication of Flint's TFA? No doubt. A ludicrous implication of Flint's TFA? Not obviously.

Second, Mullins thinks that Flint's position is unorthodox because according to the Fifth Ecumenical Council of Constantinople, the human nature assumed by Christ is made personal, so to speak, by its union with God the Son. It is said to be anhypostatic (without personhood) in abstraction, as it were, from the incarnation, and enhypostatic (made personal) by its union with a divine person. But Flint's position does not fall foul of this theological distinction. For suppose that the an-enhypostatic nature distinction is right. That just means that Christ's human nature is made personal by its union with God the Son. True, Flint seems to think that Christ's human nature would form a mere human person independent of assumption in possible worlds at which Jesus of Nazareth obtains without the act of incarnation.[27] But the logic of the TFA taken as a stand-alone argument for the conclusion that the redeemed are eventually hypostatically united to God the Son doesn't *require* that concession. A defender of such a stand-alone version of the TFA could affirm the following:

1 Christ's human nature is formed for God the Son.
2 Christ's human nature only exists at worlds where God the Son assumes it.
3 There are no worlds at which the human nature of God the Son exists unassumed, and forms a mere human person independent of incarnation.

Whatever the metaphysics of assumption in the case of Christ's human nature turn out to be, the interesting theological question for our purposes is whether *we* could be assumed by God the Son in the eschaton. I don't see why something like Flint's TFA couldn't be taken up with the an-enhypostatic nature distinction in place so that in the case of Christ his human nature is made personal through union with God the Son (and there are no worlds at which his human nature exists unassumed), but my human nature is rendered non-personal by being assumed by God the Son. In fact, that is what we would expect to happen given that in the case of Christ God the Son assumes an 'impersonal' human nature generated for assumption, whereas in the case of Eschatological Crisp (and all other redeemed human beings) an existing human person loses that personhood in being assumed by a divine person, on analogy with the heretical doctrine of adoptionism in Christology.

Now, at first blush it seems odd to think that something like adoptionism obtains in the case of the redeemed though it is a heresy when applied to Christology. But there are good theological reasons for that, reasons having to do with ensuring that there is only one (divine) person in Christ from the get-go in order that the person who is incarnate is a suitable candidate for being the mediator of human salvation. These considerations clearly do not apply to the assumption of my human nature or yours.[28]

Nevertheless, I am leery of the prospect of being assumed by a divine person, although the reasons for my concern are rather different from Mullins'. To see why, let us return to Flint's claim that personhood may be an accidental quality in human beings that human beings can lose without ceasing to exist altogether. That is, let us return to his claim that *human beings cannot exist without either being a person or being assumed by a person.* Note that Flint here makes sufficient metaphysical room, so to speak, for the theologian to affirm the following. The concrete particular that is a human nature is such that it either is a fundamental substance independent of a divine person, and thereby is a human person, or it is assumed by a (divine) person. If it is assumed by a divine person then the human nature in question either never is a human person (because assumption occurs at the moment the human nature is generated), or it ceases to be a human person (because it is assumed by a divine person at some moment later than the first moment at which the complete human nature began to exist). So the defender of the TFA can accommodate the classical orthodox theological notion that all human natures are in principle assumable by a divine person. It is just that the TFA advocate denies the classical theological assumption that in fact this only obtains in the case of one individual, namely, Christ.

My concern with this reasoning is that it is not clear what is left of a human being once personhood is removed through assumption. In the case of Christ, there is only one person present, though he has two natures. There are at least two concrete particulars (his human nature and his divine nature), but not two persons present in Christ on pain of Nestorianism. But that is because in the case of Christ, assumption takes place from the first moment at which Christ's human nature begins to exist. There is no period in which the human nature of Christ exists independent of a divine person prior to assumption. But what would it mean for an existing human person to cease to be a person while remaining a distinct individual assumed by a divine person? Flint seems to think that assumption by a divine person will enhance the lives of the redeemed in a way analogous to the optimism transhumanists have about enhancing and enlarging human capacities by adding and integrating new technologies into human organisms. Putting it in the parlance of Boethian persons once more (something Flint himself does not do), we might say that according to the TFA, redeemed humans remain distinct substances of a rational nature, but lose the property of being subsistent beings – that is, of being fundamental substances or supposits that are independent of a divine person.

Still, even if we grant this it is difficult to see how Christology alone will provide the apparatus by means of which we can explain how the redeemed can be assumed entities that remain human beings without being human persons. How am I still present in the eschaton if I am assumed and lose my personhood in the process, being 'personalized' by God the Son? We don't want to apply similar reasoning in the case of Christ because it implies adoptionism. How is this any better in the case of the assumption of mere humans who are existing persons? To put it another way, Flint wants to resist adoptionism in the case of Christ. However, in the case of the redeemed, what obtains in the eschaton looks a lot more like a case of the divine assimilation of an existing person than it does assumption as in the case of a theologically orthodox doctrine of incarnation. This is not so much a problem as a theologically curious consequence of Flint's position. But it is one with which I am rather uncomfortable.

These are not knock-down-drag-out reasons for rejecting Flint's position. There is much that is intriguing about his view, not least because it provides a model for understanding the sort of strong language of participation in the divine life that a doctrine of theosis presumes. But in my judgement the conclusion he draws raises more problems than it solves – particularly in terms of trying to provide some reason to think I may continue to exist in an eschatological state where I cease to be a subsistent entity, becoming an assumed human nature of a divine person. This, it seems to me, is tantamount to too much participation in the divine, or what we might think of as a limit case to the sort of doctrine of participation that I set out to analyse. Although I understand Flint's claim that this might be regarded not so much as a loss but as a gain – the loss of my personhood to gain immediate participation in the divine life through assumption – it amounts to a doctrine of participation at the cost of eliminating or effacing creaturely personhood. Few theologians will want to follow Flint in embracing that eschatological upshot to his position.

Conclusion

I have argued that the doctrine of theosis can be understood in such a way that it encapsulates the broad sweep of God's action in reconciling fallen human beings to Godself via the work of Christ by the power of the Holy Spirit. We could summarize much of the foregoing in the following:

> THEOSIS: The doctrine according to which redeemed human beings are conformed to the image of Christ in his human nature. By being united to Christ by the power of the Holy Spirit, redeemed human beings begin to exemplify the qualities of the human nature of Christ, and grow in their likeness to Christ (in exemplifying the requisite qualities Christ's human nature instantiates). This process of transformation and participation goes on forevermore. It is akin to a mathematical asymptote.

A key notion at work in this way of thinking about the reconciling action of God in Christ is participation in the divine nature. In keeping with some recent work in the area, I have suggested several ways in which the relation of participation may be construed: in terms of a hub-computer analogy; in terms of dispositional properties or powers; and in terms of extended minds.[29] These are conceptual building blocks that might form the basis of a model of participation in the divine life consistent with theosis – first steps along the way, so to speak, that are supposed to be indicative rather than normative. Finally, I have addressed one recent and interesting argument from Tom Flint that supposes it is metaphysically possible, and perhaps desirable, for multiple incarnations to obtain simultaneously by means of the hypostatic union of the redeemed. Although this is a model of participation that is consistent with the view of theosis outlined here, in my view it is too strong because it requires the loss of human personhood in order for union with God to occur. Thus, I suggest that a plausible doctrine of theosis will be one that takes seriously the need to provide an account of participation that is more intimate than the most intimate human relationships (as per Ephesians 5), that is unitive in nature, but that falls short of a loss of the human individual in the divine life. This is also consistent with several ways of thinking about the atonement, including the union account I have outlined elsewhere.[30] But I shall leave specifying how theosis and atonement are related for another occasion.[31]

Notes

1 See, for example, Roger E. Olson, 'Deification in Contemporary Theology', *Theology Today* 64 (2007), pp. 186–200; Paul L. Gavrilyuk, 'The Retrieval of Deification: How a Once-Despised Archaism Became an Ecumenical Desideratum', *Modern Theology* 25 (2009), pp. 647–59; and Gösta Hallonsten, 'Theosis in Recent Research', in Michael J. Christiansen and Jeffrey A. Witting (eds), *Partakers of the Divine Nature: The History and Development of Deification in the Christian Traditions* (Grand Rapids, MI: Baker, 2007), pp. 281–93. (The literature is large and expanding.) See also these representative examples of engagement with the topic from within my own Reformed tradition: Gannon Murphy, 'Reformed *Theosis?*', *Theology Today* 65 (2008), pp. 191–212; Myk Habets, '"Reformed *Theosis?*" A Response to Gannon Murphy', *Theology Today* 65 (2009), pp. 489–98; and Kyle Strobel, 'Jonathan Edwards's Reformed Doctrine of Theosis', *Harvard Theological Review* 109.3 (2016), pp. 371–99.

2 This is not the only way to construe theosis, of course. See Habets, '"Reformed *Theosis?*"' for more on this.

3 See, for example, the discussion of the work of Robert Caldwell III and Bruce McCormack in Oliver D. Crisp, *Jonathan Edwards on God and Creation* (New York: Oxford University Press, 2012), ch. 8.

4 Timothy [Kallistos] Ware, *The Orthodox Church, New Edition* (London: Penguin, 1997 [1963]), p. 231.

5 This is consistent with Ware's remarks about becoming 'gods'. The idea is not that redeemed humans become divine as God as divine, but rather that redeemed humans participate in the divine nature in an intimate relation by means of which they acquire certain divine qualities – becoming like little 'gods' (cf. Ps. 82).

6 Sometimes Orthodox and patristic writers say that theosis means that what God is by *nature* redeemed humans become by *grace*. But I'm not clear how helpful this distinction is without a lot of further qualifications. For it cannot be the case that human beings become divine by an act of grace. The metaphysical bootstrapping issue would still obtain if this was the claim being made, and I'm not sure what it means to say an entity of one sort or kind is transmuted to another kind by an act of divine fiat. So I have left out discussion of this oft-cited distinction here.

7 At one point John Calvin suggests that the distinction has to do with what some contemporary metaphysicians would call a kind essence and an individual essence: 'The word *nature* does not denote essence but kind.' John Calvin, *The Epistle of Paul the Apostle to the Hebrews and the First and Second Epistles of St. Peter*, ed. David W. Torrance and Thomas F. Torrance, trans. William B. Johnston (Edinburgh: Oliver and Boyd, 1963), p. 330.

8 It has been suggested to me that the Palamite distinction between the incommunicable divine essence, and communicable divine energies, might be a better way to carve this distinction because it does not raise the worry of a distinction without a difference. I invite the reader who agrees with this to make the relevant mental adjustment in what follows.

9 Carl Mosser, 'The Metaphysics of Union with God', unpublished paper, p. 4. Cited with permission of the author.

10 A full explication of this point would take up much more space. Interested readers may consult Oliver D. Crisp, *Divinity and Humanity: The Incarnation Reconsidered* (Cambridge: Cambridge University Press, 2007), ch. 4, where I give some account of a krypsis Christology. This is also related to my argument in *The Word Enfleshed: Exploring the Person and Work of Christ* (Grand Rapids, MI: Baker Academic, 2016) for the conclusion that we are made in the image of Christ, who is the image of God.

11 Thanks to Christa McKirland for raising this worry about conformity to the glorified human nature of Christ.

12 Edwards, *God's End in Creation*, in *The Works of Jonathan Edwards, Vol 8: Ethical Writings*, ed. Paul Ramsey (New Haven, CT: Yale University Press, 1989), p. 527.

13 Bruce L. McCormack, 'Union with Christ in Calvin's Theology: Grounds for a Divinization Theory?', in David W. Hall (ed.), *Tributes to John Calvin: A Celebration of His Quincentenary* (Phillipsburg, NJ: P&R, 2010), pp. 504–29, 505. Italics original.

14 See Eleonore Stump, *Wandering in Darkness: Narrative and the Problem of Suffering* (Oxford: Oxford University Press, 2010), p. 91.

15 See Crisp, *The Word Enfleshed*.

16 William Alston, 'The Indwelling of the Holy Spirit', in Thomas V. Morris (ed.), *Philosophy and the Christian Faith* (Notre Dame, IN: University of Notre Dame Press, 2006).

17 Mosser, 'The Metaphysics of Union with God'.

18 Mosser, 'The Metaphysics of Union with God'. Mosser also considers the notion of union as instrumental agency whereby human beings may be God's instruments or vice-regents in the created order as a number of recent biblical-theological studies of the image of God in human beings have concluded. But I shall leave this to one side here as a model that I find less conducive to the present work.

19 A recent accessible account of powers-metaphysics can be found in George Molnar, *Powers: A Study in Metaphysics* (Oxford: Oxford University Press, 2003).

20 A useful recent discussion of such instrumental union in relation to the incarnation can be found in Richard Cross, 'Vehicle Externalism and the Metaphysics of the Incarnation: A Medieval Contribution', in Anna Marmadoro and Jonathan Hill (eds), *The Metaphysics of the Incarnation* (Oxford: Oxford University Press, 2011), p. 190.

21 See: Thomas V. Morris, *The Logic of God Incarnate* (Ithaca, NY: Cornell University Press, 1986).

22 Flint, 'Molinism and Incarnation', in Ken Perszyk (ed.), *Molinism: The Contemporary Debate* (Oxford: Oxford University Press, 2011), p. 13 [Oxford Online edition]. His TFA is set in a broader context, namely, that of his Molinist account of the incarnation. But the TFA argument can be lifted from that broader context so that it stands alone as an argument for a particular eschatological view of human beings that is independent of his Molinism. That is what I shall do here.

23 Flint, 'Molinism and Incarnation', p. 13.

24 See R. T. Mullins, 'Flint's "Molinism and the Incarnation" is too Radical', *Journal of Analytic Theology* 3 (2015), pp. 1–15; Thomas P. Flint, 'Orthodoxy and Incarnation: A Reply to Mullins', *Journal of Analytic Theology* 4 (2016), pp. 180–92; and R. T. Mullins, 'Flint's "Molinism and the Incarnation" is still too Radical – A Rejoinder to Flint', *Journal of Analytic Theology* 5 (2017), pp. 515–32.

25 Flint, 'Orthodoxy and Incarnation: A Reply to Mullins', p. 184.

26 Mullins, 'Flint's "Molinism and the Incarnation" is too Radical', p. 5.

27 This has to do with Flint's commitment to a Molinist account of the incarnation, a matter that we need not enter into here. Interested readers are directed to Flint's work on this topic for more information.

28 Another objection to Flint's view was put to me by Dru Johnson. Let us call it *the multiple incarnations simpliciter objection*. Suppose that at the very moment when all human natures are assumed by God the Son, there is at least one human conceived *in utero*. This human being is immediately assumed by God the Son along with every other human nature. However, unlike these other human natures, the nature of the entity generated at the very moment of assumption is not a human person, as such, but the natural endowment of a human person. It has not existed long enough to become a human person independent of a divine person. So at the moment of assumption, this human being is hypostatically united to God the Son, who makes it 'his' human nature. But because it is not a human person independent of God the Son at the moment of assumption, it becomes his human nature in a way comparable to the assumption of the human nature of Jesus of Nazareth. The upshot: multiple incarnations *simpliciter*!

29 Recall that the latter two analogues draw upon the very helpful work of Carl Mosser.

30 In Crisp, *The Word Enfleshed*.

31 Thanks to James Arcadi, Dennis Bray, Marc Cortez, Aaron Cotnair, Joshua Farris, Thomas Flint, Jesse Gentile, Mark Hamilton, Dru Johnson, Christa McKirland, Ryan Mullins, Carl Mosser, Kyle Strobel, J. T. Turner, Jordan Wessling, Christopher Woznicki, and audiences at the Logos Institute Research Seminar in St Mary's College, University of St Andrews, and New College, University of Edinburgh, for comments on previous iterations of this chapter (or the ideas contained therein).

7

Ascension and Pentecost: A View from the Divine Missions

ADONIS VIDU

'Having Received from the Father the Promised Spirit'

It is an undisputed fact that the theological basis for understanding the nature of salvation is in the person and work of Jesus Christ. Theology must therefore seek to ground every affirmation about soteriology in a robust account of Christology. One central assertion of soteriology is that the Son and the Holy Spirit are present to the redeemed. If this is the case, it must be shown in what way the current presence of the divine persons is related to the mission of the Son and the mission of the Holy Spirit.

The present chapter seeks to provide just such an account by showing the inherent connection between the missions of the Son and the Holy Spirit. The key narrative element of this relation relates to the conditioning of the coming of the Spirit by the departure of Jesus. Jesus makes the puzzling statement: 'I tell you the truth: it is to your advantage that I go away, for if I do not go away, the Helper will not come to you. But if I go, I will send him to you' (John 16.7; cf. John 7.39). While John is the only evangelist to recount this instruction, New Testament authors treat it as a known fact that the Spirit descended after Jesus' ascension. Luke, for instance, explains the Pentecostal events in relation to Christ's exaltation: 'Being therefore exalted at the right hand of God, and having received from the Father the promise of the Holy Spirit, he has poured out this that you yourselves are seeing and hearing' (Acts 2.33).

The two events, then, are clearly correlated; but what is the logical relation between ascension and Pentecost? Couldn't Christ, the incarnate Son of God, have sent the Spirit without himself departing? Indeed, the same John records the story of Jesus breathing on his disciples and saying 'Receive the Holy Spirit' prior to the ascension (John 20.22).

I will make the case that the appropriate dogmatic way of explaining the correlation between the two events is by considering them from the standpoint of the doctrine of the divine missions. More specifically, the meaning of this correlation will only reveal itself once we understand these events in the light of the trinitarian sending of the Son and the Spirit. The analysis of these missions, particularly of the relation between the sending of the Son and the sending of the Spirit, will further ground soteriological assertions which inevitably deal with the ongoing presence of the Son and the Spirit in Christian life.

The following section explores a problematic, or at least partial, way of correlating ascension and Pentecost. Next, I introduce the doctrine of the divine missions especially as elaborated by Augustine and Aquinas. I then move, in the central constructive part of the chapter, to show how this account of the missions illuminates the logical connection between the two events, or the two sendings. Briefly put, I will be arguing that, since a mission extends a procession to include a created effect, the mission of the Spirit, extending as it does the procession of the Spirit, repeats in time the procession of the Spirit from the Father and the Son (*filioque*). This extension in time of the coming forth of the Spirit from the Father and the Son is consistent with the biblical narratives. The proposal is further clarified in conversation with a number of likeminded authors. Finally, I turn to the import of this view from the missions for the theme of this volume, soteriology.

How have the two signal redemptive historical events been correlated historically? I have identified one tradition, sometimes more suggestive than explicit, which builds on Acts 2.33, where Christ receives the 'promised Spirit', or the 'promise of the Holy Spirit'. Some authors have suggested that the reason Christ cannot send the Spirit prior to his ascension is because he has yet to receive the Spirit as a reward. It is not as if Christ did not already have the Spirit, but the ability or prerogative to send the Spirit is conditioned upon the fulfilment of certain duties. The ascended Christ, then, receives this prerogative as a reward for his obedience.

Chrysostom does not use the language of reward, but he ties the coming of the Spirit to Christ's fulfilment of his duty. The Spirit could not be sent, he writes: 'Because he could not come, since the curse had not yet been lifted, the original sin had not yet been forgiven, but all men were still subject to the penalty for it.'[1] Preaching on John 7.39, he ties Pentecost to the restoration of our favourable status and the return to friendship with God, whereupon we would receive the Holy Spirit as a gift.[2]

Protestant writers also use the language of merit in relation to Christ himself. Luther, for instance, writes: 'Therefore, these are the gifts of God's grace, which Christ received from the Father through his merit and his personal grace, in order that He might give them to us as we read in Acts 2.33.'[3]

Herman Witsius, although not asserting explicitly that Christ receives the prerogative of sending the Spirit as a gift, does nevertheless refer to the exaltation of Christ in terms of reward: 'The glory of his justice required that his well beloved Son should not be disappointed of that reward, which was due to an obedience so signal, and a service so arduous and so perfect; and which was to be enjoyed only in heaven.'[4] According to Witsius, some operations belonging to his office as mediator are only to be accomplished from heaven, including his giving of the gifts of the Holy Spirit to believers. But this exaltation is, according to Witsius, a 'right which he had procured for himself'.[5]

The nineteenth-century Church of Scotland minister George Smeaton speaks about Christ's 'power of bestowing the Spirit upon others' as 'the grandest display of Christ's exaltation – the culminating point, – arguing at once reward and divine dignity'.[6] He then goes on to state, explicitly: 'The right to send the Holy Spirit into the hearts of fallen men was acquired by atonement.'[7]

Now it is quite clear that none of the examples marshalled here indicate anything like a substantive attempt to answer my question. Overall, it can be observed that Protestant theologians retained Calvin's reserve about a substantive answer to this question. He writes: 'Here we must not put the question "Could not Christ have drawn down the Holy Spirit while he dwelt on earth?" For Christ takes for granted all that had been decreed by the Father and, indeed, when the Lord has once pointed out what he wishes to be done, to dispute about what is possible would be foolish and pernicious.'[8]

But when some of the authors do venture in this direction, the language of reward is not far off. But why should one be suspicious about it? Perhaps the most significant concern, one that has been heard increasingly in Catholic theology since Vatican II, has been one about the extrinsic nature of grace.[9] If Christ receives the Spirit as a reward, the Spirit must be seen as extrinsic to Christ, something that he receives from the outside, upon the accomplishment of his mission. This raises important Christological and Trinitarian questions. Christologically, one has to ask about the relation between the human nature of Jesus and the person of the eternal Son. Isn't Christ's human nature, by virtue of its hypostatic union to the Son, already permeated by the Spirit? The question of agency follows immediately: what is the relation between the human operations and the divine operations of the incarnate Lord? Are the divine actions somehow conditioned by the successful completion of human actions? So, for example, is the human obedience of Jesus somehow a condition of the eternal Son's sending the Spirit?

Of course, one should not presume an answer to whether the sending of the Spirit is a divine action of the Lord, or whether it is a human action. If it is a divine action, in what way may an operation of the omnipotent Lord be seen to be conditioned by something, short of saying that God acquires capacities to act, which would entail divine mutability? On the other hand, if the Son sends the Spirit through his human nature, what significant change does the ascension produce such that only the ascended Christ could send the Spirit?

This barrage of questions should at the very least alert us that we must tread very carefully over this sensitive dogmatic terrain. Trinitarian theology and Chalcedonian Christology have already laid down the ground rules for such adventures. The doctrine of the divine missions collates and applies these rules to our understanding of the temporal missions of the Son and the Spirit.

The Divine Missions

The Christian tradition understands the human history of the incarnate Son in terms of accomplishing a mission on which he is sent by the Father. This perspective is motivated by the scriptural descriptions themselves. Paul encapsulates this idea of a mission of the Son in Galatians 4.4–6: 'But when the fullness of time had come, God sent forth his Son, born of woman, born under the law, to redeem those who were under the law, so that we might receive adoption as sons. And because you are sons, God sent the Spirit of His Son into our hearts, crying out, "Abba, Father!"'

It is not necessary further to demonstrate the biblical credentials of the category of missions. This conceptuality, however, raised a number of issues during the early development of trinitarian theology, where it was taken by some to indicate a certain inferiority of the Son to the Father and the Spirit to both the Son and the Father.

Perhaps no other theologians better availed themselves of the task of showing the trinitarian character of the very category of missions than Augustine and Aquinas. It is beyond the scope of this chapter to give a complete presentation of their theology of the divine missions. Even less space exists for clarifying the distinctions between their two doctrines of the divine missions. I will have to risk taking their contributions to be coherent with each other overall. For my purposes, I will insist on two features of a doctrine of the divine missions, which are the flip sides of the same coin.

First, with Augustine and Aquinas, Western theology understands a mission to be the *temporal extension of a trinitarian procession*. One might put it this way: in a mission we have the repetition in time of an eternal relation of divine origin.

The second feature is that in a divine mission, *the creature is drawn to participate in God, as a divine person comes to exist in a new way in it, yet in such a way that the divine person does not change.*

The dogmatic reasons for this are straightforward: in a mission we are given precisely the person as he proceeds from another; that is, in his relationship of origin, yet in relation to a created term. The created term is precisely that to which, or in the form of which the divine person is sent. The sending thus coheres with the person's 'coming forth from another'. In this way is the sending an extension of a procession.

Since a divine person is nothing but a relation of origin within the unity of the divine substance, what is given in a mission is the complete substance of God, but in terms of a relation between a created term and one of the irreducible yet indivisible relations of origin within this substance. There are in God only two such relations of coming forth from another: filiation and spiration. Consequently there are only two such missions, that of the Son and the Spirit. The Father too is present in the mission; only not as sent. As I noted, the whole Trinitarian substance is present in a way fitting with its relationships of origin and mode of existence.

Augustine shows how the missions extend the processions: 'And just as being born means for the Son his being from the Father, so his being sent means his being known to be from him. And just as for the Holy Spirit his being the gift of God means his proceeding from the Father, so his being sent means his being known to proceed from him. Nor, by the way, can we say that the Holy Spirit does not proceed from the Son as well; it is not without point that the same Spirit is called the Spirit of the Father and of the Son.'[10]

What does 'extending the processions' mean? Here we are starting to wade into deeper trinitarian waters. For both Western Fathers the doctrine of the divine missions must be consistent with the doctrine of the divine attributes. One such attribute is omnipresence, or immensity. Since God is already omnipresent, what might it mean for his being to be 'extended', or for a divine person to be sent?

Both Augustine and Aquinas understand this new presence not in terms of a change in God, but rather as a change in the creature's relation to God. For Augustine, for a divine person to be sent just means for that divine person to be known. Aquinas also insists on this. It leads him to two essential insights into the doctrine: 'The divine person sent neither begins to exist where he did not previously exist, nor ceases to exist where he was. Hence a mission takes place without a separation, having only distinction of origin.'[11]

Aquinas further explains that this is a new way of existing in the other: 'Thus the mission of a divine person is a fitting thing, as meaning in one way the procession of origin from the sender, and as meaning a new way of existing in another.'[12]

The Trinity, in other words, comes to exist in a new way in another, both visibly and invisibly. Galatians 4 indicates both types of missions, visible and invisible. Both the Son and the Spirit have visible and invisible missions. The visible mission prepares the invisible missions. As Jesus puts it in John

14.23: 'If anyone loves me, he will keep my word, and my Father will love him, and we will come to him and make our home with him.'

Again, given divine immutability and omnipresence, a mission does not comport a change in God, but a new relation in the creature, whereby the creature begins to resemble God.[13] To say that God begins to exist in a new way in the creature, then, is just to say that the creature is lifted to participate in the divine relations. For this reason, Aquinas insists on defining a divine mission as 'includ[ing] the eternal procession, with the addition of a temporal effect'.[14]

These considerations merely reflect the implications of trinitarian doctrine in relation to the work of salvation of the distinct divine persons in the economy. They represent the sifting of orthodox reflection on the trinitarian nature of God in light of revelation. The Christian truth which they express is that God has made his own being available in time, he has gifted his own self, through the missions of the Son and the Spirit. Yet we are instructed to resist certain mythological conceptions of the missions, along the lines of their coming and going down and up an 'ontological ladder'. The Western tradition has always exhibited great care to preserve the ontological distinction between God and creation, not such that God is unapproachable, but that in communing with creatures he remains God.

A mythological approach will tend to regard the missions precisely in the way Augustine and Aquinas reject, as involving the divine persons in a series of departures and arrivals. The Fathers rightly sense that such a view would finally dispense with the central mystery of our faith, that in these missions we are given the indivisible God, not some intermediary, or an offshoot.

Yet at the same time, this God is giving himself to us in the only way it is fitting for him to do so, namely by drawing parts of creation into union with him.

This is rather essential for this project. In a divine mission, according to this tradition, a created effect is united to a divine person, such that this divine person comes to exist in it in a new way.

The following limited analogy might help. Take a natural magnet. The magnet is a substance that generates a magnetic field. The magnetic field comprises a relationship between two poles, negatively (S) and positively (N) charged. It must be understood that the two poles are not separable parts of the magnet, but inseparable functions of the relations, which define the magnetic field, which is the magnet itself. Now take a metallic pin to the magnet. It will become attached to only one of the poles of the magnet, depending on its own charge. In the process, the pin itself will become magnetized, meaning that it will come to exhibit the relations that constitute the magnetic field into which it participates.

This is a feeble analogy for what happens in a divine mission. The pin participates in the whole magnet, not just in one of the poles, since the poles are relational yet real distinctions within the unity of the magnet. The pin becomes attached specifically to one of the poles of the magnet, not to both of them. Finally, the pin acquires the magnetism of the magnet through its being attached to one of the poles.

Now, to cash out the analogy: the human nature of Jesus Christ is the created term that is drawn into union with the eternal Son. The whole of the Godhead resides in the human nature of Jesus Christ, since the Son is not a part of the Godhead, but the whole divine nature considered from the standpoint of relation. Even though the whole Godhead creates, attracts and unites the human nature to the divine Son, nonetheless the human nature is united exclusively to the Son, such that it belongs to him alone. The Son alone comes to exist as Jesus Christ, the Son of Man. However, what it means for the Son to exist in this human nature is precisely for this human nature to acquire the 'magnetism' of the divine relations, i.e. to become itself a channel for the relations that characterize this divine nature.

Now, just like the pin is a substance while the magnetic pole to which it is attached is only a relation, the human nature of Jesus Christ is a substance, whereas the eternal Son to which it is attached is what Aquinas calls a 'subsistent relation'. What we have here is the picture of a created substance, which comes to participate in a relation, while remaining the substance that it is. Thus, the human nature of Jesus Christ, without ceasing to be what it is, becomes hypostatically united to the Son and therefore a channel, or instrument for the Son. The Son can be said to exist in it in a new way insofar as the relation of sonship now also characterizes the human substance.

But in Western theology, it is not filiation alone that characterizes the Son. Unlike a magnet, where only two poles constitute the magnetic field, God is Trinity. The filiation of the Son further engenders the spiration of the Spirit, as the common love between the Father and the Son. But this means that the relationships into which the human nature of Jesus Christ comes to participate, united to the Logos as it is, are not only those of filiation. Not only is the man Jesus Christ the Son, that is, but he also becomes, precisely as human, breather of the Spirit. Herein, I submit, lies the key to the relation between Ascension and Pentecost. To this we can now turn.

'If I go I will send him to you'

The key question is, how is the mission of the Son related to the *human* actions and passions of Jesus Christ? I have reported a rather timid suggestion – but even in its suggestiveness still influential – that Christ is glorified as a reward, and more or less explicitly receives the prerogative to send the Spirit, also as a reward.

It may be argued that behind this answer lies a certain reflex of correlating the mission of the Spirit to the human acts and passions of Jesus. The latter are thought to somehow 'unlock' or 'enable' what is ultimately a divine action.[15] To use an analogy, it is much like before a builder puts a roof on a house, the carpenters must first frame it, the foundation must be built, and so on. And so the carpenters enable the roofing company to do their work, by having completed their part of the job.

There are solid dogmatic reasons, however, to reject this view. As we have seen, insofar as it is regarded as a divine action, it implies that God enables himself to do this or that through some created action, in this case his human obedience. This view is problematic precisely because it makes a divine act to be conditional upon the completion of a human action.

Such a view, unfortunately, has a respectable pedigree in the West, from Augustine onwards. Augustine had held that the sending of the Holy Spirit by the Son is a divine action, not one undertaken through his human nature. Augustine had argued that Christ receives the Spirit as man, but sends him as God. His reception of the Holy Spirit is conditioned, moreover, by his obedience, but also victory over the powers, etc. In his human nature, Christ removes the obstacles to grace by satisfying for our sins. In other words, he merits grace as man, to be then dispensed through his divine offices. The actions through which he merits grace, in other words, unlock the sending of the Spirit as a divine act.

Yves Congar and Dominic Legge have shown that this view has dominated Western theology up to the twelfth century, towards the end of which Robert of Melvin and Gilbert de la Porrée make an alternative suggestion. They argue that Christ, precisely in his human nature, is the cause of the influx of grace, and implicitly of the Holy Spirit.

Aquinas: Beyond Mere Merit/Reward

Thus, when Aquinas argues this same position explicitly in his later thought, he not only modifies his own earlier position, but he stands against an influential way of understanding the connection between the human nature of Christ and the dispensation of grace and the Spirit.

Dominic Legge has pointed out that for Aquinas, Christ's human nature has not only a ministerial causality, in sending the Holy Spirit, but an instrumental and efficient one as well.[16] Aquinas gently pushes against the Augustinian tradition in asserting that Christ's actions 'cause grace in us both through merit and through a certain efficiency'.[17]

The merit view, we might be reminded, holds that Christ's human actions 'unlock' a capacity to send the Spirit, or to dispense grace. The difficulty with this view, as we have seen, is that grace appears extrinsic to Christ himself. It is something that is merely bestowed on him upon the successful completion of his task.

Aquinas, on the contrary, argues that the bestowal of grace results from the overflowing fullness of grace of Christ himself. He gives us the Spirit without measure because he has the Spirit without measure. As John 1.16 says: 'From his fullness we have all received, grace upon grace.' Legge summarizes Aquinas' contribution: 'The visible mission of the Son in the incarnation brings with it, by way of intrinsic relationship grounded in the eternal processions, the invisible mission of the Holy Spirit to Christ's humanity in the fullest possible measure, and consequently every grace, gift, and charism that a human nature can receive.'[18]

This is a significant step in the direction of my proposal. Aquinas grounds the sending of the Spirit, instrumentally, in the human nature of Christ, hypostatically united to the eternal Son. However, we have also pointed out, being united to one of the persons, it is *ipso facto* united (though differently) to all the others, including the Holy Spirit.[19] The relationship between the human actions and passions of Christ and the Holy Spirit is an 'intrinsic' relation, as Aquinas holds, grounded in the processions themselves.

To speak of Christ as 'meriting' the Holy Spirit is at least partially accurate. Nevertheless, the biblical narratives seem to suggest that there is something like an 'unlocking' (of something) taking place at the ascension. If with Aquinas we hold that we receive the Spirit from Christ's own superabundance, is this superabundance something he always had? If so, why does its pouring out seem to be conditioned by the return to the Father? If not, what brings about its completion? The merit view is not without its merit in that it appears to fit aspects of the biblical teaching.

So, for example, a certain development is affirmed of the human nature of Christ. The book of Hebrews makes a particularly strong case for this, precisely in connection to Christ's heavenly session, preceded by his human obedience.[20] The author writes in 5.7–9:

> During the days of Jesus' earthly life, He offered up prayers and petitions with loud cries and tears to the One who could save Him from death, and He was heard *because of His reverence*. Although he was a Son he *learned obedience* through what he suffered. And *being made perfect*, he became the source of eternal salvation to all who obey him . . .

Similar themes are encountered in Philippians 2.6–11, where the exaltation of Christ takes place as a reward for his obedience.

The historic adoptionist and Nestorian tradition is predicated precisely on this kind of text. But how are these Scriptures to be taken, if one wishes to avoid both Nestorianism, and Docetism and a view of Christ's human nature, which makes no contribution to the ultimate salvific work of God? Aquinas' ascription of the sending of the Spirit to Christ's human nature raises the issue of whether something transpired to this human nature such that it could only send the Spirit once ascended. The older Augustinian view, as we have seen, holds that Christ's human actions merit the sending of the Spirit as a divine action. But once we make this sending a human action, why must it happen upon the ascension? If some divine capacity is not unlocked, could it be that a human capacity is?

One proposal comes from Catholic theologian Edward Schillebeeckx, an influential voice of Vatican II. His contribution to the question of how to relate ascension and Pentecost forges in the right direction, though his Christology may give us some pause.

Edward Schillebeeckx: Pentecost as Conditioned by the Realization of Christ's Sonship

In a signal piece, 'Ascension and Pentecost', Schillebeeckx addresses the question at the heart of this chapter: why couldn't Christ send the Spirit prior to his going back to heaven?[21] Schillebeeckx argues that this is not because he is on earth while the Father is in heaven, but because of a certain 'inappropriateness' or 'estrangement' from God:[22] '[A]s man, God the Son enters into a humanity which made the history of the fall, of "un-salvation", and was branded with the sign of disobedience and removal from God – death.'[23] Consequently: 'The Spirit has first to overcome the sarx-condition, the situation of non-redemption of Jesus' humanity and renew and divinize this humanity through and through into its very bodiliness.'[24] Only then can the Spirit be bestowed, Schillebeeckx argues, referencing Acts 2.33 and Hebrews 5.9.

Accordingly, Schillebeeckx treats the incarnation as a process, a 'growing reality' not so much a once and for all reality.[25] Along with Rahner and other modern Christologists, Schillebeeckx is suspicious of substance Christologies, preferring to analyse the presence of God in Jesus Christ in terms of consciousness. As a result, what Christ does is not simply a consequent of his divine identity, but what seems to be an antecedent condition of it. Such Christologies, when confronted with adoptionist-sounding texts, will tend to take Christ's obedience as what determines and constitutes his ultimate divine identity, whether by adoption, or in other terms. This is a problem for Schillebeeckx as well, and we shall return to it in due course.

However, Schillebeeckx will draw excellently on the doctrine of divine missions to explain the necessity of ascension for Pentecost. 'In the bosom of the most Holy Trinity, the Son is pure self-giving to the Father. In God, this self-giving does not imply any giving up, any self-dispossession. Still, in the sphere of the incarnation, Christ's self-giving to the Father becomes a sacrifice, a giving up, an offering of his life.'[26]

Now Schillebeeckx makes his essential move, which I think gets to the heart of the explanation: 'The actual prerequisite for the sending of the Spirit of salvation is therefore Christ's obedience and attachment to the Father.'[27] The move from the structure of the processions to the structure of the missions is transparent here: just as the Holy Spirit proceeds immanently from the self-giving of the Son to the Father, as their mutual love, so temporally the Spirit proceeds from the attachment of the incarnate Son to the Father, which, in a condition of fallenness, must be exercised as self-sacrifice.

Since in the bosom of the Trinity, the Son is the principle of the life of the Holy Spirit, 'on the level of the incarnation and thus as man, He will only be able to send us the Holy Spirit when His Sonship is completely realized in human form and therefore utterly given over in love to the Father who answers this gift in the resurrection'.[28]

Schillebeeckx demonstrates what a perspective from the missions can yield. If a mission is the repetition in time of a procession, and if the procession of the Spirit is from the Son's self-giving to the Father, it follows that the procession of the Spirit in time will also be a function of the Son's (temporal) self-giving to the Father.

Before moving on, a number of critiques need to be made to this proposal. First, Schillebeeckx's Christology is at odds with the very tradition of the divine missions that is invoked here. If a mission is the extension of a procession to include a relation to a created effect, it has been stressed that the created term does not modify in any way the divine person. Bernard Lonergan has very helpfully clarified this in his work *The Triune God*: 'the necessary external term is not a constitutive cause, but only a condition, and indeed a condition that is not prior or simultaneous, but consequent.'[29]

The distinction between an antecedent (or constitutive as Lonergan calls it) and a consequent condition may be expressed with the following example. A necessary constitutive condition of my running a competitive race is wearing quality running shoes. My using these shoes adds a capacity to my repertoire of capacities. It is, in other words, an antecedent condition of my competing to win the race. However, the fact that, necessarily, the soles of these shoes will be worn out by running in them, is a consequent condition of my using them competitively. Both are necessary conditions of my running the race, yet one is antecedent/constitutive, while the other is consequent.

The nature of consequent conditions is such that their necessity is determined by the conditions of the activity that one is engaging in. They necessarily obtain upon the acting out of the action and need not be intended. Constitutive conditions, on the other hand, refer strictly to the powers of the agent. They need to be intended as conditions for the action.

Another analogy might help. The surgeon performing the operation intends to cut through the skin to get at the tumour. Cutting through the skin enables him to operate on the patient; it creates a capacity to heal. On the other hand, causing pain to the patient is an inevitable outcome, but not something which enables the doctor to heal. Consequent conditions are necessary by-products of actions enabled by constitutive conditions.

The fundamental difficulty with Christologies such as those of Rahner, Schillebeeckx, Pannenberg and others is that they confuse the two types of conditions. More specifically, they interpret the human actions of Christ as antecedent conditions of his divine identity. *A Chalcedonian Christology, on the other hand, views the human actions of Christ as consequent terms.* In an account from the missions, therefore, Christ's human obedience is consequent upon his being what he is, namely the eternal Son of God, not a condition of his sonship!

This is related to other difficulties. Schillebeeckx argues that the giving of the Spirit is predicated upon Christ's sacrifice. But this seems to require that the fullness of the Spirit be given to Christ upon his resurrection, not upon his ascension. Now, it may be that Schillebeeckx in fact follows a modern strand that intentionally conflates the two events. Such a conflation is problematic for a number of reasons we do not have space to discuss here. More significantly, however, it reveals another confusion: Schillebeeckx tends to confuse the full realization of Christ's sonship, with the full deification, or glorification of Christ's human nature.

In his account, once his Sonship is realized, the Spirit is bestowed. Chalcedonian Christology, on the other hand, holds that his Sonship is a once-and-for-all hypostatic union from conception. The human actions of Christ are only instrumentally the actions of the eternal Son of God, since the human nature does not have its own hypostasis. As such, they are consequent conditions of his divine actions. While the distinction between the two energies, divine and human, in Christ is an important one, it must not be confused with a separation. It is beyond the scope of this chapter to engage in a discussion of Christological and Trinitarian agency. The doctrine of the divine missions intends to preserve the absolute aseity of God in insisting on the consequent nature of the created terms, as Lonergan explains: '[the created effect] is not an antecedent or a simultaneous, but a consequent condition, because the divine persons are absolutely independent with respect to all created things.'[30]

Still, the consequent nature of Christ's human act is not to be confused with mere passivity. The eternal Son instrumentalizes a human nature, which nonetheless preserves its own identity (contra monophysitism and Eutychianism), yet nevertheless is precisely the human nature of the eternal Son.

Whether or not the Chalcedonian balancing act withstands the critiques hurled at it or not, it constrains what might be said Christologically. Schillebeeckx has been found wanting in this respect. However, his account of the relation between ascension and Pentecost is appropriate.

Before moving on, one question is begged by the foregoing: if Christ is the Son through hypostatic union and not through his acts of obedience, or his divine consciousness (Schleiermacher), or his openness to transcendence (Rahner), all of which are consequent upon his Sonship, and if in virtue of this Sonship Christ also had the Holy Spirit from the beginning, shouldn't he be able to send the Spirit prior to his ascension?[31] What, in other words, is the role of the interval between conception-ascension? This problem remains outstanding.

Schillebeeckx leads us to a dead end, with his apparent confusion between resurrection and ascension.[32] He makes the giving of the Spirit a function of his Sonship, which is a result of his obedience. But the obedience is completed upon his sacrifice, and vindicated in the resurrection. Yet the narratives portray Jesus as unable to send the Spirit even after the resurrection. 'Do not cling to me, for I have not yet ascended to the Father', Jesus tells Mary (John 20.17). Certainly, the issue is complicated by the fact that, a few verses later, Jesus is recounted as breathing on the disciples and giving them the Spirit. This would seem to corroborate the lumping together of Christ's resurrection, ascension and glorification.

Nevertheless, it can be safely concluded, with the great tradition, that the resurrection and the ascension represent two different events.[33] It is also beyond doubt that Jesus did condition sending the Spirit to his having ascended. How, then, are we to understand the so-called Johannine Pentecost? Briefly stated, a significant strand of the tradition regards Jesus giving the Spirit to the disciples within the framework of the Old Testament dispensations of the Spirit. Strictly speaking, then, John 20 does not indicate an indwelling, as much as an empowering Spirit. The task for this empowering work is also immediately specified in John 20.23: 'If you forgive the sins of any, they are forgiven them; if you withhold forgiveness from any, it is withheld.'

Back to the question, then: what difference does the ascension make specifically to the humanity of Jesus, if it makes no difference to his Sonship, contra Schillebeeckx?

Kathryn Tanner: Pentecost Conditioned by the Gradual Deification of Christ's Human Nature

Kathryn Tanner's *Christ the Key* also supplies an account based on the missions of the divine persons. She writes that the relations among the trinitarian persons come to take 'humanity along for the ride', yet without changing the identity of the Son.³⁴ This happens in Christ, as 'Jesus' human life exhibits the Word's relationships with the other members of the Trinity.'³⁵

Echoing the idea that the created effect is transformed in the process of being drawn to union with God, she writes about the Son and the Spirit: 'they both return and re-ascend with us'.³⁶ There is thus a progression taking place in the human nature of Jesus Christ. She expresses this variously. At one point she indicates that there is 'some historical progression in the successful display of the Spirit's power', which is 'not apparently displayed at once', and which would seem to be related to the fact that he was sent in the form of a servant.³⁷ This seems to be a merely epistemic progress, in the way that Christ reveals the Spirit's power progressively. On the other hand, she writes about the end of his life that 'only then . . . his humanity is *genuinely full of the Spirit* in the sense of being fully transparent to it'.³⁸

'At only that point', she continues, 'is he able to send the Spirit to us through his flesh.'³⁹ There is a gradual transformation of the humanity of Christ as a precondition of his dispensing the Spirit, and this requires the passage of time.

But how are we to understand this gradual transformation in terms of Christ's relationship with the Spirit? Tanner argues, correctly in my view, that Christ has the Spirit from the beginning, in virtue of his Sonship. However, she argues that the mission of the Spirit does not commence at Pentecost. Rather, the workings of the Son and the Spirit are 'intertwined' in the very mission of redemption, which they undertake together: 'They are sent out at once together on that mission.'⁴⁰

Tanner thus challenges the received Western account of the missions of the Son and the Spirit as being sequential. She surmises the simultaneity of the missions by rightly observing that the Spirit already has an activity in Jesus' life from his very conception. The Spirit, she argues, provides the power of Sonship to the Son. The Son 'sends the Spirit from the Father, but not as the Father does. *The Spirit has already been sent out from the Father as a condition of the Son's own incarnation and mission.*'⁴¹

It follows that it is not Christ's return to the Father that procures the sent Spirit: 'The Son can send the Spirit – specifically to us – only because he has already received the Spirit and felt the effects of its working within his own human life.'⁴² The reason, then, for the ascension prerequisite is because the effects of the Spirit's mission in Jesus' own life need time. Unlike Schillebeeckx, for whom the resurrection/ascension establish Jesus' sonship and thereby lead to the spiration of the Spirit in time, for Tanner the ascension is the climax of the progressive deification of Christ's humanity, resulting in an overflowing abundance of the Spirit.

For Tanner, the Spirit does not result from the Son's love of the Father, not economically and therefore not immanently either: 'Rather than the Spirit being the love that emerges from the relationship between Father and

Son (as it usually is for Augustine), the Spirit is the love that comes forth from the Father to beget the Son.'[43] The Spirit is the love through which the Word itself proceeds, Tanner argues. It does not itself result from the Word returning to the Father in love, although the Word does return the Spirit in love. 'The Son does breathe back out the Spirit or (to change the metaphor) send back the Spirit of love to the Father, as the West stresses. But, contrary to the Western view, this is not the way the Spirit arises to begin with. The Spirit already exists in the Son; the Son has already received the Spirit as both emerge from the Father.'[44]

What may we say about Tanner's proposal? I will restrict myself to a couple of critical considerations. There is much about her proposal that resonates with my own account. She works from a perspective of missions, which repeat temporally what is the case eternally. Christ's obedience does not establish his sonship, but merely confirms it. Additionally, she rightly insists that it takes time for the deification of Christ's humanity to take place and therefore for the plenitude of the Spirit himself to be realized. But, crucially, *Christ is already the beneficiary of a mission of the Spirit, which does not issue through Christ's humanity itself.* The Son and the Spirit come together, redeeming and transforming humanity in a double helix of descent and ascent.

What Tanner has done, however, is to decouple the mission of the Spirit from the success of the Son's mission altogether. True, the Spirit does come to us because of Jesus being completely overfilled with the Spirit in his humanity. Like Aquinas and Schillebeeckx, she rightly retains the instrumental role played by Christ's humanity. Yet in Jesus' own case, there already is a mission of the Spirit in his own life, a mission not mediated by his humanity, but one which precisely enables his own humanity. What are we to make of this?

Tanner is right to insist on the work of the Spirit in the life of Jesus himself. But is she entitled to surmise that this work of the Spirit is also a *mission* of the Spirit? Certainly there is an activity of the Spirit in the Old Covenant; there is also an activity of the Spirit in John the Baptist's own life, about whom Luke recounts that he was 'filled with the Spirit' from his mother Elizabeth's womb (Luke 1.15, 41). But there is also universal agreement that these are dispensations of the Spirit that are not to be confused with the Pentecostal pouring of the Spirit, which signifies a different sort of presence, by indwelling. Strictly speaking a theology of the divine missions, such as that of Aquinas, will restrict the mission of the Holy Spirit to his visible manifestation at Jesus' baptism and Pentecost, followed by his invisible mission that commences thereafter.

The work of the Spirit in Jesus' own conception and life prior to his baptism need not be identified as a mission. Dogmatically it must be said that the whole Trinity is operative efficiently in Jesus' life. The Son too, therefore, is operative in Jesus' own life, as an efficient cause, jointly with the Father and the Spirit. But activity does not necessarily indicate indwelling.

From the fact that the Spirit is active in Christ's life from conception it is not necessary to surmise that the Spirit is sent, or indwells Christ in a divine mission. What needs to be distinguished here is an effect that is brought about by the common work of the triune persons, including the Holy Spirit, and the special union whereby a divine person comes to exist in a new way in a created term. Tanner has in other words identified a necessary though not a sufficient condition for the Spirit's indwelling, or mission: the existence of an operation of the Spirit. But *an operation does not automatically denote a mission*, as is immediately obvious from the Old Testament expectation that the Spirit which was already active then will one day be more than active, residing in the hearts.[45]

Where does this leave us Christologically? I have in fact argued that the work of the Spirit in the life of Jesus does not denote an indwelling, or a mission of the Spirit from the beginning. Does that mean that Christ was not indwelt by the Spirit? That would indeed be absurd, making him in a certain sense our inferior.

The tradition that stems from Augustine and Aquinas understands the indwelling of the Holy Spirit operationally. To be indwelt by the Spirit is to be united to the third person through a 'created grace', in this case love. Appealing to Romans 5.5, the tradition identifies love as the operation through which the Holy Spirit indwells believers.

It is only insofar as a human being returns God's love to him that she may be said to be indwelt by the Holy Spirit. Note that indwelling cannot be a matter of sheer presence, given divine immensity and omnipresence. God the Spirit is already present everywhere. It is only insofar as creatures respond operationally (that is, through their created capacities and actions) that the Spirit may be said to indwell persons.[46]

This is true for Jesus as much as it is true for us. While there is a presence and activity of the Spirit in Jesus' life from conception, leading through his circumcision and growth and so on, it is precisely at the moment of his baptism that he may be said to be indwelt by the Spirit. Not accidentally, baptism is an act of obedience for Jesus himself, as he puts it: 'it is fitting for us to fulfil all righteousness' (Matt. 3.15). Immediately after his baptism, Jesus came out of the water, 'suddenly the heavens were opened, and he saw the Spirit of God descending like a dove and resting on Him' (Matt. 3.16). The Father's voice from heaven declares that he is 'well pleased' with his Son. Jesus himself ties the coming of the divine persons to obedience and love (John 14.23).

Note that I am not making any claim for anything like a Christology from below, or a Spirit Christology. While Christ is substantially the divine Son of God from conception, the human acts he accomplishes lead to his human nature being indwelt by the Spirit. In virtue of his divinity, however, he has the Spirit fully. Yet as far as his humanity is concerned, it receives the mission of the Spirit as it learns to obey, trust and love God himself.[47]

Let me try to draw back these Christological threads in terms of the original issue. What we observe in Jesus' human life is a gradual return to the Father in love. His obedience and love for God, consolidated at his baptism, results in the mission of the Holy Spirit, as indwelling his humanity (note that it would be absurd to speak of the Holy Spirit indwelling Christ's divine nature, since that divine nature precisely is the persons in relation to each other). Not all is accomplished upon his baptism, however. Christ must still learn obedience and be thereby perfected.

The ascension, then, symbolizes the loving and obedient return of Christ to the Father, with everything the Father gave him, to present to him his completed work. The reason Christ cannot send the Spirit until he ascends is because the Spirit proceeds from the love that the Son returns to the Father. The incarnate Son obediently takes up his position at the right hand of the Father, in full submission to him, as far as his human nature is concerned.

This explains why, although there is already a pre-ascension mission of the Spirit, commencing at his baptism, Christ is still not ready to pour out the Spirit for us until the ascension. The Spirit which Jesus receives at baptism is indeed proceeding from the common love between the Father and the Son. But that which commences at baptism is only ready to be poured out once it completes the process of glorification and transformation of Jesus' own human nature. Importantly, the Spirit which Christ receives at baptism for himself is still mediated by his humanity, as it responds to the Father in love. Christ's human nature has been drawn as an external term into the trinitarian processions and shares in their own fecundity.

Tanner is right to understand that the ascension represents the climax of a process that encompassed Christ's whole human life. But we have to insist that it doesn't simply amount to a 'physical' filling up with some reified 'grace'; rather, it consists in the operational attunement of Christ's will in submission to the Father's.[48] The ascension itself may be seen as an act of obedience and submission, but this time with Christ's humanity fully transparent to the Holy Spirit, as Tanner indeed also affirms. The ascension is not simply a reward for Christ's obedience, but itself an act of obedience, in fact the culmination of Christ's education in obedience.

Christ's session at the right hand of the Father represents not only the culmination of a process, but the continuation of his mediatorship, as he serves as a 'minister [λειτουργὸς] in the holy places' (Heb. 8.2). As Christ is finally fully with the Father, he sends us the Spirit from the Father's bosom, precisely as his Spirit (Rom. 8.9; Phil. 1.19; Acts 16.7; Gal. 4.6). As man, he remains submitted to the Father as his head (1 Cor. 11.3), not usurping his glory (Phil. 2.6–11), but freely receiving it from the Father. As man, he spirates the Spirit for us, out of his continuing loving obedience to the Father.[49]

'We Will Come to Him and Make Our Home with Him'

In closing I would like to draw some conclusions in more explicit relation to the theme of the present volume. The Christian faith holds that being saved is fundamentally about union with God by the indwelling of the divine persons. Every other dimension of salvation, whether forgiveness of sin, faith, repentance, moral transformation and sanctification, deification, are predicated upon the drawing of our human nature to God, in the person of Christ and our receiving the indwelling persons and their gifts. Nothing we do, no human action enables the power of the missionary God to save. In the divine missions, there is no need to create capacities in God. Rather, everything that happens in a mission is consequent upon the free saving action of God. Yet this saving action of God (which is nothing but God himself, as pure act) draws into its orbit created realities, without dismantling them, but precisely enabling them to be what they are.

If we are to understand the indwelling of the divine persons, which constitutes the very essence of salvation, we must start with the sending of the persons. The indwelling is the consequent of the sending, hence the logic of indwelling respects the logic and order of the sending.

I will close this reflection by summarizing our findings and teasing out some specifically soteriological implications. Granted, these are not much more than promissory notes, awaiting a further unpacking, my focus having been on laying the foundations in the doctrine of the divine missions.

1 The language of merit is at best partially helpful in explaining the role of Christ's human actions and passion in his sending the Holy Spirit to us.

    Historic Reformed soteriology rightly emphasizes forensic categories in understanding our relationship to Christ. Often this creates a tension with more organic language of union with Christ, or even deification, the latter in more recent discussions. I have also suggested that in terms of the missions of the divine persons, it is misleading to say that Christ merits the Spirit, or acquires some prerogative to send the Spirit. But the language of merit must not so much be eliminated, as framed in a proper context. In such a context, the human actions and passion of Christ do indeed play a role.

2 Pentecost is a consequent of the ascension, in a temporal repetition of the eternal spiration of the Holy Spirit.

    The ascension represents the completed return and giving over of the Son to the Father in love and obedience. The framework I have presented here, from the perspective of the divine missions, encourages an understanding of salvation in terms of the drawing of created realities into the 'magnetic field', or into the orbit of the trinity, with the result that it comes to exist in us: 'we will come and make our home with him' (John 14.23). The indwelling of the divine persons, then, is a matter of our being made to resemble the divine relations, by being drawn into them. We thus come to know God (logos) and love him (Spirit).

3 Christ's human obedience and love of the Father is not a constitutive (or antecedent) condition of his divine Sonship, contra Schillebeeckx, but a consequent condition of it.

The initiative in the work of salvation and its full accomplishment rests on God (*sola gratia*). There is no human work, including that of the Son, which is autonomous from God and which procures anything on the part of God. The human actions and passion of Christ is a consequent of his action as God. Being consequent upon the divine action, however, does not rob it of its own reality and authenticity.

4 There is a real transformation and perfecting of Christ's human nature, upon the completion of which Pentecost must wait.

Christ's heavenly priesthood is conditional upon his having been made perfect, upon his learning obedience through suffering. One must account for the role of Christ's transformation, yet not in such a way that this work somehow enables God to save. On the contrary, the process of transformation is itself a result of God's active presence to Jesus' own human nature, to humanity in other words. God need not enable himself to be present salvifically to humanity. The transformation of Jesus' human nature, consisting of his active and passive obedience, results from his being the incarnate Son of God who learns to live in the power of the Spirit as man.

5 The mission of the Spirit follows the mission of the Son; it is not simultaneous with it, contra Tanner.

An account from the missions that assumes *filioque* must retain the priority of the mission of the Son to that of the Spirit.[50] The Spirit we receive at Pentecost, the Spirit of our own filiation is precisely the Spirit of Christ. The distinction between an activity of the Spirit, present in the old dispensation as much as in the new, and a mission or an indwelling of the Spirit is of essential value. It allows us to affirm that there is indeed a work of the Spirit outside of the Church, outside of the realm of salvation, in common grace, for example. But it refuses to identify this work with an indwelling of the Spirit, thus with a salvific presence of the Spirit. The Spirit does not indwell those without Christ. Rather, the Spirit's indwelling unites people to Christ. At stake in the discussion over the order of the missions is nothing else but the uniqueness of Christ himself.

Notes

1 John Chrysostom, 'Homily 78' in *Commentary on Saint John the Apostle and Evangelist, Vol. 41: The Fathers of the Church*, trans. Sister Thomas Aquinas Goggin (Washington DC: Catholic University of America Press, 1959), pp. 338–52, 345.

2 John Chrysostom, 'Homily 51', in *Commentary on Saint John the Apostle and Evangelist, Vol. 41: The Fathers of the Church*, trans. Sister Thomas Aquinas Goggin (Washington DC: Catholic University of America Press, 1960), pp. 33–43.

3 Martin Luther, *Luther's Works: Lectures on Romans*, Vol. 25, ed. Hilton Oswald (St Louis, MO: Concordia, 1972), p. 306.

4 Herman Witsius, *Sacred Dissertations on Apostles Creed*, Vol. 2, trans. Donald Fraser (Glasgow: Khull, Blackie and Co., 1823), p. 227.

5 Witsius, *Sacred Dissertations*, p. 227.

6 George Smeaton, *The Doctrine of the Holy Spirit* (Edinburgh: T&T Clark, 1882), p. 134.

7 Smeaton, *The Doctrine of the Holy Spirit*, p. 135.

8 John Calvin, *John* (Wheaton, IL: Crossway, 1994), p. 372.

9 Cf. Karl Rahner's 'Some Implications of the Scholastic Concept of Uncreated Grace', in Karl Rahner, *Theological Investigations* Vol. 1, trans. Cornelius Ernst, O. P. (Baltimore, MD: Helicon Press, 1961); Henri de Lubac, *The Mystery of the Supernatural* (New York: Crossroad, 1998); Matthias Joseph Scheeben, *The Mysteries of Christianity* (New York: Crossroad, 2008).

10 Augustine, *The Trinity*, Book IV, Edmund Hill (ed.) (New York: New City, 2012), p. 182.

11 Aquinas, *Summa Theologica*, I, Q43, A1, Ad2, in Fathers of the English Dominican Province (trans.) (Westminster: Christian Classics, 1981).

12 Aquinas, *Summa Theologica*, I, Q43 A1.

13 Aquinas includes the indwelling of the divine persons under the category of exemplary causality, a type of causality situated between the intrinsic 'formal' cause and the extrinsic 'final' cause. The driving concern here is respecting the divine transcendence. To be distinctly indwelt by the divine persons is thus to receive a participation in their personal properties, to come to resemble them distinctly, as knowledge (the Son) and love (the Holy Spirit). For more on this, see Gilles Emery, *The Trinitarian Theology of St Thomas Aquinas* (Oxford: Oxford University Press, 2007), pp. 376–7. Aquinas clarifies some of these distinctions in Aquinas, *De Veritate*, q. 21, art. 4, <http://dhspriory.org/thomas/english/QDdeVer21.htm#4>

14 Aquinas, *Summa Theologica*, I, Q43, A2, Ad3.

15 Elsewhere I have argued that a similar caution must be exercised in atonement theology. The suffering of Jesus at the cross, or any other human activity of Christ, should not be construed as antecedent, but only as consequent conditions of God's ultimate salvific action. See Adonis Vidu, 'The Cross and Necessity: A Trinitarian Perspective', *Irish Theological Quarterly* 82, 4 (2017), pp. 322–41.

16 Dominic Legge, *The Trinitarian Christology of St Thomas Aquinas* (Oxford: Oxford University Press, 2017), pp. 216–17.

17 Aquinas, *Summa Theologica*, III, Q8, A1, Ad1.

18 Legge, *The Trinitarian Christology of St Thomas Aquinas*, p. 178.

19 It needs to be said that the union with the others is different from the union with the Son, in this case. Not all divine persons are incarnate, or come to exist in the human nature of Jesus Christ, which belongs to the Son alone.

20 Cf. also Hebrews 2.10.

21 Edward Schillebeeckx, 'Ascension and Pentecost', in *Worship* 35–6 (1969), pp. 336–63.

22 Schillebeeckx, 'Ascension and Pentecost', p. 350.

23 Schillebeeckx, 'Ascension and Pentecost', p. 350.

24 Schillebeeckx, 'Ascension and Pentecost', p. 350.

25 Schillebeeckx, 'Ascension and Pentecost', p. 348.

26 Schillebeeckx, 'Ascension and Pentecost', pp. 351–2.

27 Schillebeeckx, 'Ascension and Pentecost', p. 352.

28 Schillebeeckx, 'Ascension and Pentecost', p. 352.

29 Bernard Lonergan, *The Triune God* (Toronto: University of Toronto Press, 2009), p. 441.

30 Lonergan, *The Triune God*, p. 443.

31 See, for example, Karl Rahner, *Foundations of the Christian Faith* (New York: Crossroad, 1994), pp. 206–27; Friedrich Schleiermacher, *The Christian Faith* (Edinburgh: T&T Clark, 1989), sections 93–4.

32 He writes in *Jesus* that 'broadly speaking – provisionally allowing for other positions in the New Testament – we may say that resurrection, exaltation and empowerment denote one and the same undivided reality in the New Testament profession of faith, with resurrection as the *terminus a quo* and exaltation the *terminus ad quem* of one and the same event' (Schillebeeckx, *The Collected Works of Edward Schillebeeckx. Volume 6: Jesus: An Experiment in Christology* [New York: Bloomsbury, 2014], p. 494).

33 See discussion in Douglas Farrow, *Ascension and Ecclesia* (Grand Rapids, MI: Eerdmans, 2009).

34 Kathryn Tanner, *Christ the Key* (Cambridge: Cambridge University Press, 2010), p. 145.

35 Tanner, *Christ the Key*, p. 147.

36 Tanner, *Christ the Key*, p. 161.

37 Tanner, *Christ the Key*, p. 170.

38 Tanner, *Christ the Key*, p. 171. My italics.

39 Tanner, *Christ the Key*, p. 171.

40 Tanner, *Christ the Key*, p. 172.

41 Tanner, *Christ the Key*, p. 174. My italics.

42 Tanner, *Christ the Key*, p. 174.

43 Tanner, *Christ the Key*, p. 178.

44 Tanner, *Christ the Key*, p. 193.

45 On the contrary, operations are common and appropriated, missions are unique to the persons.

46 And thus the invisible mission of the Son is through knowledge and faith, and that of the Spirit through love.

47 Yves Congar articulates a similar position. It is worth quoting him at length: 'In the case of Jesus, it is important to avoid Adoptianism. He is ontologically the Son of God because of the hypostatic union from the moment of his conception. Because of that too he is the Temple of the Holy Spirit and is made holy by that Spirit in his humanity. We have, however, as believers, to respect the successive moments or stages in the history of salvation and to accord the New Testament texts their full realism. Because of this, I would suggest that there were two moments when the *virtus* or effectiveness of the Spirit in Jesus was actuated in a new way. The first was at his baptism, when he was constituted (and not simply proclaimed as)

Messiah and Servant by God. The second moment was at the time of his resurrection and exaltation, when he was made Lord' (Congar, *I believe in the Holy Spirit*, vol. 3 [New York: Crossroad, 1983], p. 171).

48 Dumitru Staniloae refers to this as the 'state of ultimate pneumatization' of Christ's humanity. It 'consists not only in the ability to dwell in and be felt by those who believe as the body borne by Christ's person, full of helping power to do good, but also in the supreme intimacy with the Father'. He goes on to say that, "The Godhead has completely overwhelmed His body, or better said, it is transparent and irradiates unhindered through his body without abolishing it.' (Staniloae, *The Experience of God*, vol. 3 [Brookline, MA: Holy Cross, 2011], p. 150).

49 Note that I am predicating obedience to the Father strictly of Christ's human actions. Texts such as 1 Cor 15.24 and 28 are to be understood to refer to a subjection that characterizes the ongoing incarnate nature of the eternal Son.

50 An Eastern Orthodox account would also stress the link between the sending of the Spirit and its procession. So Palamas stresses that the Son must ascend as man to the Father in order to send the Spirit from the Father's bosom, from which he proceeds ('Oration 24: On Pentecost', in J.-P. Migne, *Patrologia Graeca*, vol. 151 [1865]: p. 308c). Similarly, Dumitru Staniloae: 'only when Christ, by ascending as man to the Father is filled bodily with the Holy Spirit – and as such the Father himself as God – can the fullness of the Spirit shine forth from His perfectly pneumatized body' (Staniloae, *The Experience of God*, vol. 4 [Brookline, MA: Holy Cross, 2012], p. 4).

8

Saved by Degrees?
Augustine's Ontological Pluralism

KATE KIRKPATRICK

This chapter demonstrates that the early Augustine is an ontological pluralist whose understanding of soteriology presents human beings as existing between Being and nothingness at points which are not fixed. After defining ontological pluralism and its ancient intellectual competitor, monism, I introduce Augustine's early ontology of the human person by drawing on his biographical and theological depictions of it in works written between his conversion to Christianity and the *Confessions*.[1] Attention is given to the biographical as well as the metaphysical articulations of his account in order to highlight, as Augustine himself did, that Augustine's eudaimonist soteriology combined ontology and phenomenology.

The ontological soteriology Augustine defends in this period does not clearly distinguish between salvation and sanctification. Consequently, Augustine takes human beings to be saved by degrees. Whether this view is palatable to contemporary readers will, of course, vary depending on their metaphysical and theological commitments. It may be taken to entail that either everyone is saved, or no one is. Nevertheless, I argue that Augustine's early soteriology – which combines a phenomenology of continuous conversion with a metaphysics of being saved – is of both methodological and substantive interest to contemporary theologians.

Introduction

In the fifth century BC Parmenides claimed that being is one and indivisible: that it is without beginning, without end, and immune to change. For Parmenides, although water may become steam, this is not indicative of a change from being to non-being, but a change within being. Since Parmenides this view has raised many questions, first by Parmenides' pupil, Melissus, who argued that there was no such *thing* as a vacuum – that such a thing would have to be 'a piece of unbeing'.[2] How – so the *reductio ad absurdum* goes – can nothing be something?

Much more recently, the philosopher Kris McDaniel has defended *ontological pluralism*, 'the doctrine that some things exist in a different way than other things'.³ Most people agree that there are several kinds of being: books, orchids, bricks, clouds, windows. But are there different *ways* of being? Ontological monists (such as Parmenides and Melissus) deny this possibility. On their view, there are two possibilities where being is concerned: something either is or it is not. The benefit of ontological pluralism, as McDaniel presents it, is that in addition to asking the question of whether something exists or not, the pluralist can also ask *how*, distinguishing between different kinds or ways of being. A vacuum can be said to *be*, for the pluralist, because the way it is can be distinguished from the way a book is. This view has had some advocates throughout history, including Aristotle – on some counts. His famous line in the *Metaphysics* – that 'being is said in many ways'⁴ – has had both pluralist and monist interpreters.

In the twentieth century Heidegger claimed to return to the question of being, which he thought had been neglected for too long: 'The question posed by Plato in the *Sophist* . . . "What then do you mean when you use (the word) 'being'?" In short, what does "being" mean? – this question is so vigorously posed, so full of life. But ever since Aristotle it has grown mute, so mute in fact that we are no longer aware that it is muted.'⁵ But the question was far from mute in the fourth-century soteriology of Saint Augustine, for whom (as we shall see) *Being* played an essential role in *being saved*. And, as the current volume shows, it is not mute in the Christian tradition, since many theologians and mystics have described their experiences of sin and salvation in explicitly ontological terms.⁶

For Augustine the human person, since created *ex nihilo*, exists on a spectrum between Being and nothingness – and the position they occupy on that spectrum is not fixed.⁷ But what does this mean for the sinner and the saved? The sinner tends towards nothingness, Augustine writes, but in the monist Aristotelian sense of being it is counter-intuitive to consider that they *are* less when they sin: although their accidental properties may have changed, their primary substance is unaltered. In what sense, then, can we be saved by degrees?

Augustine's Theological Anthropology

Augustine's interest in ontology was not motivated solely by the pursuit of metaphysical truth; it was also driven by his desire for anagogical ascent and a life of virtuous flourishing. From the outset, therefore, it is worth noting that Augustine presents the question of being as a question to be asked at the level of metaphysics *and* at the level of experience. In the *Confessions*, he offers an ontological account but also a phenomenology – his lived experience – of the path to salvation. The narrative of the *Confessions* shows how keenly he wanted to find an account of reality that would satisfy both his intellectual curiosity and his spiritual yearning. Augustine 'makes himself an instance of the universal human story';[8] the *Confessions* dramatize his philosophical quest for happiness, offering a typology of the soul in search of the *beata vita* (the blessed life).

In his late teens, Augustine read Cicero's *Hortensius*. Cicero's eudaimonism – the claim that all human beings seek happiness – awoke Augustine's appetite for happiness but did not satisfy it. Augustine experienced a period of spiritual lifelessness,[9] and became a Manichean.

Before becoming a Christian, Augustine famously describes encountering in the 'books of the Platonists' something that made conversion possible: a divide between the physical and the spiritual (or the sensible and the intelligible).[10] His Christian anthropology would be heavily influenced by Platonic metaphysics, and in particular by a metaphysics that distinguishes between Being and beings. The former is immutable and the latter are subject to change; the former is eternal and the latter are passing. In *The Confessions* Augustine recounts his course to this discovery. Prior to conversion, he was divided against himself 'by his own impiety'.[11] Augustine saw his existence – as a being created by Being – as good. But as fallen it was characterized by lack of being and spiritual death.[12]

The loss of his friend, Nebridius, was particularly transformative in this respect – both for Augustine and for the development of Christian theology. Augustine and Nebridius had grown up together: going to school and playing as children; sharing interests as men. Augustine describes their friendship as 'sweet to [him] beyond all the sweetnesses of life that [he] had experienced'.[13] When Nebridius died, therefore, Augustine was overcome with grief. But he also famously 'became unto [him]self a vast problem'.[14] He was in misery – 'the state of every soul overcome by friendship with mortal things and lacerated when they are lost'[15] – and beset by restlessness. He tried to find solace in beautiful places, games, feasting, sex, books, poetry but he found them empty: 'I had become to myself a place of unhappiness in which I could not bear to be; but I could not escape from myself.'[16]

Augustine's narrative is, of course, constructed retrospectively and probably with several apologetic intents.[17] Surveying his grief from a distance, Augustine attributed the depth of his distress to mistaken love: mistaken not because his friend was undeserving but because loving temporal beings does not offer the same satisfaction as loving the eternal Being, God. Augustine affirms that transient beings rightly elicit our love; they are the grounds on which the soul praises God. But the soul must take care in order not to 'become stuck in them and glued to them with love through the physical senses'.[18] When earthly loves usurp the love which rightly belongs to God, our loss of them leaves us devastated.

As a student Augustine struggled with this loss and with unanswered questions: Could he reconcile Genesis with science? Could the beauty of rhetoric be reconciled with the ugliness of its untruths? He read Aristotle's *Categories* and tried to conceive of God within this framework; he found it overrated. After moving to Rome he continued to teach rhetoric and to seek a philosophy that delivered the flourishing it promised. He had not thought, prior to his time in Rome, that there were good arguments against the Manichees' rejection of Scripture. But in Rome he read the Academics and began to see weaknesses in the Manichean position. Augustine's move to Milan brought him into the parish of Ambrose, whose sermons on salvation sowed seeds of even more fruitful doubt.[19]

However, hearing about salvation is not to be conflated with being saved. At first Augustine listened to Ambrose as one rhetorician listened to another – he described himself as 'hanging on' to Ambrose's diction 'with rapt attention' but remaining 'bored and contemptuous of the subject matter'.[20] But despite his disdain, Ambrose's well-crafted words spoke to Augustine's spiritual and intellectual questions. Ambrose's figurative reading of the Old Testament rescued the Law and Prophets from Augustine's contempt. Augustine found himself suspended in scepticism: no longer a Manichee, but not yet a Christian.

He became a Catechumen – more out of curiosity, at this stage, than commitment. He wrestled with the concepts of divine immutability and ontological monism – struggling to conceive of a being that was not physical. He encountered explanations of evil which attributed it to human free will,[21] but he found these dissatisfying – which led to the famous question: *Unde malum?* Whence evil? If God and God's creation are good, how can evil exist?[22]

In AD 386 Augustine was given some 'books of the Platonists', namely Plotinus and Porphyry. In *The Confessions*, he describes their contents almost exclusively by citing the Prologue of John's Gospel; they opened his eyes to see the eternal Word in a different light. The 'books of the Platonists' enabled Augustine to entertain the possibility of the existence of a non-physical substance. Augustine's early works encourage his readers to consider the contrast between the intelligible and the sensible: since the deliverances of the senses fail to provide the fulfilment we seek in them, ultimately only the intelligible realm offers satisfaction. The senses can give transitory pleasures and satisfactions, but the intelligible realm provides us access to eternal Good, to a love that cannot be lost as human loves can, to the source of all flourishing.[23]

Reading the books of the Platonists, Augustine was 'admonished to return into [himself]'. His description of the event merits recounting at length:

> I entered and with my soul's eye, such as it was, saw above that same eye of my soul the immutable light higher than my mind – not the light

of every day, obvious to anyone, nor a larger version of the same kind which would, as it were, have given out a much brighter light and filled everything with its magnitude. It was not that light, but a different thing, utterly different from all our kinds of light . . . It was superior because it made me, and I was inferior because I was made by it . . . When I first came to know you, you raised me up to make me see that what I saw is Being, and that I who saw am not yet Being.[24]

In the course of 'seeing Being' Augustine describes hearing God cry from afar: 'Now, I am who I am' (Exod. 3.14). He wrote that he 'heard in the way one hears within the heart, and all doubt left me'.[25]

After this moment, Augustine began to consider the being of himself and other created things differently: 'neither can they be said absolutely to be or absolutely not to be'.[26] For Augustine, to be a creature is to exist between Being and nothingness.

Augustine's Ontology

What Augustine means by this is made clearer in a text written two years later. In AD 388 Augustine wrote *De Moribus Manichaeorum* – *On the Morals of the Manicheans*, a treatise in which he refuted the heresies of his previous beliefs for the benefit of those who still held them. In particular, he focused on their teaching concerning the origin and nature of evil, free will and matters less relevant to this discussion, such as their use of symbols and bodily practices.

The Manicheans taught a gnostic doctrine of Fallenness according to which dualities that were separate in their prelapsarian existence – spirit and matter, good and evil, light and darkness – are now intermingled in the embodied existence of souls. Those who lived according to Mani's teachings would escape material entanglement and be reunited with untainted Spirit in the afterlife; those who led lives of fleshly immorality would be condemned to rebirth in another bodily prison.

Augustine begins this work by saying that the only supreme Good is that which possesses supreme existence. Only God is Being in the full sense of the term, self-contained and immutable. Then he narrows in on one of the Manicheans' apologetic strategies: the origin of evil. Augustine asks them to put aside their usual line of questioning – *whence evil* – and to focus instead on *what* evil is. For how can we know whence a thing comes without first knowing what it is? Augustine takes the Manicheans to agree that evil is hurtful, where to hurt is understood to mean a decrease or deprivation of good. But if evil is a substance (as they believed), how could it be hurt? There is no good in it to be diminished.[27]

To account for the human experience of evil Augustine proposes an alternative dualism: between what is good in itself and what is good by participation. Only God has the former kind of goodness. But the goodness of participation is mutable: it can be lost. Augustine writes:

> This second kind of good is called a creature, which is liable to hurt through falling away. But of this falling away God is not the author, for He is the author of existence and being. Here we see the proper use of the word evil; for it is correctly applied not to essence, but to negation or loss.[28]

Augustine is emphatic about two things: first, that God is not the author of evil. 'For how can He who is the cause of the being of all things be at the same time the cause of their not being, – that is, of their falling off from essence and tending to non-existence?'[29] And second, that all created things are good, and remain good by participation no matter how far they fall: 'Nothing is allowed in the providence of God to go the length of non-existence.'[30]

Hamartiology and Soteriology

Ontology thus plays a crucial role in Augustine's hamartiology and soteriology; God's grace can only truly be understood in terms of the evil it is to cure. The origin of all evil, for Augustine, is nothingness.[31] On his view, sin is 'a movement that comes from nothingness'. It involves a turning of the soul 'away from true Being, the originator of the created Being'.[32]

For Augustine, God is Being, Goodness, and Truth[33] – and presides over all that comes after God in a hierarchy that is ordained by providence and ordered by rationality and love. God is the highest human good, the Being in which flourishing can be found through participation. In *De Moribus Manichaeorum*, Augustine is explicit that sin has a corroding effect on the human being's soul's *being*; it is a 'fall movement, which brings about in the soul a failing of essence'; a 'falling away from essence and tending not to be'.[34]

As Emilie Zum Brunn has demonstrated, the theme of the growth and reduction of the soul's essence or being – *magis esse* and *minus esse* – recurs in Augustine's early work.[35] The soul can turn in either of two directions, towards or away from God. If it turns toward God, it increases in being: the soul

> 'is more' (*magis esse, magis magisque esse*); it 'possesses being itself' (*obtinere ipsum esse*) in which it is 'constituted' (*constitui*), 'edified' (*exstrui*) 'stabilized' (*stare*), 'solidified' (*solidificari*), or even 'restored' (*refici*), re-formed (*reformari*).

When the soul turns away from God, it is made to

> 'be less' (*minus esse*), 'take a lesser part in Being itself' *idipsum esse minus habere*), 'fall, suffer a deficiency' (*defici*), 'lead toward nothingness' (*tendere ad nihilum*), 'become nihilated' (*inanescere*).[36]

In the early Augustine, therefore, to be saved is to be restored to one's own essence, to perfect the being for which the human person was created. To be restored to one's own essence, however, is simultaneously to be brought closer to Essence – to the eternal uncreated Being that Augustine identifies with Moses' God, 'I am that I am'. In Sermons 6 and 7 Augustine offers an anagogical interpretation of Exodus 3.14–15 as expressing both who God is in Godself ('I am that I am') – and God as he is for us, in the economy of salvation ('the God of Abraham, Isaac, and Jacob').[37]

The former of these – that God in himself is 'He who is' – is 'too much to understand, too much to grasp'.[38] But on Augustine's Christological interpretation, God reveals himself in a manner that is humanly comprehensible:

> How is it that there I am called this name that shows *I am*, and lo and behold here is another name: *I am the God of Abraham, the God of Isaac and the God of Jacob*? It means that while God is indeed unchangeable, he has done everything out of mercy, and so the Son of God himself was prepared to take on changeable flesh and thereby to come to man's rescue while remaining what he is as the Word of God. Thus he who is, clothed himself with mortal flesh, so that it could truly be said, *I am the God of Abraham, the God of Isaac and the God of Jacob*.[39]

We will return to the role of Christ in salvation shortly, but before doing so it is worth saying more about the problem to which Christ is the solution. Zum Brunn describes Augustine's ontology as offering a 'metaphysical meaning of spiritual death'.[40] It captures something about human experience when we seek but fail to flourish, a yearning which Zum Brunn has coined 'ontological hunger'.[41]

Ontological Hunger

Ontological hunger – or in Augustine's phrase, *wanting-to-be* (*esse uelle*) – is discussed at length in *De Libero Arbitrio* (3, 6, 18, 23), where Augustine discusses the paradigm case of someone who contemplates suicide.

It is commonly supposed that someone who contemplates suicide wants to cease being. But Augustine argues that what the suicidal person wants is not nothingness, but rest. Rest, Augustine writes, is more than nothingness, for there must be a being to be at rest. In life we may suffer at the variance of our affections and attachments. Rest, by contrast,

> is characterized by constancy which, better than any other thing, makes us understand what being is. It is why the entire wish of the one who wants to die goes, not to stop being in death, but to find rest there. And while his error makes him believe that he will no longer be, his nature makes him wish for rest, that is to say an increase in being. It is why, since it is impossible not to love being, the fact that we are must not be a reason for us to show our ingratitude toward the goodness of the creator.[42]

The problem is that our wanting-to-be can only be understood rightly through conversion, through turning towards God. Prior to conversion the threefold concupiscence – sensuality, the desire to dominate, and unredeemed curiosity – lead human beings to choose the 'nothingness' that leads the soul astray into demeaned corporeality.

Being Material and Immaterial

Augustine does not condemn the body altogether. He was accused of this by his contemporaries, and he has been accused of this since.[43] But in *On the Morals of the Manicheans* and elsewhere he takes pains to affirm the goodness of the body as God's creation. What he condemns is the subordination of 'spiritual being' to corporeal. In the *Letter to Secundinus* he wrote that:

> To fall is not to be nothing but to get closer to nothingness. For when what is more leans towards what is less, it is not the second but the first of these realities that falls and begins to be less than before. As a matter of fact, it does not become identical to that towards which it leans, but its own nature has less being. When the soul leans towards the body, thus it does not become body, but, under the effect of this desire that lessens it, it corporealizes in some way.[44]

Augustine's message to the Manicheans is that evil as a failing consists not in any substance but in a failing of one's own nature. Under the guise of the good, we pursue things in the world which lead us farther from God and ourselves.

All human beings desire being – though their *wanting-to-be* is expressed in diverse pursuits. On Augustine's view, the way to address the desire-to-be must be freely chosen in order for them to participate in God. Those 'who refuse the being that they could acquire if they wanted' cannot lose their spiritual nature.[45] The soul, even turned away from God, is of a different order of being from the body. In this respect Augustine is a substance dualist, admitting different types of substance for the body and the soul. On this subject he followed not only 'the Platonists' but also the teaching of Ambrose.[46]

It is in the domain of the immaterial soul that Augustine is an ontological pluralist. Each human soul has more choices than to be or not to be – its question is: *how?* Turning away from God does not entail that you will be nothing, on Augustine's view. But it does entail that 'you will be unhappy'.[47]

Being Free to Be or Not to Be

Rowan Williams has written that 'it may occasionally sound as though Augustine is confusing the "axiological" sense of "existence" – the degree of intensity or energy of being that might allow us to say that an artist, for example, lives more fully than another person – with the sense of existence as sheer thereness: a "lower" form of existence is not less *existent*.' He claims that Augustine does 'not have a concept of sheer thereness', since to be (for Augustine) is to occupy a specific place in the order of creation.[48]

But that 'specific place' is not fixed in all respects. On Augustine's view every existent has measure, form and order – but they may not have the measure, form and order the Creator intended. Thus the failure of beings to be what they were created to be entails the disorder of their relation to God and the world, and – in the case of human beings – their own unhappiness. Unlike later statements in the Augustinian corpus, particularly those arising in the conflict with Pelagianism, passages in *De Libero Arbitrio* imply that soteriology is only partly a matter of God's action: the human will must turn towards God to receive this gift. Again, Augustine presents his account of created existence in explicitly ontological terms, distinguishing between kinds (1 and 2) and degrees (a and b) of being:

1. Created beings that do not have the *will for happiness* (the *voluntas beatitudinus*), such as non-human animals.
2. Spiritual created beings (e.g. humans) who can be divided into two further stages (or levels) of being:
    a. Existence, the fact of being; at this stage spiritual beings experience the 'wanting-to-be' that urges them to pursue happiness or peace.
    b. Through the conversion of the will, human beings have access to the second stage: participation in being. When free will is exercised to choose God, human being is perfected.[49]

All beings owe their being to God. But the second kind of being admits of degrees – here being can increase, it can be *improved*[50] and even perfected.[51]

As Zum Brunn notes, in the form discussed in *De Libero Arbitrio*, Augustine's wanting-to-be 'gives place to the action of the free will, which, powerless to separate us from God on the level of existence, nevertheless has the power to accept or to refuse our vocation for being'.[52] We may freely turn from God. But to do so is to turn from our own completion and flourishing. For this reason, the *aversio* – the turning away from God – is immanent punishment: 'Man remains with his ontological hunger, for he no longer receives anything but the inconsistent sustenance of the values here below.'[53]

If you want to be happy, Augustine says, you must 'love in yourself the very fact that you want to be. For if you want to be still more, you will come closer to what is in a supreme way.'[54] Moreover, you must be grateful to God for being – since we are superior to those creatures who do not possess the desire for happiness.

Knowing Salvation Versus Being Saved

Having discussed Augustine's Christian interpretation of the 'books of the Platonists', we will now return to the narrative of the *Confessions* in order to see how this ontology shaped his theology of continuous conversion – and salvation by degrees. Drawing on and developing the views he articulated in *De Moribus Manichaeorum* and *De Libero Arbitrio*, in the *Confessions*, Augustine affirmed that all of God's creation – even those things which are liable to corruption – are good.[55] He argued that corruption does harm, and all things which are corrupted suffer a *privation* or diminishment of good. But they cannot be deprived of all goodness, since that would lead to their non-existence: 'as long as they exist, they are good'.[56]

What the *Confessions* tell us that the treatises do not is that even once Augustine had recognized this ontology – at the level of metaphysics – he did not *live* it, as anagogical ascent, until he had experienced the mediation of Christ. He struggled with his sexual desire. He described himself as catching glimpses of the view that the unchangeable was preferable to the changeable. But he couldn't 'keep his vision fixed' on it, lapsing again into his mundane habits. He described himself as bound by the irons of his own choice – the repetition of his sins made them so habitual as to seem necessary. Here and in later works, Augustine assigns *habit* a significant role in our *aversio* or *conversio* to God.

In *Confessions* VIII, Augustine says that Christ is the only means by which human beings can be released from the chains of fallen habituation. 'I sought a way to obtain strength to enjoy you; but I did not find it until I embraced "the mediator between God and man, the man Christ Jesus"' (1 Tim. 2.5).[57] His famous and much discussed 'conversion' took place in a

Milanese garden, surrounded by fig trees. He heard the words 'take, read; take, read', and understood them to be an injunction to pick up the Bible. He read Romans 13.13–14: 'Not in riots and drunken parties, not in eroticism and indecencies, not in strife and rivalry, but put on the Lord Jesus Christ and make no provision for the flesh in its lusts.'[58]

But to describe his 'conversion' as a decisive moment in the Protestant sense is misleading in this context. Just as it is anachronistic to take Augustine to distinguish between an event of justification and a process of sanctification, it is anachronistic to read Augustine's 'conversion' in Book VIII as a single and irreversible event.

In Classical Latin, the words *conversio* and *convertere* designate the act of 'returning or becoming'. The words can be used in both spiritual and material senses. The Greek words from which these Latin terms were derived convey movement – not a transition from one static state to another.[59] That Augustine's 'conversion' should not be understood in the post-Reformation sense is illustrated by a passage in *Ad Simplicianum*, a text written very near the *Confessiones*, where Augustine uses the language of conversion to describe not the turn to God but the turn to sin.[60]

After reading the injunction to 'put on' Christ, Augustine recognized a gap between his intellectual assent to the metaphysics of salvation and his anagogical ascent to participating in God's Being. Augustine attributed the gap between knowing and living salvation to a faulty Christology: before he had believed that Christ was merely an excellent man of unparalleled wisdom.

At the conclusion of Book X of the *Confessions*, by contrast, Augustine affirms that Christ is:

> The true Mediator you showed to humanity in your secret mercy. You sent him so that from his example they should learn humility. He is 'the mediator between God and men, the man Christ Jesus' (1 Tim. 2.5). He appeared among mortal sinners as the immortal righteous one, mortal like humanity, righteous like God. Because the wages of righteousness are life and peace (Rom. 6.23), being unified with God by his righteousness he made void the death of justified sinners, a death which it was his will to share in common with them. He was made known to the ancient saints so that they could be saved through faith by his future passion, just as we are saved through faith in his passion now that it is past. It is as man that he is mediator. He is not midway as Word; for the Word is equal to God and 'God with God' (John 1.1), and at the same time there is but one God.[61]

Augustine never wrote a treatise on the atonement. As David Vincent Meconi writes, his views on this subject are 'a theological kaleidoscope with many moving parts found in several different places'.[62] Augustine's description of atonement – here and elsewhere – contains the language and themes of the

'Latin' doctrine, including *justitia*, propitiatory and substitutionary sacrifice, and satisfaction. But it is also possible to see the 'classic' and 'subjective' doctrines here too. For Augustine, the work of Christ is a cosmic triumph over the powers of darkness; but his life – and particularly his *humility* – also sets us a salvific example. Whereas later theorists of the atonement split these theories into opposing models (often taking proof texts from Augustine's writings), for Augustine they are complementary elements of the same dynamic. Conversion, for Augustine, is continuous – salvation is an ongoing process of becoming.

For Augustine, Christ's sacrifice satisfies both divine justice and the human *wanting-to-be* – it combines soteriology and eudaimonistic ontology. As Meconi writes, in the life of the believer Christ's mediation takes place in three moments: identification, incorporation and transformation. The latter two are discussed much more in Augustine's later works, especially his sermons,[63] but in the *Confessions* Augustine explores the first step – identification – because it is precisely what he found lacking in the books of the Platonists.

Their books could not teach him the love and humility of Christ. In order for human persons to conceive of ourselves truly we must identify that we have become less than fully ourselves, falling short of the end for which we were created. We must see ourselves 'with the soul's eye'.[64] This involves admitting our shortcomings – that is, it involves *humility*. In the writings of the Platonists, Augustine wrote, 'no one sings: "Surely my soul will be submissive to God? From him is my salvation; he is also my God and my saviour who upholds me; I shall not be moved any more"' (Ps. 61.2–3).

The end for which we were created, as Augustine writes in Book X, is 'the happy life', but this life does not consist in material pleasures or conditions. Rather, it is – in humility and *caritas* – a life habituated to finding joy in God.[65] The blessed life involves participation in Being and the *regula amoris*: its promise is that human persons can participate in the love of God, loving created beings through God.

Human choices therefore have ontological consequences, for their *aversio* or *conversio* to God will lead to either privation of or participation in Being. But in this life neither full privation nor full participation is possible: as long as the saved human has and exercises a capacity to sin we can only be saved by degrees. Augustinian salvation is thus lived in continuous conversion. There is no 'timeless and stable goodness in this world',[66] and as temporal creatures we must continuously choose whether to cultivate virtue or sin through our habits. As in the case of participation in Being: 'It is in the person of Christ, manifested in his teachings and example, that the meaning and proper order of virtue clearly emerge.' Habit (*habitus*) explains both the unity of the two natures of Christ and the acquisition of virtue in other human souls. Just as the Eternal Word is not modified by the assumption of Christ's human nature, a virtue such as Wisdom is not changed by the change it effects in the person who possesses it: 'God is love and created in love; the Christian soul returns to God in love by means of virtue, for virtue is the "ordering of love".'[67]

His view is concisely encapsulated in Epistle 18.2:

> There is a nature mutable in space and time, namely body. And there is a nature which is not at all mutable in space, but only in time is it also mutable, namely soul. And there is a nature which cannot be changed in space or in time, and this is God. What I have suggested here is mutable in any way, is called creature; what is immutable is the Creator.
>
> Now, since everything that we say exists, we would say exists insofar as it remains and insofar as it is one thing, and moreover unity is the form of all beauty, you can see in this arrangement of natures what is highest, what is lowest (and yet still exists) and what is in the middle, greater than the lowest and less than the highest.
>
> The highest is Happiness itself; the lowest is that which can be neither happy nor miserable; but the middle nature lives in misery when inclined toward the lowest, in happiness when turned toward the highest. Whoever believes Christ does not love the lowest, is not proud in the middle, and thus is made capable of clinging to the highest – and that is all we are commanded, admonished, incited to do.[68]

Augustine's Ontological Pluralism: Metaphor or Metaphysics?

In the *Soliloquies* Augustine claimed that 'Wisdom is not reached by one road alone', introducing the theme of the 'two ways'.[69] The way of the intellect seeks to understand with all of the powers of the mind; the way of the Church, for those less inclined to the first way, was to accept things on authority. As Joanne McWilliam writes: 'If Augustine had by this time read Tertullian, he would have disagreed with him on one point at least: he saw no reason to renounce Athens because Jerusalem was in sight. His intention was to show the possibility of dual citizenship.'[70]

Dual citizenship today involves a context where 'most contemporary metaphysicians believe that the idea that different kinds of beings can enjoy different ways of being is metaphysically bankrupt, and probably even meaningless.'[71] For those inclined to Parmenides' way of thinking, one economical way of dealing with Augustine's claim that created beings can neither 'be said absolutely to be or absolutely not to be' is to dismiss it as nonsense.

But there are methodological and substantive reasons to recommend further exploration of Augustine's early soteriology. Methodologically, it is an admirable example of theology that is embedded in experience – in this case, experience of salvation as a continuous conversion to God. Substantively,

I propose two avenues for future discussion of continuous conversion and salvation by degrees: one metaphorical and the other metaphysical.

Some theological definitions of metaphor describe it as a way 'of looking at a reality which cannot be reduced to terms of the metaphor itself'.[72] On such a definition, Augustine's account of being between 'being and not being' could be taken as an attempt to describe his irreducible experience – good as phenomenology but not as metaphysics because the latter (where soteriology is concerned) is beyond our ability to articulate.

In classical writings on rhetoric such as Cicero's *De Oratore*, metaphor was thought to differ from literal speech in its capacity to be beautiful or puzzling – for its greater evocative potential.[73] For Aristotle before him, metaphor engages us in analogical problem solving. When we think about 'evening' as a metaphor for old age, to borrow Aristotle's example, we liken the way that the sun rises and sets each day to the cycle of beginnings and endings that punctuate human lives.[74] The effort that we go to in understanding the metaphorical meaning (evening) for the target term (old age) is pleasurable and complex. Consequently, the meaning of the metaphor is not the only thing that is valuable about it, for the process of retrieval is also enriching.

More recent theories of metaphor offer a much wider range of interpretive possibilities: a metaphorical reader of Augustine could follow the hermeneutic fictionalist path, taking such language as an invitation to participate in a useful fiction[75] rather than outlining the possibility for a literal ontological transformation. On this approach Augustine's 'wanting-to-be' could be interpreted as a metaphor for what he describes elsewhere as *yearning* – the affective lack and unmet desire that characterizes human selfhood (whether or not one is committed to a historical or mythological fall). Augustine took it to be the case that human beings could feel less-than-themselves or not themselves, and that they suffered on account of this. The fictionalist could argue that the merit of Augustine's account is independent of the success of his metaphysics (or indeed of Augustine's intended wedding of ontology and soteriology), since his metaphor is rich with possibilities conducive to the pursuit of human flourishing.

The metaphysical avenue might build on recent arguments in favour of seeing ontological pluralism as 'a serious metaphysical option'.[76] Kris McDaniel's work discusses physical '*almost nothings*'. He points out that humans believe in holes, cracks and shadows, and we treat them in many of the same ways we treat beings: we quantify them, count them, ascribe features to them, including relational features such as size and location. We talk about them as persistent, or capable of effecting causes.[77]

On McDaniel's view, the ontological pluralist has an easier time explaining 'almost nothings' because she does not have to ascribe existence to almost nothings in the same way that she ascribes existence to presences.[78] Clearly, holes, cracks and shadows are in many respects dissimilar from Augustine's 'spiritual created beings' (kind 2, designated above). However,

Augustine shares with contemporary ontological pluralists an interest not only in *whether* things exist, but *how*. Augustine's metaphysics involves ascribing casually efficacious existence to both absences and presences. Most significantly, Augustine describes not only the presence of God – but the absence of God, the *privatio boni* – as causally efficacious in human life.

This chapter opened by saying that in a monist Aristotelian sense of being it is counter-intuitive to consider that someone *is* less when they sin. Augustine's substance dualism allows for the persistence of being in the physical sense, and for losses and gains of being in the spiritual. A reconstruction of Augustine's early soteriology in light of contemporary metaphysics is beyond the scope of this chapter. But the pluralist point of Augustine's (at this stage, far from systematic) soteriology is that each human soul *is* more or less depending on its relation or misrelation to God.

Michael Hanby has recently described Augustine's thought as 'decidedly anti-metaphysical'.[79] But it is clear from the foregoing that Augustine's early theology is decidedly metaphysical: it is an attempt to account for both the ontology and the phenomenology of salvation because one of the 'two ways' involves investigating both. Zum Brunn called this 'Augustine's central metaphysical intuition concerning spiritual life', namely 'that of *magis esse* and *minus esse*, in which anagogy and ontology coincide'.[80]

However, the success of the metaphysical articulation of Augustine's view should not distract us from the practical and ethical demands he took it to entail. As Mary Clark notes, Augustine's continuous conversion encompasses 'a Christian vision of life to which one commits oneself by actions'.[81] Augustine's ontological eudaimonism does not concern only the inner life of the believer, but her actions in the world. Contemporary readers of Augustine may therefore find in his thought a resource for combining the Pauline antithesis of sin and faith (as ways of being) with the language of habituation and virtue – as the means by which we participate in one or the other, by degrees. In later works – especially *De Civitate Dei* – he would develop an account of virtue as 'loving God', the ordering of love.[82]

With the arguable exception of *De Trinitate*, Augustine's works are not systematic. Augustine's discussions of salvation – and grace – are much more attentive to its relation to faith and love than to that particularly Protestant preoccupation, justification. His 'kaleidoscopic' presentation of the atonement may be dissatisfying to those who want a coherent metaphysics of salvation. But nevertheless he offers a fascinating description of an inquisitive soul in search of it. Whether our commitments lead us to consider his claims more fruitful as metaphor or as metaphysics, Augustine's eudaimonistic ontological pluralism may continue to stimulate our own thinking about the metaphysical and phenomenological differences between knowing about salvation and being saved.[83]

Notes

1 This chapter focuses on the early, fourth-century Augustine – the anti-Manichaean Augustine of *De Moribus Manichaeorum*, *De Libero Arbitrio* and *Confessiones* – rather than the fifth-century Augustine of anti-Pelagian polemic.

2 See Anthony Kenny, *Ancient Philosophy* (Oxford: Clarendon Press, 2004), p. 19.

3 Kris McDaniel, 'Being and Almost Nothingness', *Noûs* 44, 4 (2010), pp. 628–49, at p. 628; see also Kris McDaniel, 'Ways of Being', in David John Chalmers, David Manley and Ryan Wasserman (eds), *Metametaphysics: New Essays on the Foundations of Ontology* (Oxford: Oxford University Press, 2009).

4 Aristotle, *Metaphysics*, trans. Hugh Tredennick, Loeb Classical Library (Cambridge, MA: Harvard University Press, 1979), 1003a33.

5 Martin Heidegger, *The History of the Concept of Time, Prolegomena*, trans. Theodore Kisel (Bloomington, IN: Indiana University Press, 1992), p. 29.

6 Given Heidegger's exposure to Augustine, this claim is very strange: see J. K. A. Smith, 'Confessions of an Existentialist: Reading Augustine after Heidegger, Part I', *New Blackfriars* 82 (2001), pp. 273–82; and Part II, *New Blackfriars* 82 (2001), pp. 335–47.

7 I will outline Augustine's distinctions between Being, being and beings after introducing the biographical context in which he developed them.

8 Frances Young, 'The Confessions of Saint Augustine: What is the Genre of This Work?', *Aug Stud* 30, 1 (1979), pp. 8–16.

9 See Augustine, *Confessions*, trans. Henry Chadwick (Oxford: Oxford University Press, 2008), III.iii.5; he discusses *Hortensius* again in book VIII.vii.16.

10 See Augustine, *Confessions* VII.x.16.

11 Augustine, *Confessions* V.ix.18.

12 Augustine, *Confessions* V.viii.16.

13 Augustine, *Confessions* IV.iv.8.

14 Augustine, *Confessions* IV.iv.9; this phrase is repeated in X.xxxiii.50.

15 Augustine, *Confessions* IV.vi.11.

16 Augustine, *Confessions* IV.vii.12.

17 On the questions of genre, audience and historicity, see Allen D. Fitzgerald, OSA, '*Confessiones*', in *Augustine Through the Ages: An Encyclopedia* (Grand Rapids, MI: Eerdmans, 2009), esp. pp. 228ff.

18 Augustine, *Confessions* IV.x.15.

19 See Augustine, *Confessions* V.xi.21–xiii.23.

20 Augustine, *Confessions* V.xiii.23.

21 In Ambrose's sermons, Plato or Plotinus – see Augustine, *Confessions* VII.iii.5 and Chadwick's n. 4 on *Confessions*, p. 113.

22 Augustine, *Confessions* VII.v.7.

23 Augustine, *Confessions* XI.xxxix.39; see also IV.xii.18.

24 Augustine, *Confessions* VII.x.16.

25 Augustine, *Confessions* VII.x.16.

26 Augustine, *Confessions* VII.xi.17.

27 See Augustine, *De Moribus Manichaeorum*, trans. Richard Stothert, in *Saint Augustine: The Writings against the Manicheans and Against the Donatists*, ed. Philip Schaff (New York: Charles Scribner's Sons, 1901), chs 2 and 3.

28 Augustine, *De Mor. Man.* IV.vi.

29 Augustine, *De Mor. Man.* II.ii.

30 Augustine, *De Mor. Man.* VII.ix.

31 Augustine's claim that 'nothingness' can exercise causality is contested, as is absence causation in contemporary philosophy. We frequently say that the absence of something (or the lack of something's occurring) causes other things: e.g. failing to eat causes hunger; failing to vaccinate causes illness. But whether absences exist and are causally efficacious is disputed. See Brannon McDaniel, 'Presentism and Absence Causation: An Exercise in Mimicry', *Australasian Journal of Philosophy* 88, 2 (2010), pp. 323–32.

32 Augustine, *De Libero Arbitrio*, trans. Robert P. Russell, in *The Teacher; The Free Choice of the Will; Grace and Free Will*, The Fathers of the Church 59 (Washington, DC: Catholic University of America Press, 2004), II.xx.54.

33 See e.g. *Confessions* VII.x.16 on Being; *De Trinitate* VIII.5 on Goodness; and *Confessions* X.xxiii.33 on Truth.

34 Augustine, *De Mus.* VI.xi.33 ; *De Mor. Man.* 2.ii.

35 The texts discussed here were written in the period leading up to (and including) the *Confessions* (AD 397); the discussion of the texts from the late 380s is indebted to Emilie Zum Brunn's landmark study, *Saint Augustine: Being and Nothingness* (New York: Paragon House, 1988).

36 Zum Brunn, *Saint Augustine*, p. 1.

37 Sermon 7.7. *Sermons on the Old Testament*, ed. John E. Rotelle, OSA, trans. Edmund Hill, OP, The Works of Saint Augustine III/1, ed. Boniface Ramsey, 2nd release, electronic edn (Charlottesville, VA: InteLex Corporation, 2001; originally published by New City Press in 50 vols, 1990–).

38 Augustine, *Sermons*, Sermon 6.5.

39 Augustine, *Sermons*, Sermon 7.7.

40 Zum Brunn, *Saint Augustine*, p. 57.

41 See Zum Brunn, *Saint Augustine*, p. 38.

42 Augustine, *De Lib. Arb.* III.viii.23.

43 Julian of Eclanum accused Augustine of crypto-Manicheanism in the context of the Pelagian controversy; for a twentieth-century view in agreement see M. Wundt, 'Augustins Konfessionen', *Zeitschrift für die neutestamentliche Wissenschaft* 22 (1923), pp. 161–206.

44 *Contra Secundium* 11, cited in Zum Brunn, *Saint Augustine*, p. 51.

45 Augustine, *De Lib. Arb.* III.xv.44.

46 See Robin Lane Fox, *Augustine: Confessions and Conversion* (London: Allen Lane, 2015), p. 214.

47 Augustine, *De. Lib. Arb.* III.xvi.45: '*non quidem nihil, sed miser tamen eris*'.

48 Rowan Williams, 'Insubstantial Evil', in *On Augustine* (London: Bloomsbury, 2016), p. 80.

49 See Zum Brunn, *Saint Augustine*, pp. 39–40.

50 See Augustine, *De Lib. Arb.* III.xvi.45.

51 This view still appears in the autobiographical part of the *Confessions* (Book III), although Augustine later (in Book XIII) considers it differently, using a Trinitarian analogy.

52 Zum Brunn, *Saint Augustine*, p. 38.

53 Zum Brunn, *Saint Augustine*, p. 51.

54 Augustine, *De Lib. Arb.* III.vii.21.

55 Augustine cites Gen. 1.31, in which the goodness of creation is affirmed (*Confessions*, VII.xii.18).

56 Augustine, *Confessions* VII.xii.18.

57 Augustine, *Confessions* VII.xiii.24.

58 See Augustine, *Confessions* VIII.xii.29.

59 See José Ortez Reta, 'Conversion', in *Augustine Through the Ages* (Grand Rapids, MI: Eerdmans, 2009), p. 239.

60 'Sin in a human being is disorder or perversity, that is, an aversion to the more preferable creator, and a conversion to the inferior creatures.' Augustine, *Ad Simplicianum*, trans. J. H. S. Burleigh, in *Augustine: Earlier Writings* (Philadelphia, PA: Westminster, 1953), I.ii.18. Although some think Augustine's position in *Ad Simplicianum* anticipates his later anti-Pelagian presentations of prevenient grace, I share Burns' view that in AD 396 Augustine's theology did not contain the resources to develop that doctrine, and that in fact *Ad Simplicianum* is even open to Pelagian or semi-Pelagian interpretations. See J. Patout Burns, *The Development of Augustine's Doctrine of Operative Grace* (Paris: Études Augustiniennes, 1980). On Augustine's later descriptions of *Ad Simplicianum* on grace, see James Wetzel, 'Pelagius Anticipated: Grace and Election in Augustine's *Ad Simplicianum*', in *Augustine: From Rhetor to Theologian*, ed. Joanne McWilliam, with Timothy Barnes, Michael Fahey and Peter Slater (Ontario: Wilfrid Laurier University Press, 1992).

61 Augustine, *Confessions*, X.xliii.68.

62 David Vincent Meconi, 'Augustine', in *T&T Clark Companion to Atonement*, ed. Adam J. Johnson (London: Bloomsbury, 2017), p. 381.

63 See Meconi, 'Augustine': by 'incorporation', Augustine means incorporation in the mystical body of Christ, who becomes our truest identity, which we receive through the Eucharist and enact through *caritas*. And by 'transformation' Augustine takes God to have promised deification.

64 Augustine, *Confessions*, VII.x.16.

65 Augustine, *Confessions*, X.xxii.32.

66 See Williams, 'Insubstantial Evil', p. 98.

67 See George J. Lavere, 'Virtue', in *Augustine through the Ages* (Grand Rapids, MI: Eerdmans, 2009), p. 874.

68 Augustine, Epistle 18.2, cited in Philip Cary, *Augustine's Invention of the Inner Self: The Legacy of a Christian Platonist* (Oxford: Oxford University Press, 2000), p. 258.

69 Augustine, *Soliloquies*, trans. T. F. Gilligan, in *Fathers of the Early Church 5* (Washington, DC: Catholic University of America Press, 1948), I.xiii.23.

70 Joanne McWilliam, '*Soliloquia*', in Allen D. Fitzgerald (ed.), *Augustine through the Ages* (Grand Rapids, MI: Eerdmans, 2009), p. 807.

71 McDaniel, 'Ways of Being', p. 291.

72 N. T. Wright, *The New Testament and the People of God* (Minneapolis, MN: Fortress Press, 1992), p. 130.

73 Cicero, *De Oratore*, in *On the Ideal Orator*, trans. James M. May and Jakob Wisse (London and New York: Oxford University Press, 2001), pp. 159–60, 271.

74 Aristotle, *Poetics*, in *Poetics I, With the Tractatus Coislinianus, a Hypothetical Reconstruction of Poetics II, and the Fragments of the On the Poets*, trans. Richard Janko (Indianapolis, IN: Hackett, 1987), 10:1457b.

75 Kendall L. Walton, 'Metaphor and Prop Oriented Make-Believe', *European Journal of Philosophy* 1, 1 (1993), pp. 39–57, at p. 46.

76 Jason Turner, 'Ontological Pluralism', p. 27.

77 See McDaniel, 'Being and Almost Nothingness', p. 628.

78 McDaniel, 'Being and Almost Nothingness', p. 629.

79 Michael Hanby, 'Desire: Augustine Beyond Western Subjectivity', in *Radical Orthodoxy: A New Theology* (London: Routledge, 1999), p. 111.

80 Zum Brunn, *Saint Augustine*, p. 42.

81 Mary Clark, 'Spirituality', in Allen D. Fitzgerald (ed.), *Augustine through the Ages* (Grand Rapids, MI: Eerdmans, 2009), p. 814.

82 Augustine, *City of God*, trans. Henry Bettenson (London: Penguin, 2003), XV.22.

83 I am grateful to the editors, to James Crocker and to Matthew D. Kirkpatrick for their comments on this chapter.

9

Spirit, Selfhood and Salvation

MYK HABETS

Despite the mistaken but perennial idea found among many Christians, theology is not static – it changes, develops, repents and progresses. As a case in point, 50 years ago the formal study of the Holy Spirit – pneumatology – was reserved for a very few scholars working in what seemed to be remote corners of the theological cosmos. Today that has completely changed. Following the trinitarian renaissance of the late twentieth century, pneumatology arguably now occupies central stage if gauged by the flood of books, theses and essays that now appear on the topic. This is a welcome trend, in my opinion, and quite frankly it is about time. In 2001, Lyle Dabney prophetically and boldly called for the Church to grow up and 'act its age' and argued that: 'Christian theology should begin its task, that is to say, with an account of the Spirit; and thus that should now be *first* which has traditionally been *last*.'[1] Nearly two decades later, Ben Pugh in his survey of theology in the contemporary world concludes that there is now 'a massive and long-overdue shift in theology *as a whole* towards an interest in pneumatology'.[2] Pugh is referring to what is now termed a Third Article Theology (TAT).

TAT is not simply a study of pneumatology but is, rather, a conscious and considered approach to conceiving of theology and witnessing to God's self-revelation in Word and works, from the perspective of the Spirit where questions of pneumatology set the agenda and control the trajectory of the dogmatic enterprise, rather than pneumatology being the sole focus. As such, TAT is a specific and technical name for a method of theology. It seeks to articulate the contours of a Christian theology in a Trinitarian fashion, but one that starts with the Spirit.[3] TAT invites a different way of doing theology; one based more upon the actual experience of disciples of Christ. As Pugh observed: 'This new paradigm promises to bring us right back to the way the first Christians themselves theologized: they began with their experience of the Spirit.'[4] He concludes: 'This shift of perspective also offers a way of doing "theology from below" . . . This style of theology prompts the question of us all: are we missing the point of theology?'[5] In the same vein, Cornelis van der Kooi, an advocate of TAT, notes that theology, especially soteriology, should not limit itself to the abstract or theoretical: 'It is also a question of practical life whether we in our time see the benevolent work of that Spirit.'[6]

In what follows I outline a framework for thinking about selfhood and salvation by detailing a reading of Scripture that moves from *protos* to *telos* before defining what an anthropological duality looks like. After that it is possible to speak of salvation as a transformative theopoetic journey into God's triune life. In each section, the work of the Spirit forms the interpretive theological key, making this a species of TAT. Kooi presents it this way: 'In the words of the ancient hymn in 1 Timothy 3.16, a history of salvation has been put in motion in which the Spirit is the driving force; this history includes Christ justified and glorified, which is meant to become public for all powers, times, and nations.'[7] I also echo Steven Studebaker's comments on this theme:

> From the perspective of pneumatology, creation, incarnation, and Pentecost are the key moments on a continuum of redemptive history. They are not discrete and disparate economies of God's work in the world. In the incarnation, the Spirit's work that began with creation finds its fullest realization in the union of the Son with the humanity of Jesus Christ. Jesus Christ's subsequent ministry, crucifixion, and resurrection are made possible by this fundamental pneumatological condition. At Pentecost, the Spirit makes the grace of union with the Son and participation in the fellowship of the triune God universally available to all people.[8]

The Spirit who anointed and directed Jesus, the Spirit who was present at creation, and the Spirit who embodies the eschaton, is also determinative for us and our salvation.

Protos to *Telos*

The recent and now flourishing movement known as the theological interpretation of Scripture (although not new at all), has gifted the Church resources old and new for reading Scripture canonically, holistically, theologically and practically.[9] To read Scripture canonically is to take seriously the final form of the canon and the way in which the many books form one book. Whether one adopts a hermeneutic drawn from the dramatic, Christology, or the Trinity (or all three), a canonical reading of Scripture treats it precisely as Holy Scripture, God's Word to us. When this is done, intertextuality and figural readings, to identify only two features, play an important role in comprehending the depth dimensions of the text. To miss the tension of promise and the resulting fulfilment from the Old to New Testament, for example, is to miss the whole.

Reading Scripture as one coherent story allows communities of faithful readers to discern the holistic message of Scripture and see the whole and not simply the parts. Such a reading strategy unearths a variety of first and second order beliefs which are subsequently formulated as doctrines. These doctrines, such as the hypostatic union, for example, are then read back into Scripture and make sense of what was previously unclear. Such theological interpretation allows readers to make sense of much of the Old Testament, for instance, where formerly ambiguity prevailed. One thinks here of how Paul speaks of Christ as the great *mystērion*, the key to Holy Scripture (Eph. 3.2–4, cf. Col. 1.25–28), or how the prophets themselves couldn't fully understand the words given them by revelation and yet we now apprehend those same texts because of Christ (1 Pet. 1.10–25).

Finally, it is not enough to read Scripture, it has to be acted on as it acts upon us. In short, all theology should be applied. The outline of an applied theology offered by Kooi is helpful here when he provides four key functions of theological reflection – the descriptive, normative, explorative and interpretive.[10] The descriptive function of doctrine seeks to make sense of what Christians have always and still do believe. Its normative function serves as a corrective tool, however unpopular that might be today. The explorative function of dogmatics requires trust and courage as God leads believers into new experiences, contexts and practices. Finally, dogmatics has the function of offering an orientation or interpretation to life, both in the pastorate but also in ethics, politics and other spheres of life. As Kooi clearly states: 'This orienting function is similar to a hiking guide. It is not the hike itself; it is a guide that can sometimes help you avoid getting lost and let you know where you are.'[11] This chapter, to adopt this metaphor, might then be seen as a brief comment on a trail hike.

What holds each of these aspects of theological interpretation and application together is a robust pneumatology. In order to answer questions such as 'What does salvation mean?' or 'What is a human person?', theologians have to explain how the biblical material is being utilized. The interpretive method outlined above is what I call a retroactive hermeneutic. To take several biblical examples, in Hebrews 3.7–11; 4.3, 5, 7; 10.16–17 and Revelation 2.7, we read that the Spirit takes the words of Scripture and speaks them into the present. The canonical authors are consciously writing to and for Spirit-inspired readers.[12] This last point has been recognized by Markus Bockmuehl, who writes: 'The implied reader is drawn into an act of reading that involves playing an active role on stage rather than the discreet spectator on the upper balcony.'[13] This is similar to the approach advocated by Thomas F. Torrance, who borrows an idea from William

Manson in which we must *indwell* the New Testament as a whole in such a way as to look *through* the various books and passages of Scripture and allow the message to be interiorized in the depths of our mind. For this reason, his approach is called 'depth exegesis'.[14] We might, then, conclude that: it is the Spirit of Light who illuminates the significance of the Christ event through Scripture (*retro*); it is the presence of the Spirit of Life that moves the Church on (*active*); and it is the Spirit of Truth who brings the word of God into new situations (*retroactive*).

A retroactive hermeneutic fills out and complements Kooi's proposal for the function of theology; especially the explorative and interpretive dimensions. In relation to the explorative function, Kooi suggests that: 'On the basis of John 16.13, church and theology must be open to new or deepened understandings of God's will provided by the Spirit through a variety of contexts, experiences, and realities.' In relation to the interpretive or orienting function, he writes: 'Dogmatic concepts can help interpret life, identify the traces of the Spirit of Christ, and encourage people and churches in making their choices and reflecting on their practices.'[15] In these ways at least, we see how the Spirit is central to the reading, interpreting, and application of Scripture and culture alike.

When this approach to the Canon is utilized we see that a deeply Christian way to read Scripture is to read it *in light of* Jesus Christ, *with* Jesus Christ, and *submitted to* Jesus Christ. The Christian reads Scripture to see what Scripture points to. Attention is directed along the line of the witness of Scripture to the self-revealing and reconciling God, which inevitably means that Scripture has a subsidiary status in the face of what is apprehended *through* Scripture – the Truth itself.[16] Seen in this way, the Holy Scriptures bear witness to the triune God of grace and glory made fully known in Christ and by the Spirit. Starting with the sending of the Son and the bestowal of the Spirit, Christians now read from the New Testament back into the Old Testament and then back to the New Testament again, only to repeat this again and again. But each reading is done in light of Christ and under his Lordship. We can, therefore, speak of the centrality of Christ for our past, our future and our present.

For our purposes, when such an approach is taken to Scripture and we ask about the self and salvation we clearly see things differently. When Christians read in Genesis 1 that God created the world by his Word and his Spirit we, with the prologue to the Gospel of John (John 1.1–18), read that in a trinitarian manner. When in Genesis 2 we read of God (*Elohim* אֱלֹהִים) creating humans in his image as male and female, we understand by this that what is meant is that humanity was created in the image of the incarnate Son, Jesus Christ – for as Paul states so emphatically, Jesus is *the* Image of the invisible God, he alone is *the imago Dei* (see Col. 1.15–20 and Phil. 2.5–11). This means that the rest of humanity are images of the Image – Jesus Christ – and that means that Jesus is the archetype of humanity and not, as many falsely assume, an afterthought in God's plan of redemption.[17]

The centrality of Jesus is equally relevant for eschatology when we come to ask what we will be like after death, for again Jesus Christ is central. In 1 Corinthians 15, for example, Paul lays out in stunning detail how Jesus and a love for him is the key to unlocking our future. If Christ has not risen our faith is in vain (1 Cor. 15.14, 17), for the gospel would not be good news and we would be hopeless: 'if we have hoped in Christ in this life only, we are of all people most to be pitied' (1 Cor. 15.19). But we are not hopeless for 'as in Adam all die, so also in Christ all will be made alive' (1 Cor. 15.22). How? By the resurrection of Jesus Christ, 'the first fruits of those who are asleep' (1 Cor. 15.20). We find here the assuring words that in the future, after death, we shall be raised to life, and shall be like Christ – our *Imago*, our *Archē* and our *Telos*. 'Just as we have borne the image of the earthly, we will also bear the image of the heavenly' (1 Cor. 15.49), and that is precisely because we shall be like Christ. We love Jesus, not simply for being our creator, but also for being our perfector!

We are told in the epistle to the Romans 5.6: 'You see, at just the right time, when we were still powerless, Christ died for the ungodly.' But we are also told, repeatedly and across different books and authors, that the cross-work of Christ and the redemption he brings, was purposed before the foundations of the world were even laid. Peter tells us that '[Jesus] was chosen before the creation of the world, but was revealed in these last times for your sake' (1 Pet. 1.20). John tells us that 'the Lamb was slain from the creation of the world', and that believers are, somehow, known to Christ before creation and their names are written in 'the Lamb's book of life' (Rev. 13.8). Because Jesus is the incarnate Son of God, he is the key to Scripture, to the cosmos, and as such he is the key to human existence.

Such a reading necessitates we stipulate the context within which a doctrine of self and salvation is positioned. Briefly put, we must see that 'it is distinctive of Christian theology that it treats of God in his relation to the world and of God in his relation to himself, not of one without the other.'[18] When doctrines of anthropology and soteriology are abstracted from a doctrine of creation (and the Creator), the resultant theology is deficient and moralistic, sentimental or mythical – it is anthropology more than theology. When a doctrine of creation is abstracted from anthropology and soteriology, it becomes equally deficient, deistic, panentheistic or syncretistic – it is ecology more than theology.[19]

Hence anthropology and creation are not two independent *loci* of theology; rather, a doctrine of creation is the *locus* of anthropological reflection, or put another way, anthropology is a *focus* of the doctrine of creation. As a concise summary, we might say with Thomas Torrance: 'Theologically speaking, man (*sic*) and the universe belong together and together constitute what we mean by "world", the world in its relation to God.'[20] This approach becomes more evident when humanity is considered in light of the eternal Word of God who became incarnate and is identified as the one through whom creation exists. Such is the context for theological anthropology and soteriology. Before commenting on soteriology directly, the next section first makes explicit the Christological anthropology implied here.

Anthropological Duality

According to the biblical testimony, human beings are not trichotomous – that is, composed of three discrete substances: body, soul and spirit.[21] Nowhere in Scripture do body, soul and spirit represent three separate constituent parts of the human.[22] Gerald Bray summarizes the point well: 'the ancient distinction between body (or flesh) and soul is not valid, because the soul is no more than the life of the body, without which we are talking only about a corpse, not about a human being.'[23]

In place of a trichotomous or even a dichotomous (body–soul) view of the human, Scripture presents a more holistic and unified description. Thomas Torrance helpfully pictures a human person as a 'body of their soul and soul of their body'.[24] Torrance's use of this phrase derives from Athanasius and Karl Barth.[25] Barth appeared to give priority to the soul whereas Torrance wishes to see the soul and body as completely coterminous and hence neither holds a priority over the other but each inherently constitutes the other. Torrance rejects a trichotomous view of the human person in favour of a description of the human as body and soul, related to God 'through the power and presence of God's Spirit'.[26] The human 'spirit' is actually an essential and dynamic correlate of the divine Spirit – not a third object distinct from body and soul. Rather than speak of some form of dualism between body and soul, it is more appropriate to speak of a duality (body and soul); and what holds these two polarities together is the Holy Spirit.

If human beings are considered along the lines of a constitutional duality then the human S/spirit is not some 'spark of the divine' (Origen)[27] but the ontological qualification of the soul brought about and maintained by the Holy Spirit. As Torrance clarifies: 'It is not through any alleged participation in the essence of God, as Hellenic religion and philosophy maintained, but through the objective orientation of man (*sic*) in soul and body to God, the Source and Ground of all creaturely rationality and freedom, that man is constituted a rational subject and agent, i.e. a *person*.'[28] Torrance wants to raise this discussion even further. What makes men and women so distinctive is that as unitary beings, body of their soul and soul of their body, they span two worlds – the physical and spiritual – and are thereby able to reach knowledge of the created contingent order and divulge the secrets of its vast intelligibility.[29] As a result a correspondence between God and humanity, Creator and creature, is spanned by the human person created in the *imago Dei*. This anthropology becomes the basis by which we can more accurately consider what it means to be saved.

Torrance understands patristic anthropology to have recast current terms from Middle Platonism into a distinctively Christian anthropology, the two most important aspects being *soul* and *person*. Like the rest of creation, the soul and body are created and are contingent rather than immortal.[30] The soul and body of human beings are 'continuously sustained by the creative presence of God and are given immortality through the grace of a relation with God who only has immortality'.[31] This graced relation to God is initiated in space-time but extends to the eschaton in which the resurrection of the whole being of the person as body and soul is realized. Resurrection is to a creaturely participation in the uncreated eternal life of God.

The presence of the Holy Spirit in the human results in what Torrance has helpfully termed a 'transcendental determination' implanted within each of us.[32] This phrase, while clumsy, functions as a cognate for the process of *theosis*. The human person is created with a goal (*telos*) in view, to participate in the triune relationship of the Father for the Son in or by the Holy Spirit.[33]

Anthropological duality as outlined here emphasizes the differences within unity between the body and the soul animated and held perpetually together by the Holy Spirit. It also highlights the purposive nature of humanity and invites further reflection on what salvation might mean for such a view of personal selfhood.

Theopoetic Transformation

When moving from anthropology to soteriology, all within the lens of a TAT, we should most naturally think of this as a form of transformative theopoetic journey into God's triune life.[34] In what follows I will briefly outline several aspects of this way of viewing salvation, with a focus on three interrelated concepts: stewards of the mysteries of God, priests of creation, and ministers of beneficence – each of which are highlighted by a focus on the work of the Spirit.

The ressourcement and retrieval movements in recent theology have brought certain patristic emphases to the fore; one of which is Basil's insight of the Spirit's perfecting work as the one who brings creation to its destined end or *telos*.³⁵ Basil surmised that the Father is the 'original cause', the Son is the 'operative cause', and the Spirit is the 'perfecting cause' of all things.³⁶ Given the fact that all things generally operate in the world *from* the Father, *through* the Son, and *in* the Holy Spirit, we can affirm several corollaries. First, the work of the Spirit co-indwells that of the Son. Second, the work of the Son is understood to be that of the *incarnate* Christ, thus the vicarious humanity of Christ is important. Third, the work of the Spirit is to sustain the relationship between the triune God and contingent creation. Fourth, the incarnation is a union not only with all human creatures but with *all* creation – the entire ecology of life. The Spirit unites us to *this* human (Christ), and unites all creation through *this* (Christ's) humanity. Here the God-world-humanity triadic is respected.

This is reminiscent of the *Spiritus Vivificans* who works not only in the church but throughout the entire world, bringing order out of chaos as in the first creation account, and bringing all things to their providential end – communion (*theosis*) with God. As Torrance writes:

> The supreme end for which God has designed his creation and which he activates and rules throughout all his relations with it is the purpose of his Holy Love not to live for himself alone but to bring into being a creaturely realm of heaven and earth which will reflect his glory and within which he may share with others the Communion of Love which constitutes his inner Life as Father, Son and Holy Spirit. It is in the incarnation of God's beloved Son in Jesus Christ, and in our sharing in that relation of the Son to the Father through the Holy Spirit, that the secret of the creation, hidden from the ages, has become disclosed to us.³⁷

Here the transformative theopoetic journey into God's triune life is a direct result of the creation from the love of the Father through the omnipotent grace of the Son and realized by the life-giving work of the Holy Spirit.

Living within the overflow of God's boundless love, united by the one Christ through the communion of the Holy Spirit, brings into focus the true dimensions of the Christian life.³⁸ Of course, the Christian life cannot exist in a vacuum, sealed off from the foundational doctrines of Trinity and Christology, and so even here, when thinking of our actual lives, we are still talking about Christ and the Spirit. All being must be thought of as caught up into the workings *ad extra* of the Holy Trinity, for 'in him we live and move and have our being' (Acts 17.28).

What, then, is life for? A properly Christian reply has to be: a Christ-like life is the only life worth living. And so Christology becomes the controlling norm for anthropology and soteriology, as the doctrine of God becomes the controlling norm for Christology. The God of triune life and love creates out of nothing for the sole purpose of ecstatic love. The creature exists to experience the love of God and to reflect this love back to him and all of creation. It is not that God needs creatures or their love – God is replete within his own triunity. It is out of such infinite and boundless love that God creates in the first place. And it is within the life and love of God that creatures find their being, their purpose and their ends.

Creaturely life has no end in itself but exists to bring glory to God. On its own, apart from intimate communion with God, creatures merely serve themselves or create idols of their own to worship. We are, as Luther said, *in curvetus se* – creatures turned in upon ourselves. Created to participate in the divine life and love, we have become miserable little gods, attempting to establish our own counter-kingdoms, and in such enterprise, find fulfilment. We know this doesn't work, but due to the surd that sin is, we continue the pathetic attempt to live life without reference to God.

Only Christ is *the* Image of God, and only Christ is able to live a life well-pleasing to God. All others must find their life hidden in his and from within his godly vocation, live a life worth living that glorifies God. United by the Spirit to Christ, we are only then able to offer to the Father a life that would bring him glory. We know who God is through knowledge of the incarnate Son, Christ shows us what it means to be human, and united by the Spirit to him and other believers we are the body of Christ on earth, the Church. Only then does ministry, mission, and ethics have a place. As a piece of theological summary, we might say that the *imitatio Christi* follows upon a *participatio Christi* – it never precedes it.

The Christian life is lived out of Christ and by the Spirit. This can suggest, and often has, a certain passivity on the part of the believer; a 'let go and let God' attitude. But it is not at all clear that this is the corollary of such a view. Rather, this calls for some sort of clarity over divine and human agency. The Apostle Paul was clear that all we do in the Christian life is attributable to God when he wrote: 'I am crucified with Christ: nevertheless I live, yet not I but Christ lives in me; and the life which I now live in the flesh I live by faith, the *faithfulness* of the Son of God who loved me and gave himself for me' (Gal. 2.20). As Torrance reflected upon this passage, a favourite of his, he writes:

> This is surely the insight that we must allow to inform all our human responses to God, whether they be in faith, conversion and personal decision, worship and prayer, the holy sacraments, or the proclamation of the Gospel: *'I yet not I but Christ'* . . . this applies to the whole of my life in Christ and to all my human responses to God, for in Jesus Christ they are laid hold of, sanctified and informed by his vicarious life of obedience and response to the Father. They are in fact so indissolubly united to the life of Jesus Christ which he lived out among us and which he has offered to the Father, as arising out of our human being and nature, that they are

our responses toward the love of the Father poured out upon us through the mediation of the Son and in the unity of his Holy Spirit.[39]

Torrance developed a maxim for this sort of thinking: all of grace does not mean nothing of me. All of grace means all of me. By this he means to express that in the Christian life all we do is attributed, as St Paul wrote, to Christ, but at the same time we are free agents and so it is genuinely our acts we are speaking of. As Kathryn Tanner has reflected upon this same theme she helpfully reminds us that:

> If Jesus' perfection as an agent cannot be understood apart from the assumption of his humanity by the Son of God or apart from his relation to the Father, then neither should ours. Short of an achieved perfection that is ours only eschatologically, we are sanctified through life in Christ not in virtue of being morally perfect but in virtue of the eccentric, Godword reference of our efforts, clinging to Christ in the Spirit, and invoking the Father's aid in union with Christ, in our dedication to the Father's own mission of beneficent gift-giving.[40]

Tanner settles upon the following summary of the Christian life lived out of Christ and by the Spirit as: 'one that ministers divine beneficence to others, in correspondence to Jesus' own ministering of the Father's beneficence to humanity – healing, nourishing, attending to the needs of the world – what Jesus did in his own life, a prior ministry that empowers our own'.[41]

This ministry of beneficence corresponds to certain themes found in the writings of Orthodox writers and Thomas Torrance, that of being 'priests of Creation', and with a saying of St Paul's that we are 'servants of Christ and stewards of the mysteries of God' (1 Cor. 4.1). As servants (*hyperetas*) of Christ and stewards of the mysteries of God, we have received the message of salvation in Christ alone passed on to us by the Spirit (1 Cor. 2.7–10). As priests of creation it is our calling to steward creation and offer it back to God in an act of continuous worship. As ministers of God's beneficence, it is our privilege to be like ministers at the Lord's banquet, distributing outward, to others, the gifts of the Father that have become ours in and through the Son by the power of the Holy Spirit.[42] Together these three powerful ideas provide an orientation to the sort of transformative theopoetic journey into God's life suggested by Holy Scripture.

Such a vision for the Christian life is not one conceived by way of a contract between God and the individual. Contractual thinking involves external relations founded upon a legal basis. God is not a contractual God but a covenanting one. God enters into a covenant of grace with humanity (Adam), a national covenant with Israel (Abraham), and a covenant of redemption with all flesh (Jesus), and in such covenantal relations we find the stipulations and conditions of holy living. We do not condition God's love, God's grace or God's forgiveness; each is freely given. We do not merit salvation by our works or even by our intention to do good works; salvation is freely given also. And we do not share God's good gifts with all creation to accrue merit or favour with God; 'every good and perfect gift comes from above, from the Father of lights' (James 1.17). Tanner again reminds us that 'this way of life is not an obligation, or the fulfilment of a debt, to God. It is simply the only way of life appropriate to the way things are; it is simply our effort, as Karl Barth would say, to be what we already are.'[43]

Where might the Christian find the resources to live lives of stewards, priests and ministers? Only in Christ by the power of the Spirit. The life, death and resurrection of Jesus Christ show us not only how to live, but in whom to live. United to Christ by the Spirit, we have communion with the Father and are reborn, recreated and reconstituted for a life of godly loving and sharing. As such, Christians are ministers of divine benefit, as Tanner says, gifting creation back to God and in the process gifting it to each other so that others in turn become ministers of divine beneficence as well. C. S. Lewis spoke of this as being concerned with the weight of our fellow human being's glory.[44] By weight of glory he meant that burden we face for our fellow human and for all creation, for them to realize their vocation and calling before God, for them to flourish in union and communion with God, and to become stewards, priests and ministers too.

Conclusion

Much more can and should be said about this transformative theopoetic journey into the life of the triune God, but this précis will have to suffice for now. When starting with the Spirit, traditional doctrines, such as the self and salvation, are opened up to new insights and nuance. As Steven Studebaker reminds us as he concludes his own examination on this theme:

> Soteriology is a story of the Spirit. It begins with the Spirit of God hovering over the primeval abyss. It continues in the history of Israel and reaches fullness in the incarnation of Christ and the outpouring of the Spirit of Pentecost. Although different moments in the story, they are all part of one story, the story of the Spirit. A Third Article soteriology does not displace Christology, but rather shows the synergy and symmetry between Christology and pneumatology. The Spirit's work in the incarnation of Christ and as the gift of Pentecost continues and clarifies the narrative of the Spirit that begins with creation. The Spirit creates human beings to enjoy fellowship with their triune Creator and each other and

for abundant life in this world. The Spirit's work in the incarnation of Christ gives this dream for human life its fullest manifestation. With the outpouring of the Spirit of Pentecost, the Spirit's work in the life of Christ achieves a universal horizon and becomes available to all people.[45]

The same Spirit that settled upon Christ at his baptism, empowered his messianic ministry and raised him from the dead, is now given to us by the ascended Christ (John 14.16–17). As with Christ, so too we are empowered to live a life devoted to the Father, empowered to resist temptation and serve Christ, and filled with the Spirit to live lives worthy of our calling. Such Spirit-filled and Christ-shaped lives concern our own sanctification as much as they do a hospitality and care for others, and a stewarding of all creation, offering it up to the Father, in Christ, by the Spirit. Such a rich gospel reinterprets who we are, what we are, and what we are created to be and do; and such a reframing calls for a response of obedience and worship.

Notes

1 D. Lyle Dabney, 'Starting with the Spirit: Why the Last Should be First', in Stephen Pickard and Gordon Preece (eds), *Starting with the Spirit: Task of Theology II* (Hindmarsh, South Australia: Australian Theological Forum, 2001), p. 4 (3–27).

2 Ben Pugh, *SCM Studyguide to Theology in the Contemporary World* (London: SCM Press, 2017), p. 46. Pugh's assessment is largely based upon the publication of a landmark work, *Third Article Theology: A Pneumatological Dogmatics*, ed. Myk Habets (Minneapolis, MN: Fortress Press, 2016).

3 See further in Myk Habets, 'Prolegomenon: On Starting with the Spirit', in *Third Article Theology*, pp. 1–19.

4 Pugh, *SCM Studyguide*, p. 51.

5 Pugh, *SCM Studyguide*, p. 52.

6 Cornelis van der Kooi, *This Incredibly Benevolent Force: The Holy Spirit in Reformed Theology and Spirituality* (Grand Rapids, MI: Eerdmans, 2018), p. xiv.

7 Kooi, *This Benevolent Force*, p. 3.

8 Steven M. Studebaker, 'Soteriology: A Story of the Spirit', in *Third Article Theology*, p. 234.

9 Elsewhere I have dealt with many of these themes around what I term a 'retroactive hermeneutic of triune discourse'. See Myk Habets, 'Developing a Retroactive Hermeneutic: Johannine Theology and Doctrinal Development', *American Theological Inquiry* 1, 2 (2008), pp. 77–89; and Myk Habets, 'That was Then, This is Now: Reading Hebrews Retroactively', in Oliver D. Crisp and Fred Sanders (eds), *Hearing the Voice of God in the Text of Scripture: Explorations in Constructive Dogmatics* (Grand Rapids, MI: Zondervan, 2016), pp. 94–111.

10 Kooi, *This Benevolent Force*, pp. 19–21.

11 Kooi, *This Benevolent Force*, p. 21.

12 I have developed this hermeneutic in dialogue with the Johannine writings in Habets, 'Developing a Retroactive Hermeneutic'.

13 Markus Bockmuehl, '"To Be Or Not To Be": The Possible Futures of New Testament Scholarship', *Scottish Journal of Theology* 51, 3 (1998), p. 300.

14 Thomas F. Torrance, *The Christian Doctrine of God, One Being – Three Persons* (Edinburgh: T&T Clark, 1996), p. 37. He also draws heavily from the work of Michael Polanyi; see Thomas F. Torrance (ed.), *Belief in Science and in Christian Life: The Relevance of Michael Polanyi's Thought for Christian Faith and Life* (Edinburgh: Handsel Press, 1980).

15 Kooi, *This Benevolent Force*, p. 20.

16 Consult Thomas F. Torrance, 'Truth and Authority: Theses on Truth', *Irish Theological Quarterly* 39 (1972), pp. 215–42.

17 For a full account see Myk Habets, 'On Getting First Things First: Assessing Claims for the Primacy of Christ', *New Blackfriars* 90, 1027 (2009), pp. 343–64.

18 Thomas F. Torrance, *Reality and Evangelical Theology* (Downers Grove, IL: IVP, 1999), p. 21.

19 See Kathryn Tanner, 'Is God in Charge? Creation and Providence', in William C. Placher (ed.), *Essentials of Christian Theology* (Louisville, KY: Westminster John Knox Press, 2003), p. 119 (92–131). See also, Tanner, 'Creation and Providence', in John Webster (ed.), *The Cambridge Companion to Karl Barth* (Cambridge: Cambridge University Press, 2000), pp. 111–26. When theology simply capitulates to science, Tanner believes it can often take on an arbitrary stance, or even a fantastical one.

20 Torrance, *Reality and Evangelical Theology*, p. 27.

21 I have drawn here on Myk Habets, 'Naked but not Disembodied: A Case for Anthropological Duality', *Pacific Journal of Baptist Research* 4, 1 (2008), pp. 33–50.

22 For biblical surveys which highlight these points in detail, see Joel B. Green, '"Bodies – That Is, Human Lives": A Re-Examination of Human Nature in the Bible', pp. 149–73; and Ray S. Anderson, 'On Being Human: The Spiritual Saga of a Creaturely Soul', pp. 177–94, both in W. S. Brown, N. Murphy and H. N. Malony (eds), *Whatever Happened to the Soul? Scientific and Theological Portraits of Human Nature* (Minneapolis, MN: Fortress Press, 1998).

23 Gerald Bray, 'The Work of the Spirit (Rom. 8.1–17)', *Evangel* (Autumn 2001), p. 68. See further in F. Leron Shults, *Reforming Theological Anthropology: After the Philosophical Turn to Relationality* (Grand Rapids, MI: Eerdmans, 2003), p. 178.

24 Thomas F. Torrance, *The Christian Frame of Mind: Order and Openness in Theology and Natural Science* (Edinburgh: Handsel Press, 1985), p. 29 (slightly altered).

25 Athanasius, *De Incarnationis* 15; *Contra Arianos* 2.53–54; 3.20, 30–35. Karl Barth, *Church Dogmatics*, 4 vols (Edinburgh: T&T Clark, 1956–1975), III/2, p. 325.

26 Thomas F. Torrance, 'The Soul and Person in Theological Perspective', in S. R. Sutherland and T. A. Roberts (eds), *Religion, Reason, and the Self: Essays in Honour of Hywel D. Lewis* (Cardiff: University of Wales Press, 1989), p. 110.

27 David Cairns, *The Image of God in Man*, 2nd edn (London: Collins, 1973), pp. 66–78.

28 Torrance, 'The Soul and Person in Theological Perspective', p. 113.

29 Torrance, *The Christian Frame of Mind*, p. 33.

30 See Thomas F. Torrance, *Transformation and Convergence in the Frame of Knowledge: Explorations in the Interrelations of Scientific and Theological Enterprise* (Grand Rapids, MI: Eerdmans, 1984), pp. 333–49.

31 Torrance, 'The Soul and Person in Theological Perspective', p. 105.

32 Thomas F. Torrance, 'The Goodness and Dignity of Man in the Christian Tradition', *Modern Theology* 4, 4 (1988), pp. 309–22.

33 For a related idea see Ted Peters (ed.), Wolfhart Pannenberg, *Toward a Theology of Nature: Essays on Science and Faith* (Louisville, KY: Westminster John Knox Press, 1993), p. 133.

34 Variously defined as theosis, theopoiesis, Christification, deification or divinization.

35 On recent trends see Dabney, 'Starting with the Spirit', pp. 3–27.

36 Basil of Caesarea, *On the Holy Spirit*. Popular Patristic Series 42, trans. Stephen Hildebrand (Crestwood, NY: St Vladimir's Seminary Press, 2011), pp. 16, 38 (p. 71).

37 Torrance, *The Christian Doctrine of God*, p. 218. Torrance goes on to quote in full Ephesians 1.3–14.

38 The following is adapted from Myk Habets and Bobby Grow, 'Introduction: On Dogmatics and Devotion in the Christian Life', in Bobby Grow and Myk Habets (eds), *Evangelical Calvinism, Volume 2: Dogmatics and Devotion* (Eugene, OR: Pickwick Publications, 2017), pp. 1–14.

39 Thomas F. Torrance, *The Mediation of Christ*. New Enlarged Edition (Edinburgh: T&T Clark, 1992), p. 98.

40 Kathryn Tanner, *Jesus, Humanity and the Trinity: A Brief Systematic Theology* (Minneapolis, MN: Fortress Press, 2001), p. 75.

41 Tanner, *Jesus, Humanity and the Trinity*, p. 79.

42 Tanner, *Jesus, Humanity and the Trinity*, p. 80.

43 Tanner, *Jesus, Humanity and the Trinity*, p. 85 (with reference to Barth's *Ethics*, pp. 404, 462).

44 C. S. Lewis, 'The Weight of Glory', in *Screwtape Proposes a Toast and Other Pieces* (London: Fontana, 1965), pp. 94–110.

45 Studebaker, 'Soteriology', p. 249.

10

Christian Doctrines of Humanity and Salvation Provide Theological Foundations for Virtue Epistemology

BENJAMIN H. ARBOUR

It seems that the majority of work in analytic theology primarily involves philosophy informing theology. In what follows, I suggest that Christian theology offers foundations for some conceptions of virtue epistemology (VE). Moreover, Christian theology shows how and why VE is best poised among theories of knowledge to account for a uniquely Christian understanding of belief formation. Specifically, Christian theology, together with even the most basic aspects of VE, explains how indirect doxastic volunteerism fits into a Plantingean schema of proper functionalism concerning belief in God.[1] Human cognitive faculties, tainted as they are by the noetic effects of sin, generally function properly or improperly in proportion to the cultivation of intellectual virtue and the suppression of intellectual vice.

Whereas the majority of epistemologists discuss VE by focusing mostly on the positive aspects of VE (the virtuous side), I suggest that an equal treatment be given to the intellectual vices opposite the virtues espoused by VE. As I will demonstrate, Christian hamartiology can help explain what advocates of VE would have us believe about how even those who bear the divine image can fail to believe that God exists. I conclude by showing how 'being saved' further assists us in understanding what leading virtue epistemologists teach about both the individual and social dimensions of knowledge.

Before discussing the specific contribution of VE to the aspects of belief formation and doxastic responsibility, a few introductory remarks are in order. It also seems prudential to consider the nature of intellectual virtues before turning to the specifics of virtue epistemology. Kvanvig suggests that intellectual virtues:

> are a subclass of the class of admirable characteristics: persons can be admired for their cognitive powers, their intellectual insight, their ability to find the truth, as well as other sorts of qualities. A person can

be acutely perceptive, or have a memory like an elephant; she can be exceptionally intelligent or original in her thinking. Some persons are especially scrupulous in collecting available evidence before jumping to conclusions; others consistently avoid the inferential errors to which most of us are liable.[2]

Zagzebski agrees, and clarifies; an intellectual virtue is 'is roughly a disposition toward or ability to acquire justified beliefs'.[3] Sosa offers a still more precise definition of virtue, bringing environment into account. 'One has an intellectual virtue or faculty relative to an environment E if and only if one has an inner nature I in virtue of which one would mostly attain the truth and avoid error in a certain field of propositions F, when in certain conditions C.'[4] With this understanding of intellectual virtues in mind, we can now consider how these virtues fit into a robust theory of knowledge.

Aristotle long ago advocated that epistemic virtues are significant in two ways: 1) character traits such as wisdom and discernment are conducive to our striving to live a happy life; and 2) other epistemic virtues 'are conducive, we think, to the discovery of truth (and the avoidance of error)'.[5] Given that this isn't exactly a new idea, what is virtue epistemology? In a sentence, '[t]he central idea of virtue epistemology is that justification and knowledge arise from the proper functioning of our intellectual virtues or faculties in an appropriate environment.'[6] Ernest Sosa gets a bit more specific by distinguishing between animal knowledge and reflective knowledge. For Sosa, S has animal knowledge regarding p if:

1 p is true, and
2 S's belief B(p) is produced by one or more intellectual virtues of S.

However, for some piece of knowledge to qualify as reflective knowledge, it must meet the additional criteria of:

> S has a true perspective on B(p) as being produced by one or more intellectual virtues, where such a perspective is itself produced [one or more] intellectual virtue[s] of S.[7]

Advocates of VE are divided about whether or not the instancing of intellectual virtues is sufficient to guarantee knowledge, or whether something else is also necessary. Those who think instancing virtue is sufficient are known as virtue reliabilists, whereas those who think that intellectual virtues must be instanced in the right way to guarantee knowledge are known as virtue responsibilists.[8] An example from Sosa comparing the actions of an archer to knowledge illustrates what is at issue here.

Consider a lucky shot by an unskilled archer. Even if the arrow hits a bulls-eye, the accuracy is accidental. But a skilled archer may be able to hit a bulls-eye consistently. But suppose that an incredibly skilful archer decides to whimsically let an arrow fly, and by happenstance the arrow hits the bulls-eye of a target – but not because the archer aimed. Not every accurate arrow shot by an adroit archer qualifies as an instantiation of magnificent skill. Aptness is the key; when the accuracy of the arrow hitting the bulls-eye is caused by the archer's adroitness, then we have a case of apt skill. Sosa suggests that we conceive of a theory of knowledge similarly. It isn't enough for someone to believe something truly, nor is it enough that such a person is epistemologically competent. For knowledge, the person's believing something that is true needs in some measure to be brought about because of that person's instancing one or more intellectual virtues.[9]

Despite the significant differences between virtue epistemologists as to what they hope VE accomplishes, they can all agree that the central idea of VE is that knowledge arises from the proper functioning of our intellectual virtues in an appropriate environment.[10] In light of this consensus, while I personally favour Linda Zagzebski's motivational/responsibilist account of VE over alternatives, I will make use of not only her take on VE, but also that of John Greco, Jonathan Kvanvig and James Montmarquet along the way. I recognize that these thinkers disagree with each other on significant points, but my use of their ideas does not raise tensions that require us to choose a singular account of VE in showing how certain Christian doctrines serve as foundations for VE.

In order to understand my proposal more clearly, let us consider one particular intellectual virtue, namely intellectual humility, which I will use to develop an example later. Roberts and Wood offer a lucid account of this virtue, as well as corresponding intellectual vices such as pride, egotism, vanity, haughtiness, snobbery, and so on. They write:

> The intellectually vain person is overly concerned with how he 'looks' to the people who count: he wants to impress, and is very concerned not to look silly at conferences and in front of his bright students. This concern may incline him not to admit, and maybe not even notice, when someone has raised a good objection to his views. It may also incline him to fudge arguments when he thinks he can make them look good enough to get away with.[11]

In contrast:

> The humble person will be free to test his ideas against the strongest objections. His humility may also make for an intellectual adventure: he

will not be afraid to try out ideas that others may ridicule (here, if one lacks humility, courage may be a substitute).[12]

Let us add intellectual diligence/scrupulousness to the list of intellectual virtues. These virtues, together with their corresponding intellectual vices, form a helpful starting point in understanding Christian approaches to belief formation. Next, consider the vice of epistemic snobbery (and its corollaries, opposite intellectual humility) and how it might prevent someone from arriving at truth for want of believing testimony. Perhaps arrogance and haughtiness combine such that a person is intellectually unable (or even unwilling) to see what is true, all because of a lack of instancing the virtue of humility, which does seem to be the antidote for all of the varieties of epistemic pride. These vices inhibit a person's ability to gather evidence. As a result of these vices, people often fail to instance the virtue of intellectual diligence/scrupulousness and thereby shape their beliefs wrongly.

The role that evidence plays in coming to believe something is complicated, and what exactly it means for a belief to be based on evidence is even more complex. According to Robert Audi, '[t]he majority view is that it is for the evidence to be causally responsible (in the right way) for the belief'.[13] However,

> motivational virtue theorists deny that being caused by the evidence is the right way to account for a properly based belief; instead, they claim that the causal route must be described as going through some of the intellectual virtues to belief. . . . According to such a virtue theory, we determine what classification to give a belief by noting what cognitive characteristics were responsible for its formation or sustenance, and then we determine whether the belief is doxastically justified by determining whether the cognitive characteristics responsible for the belief count as intellectual virtues.[14]

What, then, are we to make of evidence? VE does not ignore the role that evidence plays in the causal chain of knowledge, or the role of evidence in doxastic justification. Rather, VE partially accounts for what occurs when a person instances the intellectual virtues of humility and diligence, such that a person seeks out evidence and makes a decision regarding what ought to be concluded accordingly in light of the evidence gathered.

Indirect Doxastic Volunteerism and Weak Foundationalism

The aspects of motivational virtue epistemology held by Zagzebski relating to evidence are extremely interesting, especially if we adopt a noetic structure of weak foundationalism akin to that advocated by Plantinga, now common among reformed epistemologists. Weak foundationalism, unlike classical foundationalism, widens the parameters of what counts as a properly basic belief such that memory and other properly functioning cognitive faculties count as reliable sources of knowledge. Even on this view, many beliefs are held involuntarily and are beyond anyone's doxastic control. I cannot help but believe, for example, that the colour of my car is silver when I see it; I do not 'choose' in any real sense of the word to believe that my car is silver; rather, I just find myself believing that it is, in fact, a silver car, on the basis of my sense perception. The same lack of direct doxastic volunteerism might apply equally to all properly basic beliefs – including memory beliefs. If I find myself recalling that I ate fish for dinner last Friday, it does not appear to be within my cognitive powers to choose to believe differently, at least not without a lot of work to distort and mar both my cognitive faculties and the deliverances thereof.

But this inability does not seem to hold in a parallel way for based beliefs. Because based beliefs are 'based' upon other beliefs, these more basic beliefs count as evidence, so some action of synthesis is required in order to form based beliefs. Cases in which based beliefs are true, then, are the result of the instancing of intellectual virtues, and are examples of reflective knowledge, at least insofar as motivational aspects of VE account for our pursuit of knowledge. Knowledge of based beliefs is voluntary. Unlike properly basic beliefs or direct knowledge, based beliefs are indirect, and as a result, someone chooses in some sense whether they hold a based belief. Said differently, because we choose to instance intellectual virtues which are partially responsible in the causal chain of gathering evidence upon which we come to form based beliefs, we possess some kind of doxastic control (albeit indirectly) over our based beliefs.

Montmarquet believes that the exercise (or non-exercise) of intellectual virtues is voluntary and under our control; that is, we can choose whether to employ our intellectual virtues in our pursuit of the truth. If intellectual virtues are part of our belief-forming faculties, and if we exercise some control over whether or not to instance intellectual virtues, then we exercise some control (at least indirectly) over what we choose to believe. This conception of intellectual virtue, along with Montmarquet's and Zagzebski's, bears an affinity to Aristotle's account of moral virtue.[15]

Another important dimension to this discussion concerns rationality as an epistemic desideratum. Richard Foley writes:

> Rationality is a function of an individual pursuing his goals in a way that on reflection he would take to be effective. Since epistemic rationality is concerned with the epistemic goal of now believing truths and now not believing falsehood . . . it is epistemically rational for an individual S to

believe p just if he on reflection would think that believing p is an effective means to his epistemic goal.[16]

Roberts and Wood note that:

> defining epistemic rationality in terms of what a truth-seeker, upon reflection, would consider an effective means to his end allows for some pretty strange cases of rationality . . . persons may be found who, on reflection, deny that they have intellectual peers, deliberately insulate their views from helpful criticism, and habitually excuse themselves from dialogue with others that would in fact further their pursuit of the truth. But if it is true that intellectual vanity, arrogance, domination, and snobbery tend to impede the pursuit of true beliefs, the person with those traits is to that extent irrational and the person of epistemic humility rational.[17]

Expanding Virtue Epistemology to Include Theology, or Theology's Contribution to Virtue Epistemology

After explaining why many virtue epistemologists overstate their claims, Kvanvig offers an alternative account of VE that avoids certain errors. He appeals to modal ontological arguments to show that knowledge is a great-making property.[18] Accordingly, knowledge is the sort of thing that contributes to the overall value, or greatness, of a being. On this basis, the possession of knowledge becomes part of what Kvanvig calls a cognitive ideal option, which allows VE to completely redefine the epistemological enterprise without redefining knowledge itself.

> As we shall see, affirming the cognitive ideal options leads straightforwardly toward a denial of the Cartesian perspective which sees fundamental structural epistemology as foundational. My aim is to show that the cognitive ideal option must be accepted and that once it is accepted we will be in a position to begin to see why the Cartesian perspective must be abandoned.[19]

Abandoning the Cartesian perspective is a tall order. Another quote clarifies what Kvanvig is pursuing:

> The conclusion to be drawn is that the importance of the virtues can only be explained by holding that they compose a part of the cognitive ideal not reducible to, or explainable in terms of, the traditional epistemological

notions of knowledge and/or justification. Instead, the importance of the virtues is that they tell us something important about the person who has them, rather than something about the particular beliefs of that person. Because of their connection to the project of finding the truth and avoiding error, they are of interest to epistemologists, but not in terms, at least not solely in terms, of their traditional task of clarifying the nature and scope of knowledge. The general lesson to be learned here is that the importance we attach to the intellectual virtues is independent, to a great extent, of traditional epistemological concerns.[20]

Kvanvig goes on to show that other attempts to reform and/or reject the Cartesian perspective offered over the last few decades haven't gone far enough; instead, they only show where epistemology is mistaken without putting forward an alternative. Kvanvig says that what is needed in such an alternative is nothing short of abandoning any approach that begins by asking what it means for an individual to be warranted in believing some proposition at some point in time.[21] He concludes by offering such an alternative:

> I want to suggest that perhaps a better picture of an ideal cognitive life is one which does not emphasize individual propositional warrant, knowledge-that, and the cementing of time-slice relations between warrant, the individual, and belief. Perhaps, instead of beginning from the Cartesian perspective, we should think more realistically of what human beings are like without abandoning the attempt to understanding (*sic*) systematically the life of the mind. What I am suggesting is meta-theoretical advice about how theory construction in epistemology should begin.[22]

It is this last point that is so vital to a theological approach to VE. If we truly reflect upon 'what human beings are like', we might find that theological anthropology leads us to study not only personal ontology, but also the divine nature, especially given the *imago Dei* tradition.

Christian theology teaches us that God is a rational, knowing being – and maximally so. Because Christians believe that humans are made in the image of God, Christians insist that we, too, are rational beings who are capable of knowledge. Insofar as humans are called to be perfect as God is perfect (cf. Matt. 5.48), we should strive to perfectly exhibit the virtues, including intellectual ones. What theologians have called the structural approach to understanding the *imago Dei* allows us to approach the entire epistemological enterprise from a different vantage point in just the way Kvanvig suggests is necessary. By understanding humans as made in the image of God, we can begin such an approach by asking how human knowledge reflects

God's perfect knowledge (cf. Job 37.16) rather than focusing primarily on issues surrounding epistemological warrant and/or justification.[23]

If we bring theology proper into conversation with various aspects of epistemology, Kvanvig's cognitive ideal approach to VE and knowledge also allows us to suggest that the will plays a significant role in how we come to form beliefs. This is true because we have been created in God's image. God, as a rational being, has a will; if we are divine image bearers, presumably we also have a will. If the *imago Dei* tradition is correct, as the Christian faith maintains, it seems perfectly reasonable that rational creatures are uniquely suited to achieve knowledge only upon the instancing of the intellectual virtues as Zagzebski describes. She maintains that knowledge must manifest dispositions that both (a) involve certain motivational structure, and (b) involve relevant kinds of voluntary control.

Furthermore, if we understand God to eternally exist as three distinct Persons as orthodox Trinitarianism demands, then a relational approach to the *imago Dei* also paves the way for other advantages of VE over traditional approaches to a theory of knowledge by discussing the role of a community in the formation of beliefs.[24] Kvanvig notes this possibility as it relates to VE, saying:

> What I am arguing for is an approach that pays attention to the possibility of finding cognitively ideal mental lives in the case of individuals who depend on a social structure to become competent in the search for truth. Such a perspective would foster an initial wonder concerning how human beings come to be competent truth-seekers, in much the same way that they become competent language speakers.[25]

Christian theology, then, serving as a foundation, helps to verify the claims of VE. Moreover, incorporating theological truths as premises for building a VE actually strengthens VE.

Finally, a Christian theological approach to VE presupposes the virtue of knowledge and the vice of ignorance. How do we know? In the words of the children's song, 'For the Bible tells me so.' Consider a sampling of verses of Scripture that display the importance of the life of the mind in Christianity: 'You shall love the Lord your God with all your heart and with all your soul and with all your mind' (Matt. 22.37); 'Do not be conformed to this world, but be transformed by the renewal of your mind' (Rom. 12.2a); 'grow in the grace and knowledge of our Lord and Saviour Jesus Christ' (2 Peter 3.18). Consider also the cautions of Scripture against ignorance (Prov. 19.2; Hos. 4.6; Acts 17.30; and Eph. 4.18). We see, then, that humans are commanded by God in Scripture to pursue knowledge for the cultivation of virtue. Thus, a teleological, or functional, view of the *imago Dei* lends additional support to VE.[26]

Biblical theology certainly provides reasons for thinking that these different aspects of humanity might be part of what it means for mankind to bear the image of God. Various scholars have favoured one understanding of what it means for humans to be image bearers of God over the other positions, and a long literature exists of defence of these various positions.[27] But as far as I can see, there is nothing that makes any particular understanding of the *imago Dei* mutually exclusive of other views. Thus, I follow J. I. Packer in advocating for a synthetic approach, which might be described as a kaleidoscopic view, and it combines multiple views into a collective understanding of the *imago Dei*.[28] This position allows for all of these anthropological understandings to serve as theological foundations to VE. Having discussed the doctrine of humanity, let us now incorporate other doctrines into VE to offer at least an explanation, but not a justification, of why we don't live out VE well.

Virtue Epistemology and the Noetic Effects of Sin

Although theological reflections on the noetic effects of sin go back at least as far as Augustine, the reformer John Calvin developed a famous account of the effects of the Fall on human cognitive faculties. He explained that although we know the truth of God's existence by virtue of our conscience, 'we do not naturally come to a proper knowledge of God'. The reason is that through this sense and this seed we come to feel a truth 'which [we] are desirous not to know', with the result that 'the knowledge of God [is] stifled or corrupted'.[29] According to Calvin, that we are desirous not to know should not be understood merely as not desiring to know a bit of knowledge, but as specifically desiring to *not* know what we already 'know' to be true. Calvin's account elucidates the meaning of Paul's verbiage concerning the suppression of the truth in unrighteousness (cf. Rom. 1.18).

Most segments of animal knowledge seem unaffected by the noetic effects of sin – at least for most people.[30] Thus, for many, it doesn't make sense to speak of a uniquely Christian mathematics. However, according to one model of cognitive impairment, the closer a subject is to our own identity, the more likely the noetic effects of sin impair our ability to rightly discern truth from error apart from special divine assistance.[31] Thus, '[w]e can be reasonably rational at the periphery of our interests, where opportunities for prideful self-assertion are limited. But the closer the topic to the core of our being, the greater the tendency to subordinate truth to other values.'[32]

Westphal, making use of the concept of sin, notes that the noetic effects of sin force us to take postmodern deconstruction seriously, especially as it relates to perspectivalism and the lack of epistemological objectivity.[33]

Westphal notes that 'to speak this way [about the noetic effects of sin] is to suggest that when we "do" epistemology, Christian philosophers should listen carefully to what their theologian colleagues (sometimes) say about the noetic effects of sin.'[34] He also argues that reformed epistemology 'shows the failure of foundationalism with exceptional clarity, [but] the alternative it proposes does not take advantage of the new opportunity to make sin an essential epistemological category'.[35] So if one were to couple reformed epistemology (with its unique appropriation of the doctrine of the noetic effects of sin) together with some version of VE, the results would be a uniquely Christian theory of knowledge.

Admittedly, my discussion of evidence might not play directly into the schema I'm now constructing all that easily, for the Pauline idea of suppressing the truth in unrighteousness does not stem from a problem involving the lack of evidence. As it turns out, we sometimes use certain types of evidence and even the truth itself to suppress other truths, as Marx and Freud persistently and pointedly illustrated.[36] However, let us consider one well-known example to illustrate the functionality of a Christian VE.

Virtue Epistemology, Christian Theology and the Ethics of Belief

William Clifford offered what he believed was an example analogous to making a decision about whether or not to believe in God. Clifford's story is well known: a ship owner who, knowing fully well on the basis of expert testimony that his ship is not seaworthy, risks the lives of numerous people by sending the ship out on another voyage.[37] Clifford notes that regardless of whether the ship makes the journey or not, the ship's owner has behaved immorally and irresponsibly; he did not act on the basis of the evidence.[38] Let's consider a slight modification to Clifford's example. Suppose that the same ship owner is aware of significant problems with his vessel, but is unsure as to whether these problems render his ship unsafe of another voyage. Suppose also that an expert engineer who focuses on examining the seaworthiness of ships is available for a nominal fee, and that the time it takes her to conduct her examination would not in any way impede the schedule of business for the ship's owner. Finally, let us consider whether the actions taken by the ship owner are ethical if he concludes on the basis of simple reflection that his intuitions that the ship is seaworthy are correct, and sends the ship out on another voyage without employing the engineer to offer her expert opinion.

One might argue that the owner's immediate, intuitive perception of the ship's seaworthiness outweighed any concerns created by other testimony, thereby exonerating him. However, if Christian VE is correct, it is just as likely that this person is guilty of epistemological sin for the following reasons. First, and perhaps most obviously, this example does not illustrate the use of intellectual virtues in diligently seeking to ascertain whether or not the ship was seaworthy or not. Hence, the ship owner exhibits no real motivation for truth, and no excellencies in diligently supporting his beliefs with any kind of evidence/justification. He fails to image God correctly in the structural sense of the *imago Dei*; that is, he does not utilize his will in coming to form beliefs in the most reliable way possible.

Second, the ship owner chooses to suppress the truth (cf. Rom. 1.18) in an effort to gain something else, foregoing the costly expense of ship repair. Thus, he could have used 'truth' to suppress other truth; for all we know, the ship owner really did intuitively consider the ship seaworthy. But if a Zagzebskian model of VE is correct, and a theory of indirect doxastic volunteerism bears this out, then although the ship owner doesn't exert any control over first-order beliefs (including properly basic beliefs such as intuition), his beliefs based on evidence are indirectly under his control. By not exercising diligence in seeking out additional evidence, the ship owner sins not only in jeopardizing the lives of the ship's passengers, but also in that he prevents himself from arriving at the truth. The ship owner's actions militate against correctly mirroring God's perfections as image bearers on the teleological understanding of the *imago Dei*.

Third, and finally, the owner does not listen to any other voices from his community who might warn him about the condition of his ship. Thus, his preoccupation with individual belief drowns out the community in helping him form beliefs. This undermines the epistemological realities gleaned from Trinitarian theology, the relational model of the *imago Dei* tradition, and social epistemology.[39]

Everyone knows that Clifford wasn't primarily concerned with the ethics of believing whether or not some imaginary ship was seaworthy or not. Rather, Clifford constructed his example in order to show by parallel example the proper ethics of belief with regard to religious belief in God. A Christian approach to VE helps to explain (at least in part) why some atheists, especially those who are not professional philosophers, insist that God does not exist in spite of so much evidence to the contrary. Some atheists, but certainly not all, simply fail to exhibit the intellectual virtues that would motivate them to seek out the truth. Instead, with minds darkened by the noetic effects of sin, they suppress the truth in unrighteousness, either by choosing to ignore evidence or by not seeking it out in the first place. Again, I cannot overstate how clearly I am aware that this is not true of all atheists, but it is true of many people we meet outside of academic contexts – *and the same can be said of many theists*.[40]

When confronted with powerful arguments for (or against) the existence of God, rather than believe (or abandon faith) in the face of such evidence, because he desires to *not* believe in God (or desires to maintain faith), someone might go online and look deliberately and only for material that would undermine (or refute) arguments for (or against) God's existence. Hence, intellectual snobbery combined with a lack of intellectual diligence prevents someone from arriving at the truth concerning God's existence. The virtuous person remains open-minded, and would seek out evidence regardless of where it leads. Anyone who behaves like the person described above fails to instance intellectual virtues, and thereby fails to arrive at the truth at least in part because he chooses to not instance various intellectual virtues, and thereby exercises indirect doxastic control over his beliefs concerning the existence of God.

According to any biblical understanding of what happens when people 'get saved', God supernaturally works in their lives. To whatever degree the image of God was marred by sin, salvation begins a process of healing and restoring that image. We have already seen how intimately the *imago Dei* is linked to VE's account of knowledge; and we have seen how important knowledge is to the Christian life. Therefore, it's no big secret that being saved is an important part of helping us instance virtues well and attain knowledge. But Christian understandings of salvation don't affirm that we are perfected when we get saved (e.g. justification and being born again). Rather, being brought out of the domain of darkness and into the kingdom of the beloved Son begins a process of sanctification where we grow in Christ-likeness.

This process of sanctification involves working towards attaining virtues, including intellectual virtues. Furthermore, although individuals are saved by God, they are saved into a community – the Church. There is a corporate dimension to the salvation of individual people. The Church is an important place where the social dimensions of virtue epistemology are played out by the people of God. One could go on about other connections between soteriology and VE, but I trust it's clear from the examples listed above that being saved is an important part of a robustly Christian approach to VE.

Conclusion

We have seen that VE has much to offer not only in the way of correcting contemporary epistemological discussions gone wrong, but also in pointing us towards a more fruitful path. I have argued that a theological approach to VE validates and clarifies some of its claims, and that traditionally accepted Christian doctrines make even more sense for the virtue epistemologist. A theological version of VE has numerous applications, especially when it comes to explaining the ethics of belief and how Christians (i.e. the 'saved') seek to cultivate intellectual virtues which are vital to achieving reflective knowledge. What I am calling for is more interdisciplinary discussion between theology and epistemology, and not merely for the sake of religious epistemology. For too long philosophers have ignored the fruits of rigorous theological reflection based on critical study of the Bible; philosophers rightly believe that philosophy can inform theology and/or biblical studies beneficially, but they are often mistaken in thinking that this is a one-way street. Theology has lots to offer philosophy, and if even some of what I've written here is true, then perhaps theology can and should inform epistemology in particular.

Of course, the same can be said of certain biblical theologians who operate oblivious to the findings of contemporary philosophy – analytic, continental, or otherwise – and this is undoubtedly a regretful and tragic situation. Regardless of whether someone identifies primarily as a theologian or a philosopher, Christians can and should rebuke the anti-intellectualism and closed-mindedness so rampant among segments of the Church. Additionally, VE allows us to see the value of pursuing not only knowledge, but also wisdom, understanding, and the very God upon whom these theological foundations rest. If we distinguish knowledge from wisdom while incorporating the theological doctrines discussed above, perhaps Christians will agree that 'wisdom unifies the knowledge of the wise person'.[41]

Notes

1 For the purposes of this chapter, I assume some approaches rather than defend them even though some of my views are not currently the most popular. Far too much has been written on belief formation, epistemological responsibility, and theories of epistemic responsibility to discuss in this chapter.

2 Jonathan L. Kvanvig, *The Intellectual Virtues and the Life of the Mind: On the Place of the Virtues in Contemporary Epistemology* (Savage, MD: Rowman & Littlefield, 1992), pp. 7–8. Kvanvig later (p. 141) offers a functional definition, noting that an intellectual virtue 'is roughly a disposition toward or ability to acquire justified beliefs'.

3 Linda Trainkaus Zagzebski, *Virtues of the Mind: An Inquiry into the Nature of Virtue and the Ethical Foundations of Knowledge* (New York: Cambridge University Press, 1996), p. 137.

4 Ernest Sosa, *Knowledge in Perspective* (New York: Cambridge University Press, 1991), p. 284. Consider the importance of the way that environment can help make room for proper functionalism and the noetic effects of sin, which I discuss later.

5 James A. Montmarquet, 'Epistemic Virtue', in Jonathan Dancy and Ernest Sosa (eds), *A Companion to Epistemology* (Cambridge, MA: Blackwell, 1992), pp. 116–18, at p. 116. The appeal to Aristotle is taken from the *Nicomachean Ethics*, Book VI, chapter I. Of course, Aristotle's position is not without its own problems. As Kvanvig notes: 'Aristotle's account of knowledge proceeds by discussing five faculties of the soul that express truth, *which are held to be infallible*.' Kvanvig, *The Intellectual Virtues*, p. 15, emphasis mine.

6 John Greco, 'Virtue Epistemology', in Jonathan Dancy and Ernest Sosa (eds), *A Companion to Epistemology* (Malden, MA: Wiley-Blackwell, 1992), pp. 520-2, at p. 520.

7 This summary of Sosa's positions, as outlined in his 'Knowledge and Intellectual Virtue' and his 'Intellectual Virtue in Perspective', is taken from John Greco, 'Virtues in Epistemology', in Paul K. Moser (ed.), *The Oxford Handbook of Epistemology* (New York: Oxford University Press, 2002), pp. 287-315, at p. 291.

8 Reliabilists include John Greco and Duncan Pritchard. Responsibilists include Lorraine Code, James Montmarquet and Linda Zagzebski. Ernest Sosa splits the horns of the dilemma by suggesting the reliabilism is true for animal knowledge, whereas responsibilism is true for reflective knowledge.

9 Sosa, *A Virtue Epistemology*, pp. 22-4.

10 Cf. John Greco, 'Virtue Epistemology', p. 520.

11 Robert C. Roberts and W. Jay Wood, 'Humility and Epistemic Goods', in Michael DePaul and Linda Zagzebski (eds), *Intellectual Virtue: Perspectives from Ethics and Epistemology* (New York: Oxford University Press, 2003), pp. 257-79, at p. 272.

12 Roberts and Wood, 'Humility and Epistemic Goods'. James Montmarquet agrees that courage counts as an intellectual virtue. See his 'Epistemic Virtue', *Mind* 96 (1987), pp. 482-97. Cf. Greco, 'Virtues in Epistemology', p. 293.

13 Robert Audi, 'The Causal Structure of Indirect Justification', *Journal of Philosophy* 80 (1983), pp. 398-415. Cf. Kvanvig, *The Intellectual Virtues*, p. 37. There exists a massive literature on the subject of evidence and epistemology. I make no effort to engage that literature here and insist on one and only one particular position on the matter, which may be a concern to some; but I maintain that the central thesis of this chapter holds regardless of whether one finds evidentialism or some other position more compelling.

14 Kvanvig, *The Intellectual Virtues*, p. 40.

15 'According to Greco's understanding of Zagzebski, all virtues are acquired traits of character that involve both a motivational component and reliable success component.' Additionally, Zagzebski notes four characteristics of intellectual virtues: 1) they are acquired traits; 2) people are responsible (at least in part) for their acquisition; 3) possessing and exercising these virtues rightly deserve moral praise; and 4) lacking/not exercising them rightly solicits moral blame. Cf. Greco, 'Virtues in Epistemology', p. 294.

16 Richard Foley, *The Theory of Epistemic Rationality* (Cambridge, MA: Harvard University Press), p. 66. Cf. Roberts and Wood, 'Humility and Epistemic Goods', p. 275.

17 Roberts and Wood, 'Humility and Epistemic Goods', pp. 275-76.

18 Modal ontological arguments seek to prove God's existence by explaining the greatness of the divine nature, specifically the necessary existence of a maximally great being.

19 Kvanvig, *The Intellectual Virtues*, p. 150.

20 Kvanvig, *The Intellectual Virtues*, pp. 156-7.

21 Kvanvig, *The Intellectual Virtues*, p. 168. But this approach, for Kvanvig, does not abandon the idea that knowledge is rightly defined as a justified true belief.

22 Kvanvig, *The Intellectual Virtues*, p. 169.

23 Cf. Millard J. Erickson, *Christian Theology*, 2nd edn (Grand Rapids, MI: Baker, 1998), p. 521.

24 Cf. Erickson, *Christian Theology*, pp. 525–6. I do not believe that these relational aspects of the *imago Dei* necessarily entail social Trinitarianism, although some would want to make that connection.

25 Kvanvig, *The Intellectual Virtues*, p. 170.

26 Cf. Erickson, *Christian Theology*, pp. 527–9. Alternative accounts of the *imago Dei* would also lend support. Cf. Joshua Farris, 'An Immaterial Substance View: *Imago Dei* and in Creation and Redemption', *Heythrop Journal* (2015), published online, DOI: 10.1111/heyj.12274.

27 For a lucid discussion of the issues in theological hermeneutics concerning interpretation of the relevant biblical passages about the image of God, see Daniel J. Treier, *Introducing Theological Interpretation of Scripture: Recovering a Christian Practice* (Grand Rapids, MI: Baker Academic, 2008). Treier uses the subject of the image of God as a running example throughout his book.

28 J. I Packer, 'Reflected Glory', *Christianity Today* 47, 12 (December 2003), p. 56.

29 Merold Westphal, 'Taking St Paul Seriously: Sin as an Epistemological Category', in *Christian Philosophy*, Notre Dame Studies in the Philosophy of Religion, No. 6, ed. Thomas P. Flint (South Bend, IN: University of Notre Dame Press, 1990), pp. 200–26, at p. 201. All bracketed insertions are Westphal's modifications of John Calvin's *Institutes of the Christian Religion*, trans. Henry Beveridge (London: James Clarke, 1957).

30 One might be inclined to think of lunatics and other mentally disabled persons as those manifesting the noetic effects of sin particularly sharply, even in regards to those areas that remain unaffected by the noetic effects of sin in the vast majority of people, religious or irreligious.

31 This model, which many attribute to Emil Brunner, means that the study of mathematics is largely unaffected by sin, but the humanities are more so, and theology especially so. Cf. Brunner, *Revelation and Reason: The Christian Doctrine of Faith and Knowledge* (London: SCM Press, 2012). Additionally, we can see how when someone uses a more technical discipline (which would be relatively unaffected) in a way to define their identity without God (such as Richard Dawkins using 'science' to deny the existence of God), the noetic effects of sin blind such a person to what is obvious to many outsiders.

32 Westphal, 'Taking St Paul Seriously', p. 205.

33 Westphal, 'Taking St Paul Seriously', p. 207.

34 Westphal, 'Taking St Paul Seriously', p. 201.

35 Westphal, 'Taking St Paul Seriously', p. 211. When discussing 'Reformed' epistemology, Westphal specifically references Plantinga and Wolterstorff in a footnote. Since the publication of Westphal's essay, Plantinga has expanded his epistemological model significantly, thereby offering a better accounting of the noetic effects of sin. Cf. Alvin Plantinga, *Warranted Christian Belief* (New York: Oxford University Press, 2000), especially chapter 7 entitled 'Sin and Its Cognitive Consequences', pp. 199–240, as well as pp. 280–2.

36 Westphal, 'Taking St Paul Seriously', p. 218.

37 William Clifford, 'The Ethics of Belief', in Michael Peterson, William Hasker, Bruce Reichenbach and David Basinger (eds), *Philosophy of Religion: Selected Readings*, 3rd edn (New York: Oxford University Press, 2007), pp. 104–9.

38 Not only was the evidence available for the ship owner to gain if he chose to seek it out, but he was in possession of the evidence when he understood what he was told by the experts who determined that the ship was not seaworthy.

39 Cf. Adam Green, *The Social Contexts of Intellectual Virtue: Knowledge as a Team Achievement*, Routledge Studies in Contemporary Philosophy (New York: Routledge, 2016).

40 As a Christian, I find the evidence for the existence of God extremely compelling. But in order to accommodate some of my claims to allow for how the same truths might apply equally against an irresponsible theist who maintains faith despite overwhelming evidence to the contrary, it's important to consider how such an individual's behaviour, even if virtuous in the sense of piety, does not accord with a robust Christian understanding of intellectual virtue.

41 Greco, 'Virtues in Epistemology', p. 298.

PART 3

The Process of Salvation

11

The Doctrine of Predestination and a Modified Hylomorphic Theory of Human Souls

ANDREW LOKE

Issues concerning divine predestination with respect to salvation have been debated among Christians for centuries. For example, theologians following the Synod of Dort (1618–19) have argued that God's predestination of events entails that the freedom of humans is significantly constrained, but others have objected that this account is incompatible with moral responsibility and the love of God as manifested by the extent of the atonement.[1]

Molinism, which proposes that God's decision to create was based on his Middle Knowledge of what a particular person would freely choose in a particular circumstance, offers an account of divine predestination which seeks to avoid the significant constraint on human freedom that beset Dort's account of divine predestination.[2] A Molinist would understand Divine predestination as follows: 'God actively bringing about certain events in the world, while for other events God places agents who are free in a libertarian sense in circumstances in which he knew they would freely and actively choose certain courses of actions, and God allows them to do that, thus bringing about these events in accordance with his plan.'

Proponents of Libertarian freedom affirm that a person is in some sense the 'first cause' of his/her free decisions and that he/she could have chosen otherwise. This is different from a compatibilist's understanding of free will, which affirms that a person's decision is ultimately determined by prior circumstances, given which he/she could not have chosen otherwise.[3]

The doctrine of Middle Knowledge was classically proposed by Luis de Molina (1535–1600), a Spanish Jesuit theologian and the author of the *Concordia liberi arbitrii cum gratiae donis* (1588). According to this doctrine, God knows what any particular person would freely do in any circumstance. As Molina explains, Middle Knowledge is that

> by which, in virtue of the most profound and inscrutable comprehension of each faculty of free choice, He saw in His own essence what each such

faculty would do with its innate freedom were it to be placed in this or in that or, indeed, in infinitely many orders of things – even though it would really be able, if it so willed, to do the opposite.[4]

This knowledge is 'middle' in the sense that it is conceptually between God's Natural Knowledge (i.e. knowledge of all possibilities, including what any free creature *could* do in any set of circumstances) and God's Free Knowledge (God's knowledge of what are in fact true states of affairs in the actual world). According to Molina, God freely decreed to actualize a world known by him to be realizable on the basis of his Middle Knowledge.

With regards to a person's response to God, the Middle Knowledge account would hold that God's enabling grace is a necessary, but not a sufficient condition. As Molina puts it:

The assistance through which we are helped by God toward justification is not efficacious intrinsically and by its nature; rather, its being efficacious depends on the free consent of the faculty of choice, a consent that the will is able not to give despite that assistance – indeed, when it consents, it is able to dissent.[5]

Hence, in Molina's account, a limited libertarian human freedom is included within God's providential will (this freedom is limited, because there are many other events, such as the time and place at which an individual is born, which are beyond the ability of an individual to freely decide). On this Middle Knowledge understanding, it is not the case that 'God actively brings about everything that happens in the world'. Rather, some events are not actively brought about by God, but by free agents, and God allows them to make the choices and carry out their free actions. By virtue of placing free agents in circumstances in accordance with his Middle Knowledge of how they would freely act, God is able to guarantee that events come to pass in accordance with his providential will.

This does not imply that all the events actualized are exactly what God desires. On the Middle Knowledge account, there may well be many aspects of this world (the world God has chosen to actualize) – such as morally evil free actions – that are undesirable by-products of the world which God regarded was the best overall creative option, a world which contains creatures who are free in a libertarian sense. The counterfactuals of freedom of which the God of Middle Knowledge was aware prior to creation and utilized in creating the actual world of God's choice are not themselves in any way subject to divine control. God simply knew what humans would do (and not do) if granted freedom in a given context. What this means is that God's ability to create a world that contains what he would have it contain is restricted by the true counterfactuals that are available.[6] Nevertheless, proponents of Middle Knowledge account would say that the granting of freedom to humans is in accordance with God's providential will. God is still in sovereign control in the sense that he could have freely chosen not to create creatures with such freedom.[7]

The Middle Knowledge view offers a possible account of how Libertarian free will is compatible with those scriptural passages that apparently indicate that God predestined that certain people would reject Jesus, including one of the Twelve whom Jesus predicted would betray him. For according to this account, God has Middle Knowledge such that he knows how each person would respond in any circumstance before they were even created. Furthermore, God is the one who determined the time and place where each person would live (Acts 17.26). From these considerations, the Middle Knowledge account would propose that God placed a person whom he knew would freely determine to reject Jesus to be born in first-century Palestine and that this person would eventually be one of the Twelve; that is, Judas Iscariot. On the Middle Knowledge account, Judas cannot complain that his rejection of Jesus was determined by God, for his rejection of Jesus was freely determined by himself.[8]

It is beyond the scope of the present chapter to provide a comprehensive assessment of the contemporary debate concerning the Middle Knowledge account.[9] I have previously argued in another article that the Middle Knowledge account is consistent with what the Scriptures say concerning human depravity, divine sovereignty, omnipotence, freedom, election, love and grace, and that this account is to be preferred to the one endorsed by the Synod of Dort, which is inconsistent with the love of God as manifested by the extent of the atonement.[10] In this chapter I shall focus on addressing the following question for the Middle Knowledge account: What explains the counterfactuals of freedom which are not subjected to divine control? To pose the question more concretely: Why is it the case that Judas was someone who would freely choose to reject Jesus? On the other hand, if one rejects the postulation that the counterfactuals of freedom are not subjected to divine control or to other controls, might one say that God created Judas this way, or that his parents procreated him this way? If either of these were true, could Judas justifiably shift the blame back to his parents or to God?

The Origin of Human Persons

The above questions are related to issues concerning the origin of human persons. In the Early Church there were three competing views concerning the generation of human persons after Adam and Eve: Traducianism, Creationism and Pre-existence. All of these views are based on the assumption of substance dualism which – contrary to physical reductionism – affirms that humans have immaterial souls which cannot be reduced to their material bodies. Substance dualism arguably offers a more compelling account of what grounds personal identity across time compared to alternative accounts, and its current lack of popularity among philosophers is explicable by a materialistic prejudice[11] which is insufficiently motivated.[12] New Testament scholar Craig Keener observes that most Jews during biblical times accepted this distinction between soul and body, and that the soul remained immortal after death.[13] This dualism is also implied by biblical texts which indicate the possibility of human existence outside the body (e.g. 2 Cor. 12.2), and fits with a coherent understanding of the Incarnation.[14]

Concerning the distinctions between Traducianism, Creationism and Pre-existence, on Traducianism human souls are propagated from parents to children, while on Creationism these are directly created by God. Pre-existence is the doctrine that God has a 'stock of souls from eternity and allocates them as needed'.[15] Oliver Crisp observes that Pre-existence is widely regarded as unorthodox, while theologians have been divided on Traducianism and Creationism and some, like Augustine, were unable to decide which view of this matter is the correct one.[16]

One of the arguments which have been offered for Traducianism is that it offers a basis for how the corruption of human nature could be passed down from Adam to his descendants, in accordance with a certain interpretation of the theory of Original Sin. Another argument for Traducianism is based on the interpretation of scriptural passages such as Genesis 25.23, according to which nations that descended from Esau and Jacob are described as within their ancestors, and Hebrews 7.10 which states that Levi was within the loins of his ancestor Abraham before he was born. Nevertheless, a Christian who accepts Traducianism on the basis of the above-mentioned arguments might wonder how God could have determined the time and place where each person would live, including creating Judas and placing him in first-century Palestine, if it were the case that the soul of each person is passed down from parents to children.

In what follows, I shall offer a solution to the question concerning why it is the case that Judas was someone who would freely choose to reject Jesus. Subsequently, I shall show that a modified hylomorphic theory of the origin of human souls can offer a promising way of demonstrating the compatibility between Molinism and Traducianism and resolving the centuries-old debate between Traducianism and Creationism.

A Modified Hylomorphic Theory of the Origin of Human Souls

The Molinist can begin his/her reply to the first question by postulating agent-causal theory. Randolph Clarke and Justin Capes explain that on agent-causal theory, a free decision (or some event internal to such a decision) is caused by the agent; and it must not be the case that either what the agent causes or the agent's causing that event is causally determined by prior events. Thus an agent is in a strict and literal sense an originator of her free decisions. This combination of *indeterminism by prior events and cause* (origination) is thought to capture best the idea that, when we act freely, a plurality of alternatives is open to us and *we determine*, ourselves, which of these we pursue. In response to the objection that the explanatory role of reasons seems to be excluded, Clarke and Capes suggest an account in which a free action is caused by the agent *and* non-deterministically caused by agent's recognizing certain reasons for which she acts.[17]

The Molinist can then add that the counterfactuals of freedom involving Judas is an essential property of Judas' personhood as a free agent, just as having four angles is an essential property of a square. Just as there are different shapes (squares, triangles, circles etc.), likewise there are different persons (Judas, Peter, John etc.), each of whom is unique. What Judas would freely choose is an essential and unique property of his personhood, and is different from what Peter would freely choose. In the case of shapes, if a shape does not have four angles, then it is not a square. It would be false to say that God made it this way, for it is necessarily so. Rather, what one should say is that, if God chooses to create a square-shaped object, then there would be four angles. Likewise, the Molinist can say that, if a person does not freely reject Jesus given the circumstances Judas had, then that person would not be Judas.[18] Given this account, it would be false to say that God made Judas this way. Rather, what one should say is that, if God chooses to create Judas, then there would be someone who would freely choose to reject Jesus given the circumstances Judas had. Thus God would not be the one who caused Judas to reject Jesus. Rather, given that Judas possessed libertarian freedom in accordance with agent-causal theory, Judas would be the 'first cause' of his choice to reject Jesus, and he would be responsible for his choice.

As for the compatibility between Molinism and Traducianism, I shall now explain how a modified hylomorphic theory of the origin of human souls can provide a way to demonstrate their compatibility. It should be noted that the modified hylomorphic theory defended here is different from the hylomorphist account of the origin of the soul proposed by Odo of Tournai (d. AD 1113).[19] Odo's view is based on the Aristotelian hylomorphic view, according to which forms are universals and ordinary physical matter is the only stuff of which individuals are made. By contrast, the modified hylomorphic theory offered here applies to immaterial souls rather than physical matter.

In a previous article,[20] I argue that a modified hylomorphic theory developed from the writings of Richard Swinburne provides an illuminating account of how a paradox against concrete-composite Christology can be solved, and how a person can gain (or lose) parts over time but remain numerically identical. Basically, my account proposes that the Second Person of the Trinity (the Son) and his concrete-divine nature and are different things pre-incarnation. One would ask, 'But how can they be different things?' An analogy from material coinciding objects would help us see how this can be the case. The typical case is that of a lump of clay and a statue (e.g. David) which the sculptor sculpts the clay into. As Wasserman explains, pursuing the familiar Aristotelian idea that material objects are compounds of matter and form – where forms are conceived of as abstract entities of some sort (e.g. 'guiding principles' or 'universal properties') – one could say that David and Lump differ because David, but not Lump, has the form Statue as a non-material part. Thus, material coinciding objects can share all of their proper material parts but differ in some non-material aspect.[21]

Of course, the Son and the divine nature are not material objects. Nevertheless, one can postulate an analogous account for immaterial entities similar to the hylomorphic theory described in Richard Swinburne's *The Christian God*. As Swinburne explains: 'On this theory, individuals are the individuals they are in virtue of the stuff (*hyle*) of which they are made, and the form or nature or essence (*morphe*) imposed upon it.'[22] Swinburne notes that on an Aristotelian view, forms are universals and ordinary physical matter is the only stuff of which individuals which have this-ness are made; but Swinburne suggests that the hylomorphic theory can be applied to an immaterial individual by understanding it in a more liberal way than the normal Aristotelian way. Thus, one can postulate a different kind of stuff from physical matter (call this different kind of stuff 'soul-stuff') or a different kind of form from universals, such as individual essences ('Maybe there is an essence not just of humanity or being a philosopher, but of Socrates').[23] Therefore, it can be postulated that the ultimate reality of a being which does individuate is a particular restriction on the specific form, and that restriction is the 'individual essence'. It is the union of the individual essence with stuff that brings into being particular individuals. In the case of Socrates, the essence of Socrates is a particular restriction on the form of humanity – it is a particular way of being human – and its union with stuff gives rise to Socrates. Granting the possibility that the human soul can exist apart from the body, that existence would consist in the instantiation of the form in immaterial soul-stuff.[24]

Swinburne eventually concludes that it would be better to say that the hylomorphic theory does not apply to souls, for the reason that: 'A hylemorphic [i.e. hylomorphic] theory has its natural application to inanimate material objects . . . If we extend it to souls we have to postulate a soul-stuff, whose existence we have no reason to postulate other than to preserve the hylemorphic theory.'[25]

However, in a previous article,[26] I argue that there is an independent reason for postulating the existence of soul-stuff and extending the modified hylomorphic theory to immaterial entities, namely that it provides a helpful account of not only how a paradox against a concrete-composite Christology can be solved, but also in general how persons can increase (or decrease) in size over time but remain numerically identical. By proposing that the immaterial 'individual essence of the Son' is what grounds the identity of the person pre- and post-Incarnation, the modified hylomorphic account affirms that a person (the instantiated 'form') can grow bigger or smaller by acquiring or losing parts (e.g. by acquiring a human nature at the Incarnation), but remain numerically the same person because the immaterial individual essence (a particular 'restriction' of the instantiated 'form') endures through time.

Here, I shall provide another independent reason for extending the modified hylomorphic theory to immaterial entities, namely that the hylomorphic account provides a solution to the difficult issues concerning the origin of human persons.

As explained earlier, the modified hylomorphic theory applies to an immaterial individual by postulating a different kind of stuff from physical matter (call it 'soul-stuff') and a different kind of form from universals, such as individual essences. It postulates that the ultimate reality of a being which does individuate is a particular restriction on the specific form, and that restriction is the 'individual essence'. It is the union of the individual essence with soul-stuff that brings into being particular individuals.

This modified hylomorphic theory of human souls can be developed to formulate a view concerning the origination of human souls, according to which soul-stuffs are passed down from parents to children, while the particular restrictions on the form of soul-stuffs are created by God to bring into existence particular individuals. Crisp observes that a possible mechanism for how human souls are propagated from parents to children is that individual souls are generated when their soul-stuff split off from the soul of the parents,[27] and on the assumption that ensoulment begins at conception, it could be that human gametes are 'carriers' of soul-stuff as well as DNA, which, when syngamy takes place, generates a new immaterial, as well as material, substance.[28] I shall illustrate the modified hylomorphic theory concerning the origin of human souls using the analogies of shapes for persons and the waters of a river for the soul-stuffs passing down from parents to children.

Just as there are different shapes such as squares, triangles and circles, likewise there are different persons such as Judas, Peter and John. If we think of each unique 'person' to be a unique 'shape' of a soul as a result of a particular restriction on the form of soul-stuffs, and soul-stuffs as the water of a river flowing down from parents to children in accordance with

Traducianism, the Molinist can say that, as the gametes of the human parents meet, God causes the water that split off from the river to take a particular shape. In this way, different persons are directly created by God in accordance with Creationism, and God could have determined the time and place where each person would live. On the other hand, the soul-stuffs which constitute the descendants (as well as the corruption of human nature, in accordance with a certain interpretation of the theory of Original Sin) are passed down from ancestors to their descendants in accordance with Traducianism. In this way, the Traducianist and the Creationist accounts can be combined, and the merits of both can be retained.

Conclusion

The Middle Knowledge account of divine predestination seeks to avoid the significant constrain on human freedom which besets Dort's account, but faces the problem of providing an explanation for the counterfactuals of human freedom which are not subjected to divine control. I propose that the counterfactuals of freedom are an essential property of an individual's personhood. Utilizing a modified hylomorphic theory of human souls, I further propose that, while soul-stuffs are passed down from parents to children in accordance with Traducianism, the particular restrictions on the form of soul-stuffs are created by God so as to bring into existence particular individuals. This proposal provides a metaphysical explanation for the counterfactuals of human freedom and resolves the centuries-old debate between Traducianism and Creationism.

Notes

1 See, for example, the discussions in James Beilby and Paul R. Eddy (eds), *Divine Foreknowledge: Four Views* (Downers Grove, IL: InterVarsity Press, 2001); Andrew Loke, 'Is the saving grace of God resistible?', *European Journal of Theology* 22 (2013), pp. 28–37.

2 For an explication of Molina's ideas, see Alfred Freddoso, *Luis De Molina, On Divine Foreknowledge: Part IV of the Concordia* (Ithaca, NY: Cornell University Press, 1988); Thomas Flint, *Divine Providence: The Molinist Account* (Ithaca, NY: Cornell University Press, 1998).

3 See Randolph Clarke and Justin Capes, 'Incompatibilist (Nondeterministic) Theories of Free Will', *The Stanford Encyclopedia of Philosophy* (Spring 2013 Edition), Edward N. Zalta (ed.), URL = <http://plato.stanford.edu/archives/spr2013/entries/incompatibilism-theories/>.

4 Freddoso, *Luis De Molina, On Divine Foreknowledge*, Qu. 14, Art. 13, Disp. 52, No. 9.

5 Freddoso, *Luis De Molina*, Qu. 14, Art. 13, Disp. 53, Part 2, No. 30.

6 This point was highlighted by a referee in Andrew Loke, 'On the doing-allowing distinction and the problem of evil: a reply to Daniel Lim', *International Journal for Philosophy of Religion* (2017). DOI:10.1007/s11153-017-9614-5.

7 See further, Loke, 'Is the saving grace of God resistible?'.

8 For how Molinism resolves this and other scriptural difficulties, see Loke, 'Is the saving grace of God resistible?'.

9 For a survey of the contemporary debate, see Ken Perszyk (ed.), *Molinism: The Contemporary Debate* (Oxford: Oxford University Press, 2011).

10 Loke, 'Is the saving grace of God resistible?'.

11 C. Stephen Evans 'The self-emptying of love: some thoughts on kenotic Christology', in S. T. Davis, D. Kendall and G. O'Collins (eds), *The Incarnation: An Interdisciplinary Symposium on the Incarnation of the Son of God* (New York: Oxford University Press, 2002), pp. 267–71.

12 George Bealer and Robert Koons (eds), *The Waning of Materialism* (Oxford: Oxford University Press, 2010), pp. xviii–xix. See further Joshua Farris, *The Soul of Theological Anthropology: A Cartesian Exploration* (London: Routledge, 2017).

13 Craig Keener, *The Gospel of John: A Commentary* (Peabody, MA: Hendrickson, 2003), pp. 538, 553–54.

14 Andrew Loke, *A Kryptic Model of the Incarnation* (London: Routledge, 2014).

15 Lynne Rudder Baker, 'Death and the Afterlife', in William J. Wainwright (ed.), *The Oxford Handbook of Philosophy of Religion* (Oxford: Oxford University Press, 2005), p. 370.

16 Oliver Crisp, 'Pulling Traducianism out of the Shedd', *Ars Disputandi* 6 (2006) ISSN 1566–5399.

17 See Clarke and Capes, 'Incompatibilist (Nondeterministic) Theories of Free Will'.

18 Following Saul Kripke, 'Judas' is used here as a rigid designator. See Joseph LaPorte, 'Rigid Designators', *The Stanford Encyclopedia of Philosophy* (Summer 2011 Edition), Edward N. Zalta (ed.), <http://plato.stanford.edu/archives/sum2011/entries/rigid-designators/>.

19 Odo of Tournai, *On Original Sin and A Disputation with the Jew, Leo, Concerning The Advent of Christ, the Son of God, Two Theological Treatises*, trans. Irven M. Resnick (Philadelphia, PA: University of Pennsylvania Press, 1994).

20 Andrew Loke, 'Solving a paradox against concrete-composite Christology: a modified hylomorphic proposal', *Religious Studies* 47 (2011), pp. 493–502.

21 This is discussed in Ryan Wasserman 'Material constitution', in E. Zalta (ed.), *The Stanford Encyclopedia of Philosophy* (Spring 2009 edn), available at <http://plato.stanford.edu/archives/spr2009/entries/material-constitution/>. Wasserman's worry concerning this view is that it gives up the popular idea that things like statues and lumps of clay are wholly material objects. However, this worry is not applicable for immaterial entities like divine nature and divine person, and it is not applicable to a substance dualist view of Christ (see below).

22 Richard Swinburne, *The Christian God* (Oxford: Clarendon Press, 1994), p. 46.

23 Swinburne, *The Christian God*, pp. 46–7. Individual essence is also called haecceity, a term introduced by Duns Scotus for that in virtue of which an individual is the individual that it is: its individuating essence making it this object or person. See Simon Blackburn, 'Haecceity', in *The Oxford Dictionary of Philosophy* (Oxford: Oxford University Press, 2008).

24 Swinburne, *The Christian God*, pp. 47–9. Swinburne attributes the view on the ultimate reality of being to Duns Scotus, although he observes that it is disputable that Scotus held a hylomorphic theory. It should also be noted that Swinburne's idea of instantiation of the form in immaterial soul-stuff assumes substance dualism, but certain versions of hylomorphic theory deny this and affirm that the form just is the soul. There is disagreement among scholars concerning whether Aristotle affirmed or denied substance dualism; see the discussion and literature cited in Howard Robinson 'Dualism', in E. Zalta (ed.), *The Stanford Encyclopedia of Philosophy* (Fall 2009 edn), available at: <http://plato.stanford.edu/archives/fall2009/entries/dualism/>.

25 Swinburne, *The Christian God*, p. 50.

26 Loke, 'Solving a paradox against concrete-composite Christology'.

27 Loke, 'Solving a paradox against concrete-composite Christology'. Crisp observes that a similar view is given by Tertullian, citing Tertullian, *On The Soul*, section 25 in A. Roberts and J. Donaldson (eds), *Latin Christianity: Its Founder, Tertullian, Ante-Nicene Fathers Vol. III*, trans. P. Holmes (Grand Rapids, MI: Eerdmans, 1981 [1885]).

28 See J. P. Moreland and Scott B. Rae, *Body and Soul: Human Nature and the Crisis in Ethics* (Downers Grove, IL: IVP, 2000), p. 221.

12

The Priority of Justification to Sanctification

JOHN V. FESKO

Justification *sola fide* is one of the hallmark doctrines of the Protestant Reformation. In contrast to Roman Catholic doctrine codified at the Council of Trent, the Reformers highlighted that justification is by grace alone through faith alone in Christ alone.[1] A comparison of Roman Catholic views with Reformed confessions, such as the Gallican (1559), Belgic (1563) or Second Helvetic (1566), reveal differences between the two positions.[2] The Council of Trent does not distinguish between justification and sanctification. Believers receive their initial justification in baptism and then by faith working through love seek their final justification at the consummation.[3] Protestant theologians, on the other hand, distinguish between justification and sanctification and characterize justification as a complete, irreversible, once-for-all event.[4] The Westminster Shorter Catechism, for example, defines justification as 'an act of God's free grace', whereas sanctification is a 'work of God's free grace'.[5] The distinction between an *act* and a *work* is an important one. An act is once-for-all and forensic, whereas a work is transformative. In many common early modern treatments of union with Christ, theologians typically treat justification as the first and sanctification as the second of the twofold benefits of union with Christ.

In recent years Evangelical theologians have been less interested in maintaining the priority of justification to sanctification. The thesis of this chapter is that a biblical understanding requires the prioritization of justification to sanctification. To say that justification takes priority to sanctification does not sideline the doctrine of union with Christ. In line with classic Reformation formulations, justification and sanctification are the *duplex gratia*, which come through union with Christ. To prioritize justification also does not mean that justification is the efficient cause of sanctification but is rather the necessary or sufficient cause. In other words, to prioritize justification to sanctification means that the believer's justification is the necessary judicial prerequisite that creates the legal context for his sanctification; justification is the determining condition for sanctification. The demands of the law stand as a twofold obstacle to the sinner's access to the eschatological work of the Spirit: the law demands fulfilment as well as satisfaction for its transgression. Since the Fall, human beings cannot meet either requirement, and thus, only Christ can. Not even redeemed sinners can fulfil the law's demands by their Spirit-wrought good works. This does not mean that justification therefore has a temporal priority to sanctification. Except for the temporally distinct benefits of election and glorification, the Spirit communicates the whole Christ through union with him (effectual calling, faith, justification, adoption and sanctification). Justification takes a relational priority to sanctification.[6] By *relational*, I mean the doctrinal relationships between the different benefits of union with Christ. For example, one cannot discuss faith prior to effectual calling because effectual calling is the necessary prerequisite; a person cannot exercise faith apart from the effectual regenerative call of the Spirit (John 3.3). Likewise, one cannot speak of justification unless he first presupposes faith, the instrumental cause of justification (Rom. 3.21–22). So one cannot posit sanctification unless he first presupposes the sinner's justification. In the language of older formulations, justification precedes sanctification in the *ordo naturae* ('order of nature'), or more familiarly, in the *ordo salutis* ('order of salvation'), or the golden chain.[7]

In order to prove this thesis, the chapter first examines a representative claim from an Evangelical theologian who eliminates justification's priority to sanctification, Marcus Johnson.[8] Second, the chapter surveys the role of the law in soteriology in order to establish the necessary exegetical footing for recognizing the priority of justification to sanctification. This section surveys four key texts: 1 Corinthians 15.56, Acts 13.39, Romans 6.7 and Romans 8.10. Third, the chapter then explores the two corollaries of recognizing justification's priority: preserving the work of Christ as the sole material cause of justification and guarding the irreversibility of justification.

To recognize that justification takes priority to sanctification does not privilege one benefit of union with Christ over another, as if justification is more important. Rather, exploring the order that exists between these two benefits is an exercise in understanding the apostle Paul's profound statement: 'And to the one who does not work but believes in him who *justifies the ungodly*, his faith is counted as righteousness' (Rom. 4.5). In other words, comprehending the natural, or relational, order between justification and sanctification preserves the fact that God does not justify the godly. As important and necessary as sanctification is for a complete soteriology, God does not take it into account in our justification. Or, in the words of the Westminster Larger Catechism, God accepts as righteous and pardons a person's sin 'not for anything wrought in them, or done by them, but only for the perfect obedience and full satisfaction of Christ, by God imputed to them, and received by faith alone'.[9]

Union with Christ as Central

Marcus Johnson claims the doctrine of union with Christ is a panacea for all that ails evangelical misunderstandings of biblical soteriology. Johnson employs the term *union with Christ* to encompass all of the varied terms and images in the Pauline and Johannine writings that refer to the believer's oneness with Christ.[10] Johnson believes that the doctrine of union with Christ has been largely ignored because participatory categories supposedly have a secondary role in many evangelical doctrines of salvation.[11] In his analysis, Johnson finds that evangelical theologians place heavy emphasis on legal categories because of the importance assigned to penal substitution and forensic justification. Johnson believes these are necessary doctrinal categories but that union with Christ is not merely legal. Some supposedly present the legal union as the basis for any subsequent (personal, real or intimate) relation to him.[12] Johnson objects to the two viewpoints that dominate Reformed theology, namely federalism and realism, and instead promotes his own *Christological realism*. The believer shares a vital, organic and personal union with Christ, which transcends mere federal or realistic categories.[13]

Johnson contends that, by virtue of the believer's union with Christ, he shares in the legal and transformative blessings of redemption, both justification and sanctification. Justification brings the forgiveness of sins and Christ's imputed righteousness and sanctification brings the newness and holiness of life. The two benefits are inseparable but nevertheless distinct because the believer receives both through his union with Christ.[14] In one sense, Johnson's formulation sounds traditional and echoes John Calvin's (1509–64) *duplex gratia*.[15] But at several points he makes a few statements that reveal his formulation's distinct features. He defines justification as 'that benefit of our union with Christ, in his life, death, and resurrection, in which God declares us to be righteous through the forgiveness of our sins and the imputation of Christ's righteousness'.[16] Because justification finds its fount in the believer's union with Christ, Johnson believes that this union 'provides the basis for our justification'. Johnson writes: 'The definition above purposely prioritizes union with Christ to indicate that it is the basis upon which God justifies us.'[17] While Johnson rests justification in the imputed righteousness of Christ, he blurs the lines when he states that union with Christ is its basis. This is deliberate, not a slip of the pen: 'In justifying us, God does in fact take into account the presence of the indwelling Christ.'[18] Hence, given the foundational relationship between union with Christ and justification, union must take causal priority and precede justification.[19] Union with Christ negates any claim that justification takes priority to sanctification because God cannot justify a person without factoring the indwelling presence of Christ. The believer's transformation lies at the basis of his justification.

Johnson believes that one of the reasons why theologians erroneously prioritize justification to sanctification is that they affirm the concept of the order of salvation (*ordo salutis*). Johnson believes that the *ordo* is a useful way to differentiate the variegated blessings of union with Christ. Sanctification, for example, is not the cause of justification or adoption. It also helps distinguish between logical and temporal priority among the benefits of union with Christ. Faith logically precedes adoption, not temporally, whereas election precedes justification logically and temporally. But at the same time, Johnson warns that the *ordo* is unhelpful if conceived in a linear fashion in which the application of Christ's benefits proceeds as a logical or causal sequence of events. In so doing, we risk losing sight of Christ in the effort to understand the variegated blessings of redemption. The blessings of redemption lose their foundation in Christ and become abstract benefits.[20]

On the whole, Johnson attempts to maintain the doctrine of union with Christ in concert with the twofold grace of justification and sanctification, and he states that these two benefits are inseparable yet distinct. But at the same time, a fog settles over his otherwise clear statements when he claims that God takes the indwelling presence of Christ into account in the believer's justification. Historically, the material cause of justification is an *iustitia aliena* and is *extra nos* because it is Christ's righteousness and not our own.[21] We lay hold of this righteousness by faith alone, but even then, faith is an instrumental, not material, cause of justification. A contributing factor to Johnson's confusing formulation is his unfamiliarity with classic uses of cause and effect language. He also does not demonstrate understanding of historic formulations and uses of the *ordo salutis* or the *ordo naturae* to explain the relationship between justification and sanctification. As much as Johnson relies on Calvin for his own formulation, he never asks or explains why Calvin denominates justification as the first and sanctification as the second benefit of the *duplex gratia*.[22] Once he removes justification's priority to sanctification, he leaves the doctrine of justification vulnerable because he inadequately explains how he preserves the *sola* in *sola fide*. Again, in Pauline terms, if God takes the indwelling presence of Christ into account, then in what sense does he justify the *ungodly*? Justification is no longer *sola fide* but by faith and the indwelling presence of Christ.

The Role of the Law

Far from an imposition upon the text, the relational priority of justification to sanctification organically grows from numerous points in the

Scriptures. But in this particular case, this section investigates four key biblical texts that establish the relationship between justification and sanctification: 1 Corinthians 15.56, Acts 13.39, Romans 6.7 and Romans 8.10. The first three texts deal with the sinner's relationship to the law and the power of sin. The last text deals with the relationship between righteousness and life.

The Power of Sin (1 Cor. 15.56)

First Corinthians 15.56 is a seldom-factored verse in the effort to establish the relational priority of justification to sanctification: 'The sting of death is sin, and the power of sin is the law.'[23] This verse has relevance for the question of the priority of justification to sanctification because, as long as sin has dominion over a person, the subjective ontological changes included in one's sanctification cannot take place. In this tiny compact statement Paul connects death, sin and law, but understanding how the connection works is all-important. A number of passages of Scripture address the connection between sin and death, whether in God's initial warning to Adam in the garden: 'In the day that you eat of it you will surely die' (Gen. 2.17), or Paul's pithy but nevertheless powerful statement 'For the wages of sin is death' (Rom. 6.23). Sin arms death with the power of destruction, that which corrodes and extinguishes life. Apart from sin, death has no claim upon a person. Those indwelled by the Holy Spirit and united to Christ are 'dead to sin and alive to God' (Rom. 6.11).[24] Sin and death stand opposed to righteousness and life under the respective representative actions of Adam and Christ (Rom. 5.12–21; 1 Cor. 15.20–28, 45–49). But if death receives its power from sin, whence arises the power of sin?

Paul reveals that the power of sin is the law, but in what way does the law empower sin? How can God's 'good' law be the animating force behind sin (Rom. 7.12)? As Paul writes in his epistle to Rome, apart from the law sin lies dead: 'If it had not been for the law, I would not have known sin. For I would not have known what it is to covet if the law had not said, "You shall not covet." . . . For apart from the law, sin lies dead' (Rom. 7.7–8). In this respect, 'through the law comes knowledge of sin' (Rom. 3.20).[25] This means, 'where there is no law there is no transgression' (Rom. 4.15). If there is no standard to which people must conform, then there can be no want of conformity to it. And if there is no law, there is no attending condemnation for its violation. 'Sin is not counted where there is no law' (Rom. 5.13).[26] The law arms sin with its death-producing power. As long as Christians live under the aegis of the law, they lie under the power of sin. Thus, the law demands satisfaction, apart from which sinners remain trapped and barred from eschatological life. No moral or transformative changes can occur unless something satisfies the law's demands (Rom. 7.4–6). The law, therefore, is an obstacle to the believer's sanctification.[27]

Justified from Sin (Acts 13.39; Rom. 6.7)

The second of four key texts appears in the book of Acts where Luke narrates one of Paul's addresses where he states: 'And by him everyone who believes is justified from everything from which you could not be justified by the law of Moses' (Acts 13.39, trans. mine). Some English translations render Paul's term *dikaiothenai* (aor. pass. inf.) and *dikaioutai* (3s pres. mid. indic.) not as *justified* but as *freed* (so NIV, NAS, for example), whereas others opt for *justified* (so KJV, NLT). To choose *freed* versus *justified* still captures a sense of Paul's statement but *justified* is the preferable translation. The term *justified* leaves intact the legal-forensic significance of Paul's term *dikaiow*, which the term *freed* otherwise partially obscures. Paul calls his audience to repent and seek the forgiveness of their sins through Christ, which he highlights by means of the preposition *dia* with the genitive, *dia toutou* – the means by which something is accomplished. Jesus provides what the law of Moses cannot, namely justification, or the declaration that a person stands righteous vis-à-vis the law. Faith in Jesus provides justification. In this particular case, when God justifies a person he frees him from the claims of the law, hence some translations render the term as *freed*.[28] Nevertheless, the divine declaration releases a sinner from the law's claims, which are otherwise an impediment to his salvation.[29]

There is a similar use of the term *dikaiow* in Romans 6.7, where Paul writes: 'For the one who has died has been justified from sin' (trans. mine).[30] In this case most translations select *freed* (NIV, NLT, ESV, NAS, KJV) instead of *justified* (ASV, RSV). But the latter translation is the preferred choice. The opening *gar* ('for') explains the connection between Christ's death and the believer's justification. 'For the one who has died [with Christ, v. 6] has been justified from sin' (trans. mine). Christ's death is the means by which God justifies the sinner and frees him from the law's claims.[31] 'To be justified from sin' means that justification delivers a believer from sin's dominion, and this is a twofold freedom: (1) judicial, from its penalty and (2) subjective, from its power (cf. Gal. 2.19–20; 6.14; Col. 2.13; 3.3; 1 Pet. 4.1).[32] Some argue that this reading does not fit because Paul does not elsewhere connect the believer's death with his justification. Thus, Paul instead states that 'justified from sin', means 'set free from the power of sin'.[33] Yet such an objection fails to consider several points.

Paul connects death and sin in 1 Corinthians 15.56: 'The sting of death is sin, and the power of sin is the law.' The apostle identifies the connections between death, sin and the law, and only justification neutralizes the law's claims, and correlatively, only Christ's work constitutes the foundation of the sinner's justified status. Second, within the framework of the death-sin-law nexus Paul addresses the justification-death connection in his statement from Acts 13.39: 'And by him everyone who believes is justified from everything from which you could not be justified by the law of Moses.'[34] In other words, the law no longer condemns a person because Christ has met the law's demands. Paul states that justification is the remedy to both the *law* and *sin*. The sinner's justification frees him from the legal claims of the law, which are due to his sin.[35] Charles Hodge (1797–1878) explains this connection in the following manner:

> *For* he who has died (with Christ) is justified, and therefore free from sin, free from its dominion. This is the great evangelical truth that underlies the apostle's whole doctrine of sanctification. The natural reason assumes that acceptance with a holy and just God must be founded on character, that men must be holy in order to be justified. The gospel reverses this, and teaches that God accepts the ungodly; that we must be justified in order to become holy.[36]

In terms of courtroom imagery, when the judge delivers the verdict of 'not guilty', the bailiff walks over and removes the prisoner's shackles, which means he is a free man. Similarly, when God pronounces the verdict of justification over the condemned sinner, the verdict frees him from the legal demands of the law – its condemnation.[37] Freedom from condemnation and the law's demands thus opens the way for the sanctifying work of the Spirit.

Paul addresses similar points in the opening verses of Romans 7 when he explains that the law holds a person in its grip as long as he lives (Rom. 7.1). But believers 'have died to the law through the body of Christ' (Rom. 7.4). This death to the law occurs through the objective work of Christ by which 'we are released from the law' (*katergethemen apo tou nomou*) (Rom. 7.6). What releases sinners from the claims of the law and the power of sin? Their justification by faith in Christ (Rom. 6.7; Acts 13.39). But to what end does God free them from the law? 'You also have died to the law through the body of Christ . . . in order that [*hina*] we may bear fruit for God' (Rom. 7.4). 'We are released from the law . . . so that [*hoste*] we serve in the new way of the Spirit and not in the old way of the written code' (Rom. 7.6). Paul's overall intention is that the believer's sanctification is the necessary consequence of his justification, and conversely that justification (the means by which he dies to the law) is the necessary prerequisite of his sanctification. In other words, we are sanctified because we are justified, but we are not justified because we are sanctified.[38]

Some might object on the grounds that justification ceases to be a forensic declaration and becomes generative of sanctification.[39] But such an objection misses the point that Paul deals with the believer's legal state, not his subjective transformation. And in this case, justification entails two things: (1) possession of the requisite obedience that the law demands, and (2) absolution from the guilt of the law's violation.[40] Freedom from the law's demands opens the gates to the renovative subjective changes that occur through the Spirit's work of sanctification. Justification does not produce these changes but rather creates the context for transformation.[41] Paul, therefore, invokes this statement: 'For the one who has died has been justified from sin', to refute his critics. Justification does not bring antinomianism in its wake. In fact, the contrary is true; sanctification springs forth from the believer's union with Christ because justification counteracts the law's demands and its ensuing condemnation.[42] To use the courtroom analogy once again, strictly speaking, the judge's verdict does not cause the prisoner to walk out of the courtroom – he does this on his own, but the verdict creates the circumstances that enable him to do so. God's verdict legally transfers the sinner from the state of condemnation (or law) to a state of salvation (grace), from the realm of flesh to Spirit, and in this new state the Spirit freely transforms the sinner through his sanctifying work.

Righteousness and Life (Rom. 8.10)

The other side of the Romans 6.7 coin appears in Paul's statement: 'If Christ is in you, although the body is dead because of sin, the Spirit is life because of righteousness' (Rom. 8.10). In the previous verses Paul contrasts the differences between life in the flesh versus life in the Spirit. Paul points to the reality of the believer's union with Christ, which is why he reminds his recipients, 'If Christ is in you', but at the same time he recognizes the reality of the deadness of the body, a condition that comes about 'because [*dia*] of sin'. Once again, the death-sin-law nexus is relevant. The sinner lies under a state of death because of sin – because of his violation of the law. But Paul states the converse truth, namely 'the Spirit is life because of righteousness'. While some argue that Paul's reference to *pneuma* is to the person's spirit rather than the Holy Spirit, the overall context of Romans 8 favours the view that Paul has the latter in mind.[43] Paul argues that, despite the believer's dying state, he has the indwelling presence of the Spirit, a down payment of eschatological life. All of this takes place 'because of [*dia*] righteousness'. That is, believers possess life because of the imputed righteousness of Christ: 'As sin reigned in death, grace also might reign through righteousness leading to eternal life through Jesus Christ our Lord' (Rom. 5.21).[44] The subjective ontological transformation, which begins in the midst of this life and finds its consummation at the resurrection, comes about because of righteousness.

In fact, the parallel structure of Paul's statement corroborates this conclusion:

soma nekron 'the body is dead'	dia harmartian 'because of sin'
pneuma zoe 'the Spirit is life'	dia dikaiosunen 'because of righteousness'

In this vein, Jerome (347–420) translated the lexeme *dia dikaiosunen* as *propter iustificationem* ('on account of justification'). That Paul does not have the person's sanctification-sourced righteous deeds in view appears in the fact that he does not pick up this theme again until verse 12: 'So then, brothers, we are debtors, not to the flesh, to live according to the flesh.'[45] As Robert Haldane (1764–1842) explains:

> In the verse before us we have an undeniable proof of the imputation to us of righteousness, for otherwise it would be a manifest contradiction to say that we die on account of our sins, and that we have life on account of our righteousness; for what is sin but the opposite of righteousness? Whoever, then, dies on account of the sin that is in him, cannot obtain life by his own righteousness. Now, if all men die on account of sin, as the Apostle here teaches, then no man can have life by his own righteousness.[46]

The only means by which sinners can secure eschatological life is the righteousness of Christ, which they receive through their justification by faith.

Doctrinal Formulation

The four surveyed texts state that the law stands as an obstruction to any transformative changes in a sinner's life. As long as he lies under the state of law, the sinner is subject to death. Only the legal-forensic work of Christ, his obedience to the law and his satisfaction in suffering its penalty, frees sinners from the law's claims and thus opens the door for the transformative work of the Spirit. Justification by faith alone is the means by which fallen human beings lay hold of Christ's active and passive obedience, his legal work. But even though believers gain access to Christ's law-neutralizing work through their justification, over the years theologians have pondered the question as to how the legal and transformative benefits relate to one another. If the sinner enters into union with Christ at the inception of his redemption in his effectual calling and thus possesses the whole Christ, how can justification take priority to sanctification? How can sanctification, which follows effectual calling and faith and is transformative, in some sense take a back seat to justification?[47] If all of the benefits of redemption come through our union with Christ, should not union be the central category and justification a subsidiary aspect?[48]

There is a sense in which modern philosophical assumptions drive these questions and create unnecessary tensions where early modern Protestant theologians saw none. If one conceives of the *ordo salutis* as a temporal or chronological sequence of events, then there are difficulties in claiming that something later down the line serves as a basis for something that is temporally antecedent to it. Moreover, in a post-Enlightenment context in which Aristotelian fourfold causality has been whittled to efficient causes, other complications arise. Each step in the *ordo* supposedly receives its efficient causal source from the previous benefit. Another modern intrusion is the effort to locate a central doctrine for one's theology or soteriology, whether union with Christ or justification. Such a quest arises in the wake of the modern context and only creates further tensions and problems. In the effort to locate the one central doctrine, other important doctrines suffer atrophy or get subsumed into the central concept and thus lose their unique qualities. While such misunderstandings may be common, this is not how theologians historically employed the *ordo salutis*.

The *ordo* is a relational and largely non-temporal ordering of the benefits of redemption and has no doctrinal centre.[49] Rather than contradicting the doctrine of union with Christ, the *ordo* explains it. Moreover, through the heuristic use of Aristotelian fourfold causality, early modern theologians were able to delineate various causes of salvation, one from another. Faith, for example, is the *instrumental*, not the *material*, cause of justification. In other words, one's justified status does not rest in the instrument (faith), but rather in the work of Christ (the material cause).[50] Faith may represent a spiritual subjective change that is logically prior to justification, but the sinner's justified status does not rest in that subjective change but in the alien and objective work of Christ. Beyond these observations, preserving the priority of justification to sanctification addresses two important doctrinal issues: it guards the purity of *solus Christus* and *sola fide* and protects the indefectibility of a person's salvation.

The Purity of *sola fide* and *solus Christus*

Preserving justification's priority to sanctification guards the purity of *sola fide* and *solus Christus*. The point of these Reformation slogans is that Christ alone is the saviour and that one may not combine his good works with Christ's works in order to secure his salvation. Justification is by faith alone, apart from good works. If God factors a believer's good works in his justification, then the material cause of justification is no longer the work of Christ alone. Additionally, by factoring a believer's good works in justification, it creates tensions with Paul's teaching in his letter to the Galatians or with his teaching in Romans, namely that God justifies the ungodly. Johnson, for example, states that God factors the indwelling presence of Christ in the sinner's justification.[51] If God factors the indwelling presence of Christ, then how can one say with Paul that God justifies the ungodly?

Such a conception misconstrues the relationship between union with Christ and justification. Geerhardus Vos (1862–1949) was aware of this error: 'Many continue to propose that the bond with the Mediator [mystical union] is the legal basis on which God permits His merits to benefit the individual sinner.' Vos runs through the logic of such an opinion: Christ has secured eternal life, but all of this is of no benefit as long as 'Christ is a stranger who is outside of me'.[52] In words that sound very similar to Johnson's union-justification formulation, Vos describes the view in order to critique it:

> He implants Christ in me, and now declares in agreement with my actual condition that I am just. Indeed, by this implanting I have truly become a member of Christ's body, so that it is now the righteousness of the body, whose organic member I am, that is imputed to me. Union with Christ is, so it is thought, therefore the indispensable juridical basis for the justification of sinners.[53]

As attractive as this sounds, Vos rightly explains that it falsifies a fundamental element of the Christian doctrine of salvation.

'Justification', writes Vos, 'is always and everywhere in Scripture a declaration of God, not on the basis of an actually existing condition of our being righteous, but on the basis of a gracious imputation of God that is contradicted by our condition. While we in ourselves are unrighteous, God's judgement acquits us. Justification is a paradox.'[54] In Pauline terms, Vos captures the truth that God justifies the ungodly. For those who propose that God bases justification on union with Christ, Vos poses a penetrating question:

> If all the actions of grace following upon the mystical union become mine on the basis of this union, the question must still always be asked: On what basis do I share in the *unio mystica* with Christ Himself? If it is true that no grace can come to me on the basis of Christ's merits as long as I am not in Christ, how is it ever possible that I would be implanted in Him? This implanting cannot occur on the basis of being in Christ, for it is precisely the implanting that effects being in Christ. One will thus

be compelled to say that implanting occurs by way of anticipation in view of impending justification. A clear circle, for now we have justification on the basis of being in Christ and being in Christ on the basis of justification.[55]

Such circular thinking is ultimately muddled and therefore erroneous for the reasons that Vos gives. Only when one prioritizes justification to sanctification and gives full weight to Paul's statement that God justifies the ungodly can he rightly relate the two doctrines in a biblical manner.

Giving priority to justification captures the simple truth that sinners are sanctified because they are justified, but they are not justified because they are sanctified. Such a relationship preserves the *solus* of *solus Christus* and the *sola* of *sola fide*; it recognizes that Christ's work alone is the material cause of the sinner's justification. Only a perfect, alien, and imputed righteousness answers the law's demands (1 Cor. 15.56; Rom. 5.12–21; 8.1–4). Only Christ's work received by faith alone breaks the power of the law; the person's sins no longer hang over his head because he has received Christ's imputed righteousness. Because of this imputed righteousness the sinner is justified from the law (Acts 13.39) and from sin (Rom. 6.7). Believers have 'died to the law . . . in order that we may bear fruit for God' (Rom. 7.4).

An Indefectible Salvation

Prioritizing justification to sanctification effectively guards against dividing justification into two phases, initial and final. The immutable, indefectible, and irreversible verdict of a single justification by faith alone becomes a provisional declaration that awaits the verdict of one's final justification.[56] In such circumstances, believers never truly live from a certain eschatological future but rather in the uncertain present. They never stand assured of their justified status because they wonder whether they have achieved a sufficient degree of holiness in order to secure their justified status. A verdict that rests in the perfect and complete, but nevertheless alien righteousness of Christ, captures the extraspective character of our faith. Only an extraspective faith that looks to the person and work of Christ rather than the introspective gaze within provides assurance that we are justified from the law and sin. Only when believers live from the future eschatological verdict of justification in the present can they know that the subsequent Spirit-wrought transformative changes will undoubtedly occur because their salvation rests on the indefectible work of Christ.

Conclusion

Prioritizing justification to sanctification is not about sidelining the doctrine of union with Christ or making it the centre of one's soteriology. Rather, to acknowledge justification's priority to sanctification reflects Scripture's teaching when it explains the law's role in salvation. Justification's priority preserves the *solus* in *solus Christus* and the *sola* in *sola fide* and guards the indefectibility of salvation. When Paul states that God justifies the ungodly, theologians echo his claim through the *ordo salutis* by placing justification before sanctification. Or, to echo Calvin's order – justification is the first and sanctification is the second benefit of the *duplex gratia*. To negate this order compromises the biblical doctrine of salvation. It opens the door to mixing the believer's Spirit-wrought works with Christ's obedience as the solid foundation for salvation, a biblically unacceptable outcome.

Notes

1 I am grateful to David VanDrunen, Mike Allen and Brian Hecker for reading over earlier drafts of this chapter and providing helpful comments and feedback.

2 Cf., e.g., Council of Trent, 'Session 6, 13 January 1547'; French Confession, XX; Belgic Confession, XXII–XXIII, Second Helvetic, XV. All confession citations and quotations unless otherwise noted come from Jaroslav Pelikan and Valerie Hotchkiss (eds), *Creeds and Confessions of Faith in the Christian Tradition*, vol. 2 (New Haven, CT: Yale University Press, 2003). All subsequent references to confessional documents come from this source unless otherwise noted.

3 Council of Trent, 'Session 6, 13 January 1547', VIII, X.

4 For multiple examples, see J. V. Fesko, *Beyond Calvin: Union with Christ and Justification in Early Modern Reformed Theology (1517–1700)* (Göttingen: Vandenhoeck and Ruprecht, 2012).

5 Westminster Shorter Catechism, qq. 33, 35.

6 I owe the term *relational priority* to my colleague, David VanDrunen.

7 On the Scotist origins of the concept of the *ordo naturae*, or *instantes naturae* ('instants of nature'), non-temporal, logical 'moments', see Hester Goodenough Gelber, *It Could Have Been Otherwise: Contingency and Necessity in Dominican Theology at Oxford, 1300–1350* (Leiden: Brill, 2004), pp. 130–8. On the use of the *ordo naturae* in discussions of soteriology see, e.g., Thomas Goodwin, *Man's Restauration by Grace* (London: Thomas Goodwin, 1692), p. 16; William Ames, *The Marrow of Theology*, trans. John Dykstra Eusden (Grand Rapids, MI: Baker, 1968), I.ii.5; Johannes Wollebius, *Compendium Theologiae Christianae*, trans. John W. Beardslee, in *Reformed Dogmatics* (New York: Oxford University Press, 1965), I.xxx.13.

8 Marcus Johnson, *One with Christ: An Evangelical Theology of Salvation* (Wheaton, IL: Crossway, 2013).

9 Westminster Larger Catechism, p. 70.

10 Johnson, *One with Christ*, p. 19.

11 Johnson, *One with Christ*, p. 26.

12 Johnson, *One with Christ*, p. 54.
13 Johnson, *One with Christ*, p. 69.
14 Johnson, *One with Christ*, p. 75.
15 Cf. John Calvin, *Institutes of the Christian Religion*, 2 vols, trans. Henry Beveridge (Grand Rapids, MI: Eerdmans, 1957), III.xi.1. Some have challenged Johnson's interpretation of Calvin's doctrine of union with Christ: see Thomas L. Wenger, 'The New Perspective on Calvin: Responding to Recent Calvin Interpretations', *Journal of the Evangelical Theological Society* 50/2 (2007), pp. 311–28; cf. Marcus Johnson, 'New or Nuanced Perspective on Calvin? A Reply to Thomas Wenger', *Journal of the Evangelical Theological Society* 51/3 (2008), pp. 543–58; Thomas Wenger, 'Theological Spectacles and a Paradigm of Centrality: A Reply to Marcus Johnson', *Journal of the Evangelical Theological Society* 51/3 (2008), pp. 559–72.
16 Johnson, *One with Christ*, p. 88.
17 Johnson, *One with Christ*, p. 90.
18 Johnson, *One with Christ*, p. 93.
19 Johnson, *One with Christ*, p. 95.
20 Johnson, *One with Christ*, p. 164.
21 See, e.g., Zacharias Ursinus, *The Commentary of Dr. Zacharias Ursinus on the Heidelberg Catechism*, trans. G. W. Williard (1852; Phillipsburg, NJ: P&R, n. d.), p. 329; Ursinus, *Corpus Doctrinae Orthodoxae, sive Catecheticarum Explicationum* (Heidelberg: Ionas Rhodius, 1616), p. 330.
22 Calvin, *Institutes*, III.xi.1. On the priority that Calvin assigns to justification within the context of union with Christ, see Richard A. Muller, *Calvin and the Reformed Tradition: On the Work of Christ and the Order of Salvation* (Grand Rapids, MI: Baker, 2012), pp. 202–43, esp. pp. 205–12.
23 Unless otherwise noted, all Scripture quotations come from the English Standard Version.
24 Anthony Thiselton, *The First Epistle to the Corinthians*, New International Greek Testament Commentary (Grand Rapids, MI: Eerdmans, 2000), pp. 1301–2.
25 Thiselton, *First Corinthians*, p. 1303; similarly, Gordon D. Fee, *The First Epistle to the Corinthians*, New International Commentary on the New Testament (Grand Rapids, MI: Eerdmans, 1987), pp. 806–7; John Calvin, *First Epistle of Paul to the Corinthians*, Calvin's New Testament Commentaries, ed. David W. Torrance and T. F. Torrance (1960; Grand Rapids, MI: Eerdmans, 1996), pp. 346–7.
26 Charles Hodge, *1 and 2 Corinthians* (1857–59; Edinburgh: Banner of Truth, 1994), p. 359.
27 Chris Vlachos, *The Law and the Knowledge of Good and Evil: The Edenic Background of the Catalytic Operation of the Law in Paul* (Eugene, OR: Pickwick, 2009), pp. 13–86.
28 Darrell L. Bock, *Acts*, Baker Exegetical Commentary on the New Testament (Grand Rapids, MI: Baker, 2007), 458–9; Gottlob Schrenk, '*dikaiow*', in *Theological Dictionary of the New Testament* [TDNT], ed. Gerhard Kittel, 10 vols (1964; Grand Rapids, MI: Eerdmans, 2006), vol. II, p. 218; cf. Frederick William Danker, *A Greek–English Lexicon of the New Testament and Other Early Christian Literature*, 3rd edn (Chicago, IL: University of Chicago Press, 2001), p. 249, section 3. Some prefer the term *freed* because of the combination of *dikaiow* with the preposition *apo* (so C. K. Barrett, *Acts*, vol. 1, International Critical Commentary [Edinburgh: T&T Clark, 1994], p. 650). At this point, however, Barrett believes that Luke attributes these statements to Paul when in fact they are not but are instead a garbled repetition

of Paul's words without a sufficient understanding of his theology (Barrett, *Acts*, p. 651).

29 F. F. Bruce, *The Book of Acts*, New International Commentary on the New Testament, rev. edn (Grand Rapids, MI: Eerdmans, 1988), pp. 262–3; also John Calvin *Acts 1–13*, Calvin's New Testament Commentaries, ed. David W. Torrance and T. F. Torrance (1960; Grand Rapids, MI: Eerdmans, 1996), pp. 383–5.

30 Bock, *Acts*, 459. On Romans 6.7, also see R. Michael Allen, *Justification and the Gospel: Understanding the Contexts and Controversies* (Grand Rapids, MI: Baker, 2013), pp. 141–51.

31 C. E. B. Cranfield, *Romans*, 2 vols, International Critical Commentary (1975; Edinburgh: T&T Clark, 2001), I:310–11; Joseph A. Fitzmyer, *Romans*, Anchor Bible (New York: Doubleday, 1992), p. 437; Robin Scroggs, 'Romans 6:7, *O Gar Apothanon Dedikaiotai Apo Tes Amartias*', *New Testament Studies* 10 (1963–4), pp. 104–8; N. T. Wright, *Romans*, New International Bible, vol. 10 (Nashville, TN: Abingdon, 2002), p. 540.

32 Charles Hodge, *Romans* (1835; Edinburgh: Banner of Truth, 1989), p. 199.

33 Douglas Moo, *The Epistle to the Romans*, New International Commentary on the New Testament (Grand Rapids, MI: Eerdmans, 1996), p. 377; Schrenk, '*dikaiow*', TDNT vol. II, pp. 218–19. Some note that the lexeme *dikaiothesetai apo* also appears in Ecclus. 26.29, 'a huckster shall not be declared right from sin [*dikaiotheseta kapelos apo hamartias*]' and the Testimony of Simeon, 'I have told you everything, so that I might be righteous with regard to your sin [*dikaiotho apo tes hamartias humon*]' (Robert Jewett, *Romans*, Hermenia [Minneapolis, MN: Fortress Press, 2007], p. 404).

34 Cranfield, *Romans*, vol. I, p. 311 n. 1; Robert Haldane, *Romans* (1874; Edinburgh: Banner of Truth, 1996), p. 248.

35 Thomas R. Schreiner, *Romans*, Baker Exegetical Commentary on the New Testament (Grand Rapids, MI: Baker, 1998), p. 319.

36 Hodge, *Romans*, pp. 198–9. John Murray (1898–1975) rightly explains that Paul deals with forensic matters in Romans 6.7 but erroneously assigns his statements to the doctrine of sanctification rather than justification: '"Justified from sin" will have to bear the forensic meaning in view of the forensic import of the word "justify". But since the context deals with deliverance from the power of sin the thought is, no doubt, that of being "quit" of sin. The decisive breach with the reigning power of sin is viewed after the analogy of the kind of dismissal which a judge gives when an arraigned person is justified. Sin has no further claim upon the person who is thus vindicated. This judicial aspect from which deliverance from the power of sin is to be viewed needs to be appreciated. *It shows that the forensic is present not only in justification but also in that which lies at the basis of sanctification.*' (John Murray, *The Epistle to the Romans*, New International Commentary on the New Testament [1959, 1965; Grand Rapids, MI: Eerdmans, 1968], p. 222.) Murray makes an unprecedented move in assigning the forensic to the doctrine of sanctification. Historically, the Reformed tradition recognizes that a believer's positional holiness, what Murray denominates as *definitive sanctification*, which he contrasts with *progressive sanctification*, comes through the doctrine of justification (John Murray, 'Definitive Sanctification', in *Collected Writings*, vol. 2 [Edinburgh: Banner of Truth, 1977], pp. 277–93.) Note, e.g., the Heidelberg Catechism q and a 60: 'How are you righteous before God? A. Only by true faith in Jesus Christ . . . God grants and credits to me the perfect satisfaction, righteousness, and *holiness of*

Christ, as if I had never sinned nor been a sinner, and as if I had been as perfectly obedient as Christ was obedient for me' (emphasis mine).

37 Cf. John Calvin, *Romans and Thessalonians*, Calvin's New Testament Commentaries, ed. David W. Torrance and T. F. Torrance (1960; Grand Rapids, MI: Eerdmans, 1996), p. 125.

38 David VanDrunen, *Divine Covenants and Moral Order: A Biblical Theology of Natural Law* (Grand Rapids, MI: Eerdmans, 2014), p. 437.

39 So, e.g., Johnson, *One with Christ*, p. 113.

40 Haldane, *Romans*, p. 248.

41 Allen, *Justification and the Gospel*, pp. 127–51.

42 Haldane, *Romans*, p. 248.

43 Cf. Hodge, *Romans*, p. 259.

44 Moo, *Romans*, pp. 491–2; Schreiner, *Romans*, p. 415.

45 Cranfield, *Romans*, vol. I, p. 390 n. 4; also Gordon Fee, *God's Empowering Presence: The Holy Spirit in the Letters of Paul* (Peabody, MA: Hendrickson, 1994), p. 500; *pace* Hodge, *Romans*, p. 259. Note, Fitzmeyer believes Paul employs a double entendre, with *pneuma* referring both to the Spirit and the believer's spirit (*Romans*, p. 491); similarly, Jewett, *Romans*, p. 491.

46 Haldane, *Romans*, p. 345; also C. K. Barrett, *Romans*, rev. edn, Black's New Testament Commentary (1957; Peabody, MA: Hendrickson, 2001), p. 150; cf. Ernst Käsemann, *Commentary on Romans*, trans. Geoffrey Bromiley (Grand Rapids, MI: Eerdmans, 1980), p. 224. Wright interprets Paul's statement as a reference to God's covenant faithfulness, or righteousness. This is generally true, but I take issue with Wright's definition of righteousness. Nevertheless, I agree with Wright's assessment that the lexeme refers to God's actions in Christ, not to the believer's moral activity (Wright, *Romans*, pp. 584–5). For a critique of Wright's definition of *dikaiosune*, see Charles Lee Irons, *The Righteousness of God: A Lexical Examination of the Covenant-Faithfulness Interpretation*, Wissenschafliche Untersuchungen zum Neuen Testament (Tübingen: Mohr Siebeck, 2015). Dunn offers an interpretation similar to Wright's (James D. G. Dunn, *Romans 1–8*, Word Biblical Commentaries, vol. 38a [Dallas, TX: Word Books, 1988], pp. 444–5).

47 See, e.g., A. A. Hodge, 'The Ordo Salutis: or, Relation in the Order of Nature of Holy Character and Divine Favor', *Princeton Review* 49/1 (1878), pp. 304–21.

48 So, e.g., Johnson, *One with Christ*, p. 95.

49 On the history, exegesis, and formulation of the *ordo*, see J. V. Fesko, 'Romans 8.29–30 and the Question of the *Ordo Salutis*', *Journal of Reformed Theology* 8 (2014), pp. 35–60.

50 Cf. Westminster Confession of Faith, XI.i.

51 Johnson, *One with Christ*, p. 93.

52 Geerhardus Vos, *Reformed Dogmatics*, 5 vols, ed. Richard B. Gaffin, Jr (1896; Bellingham, WA: Lexham Press, 2012–16), vol. IV, p. 21.

53 Vos, *Reformed Dogmatics*, vol. IV, p. 21.

54 Vos, *Reformed Dogmatics*, vol. IV, p. 22. Louis Berkhof makes the exact same observation (Louis Berkhof, *Systematic Theology: Combined Edition* [1932, 1938; Grand Rapids, MI: Eerdmans, 1996], p. 452). Berkhof likely relied on Vos's lectures in the formulation of his own views (see J. V. Fesko, 'Vos and Berkhof on Union with Christ and Justification', *Calvin Theological Journal* 47 [2012]: pp. 50–71).

55 Vos, *Reformed Dogmatics*, vol. IV, p. 22.

56 E.g. N. T. Wright, *What St. Paul Really Said: Was Paul of Tarsus the Real Founder of Christianity?* (Grand Rapids, MI: Eerdmans, 1997), p. 129.

13

Barth and Boethius on *Stellvertretung* and Personhood

ADAM JOHNSON

To be atoned for, to be saved, to be reconciled to God – these are profound matters, and difficult to understand.[1] At times this can feel like a burden, but it is likewise the delight of the church: to grow in understanding of our Lord and his saving work. Many of our questions pertain to how this atonement happened, whether it was necessary, and questions of that sort. In this chapter, I will turn things somewhat on their head, by working backward from Karl Barth's[2] understanding of Christ's saving work, to an understanding of ourselves as human persons: what must be true of us, and what are the implications for our identities, given the fact that we were saved in so comprehensive a manner by the substitutionary and representative work of Christ?[3] For in this work:

> we enter that sphere of Christian knowledge in which we have to do with the heart of the message received by and laid upon the Christian community and therefore with the heart of the Church's dogmatics: that is to say, with the heart of its subject-matter, origin and content. (*CD* IV/1, 3)[4]

But to be the 'heart of the message', the 'heart of the subject-matter' means that what we are here dealing with has the deepest and most profound implications for our understanding of other subjects, such as our self-understanding as those who died and rose again in Christ.

We begin by exploring the conceptual engine driving the whole doctrine of the atonement for Barth: the representative/substitutionary nature of Jesus Christ (the German word for this is *Stellvertretung*). In sum, I will unpack the thesis that *Barth develops the work of Christ as the work of the God who elects to be the representative substitute [Stellvertreter] of his people*, or put with an anthropological emphasis, *that we humans are who we are in Christ our representative substitute, and that our identity is therefore fundamentally shaped by the life, death and resurrection of this one*. This, I suggest, is the key to understanding the underlying logic of Barth's doctrine of the atonement, in which God in Christ took our place in order that we might have life in him. I will then unpack this insight in conversation with Boethius' *Consolation of Philosophy* and Alain Ehrenberg's *The Weariness of the Self*, exploring the relation between Christ's work and the contemporary question of human identity.

The Background: Election, Creation and Anthropology

We begin in the doctrine of God, for what it means to be human is rooted in what it means for God to be God. And when it comes to God, we are firmly and necessarily dealing with the category of decision, God's choice of grace, the 'divine movement and condescension on the basis of which men belong to God and God to men' (CD II/2, 19). God is a God in movement, a God who is what he is precisely in his decision, and the content of this decision is to be the God of man, 'a relationship outside of which God no longer wills to be and no longer is God' (CD II/2, 7). God is the God who lives out the divine life in the midst of this self-determination; the content of this self-determination, the gospel tells us, is that God willed to be who he is as our God, specifically to be our God in and through the incarnate Son, Jesus Christ.

God is the living God, who is free to specify or delimit his life as he sees fit, and according to Barth, God does in fact specify his eternal life, ordaining that he should not be entirely self-sufficient as he might be (CD II/2, 10). On the basis of his own free election of love and grace, the self-determining God chooses not to be the self-sufficient God, but to be who he is in relation to his people, a relation which is centred in the person and work of Jesus Christ. On the basis of God's election, God is who he is in relation – relation to his creation. The specific content of this relation is that 'within His triune being, God is none other than the one who in His Son or Word elects Himself, and in and with Himself elects His people' (CD II/2, 76). God is the God who in himself, in his Son, wills to represent a people, to elect them 'in Him'. And as Barth specifies, this does 'not simply mean with Him, together with Him, in His company'. Rather, it means 'in His person, in His will, in His own divine choice' (CD II/2, 117). Who is the God of the gospel, but the one who, on the basis of his free and gracious decision, elects and represents humankind in himself, in his person, in Jesus Christ, the incarnate Son of God? For this reason, creation and the creature:

> Is no more its own goal and purpose than it is its own ground and beginning. There is no inherent reason for the creature's existence and nature, no independent teleology of the creature . . . Its destiny lies entirely in the purpose of its Creator as the One Who speaks and cares for it. (CD III/1, 94)

And as God wills to be the one who represents humankind in himself, in his person, creation is nothing but the context, the stage, for that representation, or, more precisely, that which is represented by God. 'There is no such thing as a created nature which has its purpose, being or continuance apart from grace, or which may be known in this purpose, being and continuance except through grace' (*CD* II/2, 92), specifically the grace of the covenant fulfilled in the atonement of Jesus Christ.

As part of creation, therefore, the reality of human creatures lies in Christ (*CD* III/2, 225). No amount of biological, psychological, sociological and other insights will plumb the depths of human nature, for the answer lies not in ourselves as an object of study, but in the God who created and holds us in existence. Our being 'consists in participating in what God does' (*CD* III/2, 74), a claim of almost unfathomable range and significance for Barth (*CD* III/2, 145). We derive our human nature from Jesus (*CD* III/2, 50), the One Man (*CD* IV/1, 223). Jesus is not merely the pattern after which men and women are made, the first among many brothers and sisters; neither is Jesus the one who represents men and women in the sense that God relates first to Jesus and on that basis to other men and women. Rather, Jesus is 'the very ground and sphere, the atmosphere of the being of every man' (*CD* IV/1, 53), such that we exist 'in him' (*CD* III/2, 148, 317).

But the meaning of such statements lies deeper than mere nature: Jesus is more than a 'form' or platonic archetype of 'man'. Barth is thinking along quite different lines, for 'forms' and 'archetypes' do not live and move, do not have histories. What it means to be human, what it means to derive our nature from Jesus, is to have God see and treat us 'in and with His beloved Son' (*CD* III/2, 42), to have our own history included within the history of Jesus Christ (*CD* IV/1, 157–8), such that God relates to all others in and through this one man, Jesus Christ: 'God's relation to man, sinful man, is to this man alone and all others in and through Him' (*CD* III/2, 43). And this language is no mere 'as if' or 'as though', a divine sleight of hand, or decision to see things in a graciously 'rose coloured' manner. Not at all. It is not that God chooses to see fundamentally independent and free creatures *as though* they were in some way related to Jesus Christ. Rather, what it is to be human is to have one's history within the history of Jesus Christ, such that Jesus 'is our true existence' (*CD* IV/1, 154; cf. 160). Because this is true, 'because we are in Christ, every man in his time and place is changed' (*CD* III/2, 133) in the course of the history of Jesus, the one in whom we live and move and have our being, the one in whom we died and rose again.

The danger with this line of thought, and one which Barth is well aware of, is that humanity is simply swallowed or absorbed into Jesus, such that we are left with Jesus and nothing else: to be human simply is to be Jesus, or part of Jesus in some way. But Barth consistently eschews such a totalizing, one-sided account (despite concerns to the contrary[5]). For what Barth is after, what he finds within the gospel, is the good news that 'the being and act of God stands in relation to our own being and act – a common history which is shared' (CD IV/1, 7). Apart from such a sharing, from such a relation in which the elect creature is freed to elect God in turn as a legitimate covenant partner, the gospel fades from good news to a mere tautology, a mere restatement of a God who is God alone, without partner, without friend. How, then, does Barth safeguard the freedom and legitimacy of God's covenantal partner *within* his account of the creature receiving its being and history *in* the person and work of Jesus Christ? Briefly, the answer lies within the doctrine of the Trinity:

> He [God] willed the existence of a being which in all its non-deity and therefore its differentiation can be a real partner; which is capable of action and responsibility in relation to Him; to which His own divine form of life is not alien; which in a creaturely repetition, as a copy and imitation, can be a bearer of this form of life . . . In God's own being and sphere there is a counterpart: a genuine but harmonious self-encounter and self-discovery . . . Thus the *tertium comparationis*, the analogy between God and man, is simply the existence of the I and the Thou in confrontation. (CD III/1, 184–5)

How can we both be free and 'in Christ', or have our own history which is nonetheless a history within the history of another, of Jesus Christ? Because we are fashioned after the pattern of the Trinity. More specifically, we are fashioned after the pattern of the Son who is God, but is so in and with and from the Father; whose history is not his own free history, but a history from and within the eternal history of the Father from whom he receives his eternally begotten being. We are genuine creatures with real freedom, standing in relation to God while nonetheless living in Christ, receiving our being from him, and being represented by him, because such simultaneous otherness and in-ness is precisely the reality of the Triune life which we are meant to image forth as his creatures.

The Foundation of the Atonement: *Stellvertretung*

Stellvertretung (1): *Substitution*

With this backdrop, we are in a place to better understand some of Barth's fundamental commitments when it comes to the doctrine of the atonement. On the one hand, Barth's thought is saturated with substitutionary language, in which what happens to Christ is unique to him: we are spared that which he endures. On the other hand, his thought is equally saturated with representational language, in which that which happens to Christ therefore happens in us, because of the intrinsic relation between us – and both lines of thought are brought together in a single term: *Stellvertretung*. So which way will Barth have it? Does Jesus spare us from the fate we deserve by taking it to himself, or do we suffer our fate in Jesus? Though the editors of the *Church Dogmatics* note that *Stellvertretung* 'enshrines the notions both of representation and substitution, and never the one without the other' (*CD* IV/1, vii), their case is overstated, as Barth distinguishes between substitution and representation both linguistically and conceptually, and the term contains an inner tension we do well to explore.

We see this dynamic clearly in Barth's account of the meaning of 'for us': 'It has happened fully and exclusively in Him, excluding any need for completion. Whatever may happen in consequence of the fact that Jesus Christ is for us cannot be added to it . . . His activity as our Representative and Substitute' (*CD* IV/1, 230; *KD* IV/1, 252: *sein stellvertretendes Handeln für uns*). But how can one be both representative and substitute? A substitute, it would seem, takes the place of another so that they need not inhabit or take that place. A substitute does something for us so that we need not do it ourselves, much as a substitute teacher might cover a class for the primary teacher who is ill. A representative, on the other hand, includes the people she represents: their fate hangs together, much as when a band of soldiers eagerly awaits the results of a parley. Does Jesus' work include or exclude us? To put it succinctly, did he die for us (substitution: Rom. 5.8; 1 Pet. 3.18), or did we die in him (representation: Rom. 6.6; Gal. 2.20)? We will consider each in turn.

Barth offers a strong defence of substitution: 'In his place Jesus Christ has suffered the death of a malefactor. The sentence on him as a sinner has been carried out. It cannot be reversed. It does not need to be repeated. It has fallen instead on Jesus Christ' (*CD* IV/1, 93). In the place of man: 'Jesus Christ rendered that obedience which is required of the covenant partner of God, and in that way found His good pleasure. He did it by taking to Himself the sins of all men, by suffering as His death the death to which they had fallen prey' (*CD* IV/1, 94). In a similar vein, Barth notes that Jesus fulfils this work 'by treading the way of sinners to its bitter end in death, in destruction, in the limitless anguish of separation from God, by delivering up sinful man and sin in his own person to the non-being which is properly theirs . . . The decisive thing is not that He has suffered what we ought to have suffered so that we do not have to suffer it . . . [though] this is true of course' (*CD* IV/1, 253). This qualified affirmation takes place within Barth's nuanced affirmation of the concept of punishment within the atonement, but the point stands: Jesus suffered what we ought to have suffered, so that we do not have to suffer it.

Everything, he says, depends on the 'doctrine of substitution' (*Lehre von der Stellvertretung*), the fact that:

the Lord who became a servant, the Son of God who went into the far country, and came to us, was and did all this for us; that He fulfilled . . . the divine judgment laid upon Him. There is no avoiding this straight gate . . . If the nail of this fourfold 'for us' does not hold, everything else will be left hanging in the void as an anthropological or psychological or sociological myth, and sooner or later it will break and fall to the ground. (CD IV/1, 273; KD, 300).

Everything, for Barth, depends on the 'doctrine of substitution' (CD IV/1, 273).[6]

At the heart of this substitutionary account is the idea that our sin is transferred to Jesus, or that he bears our sin for us – for without this transfer, this exchange, it would seem impossible to explain how that which was ours can become his, that we might be spared. 'The rejection which all men must die, God in His love for men transfers from all eternity to Him in whom He loves and elects them, and whom He elects at their head and in their place . . . He, the Elect, is appointed to check and defeat Satan on behalf of all those that are elected "in Him" . . . And this checking and defeating of Satan must consist in His allowing the righteousness of God to proceed against Himself instead of them' (CD II/2, 123). 'Transfer' and 'instead' are key here – something shifted, something changed places or was exchanged, that we might be spared.

It is precisely at this point that the role of sin-bearing becomes so important. With great richness Barth explores the Pauline view that 'He has caused Him to be regarded and treated as a sinner. He was made a curse for us, as Paul unhesitatingly concluded from Deuteronomy 21.23 (Gal. 3.13)' (CD IV/1, 165). But this is no mere fiction, for the emphasis does not fall in 'regarded' but on 'was made'. Jesus makes his own 'not only the guilt of man but also his rejection and condemnation, giving Himself to bear the divinely righteous consequences of human sin, not merely affirming the divine sentence on man, but allowing it to be fulfilled on himself' (CD IV/1, 175).

> He takes upon Himself to be the bearer and Representative [*Träger und Vertreter*], to be responsible for this case, to expose Himself to the accusation and sentence which must inevitably come upon us in this case . . . He takes from us our own evil case, taking our place and compromising Himself with it.
>
> And as He does that, it ceases to be our sin. It is no longer our affair to prosecute and repent this case . . . He is the man who entered that evil way, with the result that we are forced from it; it can be ours no longer.
>
> But that means that it became His way: His the sin which we commit on it; His the accusation, the judgment and the curse which necessarily

fall on us there ... He is the condemned amongst those who are pardoned because the sentence which destroys them is directed against him. (*CD* IV/1, 236–7; *KD*, 259; cf. *CD* III/2, 48)

And once more, Barth affirms that this is no 'exchange only in appearance', a 'masquerade' or 'dressing up' – in Jesus Christ, God made our sin his own, taking the place of us sinners. 'Our sin is no longer our own. It is His sin, the sin of Jesus Christ' (*CD* IV/1, 238). Jesus, in this sense, is the 'one great sinner' (*CD* IV/1, 254; *KD*, 279: *als der des einen großen Sünders!*).

Stellvertretung *(2): Representation*

Alongside this robust account of substitution, we find an equally vigorous (if not even stronger!) account of representation, highlighting the way in which we are included in the work of Christ, rather than excluded from it. Jesus is the 'representative of all nations and stands amongst the nations as the representative of God', as such 'bearing the judgments of God' (*CD* IV/1, 35) in a way that affirms not so much his apartness as his 'solidarity with the world' (*CD* IV/1, 187). And to be clear, this is an ontological (or objectivistic)[7] and not merely emotional, poetic or political solidarity: 'In the One in whom they are elected, that is to say in the death which the Son of God has died for them, they themselves have died as sinners' (*CD* II/2, 125). The work of God in Christ is not one which sets us aside as spectators, while Jesus deals with the problem for our benefit; rather, his work is one which includes ourselves, one in which we have a necessary and intrinsic stake and connection, for this is our work – the work of our representative in whom we live and move and have our being.

This line of thought comes clearly to the fore in *CD* IV/1.3 'The Verdict of the Father'. 'That Jesus has died for us does not mean, therefore, that we do not have to die, but that we have died in and with Him, that as the people we were we have been done away and destroyed, that we are no longer there and have no more future' (*CD* IV/1, 295). As bizarre as it may seem: 'We died. This has to be understood quite concretely and literally. In His dying, the dying which awaits us in the near or distant future was already comprehended and completed, so that we can no longer die to ourselves (Rom. 14.2f.) ... His death was the death of all' (*CD* IV/1, 295). Put another way: 'In His death He dies the death of man. Order is created, then, not by any setting aside of sins, but by that of the sinner himself ... It is not by the giving of medicine, or by an operation, but by the killing of the patient that help is brought' (*CD* IV/1, 296).

It is this, more than anything, that explains Barth's *distance* and *proximity* to penal substitution.[8] Barth is in the native soil of that doctrine (dwelling on divine justice and wrath, punishment, transferred sin . . .), but he simply cannot reconcile himself to thinking of sin or punishment (let alone God's wrath!) *as the fundamental problem*, when the reality of the sinner and her relationship to God includes and transcends such realities. The problem is not simply how to punish sin: it is how to destroy sin and the sinner (and in so doing punish her), while resurrecting her for relationship with God, for salvation. Barth's answer is that this is in fact what we must do: we must die, in Christ, and rise in him – a solution that includes the central dynamics of penal substitution, while reaching far beyond in a synthesis of substitutionary and representational categories, in which the sinner truly and literally dies in Christ, thereby fulfilling the law of a God whose love is a love of law and order.[9] Barth thus takes up the concerns of penal substitution within a far more comprehensive account in which substitution plays its role alongside representation, and justice is satisfied alongside God's love,[10] to note some of the key divergences (and developments).

At root what we have here is an 'anthropology which is embraced by Christology', such that 'in His work, His death on the cross, as the death of our Representative and substitute, it came to pass that, as the sinners and enemies we are, we were delivered up to death, and an end was made of us, and we came to an end with this whole world of sin and flesh and death' (*CD* IV/1, 348).[11] Just as theology proper embraces Christology via the doctrine of election (God does not will to be God alone, but to be the God of the people he represents in Jesus), so Christology embraces anthropology via that same doctrine of election (what it means to be human is to be human in Jesus Christ, to have one's identity rooted in and shaped by the history of this particular Israelite). God did not will to be alone, and neither did he will us to be alone, nor to have an independent and discrete identity, knowable and identifiable apart from any other relation. We, by the will of God, are creatures whose identity is encompassed by a greater reality, the reality and history of our Lord Jesus Christ. On this basis, we have died in him, and risen in him (Col. 2.12):

> I am the man of sin . . . I myself am nailed to the cross and crucified (in the power of the sacrifice and obedience of Jesus Christ in my place) . . . I am therefore destroyed and replaced . . . as the one who has turned to nothingness I am done away in the death of Jesus Christ. (*CD* IV/1, 515)

It is this integration of substitution and representation seen in the concept of *Stellvertretung* that energizes Barth's fourfold account of the atonement, in which Jesus is the 'Judge Judged in Our Place' (*CD* IV/1, 211–83):

1. Jesus is the Judge among us, justice incarnate, the just God with us. His is the role to bring justice and righteousness to his creation, and as such to do away with all injustice, all the unjust.

2 But, and this is where *Stellvertretung* comes to play its vital role, Jesus is the Judge judged – the judge who takes our place as the judged, taking upon himself our sin, our guilt, our very selves.

3 And as the one who takes our place, who both represents us and is our substitute, he is judged. It is in Jesus, the one great sinner, that our sin meets it proper end, that we are judged and done away with as the sinners we are.

4 But this is not the end, for as the one who acted justly in our place, Jesus is the one in whom we are vindicated by the Father, raised from the dead and brought to a life of righteousness.[12]

In sum, *Stellvertretung* energizes the core of Barth's theology of the atonement.

Stellvertretung and Identity

Earlier we noted:

> As part of creation, therefore, the reality of human creatures lies in Christ (*CD* III/2, 225). No amount of biological, psychological, sociological and other insights will plumb the depths of human nature, for the answer lies not in ourselves as an object of study, but in the God who created and holds us in existence. Our being 'consists in participating in what God does' (*CD* III/2, 74), a claim of almost unfathomable range and significance for Barth (*CD* III/2, 145).

While such claims have profound implications for our understanding of Christ's death and resurrection, they have equally weighty implications for our understanding of human nature generally, which we will now consider in more depth, in dialogue with a broader range of ancient and contemporary sources, starting with Boethius' *Consolation of Philosophy*.

Lady Philosophy, in the beginning of the book, finds a man overthrown: a politician in exile, but more importantly, a man who has lost his bearings. At the conclusion of the first stage of their conversation, she says: 'Now I know the other cause, or rather the major cause of your illness: you have forgotten your true nature.'[13] But this is odd, for Boethius had just given a perfectly acceptable definition: 'man is a rational and mortal animal'. In fact, this seems to be a specification of his famous definition of personhood, 'an individual substance of rational nature',[14] applied to *human* persons, who are a specific kind of individual substance, namely, mortal animal substance. We are like the animals in having a body, a mortal animal substance, but we are also like the angels, having a rational nature or soul. For this reason, we stand midway in the hierarchy of creation: one foot on earth, and one foot in the heavens, so to speak. What could be missing?

Jumping forward in the argument, we find Lady Philosophy arguing that:

> Since it is through possession of happiness that people become happy, and since happiness is in fact divinity, it is clear that it is through the possession of divinity that they become happy. But by the same logic as men become just through the possession of justice, or wise through the possession of wisdom, so those who possess divinity necessarily become divine. Each happy individual is therefore divine. While only God is so by nature, as many as you like may become so by participation.[15]

To be happy, in other words, is to possess happiness – but as God himself is not merely happy, but happiness itself, to become happy is to possess God, to become God – by participation, and not by nature. But what does this have to do with human nature? The key lies in the nature of happiness. If happiness is something super-added to human nature, like optional leather seats in a luxury car, then we have made no progress in understanding what it is to be human. But this is not how the ancients thought of happiness. Aristotle, for instance, thinks of happiness as the end of action: that toward which all action aims. But action is not arbitrary – it is a matter of function, of nature. Happiness and nature are intrinsically bound together, for nature has function, and fulfilled function is function which reaches or attains its end, and which therefore attains happiness.[16]

And why does this matter? Boethius, according to Lady Philosophy, has effectively left an account of function or *telos* out of his account of human nature, resulting in a definition that has made him disastrously ill. The *telos* of humankind is to participate in God. We err by seeking various things that are 'not perfect and good, for the reason that they differ from one another, and because they are lacking to one another and cannot confer full and perfect good'.[17] That is to say, we seek wealth, friendship, security, and a host of other goods – but these, because they are not complete and self-sufficient, bring along with them a host of needs and insecurities. What we need is the true good, where these lesser goods 'are brought together into one form and efficient power, as it were, so that sufficiency becomes identical with power, reverence, glory and pleasure'.[18] Where the goods we seek stand in an intrinsic and inseparable relation to each other, where happiness, power, and the other goods of life stand in perfect harmony to each other, there and only there will we be satisfied.

The culmination of this argument leaves Boethius rather breathless: 'You are playing with me, aren't you, by weaving a labyrinth of arguments from which I can't find the way out. At one moment you go in where you'll come out, and at another you come out where you went in. Or are you creating a wonderful circle of divine simplicity?'[19] And this indeed is what Lady Philosophy has done: she has developed an account of human nature in which participation with God is a constitutive element of our very nature. Whereas we, in our sin, direct our attention to an array of goods which are not in harmony with each other, and bring us to unhappiness, humans are the kinds of creatures whose natures are only fulfilled by participation with the God who is the simple source of all those goods we seek apart from him in our sin. To be human is to be designed to participate in God's divinely simple being and character.

To be human, therefore, is not to be a rational mortal animal as Boethius had said. This may be right, so far as it goes, but what it lacks is decisive, leaving the imprisoned Boethius in shambles. We are rational mortal animals *fulfilled through participation in God*. This participation is not optional, it is not one of the things we can do as rational animals, or even one of the things we should do. This participation is what we were designed for, and therefore a core element of what we are. We are rational mortal animals designed for participation in God. And lest we think of 'design' as something akin to a plan, hope or possibility, this is clearly not how the ancients thought. This design has to do with the fabric of our being, our functions and capacities . . . everything we are is ordered toward this reality. To be a rational mortal animal *not* participating in God is to reject one's own nature, to move toward the dissolution of one's own being.

And this is precisely what we find in Barth, though with more Christological specificity: the participation constitutive of our nature and therefore happiness is not merely *in God* but *in Christ* – a participation which is not merely something we move toward, but which was elected by God before the foundation of the world, and therefore characterizes the whole shape of God's creative and redemptive project. What does it mean to be a human person? Put simply, it means to be elected by God to participate in Christ – and only in this way to be a rational animal: to be a rational animal in Jesus Christ, our *Stellvertreter*.

But this is no easy matter to accept, for the idea of having an identity which is not merely relational, but grounded in a specific relationship which is constitutive of our nature goes against a strong tide in our culture. Charles Taylor chronicles this change in his *Sources of the Self*, noting the profound transformation 'from the hegemony of reason as a vision of cosmic order to the notion of a punctual disengaged subject exercising instrumental control', which 'helps to explain why we think of ourselves as "selves" today'.[20] The turn is one from the external objectivity or order and norms to one in which we 'take charge in constructing our own representation of the world . . . by . . . associations [which] form and shape our character and outlook', subjecting our bodies, 'traditions or habits' to 'radical scrutiny and remaking'.[21] Alain Ehrenberg, in *The Weariness of the Self*, furthers this line of thought within his narrower study of the history of depression in the contemporary age, arguing that 'contemporary depression is the marriage between the traditional melancholia of the exceptional person and the modern egalitarian idea that anyone can be exceptional'. Depression is 'a mindset heavy with multiple social practices and representations of ourselves in a society in which values associated with autonomy (e.g. personal choice, self-ownership, individual initiative) have been generalized'.[22] In other words, different epochs have their attending plights, and our individualistic consumerist society, unmoored from traditional values, prizing self-realization the way it does, has generated or greatly exacerbated the phenomenon of widespread anxiety and depression. In sum, Ehrenberg argues anxiety and depression are largely a cultural phenomenon of our own making: 'liberation might have gotten us out of the drama of guilt and obedience, but it has taken us straight into the demands of responsibility and action. And so the weariness of depression took over from the anxiety of neuroses.'[23]

Assuming, for the sake of argument, Ehrenberg's thesis that anxiety and depression are to a significant degree a 'sickness of self', the attending side effects of a society driven by individualistic self-fulfilment, what might be a response rooted in the substitutionary and representative death and resurrection of Jesus – one which acknowledges participation in Christ as the single most determinative feature of our nature and identity as human beings?

It is axiomatic for the Christian faith that our identity lies not solely within our ourselves, for our identity is not located strictly within the individual, and available for the individual to discern, construct, develop or change as she pleases, whether directly or indirectly. Our identity is a social one – not constructed for us by society, not simply given to us by others, but one lived out and partially constituted by others and our relations to them. We, as Aristotle notes, are political animals.[24] But deeper still, we find that our identity is in Christ. Not that we locate our identity in him, alongside other identity-forming behaviours of self-making or self-identification, such as identification with or participation in a family, club, institution, neighbourhood or nation. What it means to be human is to be in Christ, to have one's identity in him, to receive one's identity and have it shaped and constituted by the life he lived, by his death and resurrection.[25] While Christianity affirms the individual, it rejects individualism, for individualism attempts to cut at the root of our identity in Christ. We are not who we make ourselves to be: we are who we were made to be, we are who we are in Christ. External realities such as nature, calling and law shape and form us into who we should be – but in and through all this stands the basis of all these external realities: the person of Jesus Christ, in whom we live and move and have our being. He is the source of the order we inhabit. He is the source of the laws which shape and mould our bodies and souls. He is the one in whom we die (Rom. 6.6; Gal. 2.20) and in whom we rise again (Col. 3.1), for he is our *Stellvertreter*.

And along with this rejection, Christianity rejects Western culture's emphasis on giving ourselves the identities of our choice. This is not to say that our identity simply *is* the identity of Jesus, for we are not him, we are not swallowed up to disappear in him. The love and law of God affirms the reality of the individual, of his covenantal partners made in his image, but affirms the reality of the individual *in* their constituting relation to Jesus, the one in whom all things hold together (Col. 1.17). But to understand this, we must briefly consider the nature of participatory autonomy.

Participation and Autonomy

To such a relational and participatory view of human nature, we Westerners cannot help but recoil into the arms of autonomy, for this was the milk on which we were raised. Any thesis concerning a Christologically oriented participatory account of human nature must provide a compelling account of autonomy, or find itself seeking shelter in an utterly inhospitable environment. Fortunately, Barth does not disappoint. God 'wills and fulfills and reveals Himself not only in Himself but in giving Himself, in willing and recognizing the distinct reality of the creature, granting and conceding to it an individual and autonomous place side by side with Himself'. But note carefully – this is not an individuality or autonomy side by side with his own, *simpliciter*. These gifts of individuality and autonomy are not to be:

> possessed outside Him, let alone against Him, but for Him, and within His kingdom ... The sovereignty which was to be confirmed and glorified was the sovereignty of His love, which did not will to exercise mechanical force, to move the immobile from without ... but rather to triumph in faithful servants and friends ... in their obedience, in their own free decision for Him. The purpose and meaning of the eternal divine election of grace consists in the fact that the one who is elected from all eternity can and does elect God in return. (CD II/2, 178)

Two bedrock commitments clearly emerge here. First, autonomy and individuality are vital for Barth's theology, apart from which there would be no creatures with whom God could meaningfully relate and to whom he could give himself in love and freedom. Second, this autonomy and individuality is properly understood only within, and not alongside or apart from, the life of God. This is a genuine creaturely autonomy within the life of the Creator. What then might 'autonomy *in*' mean?

One possibility lies further within Barth's treatment of election, in which he distinguishes between the being and life of the creature: 'Between the being of the elect and his life as such there lies the event and the decision of the reception of the promise. It is not for his being but for his life as elect that he needs to hear and believe the promise. Not everyone who is elected lives as an elected man' (CD II/2, 321). Our very being, and not merely that of our Creator and Saviour, stands as an object of faith: a reality we comprehend only as we receive it in the light of revelation. Our being is not accessible to us as creatures, as a matter of scientific or psychological observation, for it lies hidden in Christ. Alongside this being which is ours, hidden in Christ, is the life we live and experience, the choices we make, the autonomy we experience as creatures. The divine election consists in the determination of our being in Christ, that we can and do elect God in return, in this present life. Election is God's will and call that our life correspond to our being in Christ, that our autonomy and individuality flourish within God's life and history for us.

At root, then, Barth posits an account of human nature which we cannot perceive, and to which we have access only in faith: that we are what we are in Jesus Christ, that his history transcends and encompasses our own, and that our freedom and autonomy emerge and become what they are only within this greater reality as God elects us that we might in turn and on that basis elect him. Inasmuch as our being is in Christ, it is proper to say that the work of Christ is a representational one, one that includes and shapes our own as the reality and history in which we subsist. Inasmuch as we are autonomous and free creatures *within* this history, within this person, Christ's work is a substitutional one – one which we do not live and experience as such, for our life, our experience, is one which does not at present directly access or perceive our being in Christ.

What then is the life lived by the unrepentant? A 'lie, an absurd self-deception, a shadow moving on the wall – the being of that man who has long since superseded and replaced and who can only imagine that he is man, while in reality he is absolutely nothing' (CD IV/1, 89). As hard as it is to believe (or perhaps it isn't so hard after all), 'we cannot experience and perceive and comprehend ourselves in this our real to-day' (CD IV/1, 548), for 'we are in Him and comprehended in Him, but we are still not He Himself. Therefore it is all true and actual in this Other first and not in us' (CD IV/1, 549). Our freedom, our autonomy, or individuality – all these are real, and treasured by God, the one who seeks to be our God, to be our friend. But these realities are what they are only in a specific relation, only as they are contained within a history, within the life of Jesus, which grounds, shapes and constrains them as the kind of reality they are. The life of the unrepentant is a life which refuses to conform to its being, moving persistently into a lie, toward non-being and dissolution.

Conclusion

We are creatures whose natures and identities are not merely social and relational, but are bound up within and determined by a specific relation: the relation God determined as the very basis of his creative project. We are creatures whose nature and identities are found in Jesus. The relation here is not one of identity – we are not swallowed up within the story of Jesus, such that our own experience and identity is merely a fleeting vision, an ephemeral and ultimately false sense of personal independence that bears no semblance to reality. Not at all – but the genuine identity and autonomy we have occurs within and is shaped by a participation which is constitutive of our nature. Such an understanding gives the lie to either of two extremes. On the one hand, our nature and identity is not merely shaped and determined outside of ourselves. We have real and meaningful identity and agency in relation to Christ. The individualism of modern Western culture is not entirely without merit, for God seeks to be in relation: relation with creatures who have a real and meaningful freedom before him as his covenantal partners. But on the other hand, our autonomy, the making and shaping of our own identities, is not absolute and promethean, and neither is it a relative matter, happening amidst a range of other forces and factors mutually shaping each other. There is some truth in these matters of course – but the ultimate and decisive feature of our identity is that it is a given and shaped identity through our participation in Jesus Christ the *Stellvertreter*, the one who is simultaneously our representative and substitute. Our identity as human beings, and therefore our nature, purpose, actions and happiness are all bound up within a relationship which we do not determine, but determines us: for we are creatures made in a unique relation to Jesus, our head, the one in whom all creation holds together, the one whose life and history determinatively shapes our own as the men and women who died and rose in him. Our identity is thus a received identity, which we shape in the relative autonomy God grants to us within our relationship to Christ, and through the power of his Spirit.

Notes

1 I would like to thank Jeannine Michele Graham, Glen Johnson, Paul Nimmo, Kyle Strobel and Hannah Williamson for their comments on earlier drafts of this chapter, and George Hunsinger and Keith Johnson for granting permission to revise and expand my chapter in their edited volume for this present work: Adam Johnson, 'Atonement: The Logic of Representation and Substitution', in *Companion to Karl Barth*, ed. George Hunsinger and Keith L. Johnson (Chichester: Wiley Blackwell, 2019). Finally, I would like to acknowledge the Yale Center for Faith and Culture, whose generous summer research grant paved the way for my studies on anxiety and depression to which I briefly allude here.

2 In this chapter, I build on the foundation of Karl Barth's theology. While his thought is distinctive, it is not without precursor. His thought bears strong affinities to patristic understanding of human nature, such as we see in chapter 4 of Frances Young, *God's Presence*, esp. pp. 173–5 (Cambridge: Cambridge University Press, 2013). The writings of T. F. Torrance offer a nice bridge between Barth's views and the patristic material: Thomas F. Torrance, *The Mediation of Christ* (Colorado Springs, CO: Helmers & Howard, 1992); Thomas F. Torrance, *Atonement: The Person and Work of Christ* (Downers Grove, IL: InterVarsity Press, 2009). Cf. Alexandra S. Radcliff, *The Claim of Humanity in Christ: Salvation and Sanctification in the Theology of T. F. And J. B. Torrance* (Eugene, OR: Pickwick, 2016). We find similar lines of thought in Maximus the Confessor's integration of Christology, protology and deification, wherein human nature is bound up within Christology comprehensively. Paul M. Blowers, *Maximus the Confessor: Jesus Christ and the Transfiguration of the World* (Oxford: Oxford University Press, 2016), p. 138.

3 For more on the topic of representation and substitution, I commend the work of Jeannine Graham: Jeannine M. Graham, *Representation and Substitution in the Atonement Theologies of Dorothee Sölle, John Macquarrie, and Karl Barth* (New York: Peter Lang, 2005); Jeannine M. Graham, 'Substitution and Representation', in *T&T Clark Companion to Atonement*, ed. Adam J. Johnson (London: Bloomsbury, 2017). For more on Barth's theology of the atonement, I recommend: Nathan D. Hieb, *Christ Crucified in a Suffering World: The Unity of Atonement and Liberation* (Minneapolis, MN: Fortress, 2013); Adam Johnson, *God's Being in Reconciliation: The Theological Basis of the Unity and Diversity of the Atonement in the Theology of Karl Barth* (New York: T&T Clark, 2012); Paul Dafydd Jones, 'Barth and Anselm: God, Christ and the Atonement', *International Journal of Systematic Theology* 12, no. 3 (2010); David Lauber, *Barth on the Descent into Hell: God, Atonement and the Christian Life* (Burlington, VT: Ashgate, 2004); Bruce L. McCormack, 'The Sum of the Gospel', in *Toward the Future of Reformed Theology: Tasks, Topics, Traditions*, ed. David Willis-Watkins, Michael Welker and Matthias Gockel (Grand Rapids, MI: Eerdmans, 1999); Bruce L. McCormack, 'The Ontological Presuppositions of Barth's Doctrine of the Atonement', in *The Glory of the Atonement: Biblical, Historical and Practical Perspectives*, ed. Roger R. Nicole, Charles E. Hill and Frank A. James (Downers Grove, IL: InterVarsity Press, 2004). For an account of my understanding of the doctrine of the atonement more broadly, see: Adam Johnson, *Atonement: A Guide for the Perplexed* (New York: T&T Clark, 2015).

4 Karl Barth, *Church Dogmatics*, trans. G. T. Thompson, 5 vols in 14 parts vols (Edinburgh: T&T Clark, 1936–77); Karl Barth, *Die Kirchliche Dogmatik*, 5 vols in 14 parts vols (Zollikon, Switzerland: Evangelischer Verlag, 1932–70). Cited throughout as CD and KD respectively.

5 Dorothee Sölle, *Christ the Representative: An Essay in Theology after the 'Death of God'* (London: SCM Press, 1967), pp. 88–91.

6 Cf. Karl Barth, *Dogmatics in Outline*, trans. G. T. Thompson (New York: Harper, 1959), pp. 115–16; Karl Barth, *Dogmatik Im Grundriss* (Zürich: Evangelischer Verlag, 1947), p. 135. *Vertauschung* in place of *Stellvertretung*.

7 Sölle, *Christ the Representative*, p. 88.

8 On the range of views, see: Garry J. Williams, 'Karl Barth and the Doctrine of the Atonement', in *Engaging with Barth: Contemporary Evangelical Critiques*, ed. David Gibson and Daniel Strange (Nottingham: InterVarsity Press, 2008), pp. 256–7.

9 Barth, *Dogmatics in Outline*, pp. 48–9.

10 Shannon Nicole Smythe, *Forensic Apocalyptic Theology: Karl Barth and the Doctrine of Justification* (Minneapolis: Fortress Press, 2016); Shannon Nicole Smythe, 'Karl Barth', in *T&T Clark Companion to Atonement*, ed. Adam J. Johnson (London: Bloomsbury, 2017).

11 Note the distinction between representation and substitution in the German: *als dem Tod unseres Repräsentanten und Stellvertreters, KD*, p. 385; cf. p. 387.

12 Lest we be distracted by the overwhelming role of judicial categories, and over-emphasize the similarities with penal substitution, Barth takes a vital excursus in CD IV/1, pp. 273–83, in which he retains the fundamental structure of the fourfold work of Christ, energized by the doctrine of *Stellvertretung*, covering the same material from the standpoint of holiness and the sacrificial system: the Priest sacrificed for us (cf. Grebe, *Election, Atonement, and the Holy Spirit: Through and Beyond Barth's Theological Interpretation of Scripture* [Eugene, OR: Pickwick, 2014]). This excursus cements two vital commitments for us. First, the substitutionary/representative framework is fundamental for Barth in a way that runs deeper than the many expositions or forms by means of which that framework is developed in Scripture, such as the judicial or sacrificial views we have briefly canvassed. *Stellvertretung*, we can now see more clearly than before, is truly that on which the whole doctrine of reconciliation depends (CD IV/1, pp. 273). Second, the distinction between the formal framework (*Stellvertretung*) and material standpoints (judicial, cultic, military etc.) opens up the door for a multiplicity of perspectives on Christ's reconciling work to fund and equip the church's proclamation. *Stellvertretung* is thus the energizing centre of Barth's theology of the atonement.

13 Boethius, *The Consolation of Philosophy*, trans. V. E. Watts (New York: Penguin, 1999), I.vi.

14 Cited in: Thomas, *Summa Theologica*, trans. Fathers of the English Dominican Province (Westminster: Christian Classics, 1981), III.16.12.

15 Boethius, *Consolation of Philosophy*, III.x.

16 Aristotle, *Nicomachean Ethics*, trans. Terence Irwin (Indianapolis, IN: Hackett, 1985), 1097a15–98a20.

17 Boethius, *Consolation of Philosophy*, III.xi.

18 Boethius, *Consolation of Philosophy*, III.xi.

19 Boethius, *Consolation of Philosophy*, III.xii.

20 Charles Taylor, *Sources of the Self: The Making of the Modern Identity* (Cambridge, MA: Harvard University Press, 1989), p. 174.

21 Taylor, *Sources of the Self*, pp. 174–5.

22 Alain Ehrenberg, *The Weariness of the Self: Diagnosing the History of Depression in the Contemporary Age* (Montreal: McGill-Queen's University Press, 2010), p. xxx. Note the affinity of Ehrenberg's project with that of Boethius' 'Lady Philosophy', in their shared interest in the 'sick self'. Cf. Ehrenberg, *The Weariness of the Self*, pp. 15–44.

23 Ehrenberg, *Weariness of the Self*, p. 229. Cf. Mays' statement that 'depression may help some people see the fuzzy baffle of individualist ideology for what it is: a language that discourages our belonging anywhere. It also encourages the enmity to rootedness at the heart of depressive malignancy and the aversion to our only true human right: to be knit into the general communion of suffering, emerging and disappearing human presence.' John Bentley Mays, *In the Jaws of the Black Dogs: A Memoir of Depression* (New York: HarperCollins, 1999), p. 110. Cf. pp. 200–1, 226 on personhood.

24 Aristotle, *Nichomachean Ethics*, 1097b10.

25 Cf. Blowers, *Maximus the Confessor*, p. 199.

14

Being Christ: Salvation and Bonhoeffer's Christo-Ecclesiology

W. MADISON GRACE II

Introduction

In the third century, Cyprian famously stated, '*Salus extra ecclesiam non est*', that is, 'outside the church there is no salvation',[1] thus connecting the relationship between soteriology and ecclesiology. Cyprian's claim has since been interpreted in a variety of ways. In general, however, his claim is commonly understood as maintaining a connection between the salvation of individuals and some concept of Church. Noah's Ark has traditionally been alluded to in this regard, in that only those in the ark were saved from the deluge in a way similar to only those who are in the Church find salvation; those not in the Church, not being saved. Of course, a good bit of this assertion rests upon what is meant by 'Church' in this statement. For it has been used to limit the understanding of the saved to members of certain traditions within Christianity.

Protestants have utilized this concept too in their conceptions of Church, at least loosely. Operating with a concept of visible and invisible Church made up of the faithful (and universally applied), Cyprian's dictum finds expression within the theology of the Reformers and their heirs. For instance, the Westminster Confession of Faith (1646) states:

> The visible Church, which is also catholic or universal under the Gospel (not confined to one nation, as before under the law), consists of all those throughout the world that profess the true religion; and of their children: and is the kingdom of the Lord Jesus Christ, the house and family of God, *out of which there is no ordinary possibility of salvation*.[2]

Though there are varying degrees of understanding as to what is meant by how one attains salvation and who is admitted into the Church, there is an unmistakable historical connection between the doctrines of soteriology and ecclesiology. That is, the company of those that are, have been, or would be saved are rightly connected to the 'Church'. But is the connection between the Church and salvation more than this? Does the concept of Church, in relation to salvation, have meaning beyond the set of individuals who are being 'saved'? A variety of answers might be provided, from institutional models of the Church to more Free Church conceptions. In either case, the answers to these questions presume a notion of personhood that we will address in a moment. In this chapter, I turn my attention to Dietrich Bonhoeffer and his communal notion of personhood, which furnishes us with some unique Christological ways of forging a link between soteriology and ecclesiology. In Bonhoeffer's theology there is a close connection to the reality of the Church and the person and work of Christ. He bound up the reality of the Church into the reality of Christ and in this way conceived of what some have called *Christo-ecclesiology*. In what follows, I unpack Bonhoeffer's conception of the Church in relation to Christ, showing that he understood the Church as the place of Christ *in* the world and, as such, the place of being united to him and living in him *for* the world.[3]

Dietrich Bonhoeffer, Theology and Church

Since his death on 9 April 1945, Dietrich Bonhoeffer has been a resource for various theological, philosophical, ethical, social and political conversations.[4] While his involvement in the resistance to the Nazi regime during the Second World War earned him the posthumous label of 'hero', it is writings from prison (especially his concept of religionless Christianity)[5] for which this activist-pastor has received signal acclaim. And it was his work on and for the Church that was his major achievement.[6] As an early teen, Bonhoeffer declared his singular interest in the Church, a career choice that would create not a little objection from his family, who saw that Church fraught with problems. His response to their objection: 'Then I will reform it.'[7] A programme of reformation was indeed what he had in mind and expressed itself in his scholarship in the academy and his pastoral ministry in various churches in Germany, Spain and England. From the earliest part of his academic career to his final days, Bonhoeffer never wavered from the task of thinking and writing about the Church. His doctoral dissertations, *Sanctorum Communio* and *Act and Being*, his popular works *Discipleship* and *Life Together*, even his writings in *Letters and Papers from Prison* show Bonhoeffer's consistent engagement with ecclesiology.

The Place of Christ

If Bonhoeffer's adolescent claim to 'reform' the Church solidified his vocational pathway in life, then his doctoral dissertation established his theological programme.[8] *Sanctorum Communio: A Theological Study of the Sociology of the Church* is a work accomplishing the task of merging two disciplines together – theology and sociology.[9] His goal, on the one hand, is to look into the question of sociology from a Christian perspective and show that its answer is found in the concept of Church. On the other hand, he shows that '"Person", "primal state", "sin", and "revelation" can [only] be fully comprehended in reference to sociality'.[10] These categories become the framework for Bonhoeffer's argument of the social nature of the Church. Since the Church exists as a community, it is imperative that one also understands the nature of the individuals that constitute the community. That is, the way in which one conceives of personhood relates to how one conceives of community, which Bonhoeffer also connects to how one conceives of God. This leads him to posit, '[t]he *concepts of person, community, and God* are inseparably and essentially interrelated'.[11] It is upon this supposition that Bonhoeffer builds his social theology. In what follows we will unpack further how Bonhoeffer conceived of persons and community in relation to Church and to God. It is Bonhoeffer's social theology and the communal ontology of the Church that is, I think, one of the most intriguing aspects of his discussion on ecclesiology, and one that merits much more analytic attention.

According to Bonhoeffer, without the concept of God in the relatedness between persons (I) and others (You) there can never be any true sense of community. In other words, true community requires a sort of ontic-union, that is, an understanding of the limits of relatedness, one person to another. These limits are dictated in part by the fact that persons are in a fallen world in which true relatedness between persons is dysfunctional and deficient. An 'I' can interact with another, so Bonhoeffer asserts, but only as another 'I', not a 'You'. Thus the 'I' is unable to know relatedness to others and therefore unable to create true community. According to Bonhoeffer, when these 'I's' interact, with what he calls an 'ethical barrier', individual 'I's' recognize the existence of others. This deficiency in relatedness leaves only an activity in *concrete* realities of ethical responsibility toward one another. As a result, Bonhoeffer goes on to explain: 'From the ethical perspective, human beings do not exist "unmediated" *qua* spirit in and of themselves, but only in responsibility vis-à-vis an "other".'[12] He goes on to say that, 'everything that can be said about the Christian concept of person can only be grasped directly by the person who is facing responsibility.'[13]

From here Bonhoeffer's concept of personhood and communal ontology takes another interesting turn. Though Bonhoeffer acknowledges 'other' in a concrete, ethical encounter, he thinks that the ability to know this 'other' remains insufficient without divine mediation. Accordingly, Bonhoeffer states that '*only through God's active working does the other become a You to me from whom my I arises. In other words, every human You is an image of the divine You.*'[14] This divine activity means that the individual is consistently becoming an 'I' as it engages the 'You', and this co-relationship exists only in the relationship with God. There is in Bonhoeffer's thinking a sort of ontic-enlargement of the human-self upon the actualization of relatedness between persons. Bonhoeffer says:

> The other person presents us with the same challenge to our knowing as does God. My real relationship to another person is oriented to my relationship to God. *But since I know God's 'I' only in the revelation of God's love, so too with the other person; here the concept of church comes into play*. Then it will become clear that the Christian person achieves his or her essential nature only when God does not encounter the person as *You*, but 'enters into' the person as *I*.[15]

With this social ontology in place, Bonhoeffer examines humanity in its pre-lapsum and post-lapsum states. In the pre-lapsum or primal state, Bonhoeffer understands true community as necessarily existing between both God and humanity and between human persons, one to another. His exposition of the primal state provides a good deal of the leverage for his illustration of how humanity was intended to exist in community, a point that he also relates to the eschatological hope.[16] By seeing how humanity is intended to exist, any sense of brokenness of community highlights the fallenness of humanity.

Of all that befell humanity by the primal sin, the loss of community with God and others rank among the most severe penalties. This sense of community is clearly social, especially as it relates to a plurality of persons. But as such, it also functions socially in similar ways as an individual relates to others. When an individual engages an 'other' – that is, an existing community – that individual is then engaging, according to Bonhoeffer, the collective person, as it were, of that community. Since the community is conceived of as a collective person it carries with it all the social problems of individual persons. What is more, this means that there is a mutual social relationship between the individual and the collective person of the community. Just as the individual comes into consciousness, or becomes aware of itself, in relating to other persons or the collective person of the community, so too the collective person of the community comes into consciousness as it relates to the individual. Thus for both the individual and the collective person, the ability to 'come into being' happens in the midst of their sociality, or social relations. The relational ontology Bonhoeffer presents here raises a variety of concerns and questions like: can an individual person exist individually or are other persons necessary to their being fully human by virtue of the fact that he says that by their relatedness they 'come into being'? Though these questions are certainly important they are beside the point that Bonhoeffer is raising, namely that individuals have their existence in relation to others, that is, in community. He says:

> The universal person of God does not think of people as isolated individual beings, but in a natural state of communication with other human beings . . . God does not desire a history of individual human beings, but the history of the human community. However, God does not want a community that absorbs the individual into itself, but a community of human beings. In God's eyes, community and individual exist in the same moment and rest in one another. The collective unit and the individual unit have the same structure in God's eyes. On these basic-relations rest the concepts of the religious community and the church.[17]

Bonhoeffer's concern here is that true community in social relatedness not be confused with other forms of individuals relating to one another. We can conceive of groups of individuals en masse that exist without any sense of what Bonhoeffer regards as true community. Think of people on a train during rush hour, or groups of individuals listening to a lecture. According to Bonhoeffer, we find the existence of community when we find individuals whose wills are working in relation to other individual wills. By this he does not mean that the fullness of the realized existence of one individual is confirmed by merely having its will bump up against another's will, as it were. Such interaction as this is merely an acknowledgment that individuals exist. True community, however, requires that wills must not work against one another nor even beside one another. Rather, they must work *with* one another. By working with one another, community comes into being in its social form and, according to Bonhoeffer, it is in the Church that one should find the purest form of such a community.

Bonhoeffer goes a step further, claiming that as individual wills come alongside one another in the community of the Church, another social element is added. He claims that when two wills come together '[a] third person joining them sees not just one person connected to the other; rather, the will of the structure, as a third factor, resists the newcomer with a resistance not identical with the wills of the two individuals'.[18] This third person, he claims, can be seen as the *objectiv Geist* (objective spirit) of the community and exists in such a way that each individual in the community is able to recognize its existence apart from the community. For an individual to exist apart from this *spirit* is tantamount to removing oneself from the community. The concept, therefore, of true community, as Bonhoeffer sees it, is such that the community has a unified spirit as a collective person. Socially, one interacts with this community in the same way that one interacts with individuals. As such, Bonhoeffer rejects the notion that this sense of community should be understood in institutional forms. Rather, the Church as a collective person is to be understood, in Bonhoeffer's terms, as a body. Theologically speaking, Bonhoeffer makes the case for a particular way to understand Church in its communal – that is, social – forms.

The brokenness of community on account of the Fall does not merely have individual consequences. The collective person comprised by the community also shares in these negative consequences. Even the ideal community imaginable is still limited by the effects of the Fall. Persons existing in their old humanity, in Adam, persist in this limited sense of community until a new humanity is created for them. In that interregnum, humans persist in isolation, or at least in a less than ideal sense of community. Here Bonhoeffer says, '[e]very person exists in complete, voluntary isolation; everyone lives their own life, than all living the same life in God'.[19] The community in the state of sin is now the *peccatorum communio* or community of sinners, existing in what Bonhoeffer calls 'ethical solidarity'. He says:

> The experience of ethical solidarity is based upon the utmost singularity of the person, so that even in the awareness of the closest solidarity, the ontic-ethical separateness of individual persons caused by sin can never end, nor disappear from consciousness. One cannot avoid the boundaries of the self. Here we are faced with the I-You-relation described above but actualized in a sinful way, whose 'overcoming' [*Aufhebung*] is only possible in the concept of the church.[20]

The way forward, something ultimately found in the Church, is such that both individuals and communities, existing in their respective personhoods, find ways to repent of their sin. This is true for individuals, churches and nations. The interconnectedness between the individuals and the collective persons they constitute is at work in tandem in the activity of repentance. Individual culpability and corporate culpability are intertwined in such a way that any sense of finding relief from the state of sin has to be so that both senses of personhood – individual and collective – are able to find forgiveness in it. This concept is foreign to those operating from individualist perspectives or those who conceive of their personhood being something non-relational. However, if a person is necessarily contingent upon those with whom he or she relates, whether other individuals or communal persons as Bonhoeffer argues, then there is a shared reality with that other person. In a non-relational personhood one is removed from the joys or sins of another and only participates in the joys or sins that arise out of the individual person. Accordingly, one's engagement in a joyous or sinful activity is necessitated by the inner choice of the individual and not through an external force. For Bonhoeffer, one 'comes into being' along with the other and then shares in whatever joys or sins that that person (individual or communal) has. This social structure helps explain the nature of true community, which, I think with Bonhoeffer, should be found in Church. For it conceives of relations that break through the barrier at the edge of individual 'I's' and draw each other into mutual participation with the whole. Think of the sports spectator who believes that as her team won or lost on the field she won or lost with them. This is more than a shared emotion. It is part of how communities exist. Taking our cues from Bonhoeffer's account of true community will allow us to move beyond the individualist myopia common to much of modern theologizing and re-situate the true identity of humans in Christology and the Church.

This progression of thought leads Bonhoeffer from the reality of social relations, through broken community, to the place where one can address how individuals and communities move toward true sociality, or, as he stated earlier, move to the place where God '*enters a person as an "I"*'.[21] This place, in distinction from the *peccatorum communio*, is the *sanctorum communio*. This is where Bonhoeffer formally takes up the topic of the Church and begins to build his ecclesiology from the foundation of social relations. In this formulation he recognizes that there have been other forms of conceiving of the Church – historically or religiously speaking – but these forms fall short because he thinks they attempt to form an idea of the Church externally, that is, from without of the Church. The Church can only be understood from within, that is, from the place of faith. Because revelation is found only within the Church, the locus of the Church is the only place to comprehend faith. In this, I agree with Bonhoeffer that: 'The reality of the church is a reality of revelation, a reality that essentially must be either believed or denied.'[22] By implication, to found the Church upon an abstract thought (e.g. religion, holiness or tradition) is to lead the Church into abstraction. The concrete reality of the Church is bound up into the idea that the Church itself is revelation – the Church is itself God's revealed reality.

The correlation between revelation and Church that Bonhoeffer constructs is built upon his exegetical understandings of the nature of the Church in the New Testament as well as his own dogmatic tradition. The idea of Church (*Gemeinde*, which is often translated 'church-community') is for Bonhoeffer a biblical concept that rightly connects the community of believers to Christ himself. The Church is ordained by God, actively existing in Christ, and is actualized, or comes into existence, by the Holy Spirit. It is conceptually identified with Christ and Christ's personhood in the metaphor of the body. The Church also, and most importantly, is an active present reality of Christ today. Here Bonhoeffer states that 'Christ exists as church-community' (*Christus als Gemeinde existierend*), which he will come back to time and again in his writings. This existence does have universal (and invisible) aspects to it. But what Bonhoeffer has in mind is a visible Church, which he regards as the actual presence of Christ on earth. This is why he thinks that the Church can be conceived of as revelation itself; it exists as an ontic-relation with the one who is revealed.

For Bonhoeffer, the necessity of understanding the Church as revelation is because he believes the will of God 'must become visible and comprehensible at some point in history' as a completed act.[23] For an individual or a community to exist in a relation to God, they must, according to Bonhoeffer, at some point have some sort of access to the will of God. To this he makes his appeal to revelation. Because of the Fall, God must be the one to 'speak and act' in the world to reveal his will and he has assigned the locus of this revelation to the Church. And the Church exists as the body of Christ, which is the word or speech of God, and is revealed in time to the world through the Holy Spirit who actualizes it. For Bonhoeffer:

> The Holy Spirit is the will of God that gathers individuals together to be the church-community, maintains it, and is at work only within it. We experience our election only in the church-community, which is already established in Christ, by personally appropriating it through the Holy Spirit, by standing in the actualized Church.[24]

This actualization of the Church through the Holy Spirit is more than a potential Church. That is, it is not the community that can *become* the body of Christ; rather, it *is*, in actuality, the revelation of Christ. In this Bonhoeffer appeals to and agrees with Irenaeus that the Church has a pneumatological essence. Irenaeus says: 'The Spirit is only in the church-community, and the church-community is only in the Spirit.'[25]

Following Bonhoeffer, then, the essence of the Church is one that requires participation in the revelation of God, which is the Word, which Bonhoeffer clearly states is actualized by the Spirit. This structure places Christ at the centre, between heaven and earth as the Church's mediator. For it is only in the personhood of Christ, by which he represents humanity before God, that humanity finds its fullness. For Bonhoeffer, it is not merely the fact that Christ's person performs the work of the mediator at some point in the past. He regards this work as performed in time and space, at particular places known as church or churches. It is where the Church is, where Christ is revealed so that the will of God is made known and that individuals can know this will and can enter the ontic-relation of this new humanity. Far from being merely a religious community, Bonhoeffer sees this structure as

Church, or the place where Jesus Christ is present in concrete. Bonhoeffer states it this way: 'Community with God exists only through Christ, but Christ is present only in his church-community, and therefore *community with God exists only in the church*.'[26]

For the individual, then, the reality of the Church is the presence of Christ who is the form and means of salvation. Doing a bit of analytic speculation, one might spell out personhood in a couple of ways that are consistent with Bonhoeffer. One could understand this along the lines of a necessary causal condition. For the individual to find true expression of his/her identity, that same person must be situated in an appropriate environment to express his/her design. Otherwise, the stronger claim, and one that Bonhoeffer may not have been averse to, is that humans truly are identified when they are properly linked up to other humans in a redeemed environment, such that on this view the Christian community makes my identity sufficient. Otherwise, I am left with only a partitive notion of identity, unactualized and unexpressed. Strange as it may sound, I am like a limb with no body. For not only is there 'no salvation outside the Church' in a spatial sense for Bonhoeffer, he regards salvation as predicated upon one's ontic-participation in it. 'Faith is based on entry into the church-community, just as entry into the church-community is based on faith', he says.[27] The soteriological concepts that Bonhoeffer uses here are based upon the social structure of the reality of the Church *as* Christ, that is, as his person and those *in* him. He states that one can approach Jesus 'only in relation to that place where his person reveals himself to me as he really is. Only through Christ's own revelation do I have opened to me his person and his works.'[28] For Bonhoeffer, reality itself, not just soteriology, is bound up in Christ. An individual that would benefit from the work of Christ must find himself or herself united to the one who completed that work. In order to receive this benefit one has to encounter Christ by means of the revelation of Christ. This revelation is found only in the place of the Church. Outside of the Church one is not able to encounter the revelation of Jesus Christ.

Summarily speaking, the structure of the Church is such that as it exists in particular locations as visible communities; communities that exist as the place of Christ, so to speak. In these places Christ is the mediator between God and humanity, not so much represented in the body, but bodily present as God's revealed will actualized by the Holy Spirit. For one to be able to know God, engage his will and have access to his presence – to be thus reconciled – one must come to the place of Christ, which is the place of the Church. To this we must ask: where is the place of Christ? That the Church exists *as* Christ is important for Bonhoeffer, but it is also important for one to know how to come to this place of Christ and participate in the community where Christ and salvation are found. It is what Bonhoeffer thinks about revelation that is the key to understanding this structure of the

Church and its soteriological purpose. This revelation does not exist as a simple set of propositions to be possessed. Rather, it is a social, relational encounter with the one who creates the church-community.

Encountering Christ

For Bonhoeffer, the correlation between Christ, the Church and the individuals who make up the Church is one of *imitatio*. If Christ exists as church-community, then the Church, and the individuals who comprise it, are to be formed into the character of their foundation. In other words, not only does the Church exist because of the presence of Christ, the Church exists as part of Christ's immanent activity. The term that he uses most to describe this action is *Stellvertretung* or vicarious representative action, a term that then is applied to Christ as the *Stellvertreter*, or the vicarious representative. The activity of Christ for the world is not that he comes merely in solidarity with the world – that is, he does not merely become one of us by the incarnation. Christ comes to act for the world in ways that they cannot act. That is, Bonhoeffer's concept of vicarious representative action ought to be understood in part as in relation to responsibility. In his *Ethics*, he states: 'Vicarious representative action and therefore responsibility is possible only in completely devoting one's own life to another person.'[29]

Sociologically speaking, this connection comes through the work of God becoming the 'I' necessary to overcome the barrier of the Fall. In other words, 'since destroying the primal community with God also destroyed human community, so likewise when God restores community between human beings and God's own self, community among us also is restored once again.'[30] The problem of the Fall was that Adam acted for himself, and in doing so brought all of humanity along with him. Christ, in his vicarious representative action takes this 'humanity-in-Adam and [transforms] it into humanity-in-Christ'.[31] This typifies the essence of what the Church is, namely the 'life principle of the new humanity'.[32] This activity, or work, of Christ for humanity then becomes the action of Christ of the Church for the world. And for one to become the new humanity through the work of this activity of Christ one must enter into Christ, and his community, the Church. In this way, one may receive the benefits of Christ's work given *pro nobis* so we, 'with-one-another', in turn act 'for-one-another' as vicarious representatives for the world.

Bonhoeffer is not content with the systematic categories that traditionally help explain Christ, salvation, Church, etc. For example, in his Christology lectures (*Christ the Centre*), he begins by stating that Christological questions ought not begin with *what* Christ has done so much as *who* Christ is.

For it is in understanding who he is that his work then follows. There is no such systematic bifurcation of person and work in Bonhoeffer's Christology, particularly when it comes to Christ's ongoing activity in the world.[33] For the Church, this unity of the person and work of Christ in his personhood means that as one is united to the person of Christ one also is united to the activity of Christ. Since the Church is the place of Christ in the world, it is also the place of Christ's activity in the world. The continual activity of Christ in the world is bound to the place of Christ in the world. There, in the Church, Christ's action is continually accomplished. The action of Christ for the world becomes the dynamic action that those caught up into Christ are to continue for the world.

This is not to say that Bonhoeffer refuses the classic loci of theology altogether. By asking the question of humanity's (new) reality in Christ in terms of ecclesiology and sociology, he presents a different picture of the relationship between Christ and the Church than is normally articulated. Hereby, humanity is not a collection of individual monads walking around, nor is it a coherent set of propositions, but it is a dynamic concrete reality that only God can actualize. The work of Christ does not function merely as an objective act that individuals choose to believe in or not. The work of Christ is primarily an act of revelation that begins with the incarnation, is accomplished through the cross and resurrection, and is set to continue in the Church through the work of the Spirit. An individual's salvation is thus constituted by their participation in this community, which, for Bonhoeffer, is a participation in Christ.

This raises the question of how one then joins this community, or how does one become a part of the community where salvation exists. If we look to Bonhoeffer's literary remains for a precise answer to this question, we don't find all that much. He does not speak of conversion, nor conceive of any dramatic change in his own life except for a time when a 'turning from the phraseological to the real ensued'.[34]

Salvation for Bonhoeffer is one that is found by participating in the reality of Christ that exists in the place of churches. For it is in the churches that the two main activities of the Church actively relate the individual members with their constitutive centre: word and sacrament. To be in the Church is to be in Christ, so one must encounter Christ. The way to encounter Christ is through proclamation of the word and participation in the sacraments. This encounter, or proclamation, of Christ exists because of the nature of the Christ-church reality of revelation. In his habilitation, *Act and Being*, Bonhoeffer addresses this proclamation:

> Revelation should be thought of only in reference to the concept of church, where the church is understood to be constituted by the present proclamation of Christ's death and resurrection – within, on the part of, and for the community of faith.[35]

This proclamation of Christ is necessary for the continual process of the Church being the Church. Because the community has to deal with sin it needs the continual proclamation of the word given to it, that then leads to repentance, and through this finds itself actualized, or re-created, again through the Spirit. One way this proclamation comes is in the form of preaching. Preaching is the activity of the Church 'which it carries out and by which it is borne', Bonhoeffer says.[36] This preaching is simultaneously for those who have faith and those who have potential faith, but in either case the preaching belongs to and exists in the Church. This preaching of the word is what is holding the Church together, as Bonhoeffer explains, saying: 'The word constitutes the unity between essential and empirical Church, between Holy Spirit and objective spirit.'[37] In this community gathered around the word, through preaching, the body receives the gifts of the Spirit. This gathering for preaching becomes one of the reasons for the Church being the Church, for it is the place the Church hears from Christ. For one to claim to be part of the Church yet never assemble with the Church is utterly contradictory for Bonhoeffer: 'For it is the word *preached* according to the will of God and of the church-community that is the means through which this will is actualized.'[38] Bonhoeffer admits that there are individuals who, due to illness or some like condition, are a part of the sanctorum communio, which, of course, raises the question of the necessity of the Church for salvation. However, he stands by his belief that the Church is the place where individuals receive faith through preaching. If other cases exist it is due to God's work and they are exceptions. For Bonhoeffer, the preaching of the word brings an individual into the place where the will of God is heard, and this participation with Christ and the Spirit draws persons into the membership of the Church.

While preaching is the primary way that proclamation occurs in the Church, Bonhoeffer also understands the sacraments as effective means of engaging Christ and the Church. 'The Protestant concept of sacrament is necessarily connected with the word . . . Sacraments are acts of the church-community and, like preaching, they unite within themselves the objective spirit of the church-community and the Holy Spirit who is operating through it.'[39] Baptism is the Church activity that incorporates individuals into the community. It is an act of grace for those who participate in it. For adults this is a direct appropriation of faith and reception of grace. For infants who are baptized the objective spirit of the church-community is the one who receives the sacrament for the child who is then brought into the community where the child is to remain. When Bonhoeffer later writes *Discipleship*, he further clarifies the nature of baptism for the believer and the Church. Baptism is an act in which we become Christ's. Accordingly, he says: 'Baptism thus implies a *break*. Christ invades the realm of Satan and lays hold of those who belong to him, thereby creating his church-community.'⁴⁰ This baptism also depicts, or proclaims, the nature of the life lived with and for one another in the Church community: a life of vicarious representation. The symbol of baptism is one of death to self and thus entails the continuous work of the believer in the Church. Coming into the membership of the church-community entails encountering Christ in the midst of the church-community. Thus being baptized into Christ is, for Bonhoeffer, to become Christ, and then to act *as* Christ for the Church and for the world.

The Lord's Supper also is a participatory activity of the Church community that continually unties the social individual persons into the collective person of the Church and Christ. In the supper, as in baptism, Christ encounters the individual personally and through such encounter makes one a participant in Christ and the Church. This perpetual fellowship ritual is necessary for the assembly of the Christ-community to reconstitute and actualize itself again and again. Bonhoeffer understands that in the event of the Supper humans are performing an act before God and in doing so are identifying community in a 'publicly visible form' that 'God visibly recognizes as such'.⁴¹

In these two activities, word and sacrament, the Church community feeds the faith of individuals, by which they collectively participate in Christ. In doing so, that is, in proclaiming the word and practising the sacraments, the church-community itself becomes the body of Christ and visible in the world.⁴² Utilizing the traditional structure of theology, one might question if the sacraments are to be thought of in relation to soteriology and not just in ecclesiology or sanctification. For Bonhoeffer, these ecclesial practices are necessary to establish the Church. Without them there is no Church. For they mediate and constitute the revelation of Christ in the Church. The place of this revelation is the place of Christ and the place one comes to faith.

Conclusion

Since Bonhoeffer's otherwise brief appearance, talk of salvation has taken on an overtly individualistic character. The questions of individual salvation have become so central to many traditions that introducing a communal aspect to salvation remains mostly suspect. It is granted that Christ is the mediator, means and place of salvation. It is in him, through his accomplished work, that individuals are to be unified in order to attain salvation. Is it then appropriate to conceive of Christ in communal ways? Bonhoeffer's position is one that draws ecclesiology and Christology (both his person and work) closely together, so close in fact that Bonhoeffer is sometimes charged with being Roman Catholic. Should there not be a separation between the Church and Christ? In linking the two closely together has Bonhoeffer conflated justification and sanctification? Has he moved away from his Protestant roots to bring works into faith? It is understandable to raise these questions. However, they are not what is most pressing for him. The labour of Bonhoeffer's work was to understand the concrete reality of the world around him and find Christ in the centre of it in the place of the Church.

Notes

1 Cyprian, *Ep.* LXXII.21.
2 Westminster (emphasis added).
3 Much of this chapter is drawn from my dissertation on Bonhoeffer's conception of church. See W. Madison Grace II, 'The Place of Church in Dietrich Bonhoeffer's Theology' (PhD Diss, Southwestern Baptist Theological Seminary, Fort Worth, Texas, 2012).
4 For example, Stephen R. Haynes highlights the broad appropriation of Bonhoeffer in his work *The Bonhoeffer Phenomenon: Portraits of a Protestant Saint* (London: SCM Press, 2004).
5 See Dietrich Bonhoeffer, *Letters and Papers from Prison*, ed. John W. de Gruchy, trans. Isabel Best, Lisa E. Dahill, Reinhard Krauss and Nancy Lukens, *Dietrich Bonhoeffer Works* 8 (Minneapolis, MN: Fortress Press, 2010).
6 There are a variety of histories on Bonhoeffer in print. Two good examples are Eberhard Bethge, *Dietrich Bonhoeffer: A Biography: Theologian, Christian, Man of his Times*, rev. and ed. Victoria J. Barnett (Minneapolis, MN: Fortress Press, 2000); and Ferdinand Schlingensiepen, *Dietrich Bonhoeffer: 1906–1945: Martyr, Thinker, Man of Resistance* (London: T&T Clark, 2009).
7 See Bethge, *Dietrich Bonhoeffer*, p. 36.
8 Clifford Green states: 'Understanding the theology of Dietrich Bonhoeffer requires a thorough understanding of *Sanctorum Communio* . . . Here are found central ideas that inform all his writings – and, indeed, his life – notwithstanding theological and personal developments associated with later works such as *Discipleship*, *Ethics*, and *Letters and Papers from Prison*.' Clifford J. Green, 'Editor's Introduction to the English Edition', in Dietrich Bonhoeffer, *Sanctorum Communio: A Theological Study of the Sociology of the Church*, ed. Clifford J. Green and Joachim von Soosten, trans. Reinhard Krauss and Nancy Lukens, *Dietrich Bonhoeffer Works* 1 (Minneapolis, MN: Fortress Press, 1998), p. 1.
9 Dietrich Bonhoeffer, *Sanctorum Communio: A Theological Study of the Sociology of the Church*, Eng. edn ed. Clifford J. Green, trans. Reinhard Krauss and Nancy Lukens, *Dietrich Bonhoeffer Works* 1 (Minneapolis, MN: Fortress Press, 1998).
10 DBWE 1:21.
11 DBWE 1:34. Ital. orig.
12 DBWE 1:50.
13 DBWE 1:52.
14 DBWE 1:55. Ital orig.

15 DBWE 1:56. Ital. orig.
16 See DBWE 1:63.
17 DBWE 1:79–80. Ital. orig.
18 DBWE 1:98.
19 DBWE 1:108.
20 DBWE 1:117.
21 DBWE 1:56. Ital. orig.
22 DBWE 1:127. Italics removed.
23 DBWE 1:141.
24 DBWE 1:143.
25 Irenaeus, *Against Heresies*, 3.24.1. Translation from DBWE 1:144.
26 DBWE 1:158.
27 DBWE 1:159.
28 Dietrich Bonhoeffer, *Berlin: 1932–1933*, ed. Larry L. Rasmussen, trans. Isabel Best and David Higgins, *Dietrich Bonhoeffer Works* 12 (Minneapolis, MN: Fortress Press, 2009), p. 310.
29 Dietrich Bonhoeffer, *Ethics*, ed. Clifford Green, trans. Reinhard Krauss, Charles C. West, and Douglas W. Stott, *Dietrich Bonhoeffer Works* 6 (Minneapolis, MN: Fortress Press, 2005), p. 259.
30 DBWE 1:145.
31 DBWE 1:147.
32 DBWE 1:147.
33 DBWE 12:300–08.
34 DBWE 8:357.
35 Dietrich Bonhoeffer, *Act and Being: Transcendental Philosophy and Ontology in Systematic Theology*, ed. Wayne Whitson Floyd Jr, trans. H. Martin Rumscheidt, *Dietrich Bonhoeffer Works* 2 (Minneapolis, MN: Fortress Press, 1996), p. 110.
36 DBWE 1:220.
37 DBWE 1:226.
38 DBWE 1:227.
39 DBWE 1:240.
40 Dietrich Bonhoeffer, *Discipleship*, ed. Geffrey B. Kelly and John D. Godsey, trans. Barbara Green and Reinhard Krauss, *Dietrich Bonhoeffer Works* 4 (Minneapolis, MN: Fortress Press, 2001), p. 207.
41 DBWE 1:244.
42 See DBWE 4:229.

15

Redeeming the Eucharist: Transignification and Justification

JAMES M. ARCADI

That Jesus calls a piece of bread and a measure of wine by the terms, respectively, 'my body' and 'my blood' is not in question. This much is clear from but a moment's glance at the relevant passages of the Synoptics and 1 Corinthians.[1] Furthermore, these locutions form the heart of nearly all celebrations of the Eucharist, irrespective of the denominational locale in which these liturgical utterances are made. What, however, is in question is just what these curious utterances mean and how the realities they denote relate to the salvation of the humans who hear these words and consume the bread and wine – newly termed 'body' and 'blood'. Transignification is one attempt to address the question of what these utterances mean. The term was initially coined in the mid-twentieth-century by the Dominican Edward Schillebeeckx as he proposed to explicate a Roman Catholic understanding of Christ's presence in the Eucharist, while avoiding the challenge of deploying an Aristotelian metaphysic in a day when this ontology no longer seemed tenable. Despite the fact that the metaphysical reflections of the Stagirite philosopher are no longer seen in contemporary metaphysical circles as untenable, there is much in this proposal that can be appropriated for an account of Christ's presence in the Eucharist regardless of one's penchant for – or aversion to – a substance ontology. Further, this Eucharistic proposal has much to offer sacramentally-minded Christians not constrained by the dictates of the Roman Catholic Church. Moreover, so I will argue, there are conceptual resources within this Eucharistic proposal that can be brought to bear on soteriological issues.

The plan of this chapter is as follows. I first review Schillebeeckx's initial mid-twentieth-century proposal. This is followed by discussions of similar proposals found in the analytic literature by Michael Dummett and Harriett Baber. I then pivot to consider the phenomenon of prosthesis use and some of the psychological-therapeutic perspectives offered by prosthesis users. This will do two things. First, it will provide us with an underpinning to a straightforward, first-order discourse analysis of the curious Eucharistic utterances. Second, it will provide a model for how it might be that human beings are incorporated into the body of Christ, thus constituting a soteriological model of justification. Finally, I show how slight nuances in one's perspective on the consecrated Eucharistic elements can have implications for how one understands the status of the redeemed human.

I should note from the outset that I do not think this model makes an explicit endorsement of a particular theory of the atonement. I think that a range of standard atonement models could be consistent with the motif proffered here. If one thought, along the lines of some in the Eastern Orthodox tradition, that all one needs is a theosis model of the atonement, then one might see my prosthesis model here as telling the whole story. If, however, one was keen to include penal or satisfaction elements in one's theory of the atonement, then one could easily tell this story with these elements as the preamble and my prosthesis model as a story about sanctification. Furthermore, while I take the transignification theory of the Eucharistic presence as a serious and worthwhile one, it differs in important respects from what I have defended elsewhere.[2] That said, because I make use of some of the conceptual infrastructure of my previous work in this chapter, the distinguishing features between the two views are subtle.

Schillebeeckxian Transignification

Christ said of a piece of bread, 'This is my body' and of a measure of wine, 'This is my blood'. Ministers standing *in persona Christi* make the same utterance. Ministers might also, when distributing the consecrated elements, make the utterance, 'This is the body of Christ' or 'This is the blood of Christ'. Schillebeeckx helpfully shows that discussions of the mechanics of the Eucharist prevalent in the medieval period through the Council of Trent were primarily concerned with presenting a metaphysical state of affairs wherein these statements came out as true. The primary motivation was a positive statement, that 'This is the body of Christ' is true on the level of first-order discourse. As Schillebeeckx writes: '[W]e may say that the concept of "transubstantiation" points to nothing more, but also to nothing less, than the Catholic feeling for the biblical and distinctively Eucharistic real presence of Christ within the medieval framework of thought.'[3] This is to say that a doctrine of transubstantiation was not the end of Eucharistic ruminations, it was rather the means by which medieval Roman Catholics secured the notion of the real presence. The dispute, however, was twofold. First, as the example of John Wyclif shows, the question was raised as to whether the absence of the bread and wine was required to secure the real presence. Second, as the example of Schillebeeckx himself shows, the question was raised as to whether an Aristotelian substance ontology was a necessary philosophical framework for proper explications of the real presence.

The first component of the dispute, exemplified by the *doctor evangelicus* John Wyclif, pertains to the Roman requirement to deny that the bread or the wine continues to be present after the consecratory utterances are made by the priest. Although Pope Innocent III had used the term 'transubstantiation' at the Fourth Lateran Council (1215), no official proclamation as to the metaphysical implications of this term had been forthcoming. The Council of Constance (1418) was called in part to counter views on the Eucharist promulgated by Wyclif and his followers, including Jan Hus. This council decreed Wyclif and Hus to be heretics and the council gave these errors as the basis for their heresy. They were condemned for holding:

1 The material substance of bread, and similarly the material substance of wine, remain in the sacrament of the altar.[4]
2 The accidents of bread do not remain without their subject in the said sacrament.[5]
3 Christ is not identically and really present in the said sacrament in his own bodily person.[6]

Lateran IV and Constance required the belief that in the consecration of the bread and wine of the Eucharist, Christ became substantially present 'under the form' of bread and wine. Constance further specified that this substantial change necessitated two further beliefs. First, one had to believe that after consecration the substances of the bread and wine were no longer present on the altar. Second, that what remained on the altar was the corporal presence of the substance of the body and blood of Jesus Christ, which is identical with the body of Christ sitting at the right hand of the Father.

The second component of the dispute into which Schillebeeckx entered concerned whether an Aristotelian substance ontology is required for a canonical Roman explication of the real presence. To this, Schillebeeckx issued a resounding 'no'. Schillebeeckx concludes: 'The dogma [of transubstantiation] was thought out and expressed in "Aristotelian" categories, but the strictly Aristotelian content of these categories was not included in what the dogma intended to say. Christ's real presence in the Eucharist is therefore not tied to Aristotelian categories of thought.'[7] This interpretation of the conciliar statements allowed Schillebeeckx the freedom to pursue an explication of the real presence within a different category of thought. For Schillebeeckx, this meant a turn to phenomenology, and specifically the phenomenology of experiencing the Eucharist within the ritual of the Roman Catholic Church.

In light of Schillebeeckx's determinations regarding what is required by the Roman canons and what is untenable about Aristotelian ontology, he turns to ground an account of the real presence in other terms. This is apparent when he asks the question: 'What is the *reality* that we experience in our perception of the Eucharistic form?'[8] But reality, for the phenomenologist, is the significance of an object for the perceiver, from the perspective of the perceiver.

> What appears, in our experience, as bread and wine is the 'body of the Lord' appearing to us (as sacramental nourishment). The significance of the phenomenal forms of bread and wine changes because by the power of the creative Spirit, the reality to which the phenomenal refers is changed – it is no longer bread and wine, but nothing less than the 'body of the Lord', offered to me as spiritual nourishment.[9]

The objects that were formerly perceived as bread and wine have, for the perceiver, become phenomenally the body and blood of Christ. This would, it seems, secure both the real presence of the body of Christ and allow one to hold that the bread was no longer present, thus allowing one to maintain fidelity to the spirit of the Roman Catholic conciliar statements, even if not expressing that spirit in the idiom of Aristotelian categories. However, further specification of Schillebeeckx's suggestive theory is possible, and for this I now turn to consider some recent analytic treatments of the issue.

Recent Explications of Transignification

The touch-points between the ensuing analyses and Schillebeeckx's proposal will be apparent, but what follows makes use of not just phenomenology but a descendent of this philosophy attending to social ontology. A basic, and very rough, notion underlying the commitments of social ontology is that the nature(s) of items in the cosmos – the 'what-it-is' of things – are determined, not discerned, by humans. In the context of our social interactions and in service to them, the items that are utilized in these interactions are given meaning and their natures. In application to the Eucharist, as bread and wine take their meaning from social interactivity – as do all objects – their natures can be changed from what they are normally taken to be.

Michael Dummett approaches the question of the doctrine of the Eucharistic presence by setting up a simple interrogation of a would-be participant in the Eucharist. He writes: 'I propose to understand the doctrine as requiring no more than that the correct and unqualified answer to the question "What is it?", asked of either of the consecrated elements, is "The Body of Christ" or "The Blood of Christ".'[10] This much is straightforward and many traditions have wished to analyse the curious phrases that ministers utter on this simple level. However, Dummett's social ontological model of the Eucharist puts a great deal of emphasis on the nature of what he calls 'deemings'. I will focus on how these so-called deemings function pertaining to artefacts, such as those ordinary objects made by humans. It might be that a deeming model undergirds the ontology of natural kinds as well as artefactual kinds, but this could prove controversial and is not necessary to my project, since I take it that bread and wine are not natural kinds, but the product of human ingenuity and creativity (of course, bread and wine are made from natural kinds, such as grain, water, and grapes, but it takes human effort to bring from these natural objects the artefactual elements of bread and wine).[11] The basic idea behind Dummett's deemings is that artefacts are not any thing until humans deem or declare them to be some specific entity. Moreover, artefacts exhibit a necessary plasticity such that whereas a particular object, O, at time t_1, may be considered an X, yet at t_2 O is deemed to be Y, and hence at t_3, O is in fact a Y and no longer an X. How might this work? Dummett uses an instance of an ashtray as an illustration. Suppose we have in mind an ashtray and suppose we have a smoker in mind, call him 'Matt'. Suppose this ashtray is a shallow bowl with some notches taken out of the rim wherein cigarettes and cigars might rest comfortably when not finding a home in a Matt's mouth. It does not seem as though an ashtray is a natural kind – ashtrays are not harvested from ash trees. Hence, when the glass smith forges the tray, Matt buys the tray and then flicks his ashes into said tray, this artefact is deemed an ashtray.

Now imagine this situation. Suppose Matt accidentally knocks his ashtray off his coffee table and it smashes beyond use; he throws it in the bin, but the cigar in his mouth is growing dangerously in need of a flick of ash. Matt seeks a small bowl from his kitchen. Suppose this is a small cereal bowl having heretofore been used exclusively for breakfast foods. Matt could take this bowl, utter, 'This is an ashtray' and flick his cigar ashes into the, now known as, ashtray. Matt would be at this point deeming the cereal bowl an ashtray. Although we might frown at Matt's use of the cereal bowl as an ashtray and although we might think twice if Matt in the future were to offer us a bowl of cereal, artefacts do not carve up reality at the joints. Humans carve parts of reality into artefacts, and in so doing, at times, change artefacts from one to another.[12]

One important component to Dummett's deemings, and this is especially highlighted in Baber's appropriation of transignification (more on this anon), is that in order for these deemings to stick, they must take place within a socio-linguistic community that adopts the new status of the object in question. That is, if the rest of the members of Matt's household continued to refer to the cereal bowl-turned-ashtray as a cereal bowl, kept cleaning out the cigar ashes, kept cleaning it out and eating cereal from it, it would not seem as though Matt's deeming took. Rather, the deeming (especially of one object to another) has to be ratified, at least in language, especially in practice, by the socio-linguistic community in order for a veridical deeming to have been said to occur.

The application of this story to the Eucharist is quite simple. Prior to the utterance of the curious words at the Last Supper, both the bread on the table and the wine in the cup were certain artefacts, standard ones known as 'bread' and 'wine'. When, however, Christ took the bread in his hands, drew his fellow diners' attention to it, and uttered, 'This is my body', on this analysis, Christ was deeming the bread to be his body. Because Christ is God, his deemings are to be taken as authoritative by any who believe him to be God. Dummett even states that taking the bread as Christ's body requires the antecedent belief in the Incarnation, and thus those who do not have the requisite antecedent belief cannot be expected to hold the deeming to have obtained.

Baber follows suit in the transignification motif in her two articles, explicitly invoking Dummett at one point. Baber avers that her transignification model grounds the aptness of the liturgical utterance, and does so in a much more metaphysically simple manner than previous attempts to secure the real presence in the history of theological reflection. She construes the change in the elements to be a matter of a change in the institutional conventions respecting the elements. According to her model, 'the act of consecration is a conventionally generated action analogous to, for example, the act of writing out a cheque.'[13] By all empirical counts, a rectangular piece of paper with numbers and letters on it is literally worth no more than a piece of paper. Yet, given certain conditions constituted by particular social and institutional conventions, a cheque one writes for $200 *is*, on Baber's view, $200. The meaning of the object goes beyond its empirical makeup. Following this analogy, given the conventionally generative actions of the Eucharistic liturgy, when a minister says of a piece of bread that it is the body of Christ, the bread in fact becomes the body of Christ. Might one allege that this view is simply subjective, being based on the psychological states of the participants in the liturgy? Baber argues that the presence of the body of Christ *qua* institutional fact is similar to other standard social conventions:

> But marriage, money, boundaries, and the like are not 'subjective'. They are the products of collective rather than individual intentionality and the institutions in which it is embodied. An individual cannot by his own initiative, through believing, wishing, or acting as if it were so, enter into or dissolve a marriage, acquire citizenship or increase the value of his portfolio. And, on the account proposed here, the presence of Christ in the Eucharist is likewise secured by the collective intentionality of an institution, viz. the Church.[14]

Employing a social ontological framework, Dummett and Baber show that while some things in our world are the result of institutional or social convention, they are no less real. Hence the reality of the real presence of Christ in the Eucharist need not be construed by deploying a substance ontology, but can be explicated using well-worn social ontology. However, like Dummett's view, assenting to the truth of the metaphysical state of affairs that undergirds the liturgical utterance requires the antecedent participation in the relevant institution that sanctions the institutional fact of that object being the body of Christ.

But, one might aver, Christ presents us with a very odd situation indeed. For it is one thing to tell us that a cereal bowl has been deemed an ashtray, quite an extreme version of this to hold that a piece of bread has been deemed a human body and that we are to now consider this bread to be the body of Christ. Is this not a step too far for a deeming socio-linguistic state of affairs? Here is where we now pivot to consider the testimony of prosthesis users to push on the intuition that this situation is in fact beyond the pale. For what occurs in an instance of prosthesis use is that some artefact – the product of human ingenuity and creativity – is deemed to be part of a user's body, deemed to be a certain part of a user's body, and the user, and her socio-linguistic community, take it as such.

Prosthesis Use

In the Eucharist, Christ denotes a piece of bread – an artefact – to be his body. Understood along the lines demarcated by Schillebeeckx, Dummett and Baber, this can be taken as an act of deeming whereby the object – the piece of bread – takes on a new social ontological status. Although this kind of a linguistic situation might be easy to understand in the 'cereal bowl to ashtray' or 'piece of paper to cheque' illustrations, some might baulk at applying this state of affairs to the 'piece of bread to the body of Christ' situation. I suspect that the main area of nervousness for the detractor would be the manner in which an artefact is supposed to be conceived of as becoming a human body – something that is thought to be entirely organic. However, while it is certainly the case that human bodies are by and large constituted by organic parts, in the case of prosthesis use non-organic objects – artefactual objects – come to be incorporated into the bodily systems of the prosthesis users such that these prosthetics become, through a process of deeming, parts of the prosthesis user's body. I will exposit this phenomenon here and then make an application of this to the Eucharist before taking all these themes to the sphere of justification.

The use for a prosthetic limb comes when a person desires to accommodate their body for a limb that is missing due to limb loss or congenital limb-deficiency. A prosthetic limb serves the purpose of providing a means for an amputee, for example, to engage in the world and with her body image in a manner similar to the manner she engaged in the world prior to amputation. 'Incorporation' is a term referring to the manner in which the prosthetic device is integrated into the users' bodily system – in terms of her bodily awareness, perceptual ability, bodily self-identity, peripersonal space, and so on. Although a thorough survey of the relevant psychological literature is outside the scope of this present study, I here point to a few instances where incorporation appears to have occurred to a sufficient level that prosthesis users considered their prosthetic to be their body.

For instance, many prosthesis users report that their prosthesis is as much a component of their bodies as their organic parts. One user writes: 'Within my body schema, my prosthetic is as much a part of my body as my skin, blood, and organs.'[15] Likewise, too, another user reports on the use of a new prosthetic device that: 'One of the major factors in my satisfaction with a new prosthesis is how little I feel it. That may sound strange, but to me, my prosthesis is an extension of my body.'[16] For both of these prosthesis users, a non-organic and artefactual object has become part of their bodies. These other objects have been properly incorporated into the bodies of their users. Murray comments: 'That prostheses can complete a body, i.e. that they can become "part of" the body, is testified by both amputees and people with congenital limb absence.'[17] The result of this incorporation is that some prosthesis users even attest to considering the incorporation sufficient to the point that the prosthesis completes the body. Another user attests: 'Well, to me it's as if, though I've not got my lower arm, it's as though I've got it and it's [the prosthesis] part of me now. It's as though I've got two hands, two arms.'[18] What these testimonies indicate is that one ought not baulk at the notion that an artefact can, within a socio-ontological framework, become a veridical part of a person's body.

Now, it is not necessary for a prosthesis user to perform some explicit act of deeming. She does not need to look at her prosthetic leg and declare, 'This is my body!', although an act of this nature can certainly serve the incorporation process. What is sufficient for incorporation to have occurred is the kind of self-attestation and self-conceptualization demonstrated in the aforementioned testimonies. The lesson learned from these forays into the realm of prosthesis use, is that the kind of deeming that occurs in 'cereal bowl to ashtray' can also occur in situations of 'artefact to body part', and hence there is grounds for the application of this conception to the Eucharist to explicate a transignification explanation of 'piece of bread to body of Christ'.

This is my Prosthesis

It seems to me that there are resources within this ontological framework for following the letter as well as the spirit of the Roman canons. But this means that the difference between adopting this framework while holding to a Roman conception and adopting this framework while holding to a non-Roman conception is subtle. The difference between a Roman transignification and a non-Roman transignification turns not on the answer to the question, 'Is this the body of Christ?' – both will answer 'yes'. The difference turns on the answer to the question, 'Is this a piece of bread?' The Roman is required to answer this 'no'. The non-Roman is free to answer in the affirmative. One's intuitions on this score are revealed in how one approaches other instances of a change in signification or deeming. Is the cereal bowl-turned-ashtray still a cereal bowl? Is the small, rectangular piece of paper still a piece of paper in addition to being $200? Is the prosthetic leg still an artefact made by human hands of inorganic material as well as the amputee's leg? If one has the intuition that in the other instances of a change in signification the original item ceases to be – ceases to exist as what it once was – then it seems to me one can satisfy the desiderata of the Roman canons with a clear conscious. If, however, one has the intuition or commitment to the fact of the remaining original entity in addition to whatever other signification the object expresses by a veridical deeming, then when one applies this conception to the Eucharist one ends up with a non-Roman perspective on the consecrated bread and wine.

My concern here is not to resurrect outdated ways of maintaining fidelity to the letter or spirit of the Tridentine canons. Faithful adherents to the Roman Catholic teaching magisterium are certainly required to hold to the twin notions of the absence of the bread/wine and the substantial presence of Christ's body/blood. However, Catholics of a non-Roman variety are free to draw on these conceptual resources to exposit alternative means for securing a conception of the real presence of Christ in the Eucharist. But I note that there are Roman and non-Roman ways of applying the deeming motif to the Eucharist and this will carry over in the next section to Roman and non-Roman ways of applying this motif to justification.[19]

Regardless of what one says about the continued presence of the bread, the transignification model – with a social ontology infrastructure – can deliver on a straightforward understanding of Christ's utterance, 'This is my body'. What Christ means is that the object formerly known only as bread has, in an act of deeming, become in reality the body of Christ. I now turn to apply these reflections to the area of soteriology.

Deemed Righteous

The Eucharist has certainly been a locus for much dispute in the history of theological reflection. The disputes over the doctrine of justification do not pale in comparison. My purpose here is not to settle the disputes in either of these doctrines, but merely to draw out some level of conceptual interrelationship between the two. The preceding reflections on transignification brought about a perspective on the Eucharist that holds the minister – in the context of the ecclesial community and standing *in persona Christi* – to deem the bread and the wine as the body and blood of Christ. I showed these linguistic deemings of these specific artefacts to be related to the kind of deeming that might occur when a prosthesis user deems her prosthesis to be properly a part of her body. As the testimony of these users indicate, a deeming of this nature makes it such that when one asks of as amputee if her prosthetic is her body, she answers in the affirmative. Likewise, when we ask if the consecrated bread is the body of Christ, we too can answer in the affirmative. In the realm of soteriology, a similar phenomenon can be seen to occur. Only, in this realm it is not bread or a prosthetic leg that is being deemed, it is we humans who are *re*-deemed.

The exegetical issues pertaining to the right interpretation of Paul's letter to the Romans are deep, and the variety of interpretive motifs vast. I do not pretend that what I say here settles any of these complex issues. However, I want to point out that there is a dovetail between the transignification deeming motif and one plausible interpretation of Paul's use of *dikaioō*.[20] One way of explicating Paul's notion of justification in the Christian tradition has been to hold that God declares a Christian righteous in the act of redemption. This is a forensic explication of justification. The Christian has not merited or earned justification due to any acts she has performed, rather the righteousness belongs to Christ and this is then credited or awarded to or counted as the Christian's righteousness. But this notion of the declarative word of the righteousness of a Christian has clear resonances with the deeming motif of transignification. God declares or asserts or performs some speech act that brings it about that the Christian – within God's socio-ontological world – is righteous.

The further implications of this distinction for soteriology should be clear. If the deeming motif is to be carried along from prosthetic use to the Eucharist to the individual Christian, then the distinction between a Roman and a non-Roman perspective carries through as well. Of course, note that I am not talking about Roman or non-Roman perspectives on soteriology. I am using the term 'non-Roman' to refer to views wherein the original entity remains, and I am using the term 'Roman' to refer to views wherein the original entity does not remain. Hence, a Roman take would have it that when God deems the human being to be part of the body of Christ or to be saved or to be regenerate, that human is no longer what it once was. Whereas a non-Roman perspective would aver that, while being deemed a new entity, the human always retains, under some consideration, its original status. Let me unpack these implications in more detail.

A Roman-inspired soteriological motif would have it that Paul's description of the Christian as a 'new creation' means a completely new entity. Paul writes in 2 Corinthians 5.17: 'Therefore, if anyone is in Christ, he is a new creation. The old has passed away; behold the new has come.' As on the Roman model of the Eucharist the bread ceases to be bread, and the wine ceases to be wine, after the deeming of the entities as the body and blood of Christ, so too would the human cease to be what it once was and instead become a new entity. A non-Roman perspective on this phenomenon might look like Luther's *simul justus et peccator* motif. Although from one angle the Christian is to be seen as righteous and a new creation – redeemed – it is also understood that the Christian is still a sinner and retains something of the Christian's original unrighteousness. Regardless of whether one opts for a Roman-inspired or non-Roman-inspired application of the transignification motif, it is easy to see how a similar socio-ontological phenomenon as occurs in the Eucharistic deeming can be seen to occur in the act of justification.

Conclusion

The fact does not escape me that another Pauline motif applicable in this regard is to refer to the Church as the body of Christ.[21] Those Christians whom God has redeemed by deeming them righteous are thought by Paul to be incorporated into the body of Christ. As I indicated before, it is not necessary for a veridical act of deeming to occur that the deemer actually utter some deeming sentence. Matt can deem his cereal bowl to be an ashtray just in virtue of his use of the object as an ashtray. Sue does not have to deem her prosthetic limb in order for it to be her body, she just has to sufficiently incorporate it into her bodily system in order for this deeming to go through. In the case of the Eucharist, we do have an explicit deeming utterance, both Christ and ministers standing *in persona Christi* say of a piece of bread, 'This is my body' or 'This is the body of Christ'. On this analysis, then, Christ need not utter any explicit sentence in order for human redemption – humans being declared righteous – to occur. However, the conception of Christ uttering some form of a declarative word to the redeemed has been a part of the traditional Protestant reflection on this theological phenomenon. Hence, I might suggest that in addition to deeming a piece of bread as his body, we might see that the deeming words that Christ might speak to all the humans who are redeemed in the act of redemption could be understood to be – as in the Eucharist – 'This is my body'.

Notes

1 Matt. 26.26–28; Mark 14.22–25; Luke 22.14–20; 1 Cor. 11.23–26.
2 See my book *An Incarnational Model of the Eucharist* (Cambridge: Cambridge University Press, 2018).
3 Edward Schillebeeckx, *The Eucharist* (London: Sheed and Ward, 1968), p. 60.
4 Norman Tanner, *Decrees of the Ecumenical Councils: Vol. 1* (London: Sheed and Ward, 1990), p. 411: '*Sustantia panis materialis, et similiter substantia vini materialis, manet in sacramento altaris.*'
5 Tanner, *Decrees Vol. 1*, p. 411, '*Accidentia panis non manent sine subiecto in eodem sacramento.*'
6 Tanner, *Decrees Vol. 1*, p. 411, '*Christus non est in eodem sacramento identice et realiter in propria persona corporali.*'
7 Schillebeeckx, *The Eucharist*, p. 102.
8 Schillebeeckx, *The Eucharist*, p. 145, emphasis original.
9 Schillebeeckx, *The Eucharist*, p. 149.
10 Michael Dummett, 1987, 'The Intelligibility of Eucharistic Doctrine', in William Abraham and Stephen Holtzer (eds), *The Rationality of Religious Belief: Essays in Honor of Basil Mitchell* (Oxford: Oxford University Press, 1987), p. 234.
11 For an engaging and fascinating study of these material components of the Eucharist, see David Grummett, *Material Eucharist* (Oxford: Oxford University Press, 2016).
12 I am not here arguing that one must think that the human-to-reality relationship is one of making not matching *in toto*. Rather it is simply the case that for non-natural kinds, artefactual kinds, humans make these. It might be that humans discover oak trees, tigers and copper, but humans make cereal bowls, wooden tigers and jewellery.
13 H. E. Baber, 'The Real Presence', *Religious Studies* 51, 1 (2013), p. 21. See also her 'Eucharist: Metaphysical Miracle or Institutional Fact?', *International Journal for Philosophy of Religion* 74, 3 (2013), pp. 333–52.
14 Baber, 'The Real Presence', p. 26.
15 Elizabeth Wright, 'My Prosthetic and I: Identity Representation in Bodily Extension', *Forum: University of Edinburgh Journal of Culture and the Arts* 8 (2009), p. 1.
16 C. D. Murray, 'An Interpretative Phenomenological Analysis of the Embodiment of Artificial Limbs', *Disability and Rehabilitation* 26, 16 (2004), p. 970.
17 Murray, 'An Interpretative Phenomenological Analysis', p. 970.
18 Murray, 'An Interpretative Phenomenological Analysis', p. 970, contractions *sic*.
19 Note that I mean 'Roman' and 'non-Roman' in this instance just to refer to the absence of the bread or the continued presence of the bread. I do not mean that this will necessarily align with official Roman Catholic teaching on the theology of justification.

20 In Romans this term can be found in Rom. 2.13; 3.4, 20, 24, 26, 28, 30; 4.2, 5; 5.1, 9; 6.7; 8.30, 33. Other Pauline instances include 1 Cor. 4.4; 6.11; Gal. 2.16, 17; 3.8, 11, 24; 5.4; 1 Tim. 3.16; Titus 3.7.

21 Clear examples are Rom. 12.3, 'we, though many, are one body in Christ'; 1 Cor. 12.13, 'For in one Spirit we were all baptized into one body'; 1 Cor. 12.27, 'Now you are the body of Christ and individually members of it'; Eph. 1.22–23, God 'put all things under his [Christ's] feet and gave him as head over all things to the church which is his body'.

16

Regeneration and the Spirit

PAUL HELM

> Batter my heart, three-person'd God, for you
> As yet but knock, breathe, shine, and seek to mend;
> That I may rise and stand, o'erthrow me, and bend
> Your force to break, blow, burn, and make me new.
> I, like an usurp'd town to another due,
> Labour to admit you, but oh, to no end;
> Reason, your viceroy in me, me should defend,
> But is captiv'd, and proves weak or untrue.
> Yet dearly I love you, and would be lov'd fain,
> But am betroth'd unto your enemy;
> Divorce me, untie or break that knot again,
> Take me to you, imprison me, for I,
> Except you enthrall me, never shall be free,
> Nor ever chaste, except you ravish me.
> John Donne – Holy sonnet 14

This chapter is offered as a response to the Editors' invitation to make a contribution to the idea of regeneration at the conceptual crossroads of the doctrine of salvation and of human ontology, particularly as it concerns the nature of the Spirit's work in regeneration. I shall consider two ways of approaching regeneration; the scholastic way, taking as my example the Puritan Stephen Charnock's (1628–80) short work on regeneration, *The Nature of Regeneration*, because of its clarity and succinctness. It was one of several short pieces of his on the topic. Charnock was a well-known later Puritan, best known for his *Existence and Attributes of God*.[1] I take this short work to be typical of Reformed Orthodox theology on the subject. This is followed by a work that is much better known, Jonathan Edwards' *Religious Affections* (1746),[2] which propounds an alternative approach to regeneration.

'Being saved' is an expression of passivity. No debate on that. In Christian church history the theological issue has been that of passivity's distinctness and strength. The Augustinian tradition, of which Charnock and Edwards were exponents, upholds it in a strong, monergistic manner. In regeneration God by his gracious power brings life to dead souls. Regeneration is the act of God the Holy Spirit. What is distinctive is that in regeneration there is a moment that the soul receiving it is passive. It is passive because it is disabled or spiritually dead. Regeneration must follow. To this end, I explore Edwards' and Charnock's variant understandings of this monergism.

Christian Scholasticism

The Reformed scholastic approach to regeneration is a matter of the impartation of a new habit. Charnock's short book *The Nature of Regeneration* is a good example of such thinking. This is discussed, and certain misunderstandings identified. The meaning of 'new habit' is clarified, and its pros and cons assessed. Aristotelian opposition to the idea, based on Aristotle's dictum in the *Nicomachean Ethics*, that we become X by doing X-like things, is considered, and certain misunderstandings dispelled. By scholasticism is here meant Reformed scholasticism.

It has been held that scholasticism implies a degeneration of the purity of first-generation Reformed theology into 'rationalism' and 'logic'. From the very start of the Reformation the majority of its theologians had been educated as Roman Catholic scholastics. So it was natural that they kept the skills that they had acquired and employed them in their new, Protestant careers. But it is clear that scholastics such as Charnock had a pastoral side to their work.

Reformed Scholasticism, developed from Aristotle and Thomas Aquinas and adapted to the demands of Christian theology, proved to be quite flexible for the development of a systematic understanding of the Reformed faith in its didactic and polemical modes in the tradition of faith seeking understanding. Charnock's work is a good illustration of this theological style.

Regeneration is understood as the gracious possession of new habit infused by the Holy Spirit. As such it is not a change in the essence of the soul – that would make regeneration to consist in the development of a new soul. But it is nevertheless a radical change or set of such changes. For regeneration is a deep change of the soul, and all its faculties and powers are affected by this change. Charnock reckons it is difficult to describe so deep and broad a change. He lists some of the issues that arise in disputing its nature: '[W]hether it be quality, or spiritual substance; whether, if a quality, it be a habit or a power, or whether it be the Holy Ghost personally.'[3] Its effects can be identified, but its nature is mysterious. Not to mention the fact that we have a natural ignorance of such things, and an antipathy to them, and of course no experience of those things that others are the subject of, involving basic changes in ethical and spiritual orientation. How should we understand this vital principle and the radical changes it brings? How in this state of incomprehension and ignorance are we to cope?

Charnock begins his answer to such queries by first providing a series of negatives, what regeneration is *not*. For example, it is 'not a removal or taking away of the old substance or faculties of the soul . . . the new creation . . . gives not a new faculty, but a new quality . . . Human nature is preserved, but the corruption in it is expelled . . . The essential nature of man, his reason and understanding, are not taken away, but rectified.'[4] But (paradoxically) 'the change is so great that the soul seems to be of another species and kind, because it is acted by that grace, which is another species from that principle which acted it before.'[5] The actions of the soul, of the understanding and will and the passions remain generically the same, but following regeneration their objects, their intentionality, differ markedly in their moral and spiritual character. Acts of the soul are to be differentiated on the basis of their acts, and this principle is the same when the objects are those that are intrinsic to regeneration: '[B]ut the principle, end and objects of those objects of those acts, arising from those restored qualities, are altered.'[6]

Further, regeneration is not merely the awakening of latent principles in the self. This work, therefore, is not merely 'an awakening of good habits which lay before oppressed, but a taking off those ill habits which were so far from oppressing nature that they were connatural to it, and by incorporation with it, had quite altered it from that original rectitude and simplicity, wherein God at first created it'.[7] Nor is it brought about by baptism.[8]

So if regeneration is not any of these things mentioned, what is it? Charnock's reply is that it is a real change in the soul, an act of grace upon nature, giving the soul a new form: 'The operations of a new creature are real, and therefore suppose a real power to act, and a real habit as the spring of them.'[9] All regenerate persons have the same nature, 'which extends to every part; understanding, will, conscience, affections, all were corrupted by sin, all are renewed by grace'.[10] This is because it is the soul that is regenerated, and therefore all the powers are changed, redirected, in harmonious fashion.

At this point in his account Charnock refers to Spirit and word, in the form of the precepts and the promises to the soul of Christ's merits as otherwise revealed in the gospel. Despite the pronounced supernaturalism of the account of regeneration so far, he does not say whether the implantation of new life by the Spirit is an event that occurs apart from the influence of the word, contemporaneous with it, or caused by it. He simply refers to begottenness by the word, which suggests a causal instrumentality of the word by the Spirit. But nevertheless it seems there might be a priority in the operation of the Spirit on the soul prior to the word taking effect, a kind of enlightening, enlivening of the soul in love to and desire for the glory of God, making it appropriately effective: 'The very first motion of this new principle is towards God, to act for God; as the first appearance of the living seed in the ground is towards heaven.'[11] This is strengthened by baptism. 'Some indeed say that regeneration is conferred in baptism upon the elect and exerts itself afterwards in conversion. But how so active a principle as a spiritual life should lie dead, and asleep so long, even many years which intervene between baptism and conversion, is not easily conceivable.'[12] It seems from this that the spiritual life that is regeneration occurs in providentially effected conditions in which the gospel is available and in which the person concerned is capable of understanding it; the word understood and applied by the Spirit effects the change from regeneration to conversion.

So regeneration can be seen here in the scholastic sense of the infusing of a new habit. This is how Charnock understood the Johannine language of the reception of a new seed, but also Christ's language of a new birth (John 3) and Paul's of a new creative light (2 Cor. 4.6). What these tropes have in common is the occurrence of a radical, divine, creative impulse with permanent effects.

Within the Reformed camp more widely, some were exercised by the charge of Roman Catholic antagonists that the Reformed doctrine of regeneration was a species of enthusiasm, of God speaking directly to the soul. To answer such a charge some Reformed theologians developed congruistic tendencies, accounts of regeneration in which it was explained by unique sets of providential occurrences none of which involved a direct divine intervention.[13]

But Charnock makes his view clear, that word and Spirit are two distinct elements, in which the new habit of regeneration, the vital principle, generate new rational or intellectual appetites for the gospel. So regeneration is not, cognitively, the direct voice of God, but the indirect voice, as it applies the word of God to the mind and conscience of the individual and in turn brings changes in one's desires and emotions.

In the scheme of Reformed scholasticism, regeneration is not a theoretical matter, but has to do with the practical reason, with ends and means to ends, and particularly in the case of regeneration, with the gain of a new end, the capacity to experience and exhibit the glory of God. 'The glory of God is the end of the new creature, self the end of the old man . . . The very first motion of this new principle [of regeneration] is towards God, to act for God; as the first appearance of a living seed in the ground is toward heaven; thither it casts its look, from whence its life came . . . and therefore what he doth is for God.'[14] Changes occur in the inner self, and then follow in the outer self. These are expressed as changes in the understanding and will, variously stated.[15] So Charnock considers regeneration under the category of 'the nature of a change', the first of a series of scholastic terms that he considers. This scholastic term has something to do with a new principle, a vital principle.

He defines 'the nature of a vital principle' as a change that brings about a stream of new life in the soul:[16] 'The new creature is a vital, powerful principle, naturally moving the soul to the service and obedience of God, and doth animate the faculties in their several motions, as the soul doth quicken the members of the body. It is called the hidden man, the inward man, implying that it hath life and reason.'[17] The various out-workings of this new principle are likened to an 'inner being', the language that Paul uses in Romans 7.27, which has varied effects including lending itself to the utilization of Aristotelian fourfold causation: 'Christ is the meritorious cause of this life in his person, the efficient cause of it by his Spirit; but grace is the formal cause of this life, as God is the cause of our bodily life *efficiently*, the soul the cause of it *formally*.'[18]

However, of these different expository strategies, the term 'habit' may be the most fundamental and theologically significant idea in Charnock's account of regeneration. A habit is a disposition, 'an inward frame' enabling ready action. 'Since this new creation is not a destruction of the substance of the soul, but that there is the same physical being and the same faculties in all men, it is necessary, therefore, that this new creation consist in gracious qualities and habits, which beautify and dispose the soul to act imitation, but are divinely-infused or imparted righteously and holily.'[19] These God 'doth infuse those that he moves to the obtaining a supernatural good, some spiritual qualities whereby they may be inclined of themselves to motions agreeable to their nature, in an easy and natural way'.[20] Charnock refers to Thomas Aquinas' discussion of the infusion of grace in the *Summa Theologiae*:

> [M]an is helped by God's gratuitous will, inasmuch as a habitual gift is infused by God into the soul; and for this reason, that it is not fitting that God should provide less for those He loves, that they may acquire supernatural good, than for creatures, whom He loves that they may acquire natural good. Now He so provides for natural creatures, that not merely does He move them to their natural acts, but He bestows upon them certain forms and powers, which are the principles of acts, in order that they may of themselves be inclined to these movements, and thus the movements whereby they are moved by God become natural and easy to creatures, according to Wisdom 8: 'she ... ordereth all things sweetly'. Much more therefore does He infuse into such as He moves towards the acquisition of supernatural good, certain forms or supernatural qualities, whereby they may be moved by Him sweetly and promptly to acquire eternal good; and thus the gift of grace is a quality.[21]

'Grace' here covers different understandings of grace in Catholicism than in Reformed Protestantism, but the point of principle holds true for both. For medieval Catholics, grace includes the infusion of Christ's righteousness, whereas for the Reformed Christian Christ's righteousness is an alien, imputed righteousness. But regeneration is a subjective state, and Aquinas' idea of subjective infusion can be applied to it.

So, as Aquinas' use of the expression 'infusion' of grace makes clear, regenerate habits are not acquired through imitation or instruction but by a direct gift. This is a necessary requirement for regeneration, changing a person's nature by infusing a new habit, a participation in the divine nature (2 Pet. 1.4). This is modelled upon the divine nature, though this is never understood by Charnock in terms that approach those of *theosis*.

> [I]t is no participation of the essence of God. It is a nature, not the essence; a likeness in an inward disposition, not in the infinite substance, which is communicated by generation only to the Son, and by procession to the Holy Ghost. The divine essence is incommunicable to any creature. Rather, a likeness to Christ, and of the Spirit.[22]

It is the knowledge of God, the choice of God, the desire for God. Charnock divides it into an array of sub-habits.[23] But he tempers his descriptions, taking into account that it is concerned with growth that at first may be scarcely discernible, though it is essentially active; a kind of natural necessity of the habit, and a voluntary choice.[24] Freely, not forced. Charnock's collective term for the effects of these sub-habits is 'impressions', 'divine impressions',[25] which is the closest he comes to the distinctive language of our other theologian, Jonathan Edwards.

Jonathan Edwards

Jonathan Edwards (1703–58) grew up in a culture that was heavily influenced by Reformed orthodoxy. But as a young man he devoured Locke's *Essay* and features of his philosophy became a lifelong element in his thinking. Though we may say that theologically he remained with the Reformed Orthodox, he turned his back on scholasticism as a mode of articulating this theology in favour of elements of Locke's philosophy. For example, Locke's rejection of faculty psychology (*Essay* II, XX), his view of the motivational power of emotions (*Essay* II, XXI) and his understanding of personal identity (*Essay* II, XXV ii) are the most prominent, and undergirding these are his views of reason and revelation (*Essay* IV, XVIII).

The purpose of Edwards' *Religious Affections* was a product of the revivals of New England, and the controversy they engendered.[26] There was division between those, such as Charles Chauncy (1705–87), who dismissed the phenomena that often accompanied the effects of preaching upon a congregation, such as screaming, shouting, dancing, fainting and so forth, as fleshly. And others such as the Davenport brothers, who regarded such effects as vital evidence of the genuineness of the effects of their preaching.

The layout of the book shows that Edwards' strategy was to take a position somewhere between these two extremes. The work is in three parts. The first sets out Edwards' anthropology, particularly the affections and their religious importance. The second is entitled 'Shewing What are no certain signs that Religious Affections are Truly Gracious, or that they are not', that is, which are phenomena in assessing the genuineness of religion. The third – double in size of the first two parts together – is a 'Shewing what are Distinguishing Signs of Truly Gracious and Holy Affections'. Here Edwards sets out his views on genuine signs of true religion.

Despite being written in Edwards' distinctive prose style, I think it is fair to say that the material of Part Three – Edwards' list of positive 'signs' of regeneration – would be agreeable to Charnock, judged by the Puritans of New and Old England whom Edwards cites for support. But it is Part One and its reverberations elsewhere throughout the book that are of interest to us here.

As well as being an expansion of his 1734 sermon, 'Divine and Supernatural light', his *Religious Affections* is a thoroughly Lockean production.[27] Edwards' doctrine of the 'new sense' deliberately meets the criteria of Locke. It conforms to Locke's simple idea – it is an immediate supernatural intuition from God, not from man, validated by the reason as such. It is knowable only by acquaintance. Locke thinks that such experiences are legitimate in religion, provided that they are subordinated to and informed by revelation. Edwards provides his tests, appealing to reason[28] and revelation to do so, in a broadly Lockean fashion. For Edwards, religious experiences that Locke dismisses as 'enthusiasm' are not 'spiritual'.[29] He, like Locke, also dismisses the idea of new revelations, and the acquisition of new faculties.[30] Locke makes negative remarks in the *Essay* about new simple ideas in Book II, Chapter II. He thinks that human beings cannot invent any new simple ideas. Yet God may, he thinks, at least create creatures with more than five senses. This is all that Edwards needs for his idea of a new simple idea as the immediate gift of the grace of God. He is well within the boundaries of Lockeanism at this point.[31] It is not altogether clear why he favours the expression 'simple idea'. A simple idea for Locke was, say, an uninterpreted splash of redness. Besides 'new simple idea', in exposition of his doctrine of regeneration Edwards prefers an expression such as 'spiritual sense', which does justice to the responsive activity of the recipient in receiving divine and supernatural light. Such a person possesses 'a new, active sense'. Perhaps 'simple' is to be understood negatively, as 'without any creaturely or natural elements'.

For Edwards, its use underscored truly supernatural experiences compared with the products of the human imagination.

The new simple idea claim was not subject to issues regarding 'private language' that have concerned philosophers since Wittgenstein. Edwards has no qualms that one recipient of a new simple idea may have with others that also have one. Perhaps he could say that there is a public context sufficiently precise to support communication. Perhaps he would direct the query to the matter provided *in extenso* in Part Three of the *Religious Affections*.

Edwards' departure from the faculty psychology of scholasticism is evident in Part One of the *Affections*: 'God has indued the soul with two faculties: one is that by which it is capable to perception and speculation, or by which it discerns, views and judges of things, which is called the understanding. The other faculty . . . is sometimes called the *inclination*.'[32] He goes on to say that: 'The will, and the affections of the soul, are not two faculties; the affections are not essentially distinct from the will.'[33] Locke and Edwards sometimes use the term 'faculties', but at other times not, indicating by this not so much inconsistency in their views but an understanding of the faculties as referring to modes of the unitary self, rather than essential distinctions within the self.

The account Edwards gives of 'affection' was also largely the result of direct Lockean influence. Before the long chapter XXI of Book II 'Of Power' in his *Essay Concerning Human Understanding*, which Edwards used overtly in his account of human action in *The Freedom of the Will*, Locke placed a shorter discussion, Chapter XX, 'Of Modes of Pleasure and Pain'. I will try to display the similarity if not the identity of the views, first by quoting Locke verbatim, and then Edwards.[34] First Locke:

> Amongst the simple *ideas* which we receive both from *sensation* and *reflection*, pain and *pleasure* are two very considerable ones. For as in the body there is sensation barely in itself, or accompanied by *pain* or *pleasure*, so the thought or perception of the mind is simply so, or else accompanied also with *pleasure* and *pain*, delight or trouble, call it how you please. These, like other simple *ideas*, cannot be described, nor their names defined; the way of knowing them is, as of the simple ideas of the senses, only by experience.

Locke then goes on to illustrate this by reference to the affections of love, hatred, and so on.

Now let us compare this with what Edwards asserts in the *Religious Affections*.

> The other faculty is that by which the soul does not merely perceive and view things, but is some way inclined with respect to the things it views or

considers; either is inclined to 'em, or is disinclined, and averse from 'em; or is the faculty by which the soul does not behold things, as an indifferent unaffected spectator, but either as liking or disliking, pleased or displeased, approving or rejecting. This faculty is called by various names: it is sometimes called the *inclination*: and, as it has respect to the actions that are determined and governed by it, is called the *will*: and the *mind*, with regard to the exercises of this faculty, is often called the *heart*.[35]

So Edwards takes his new simple idea proposal along the Lockean road as far as it will take him. And later on in the book, Edwards argues that:

Nor on the other hand, do I know of any rule any have to determine, that gracious and holy affections, when raised as high as any natural affections, and have equally strong and vigorous exercises, can't have a great effect on the body ... no such rule can be drawn from reason ... none has ever been found in all the late controversies which have been about things of this nature.[36]

Here also he echoes Locke. Such a passage shows Edwards' desire to keep to an idea of the middle way between the extremes produced by the phenomena of revival.

Though Edwards used the Lockean expression 'simple idea' later on in the *Affections*, he does not do so here. Also he does not mention what is important for Locke, ideas of reflection, the production of ideas involving the mind's abstracting and generalizing and imagining from what the senses receive. As already mentioned, besides 'new simple idea' the other key expressions are those such as 'new perception', 'new sensation' and 'new principle'. These become more frequent in Part Three, wherein he is 'distinguishing signs of truly gracious and holy affections' from 'natural affections'. But he never uses the Lockean terminology of 'ideas of reflection' in the *Affections*.

We shall have this language – new simple idea, new sensation, and so on – to the forefront in trying to understand Edwards' view of regeneration. It is clear that regeneration has a character quite other from the deliverances of the five external senses and their rearrangement, hence Edwards' studied avoidance of the Lockean term 'idea of reflection'. Regeneration is purely spiritual, the result of the direct operation of the Holy Spirit. These new expressions, therefore, designate a supernatural phenomenon.

Nevertheless, despite this difference, the general Lockean outlook is clearly present. The new simple idea, or new sense, is not an instance of what Edwards called the external senses, whose internal objects are features of the external world. Perceptual ideas are of the world around us, as ideas of reflection ideas produced by the mind operating on the simple ideas of the external senses. So the 'new supernatural sense' is purely an effect on the mind, not productive of ideas of reflection, though Edwards does not press this point in the *Religious Affections*. Let us attempt to understand how Edwards works this out.

This simple idea, which is not the product of an existing faculty nor of a new faculty, is an immediate product of divine grace. It is the idea of a new sense or principle of the mind that has enlightening and vivifying effects on the soul, the understanding and the will, and especially the affections. To use a crude analogy, it is like the effect of a transmitter operating on a new wavelength giving data that no other wavelength can provide. Being a new sense, it brings with it aspirations and aversions of a distinct, corresponding kind, of sets of pleasures and pains that are purely spiritual.

> From hence it follows, that in those gracious exercises and affections which are wrought in the minds of the saints, through the saving influences of the Spirit of God, there is a new inward *perception* or *sensation* of their minds, entirely different in its nature and kind, from anything that ever their minds were the subjects of before they were sanctified.[37]

Edwards is very keen to stress that this new sensation is above nature. It is not a mere re-arrangement of the products of our minds.

> For doubtless if God by his mighty power produces something that is new, not only in degree and circumstances, but in its whole nature, and that which could be produced by no exalting, varying or compounding of what was there before, or by adding anything of the like kind; I say, if God produces something thus new in a mind, that is a perceiving, thinking, conscious thing; then doubtless something entirely new is felt, or perceived, or thought; or, which is the same thing, there is some new sensation or perception of the mind, which is entirely of a new sort, and which could be produced by no exalting, varying or compounding of that kind of perceptions or sensations which the mind had before; or there is what some metaphysicians call a new simple idea. If grace be, in the sense above described, an entirely new kind of principle; then the exercises of it are also entirely a new kind of exercises. . . . Hence the work of the Spirit of God in regeneration is often in Scripture compared to the giving a new sense, giving eyes to see, and ears to hear, unstopping the ears of the deaf, and opening the eyes of them that were born blind, and turning from darkness unto light. And because this spiritual sense is immensely the most noble and excellent, and that without which all other principles of perception, and all our faculties are useless and vain; therefore the giving this new sense, with the blessed fruits and effects of it in the soul, is compared to a raising the dead, and to a new creation.[38]

A final point on the Lockean approach to the affections has to do with the important part they play in motivation to action. Edwards comes to this aspect of his work in Part Three of the *Affections*, where he aims to show what effects the new simple idea has.

The new simple idea of this supernatural kind produces a new range of perceptions, sensations and affections, new pleasures, new pains. Edwards is emphatic that this is not from the working of any of the five 'external' senses, but from the immediate operation of the Spirit, and so its operation is that of a kind of new faculty of its own.

The new sense is 'supernatural' not in the sense that it is produced miraculously, an event contravening a law of nature, but because the gift of regeneration is 'above' the natural order and its products. Its vehicle or occasion is the transmission of the word of God in Scripture, but its coming is a separate happening. It supervenes on Bible study or on hearing preaching, occurring by God's sovereign will. Not surprising, then, Edwards' claims that it is accompanied by deep affection which may give rise to bodily agitations. Religion, which consists much in the affections, has much to do with this new simple idea, then. It brings about events in time, but neither it nor its occurrences cannot be explained naturalistically.

So a new simple idea is not an idea that is supervenient on anything natural. It does not involve any of the five external senses singly or in combination. It is not possible to summon it by an act of the will, or by any other natural state. It is self-certifying, and it is in turn productive of distinctive moral and spiritual effects.

That is, the answer to our question is to be found in the affections. The new simple idea is affectional: as Locke claimed, and Edwards agreed, it is the affections that motivate the soul or heart to actions of various kinds. He took this also from Locke's chapter on 'The Modes of Pleasure and Pain', which has to do with the power that motivation has on our actions given their arousal by the prospect of pain or pleasure.

Edwards, following Locke, had said:

Such is man's nature, that he is very inactive, any otherwise than he is influenced by some affections, either love or hatred, desire, hope, fear or some other. These affections we see to be the springs that set men agoing, in all the affairs of life, and engage them in all their pursuits; these are the things that put men forward, and carry 'em along, in all their worldly business, and especially are men excited and animated by these, in all affairs, wherein they are earnestly engaged, and which they pursue with vigor.[39]

The prospect of the occurrence of uneasiness brought about by one's new spiritual sense acts in a parallel way; it produces new affections that give rise to spiritual activity.

This accounts for the importance in Edwards' account (in Part Three) of religious affections springing from the new spiritual sensations. But besides this confident account of the unique, spiritual, entirely new work of God in the soul, Edwards is also notably cautious about whether those who possess this new life may also identify it in others. These cautions, as well as what we have noted, help us to understand the negative things he has to say about the religious dangers of relying on the imagination, are no doubt tailored by what Edwards regarded as the excesses of the revivals.

In contrast to his confidence in expounding all of this he is notably cagey about the ability of one person to detect the true spiritual states of another. The distinguishing marks are meant for one's own use; they are not meant to be used on any others. They are not to fuel the fires of censoriousness that marked the revivals. Accordingly, Edwards writes:

> That I am far from undertaking to give such signs of gracious affections, as shall be sufficient to enable any certainly to distinguish true affection from false in others; or to determine positively which of their neighbors are true professors, and which are hypocrites. In so doing, I should be guilty of that arrogance which I have been condemning. Though it be plain that Christ has given rules to all Christians, to enable 'em to judge of professors of religion, whom they are concerned with, so far as is necessary for their own safety, and to prevent their being led into a snare by false teachers, and false pretenders to religion; and though it be also beyond doubt, that the Scriptures do abound with rules, which may be very serviceable to ministers, in counseling and conducting souls committed to their care, in things appertaining to their spiritual and eternal state; yet, 'tis also evident, that it was never God's design to give us any rules, by which we may certainly know, who of our fellow professors are his, and to make a full and clear separation between sheep and goats: but that on the contrary, it was God's design to reserve this to himself, as his prerogative. And therefore no such distinguishing signs as shall enable Christians or ministers to do this, are ever to be expected to the world's end: for no more is ever to be expected from any signs, that are to be found in the Word of God, or gathered from it, than Christ designed them for.[40]

Concluding Comments

We have considered two different philosophical approaches to the idea of monergistic regeneration in Reformed theology. How are we to evaluate these? Each is an instance of supernatural immediacy, and both are varieties of Protestant Augustinianism. It might be thought that Charnock's

Reformed scholasticism is hard and formal whereas Edwards' 'Lockean supernaturalism' is affectionate, warm and pastoral. But such a case cannot be made convincingly. There is attention to formal matters in Edwards, particularly in his distinctions between natural and supernatural experience, and his contrasts between what he takes to be true spirituality and mere imagination; and a stress on the affections in Charnock.[41] Besides writing his short work on a broader canvas than Edwards, Charnock also stresses the 'new nature' that is characteristic of regeneration. He very much stresses the God-centredness of this new nature in his account of regeneration, as does Edwards, though each does his work in a particular polemical setting. So what then are the differences? Here are one or two.

Charnock develops the idea of regeneration, taking it to be an unusual event in the soul, in terms of explicating Christian doctrine onto a template of anthropology, that of scholasticism. The idea being that this can beget self-understanding. This is the language of analysis, of description, reducing the varied language of Scripture to that of an event that is caused in secret, as it were, but makes itself present in consciousness immediately, or after a short interval. By contrast, Edwards appears to have little interest in such a project; rather he marks the singularity of regeneration by a neologism, 'a new simple idea' which he derives from Locke, thereby stressing both its 'supernaturalness' and its self-presentation in the consciousness. A Lockean 'simple' idea ceases to be such as soon as it is interpreted; as the red patch is identified as a tomato skin, or as a traffic light, it informs us about the external world. Edwards' new simple idea does not function like this, but must retain its simpleness. Paradoxically he can say little of his phenomenon in itself, but has a great deal to say about the ethical and religious effects that one who is possessed of such an idea may experience.

To such an approach to regeneration, when there is no place for the cooperation of an independent, autonomous will, there is one overriding difficulty for many modern philosophical theologians: that the doctrine, however it is dressed up, treats human beings as puppets. Neither Charnock nor Edwards considers this as presenting any sort of difficulty – it scarcely ever enters their heads – any more than it enters the head of John Donne, as his sonnet, with its strikingly violent language, shows.

In the case of Edwards, a notable compatibilist, this is not perhaps surprising. But Charnock, too, has interesting remarks on freedom and voluntariness in regeneration.

> There is a kind of natural necessity of motion, from life and habit, yet also a voluntary choice; it is the power which constrains and inclines the will: Psalm cv.3. The apostle tells us there was a 'necessity laid upon him to preach the gospel,' 1 Corinthians ix.16, yet it was not a compulsion, but a voluntary act, after his will was changed. The new creature is not

constrained from without, but flows freely, is not forced; the chief work is upon the will, the proper effect of any work upon the will is voluntariness. The Spirit works to make it willing; its motion then is not by compulsion: there is a sweet necessity of the new nature, and a gracious choice of will, which meet together and kiss each other; a natural, not a coactive necessity. How freely doth the soul, winged with grace, move to and for God, as a bird in the air![42]

To this general problem the point can be made that such proponents of regeneration had a much more heightened and sensitive notion of human beings as *creatures* than is evident nowadays. They were supportive of the idea that all the creation is upheld by God in a *creatio continua*, with God as its primary cause. This is a consequence of the creator/creature distinction: the creaturely dependence of the creature on the Creator. There are contemporary philosophers who hold that it is an infringement of human autonomy to come into the world with an endowment of DNA, subject to parental example, and an early education. In their view this plight makes personal responsibility impossible. To be truly free we all ought to have a say as to what characters we are to be. What the character of the 'we' would be, who ought to select his or her own DNA, is not clear. Reasonable or not, such an outlook was not entertained by Christian theists of 200 or 300 years ago.

That apart, they also held that monergistic regeneration is wholly gracious and benign. If an everyday example may be permitted, the regenerate is like the drowning person when being pulled clear of the icy water. No one here countenances the objection that such markedly and unacceptably heteronomous effects, that occur without the consent of the patient, are inadmissible.

Notes

1 Stephen Charnock died in 1680, aged 52. Most of his work was published posthumously, including that on regeneration. He was part of Cromwell's circle, but after the Restoration eventually became co-pastor at Crosby Hall, London, from 1675. There are four connected pieces on regeneration. All of them are to be found in Volume 3 of *The Complete Works of Stephen Charnock*, intro. James M'Cosh (Edinburgh: James Nichol, 1865); hereafter, references to this work appear as *Charnock* followed by page number.

2 Jonathan Edwards, *Religious Affections*, ed. John E. Smith (New Haven, CT: Yale University Press, 1959).

3 *Charnock*, pp. 86–7.
4 *Charnock*, p. 91.
5 *Charnock*, p. 91.
6 *Charnock*, p. 92.

7 *Charnock*, p. 93.
8 *Charnock*, pp. 93-4.
9 *Charnock*, p. 94.
10 *Charnock*, p. 95.
11 *Charnock*, p. 98.
12 *Charnock*, p. 94. Such a view was held by the Westminster divine, Cornelius Burges, *Baptismall regeneration of elect infants, professed by the Church of England, according to the Scriptures, the primitiue Church, the reformed churches, and many particular divines apart* (London: Printed by I. L[ichfield] for Henry Curteyn, Ann. Dom. 1629).
13 Noteworthy in this project was the writing of the French Huguenot Claud Pajon (see Albert Gootjes, *Claude Pajon (1626-1685) and the Academy of Saumur* [Leiden: Brill, 2014]). Following the Revocation of the Edict of Nantes in 1598, which provided French Calvinists with limited legal protection, the persecution of the Reformed in France led to numbers emigrating to England and elsewhere in the seventeenth century. It is not clear, but clearly possible, that some brought this Pajonist influence with them. (A copy of Pajon's chief manuscript [He did not publish his views] was recently located in the Huguenot church in London.)
14 *Charnock*, p. 99.
15 *Charnock*, pp. 103-4.
16 *Charnock*, p. 105.
17 *Charnock*, p. 105.
18 *Charnock*, p. 105.
19 *Charnock*, p. 106.
20 *Charnock*, p. 106.
21 *Summa Theologiae*, 1.2. Q 110 Art 2.
22 *Charnock*, p. 124.
23 *Charnock*, p. 123.
24 *Charnock*, p. 110.
25 *Charnock*, p. 165.
26 The main thesis of the *Religious Affections* has a longer history than Edwards' reaction to the revivals, as evidenced by his seminal sermon, 'A Divine and Supernatural Light', published in 1734.
27 For more evidence of this, see Paul Helm, 'Jonathan Edwards, John Locke, and Religious Affections', *Jonathan Edwards Studies* 6, 1 (2016), pp. 3-15.
28 *Religious Affections*, p. 132. Edwards was to make his position even clearer in *The Freedom of the Will*, published in 1754.
29 For Edwards the term 'spiritual' invariably refers to the work of the Holy Spirit, not the powers and states of the human spirit.
30 *Religious Affections*, p. 210.
31 Locke, *An Essay Concerning Human Understanding*, Bk II, Ch. II 'Of Simple Ideas'. Hereafter referred to as *Essay*.
32 *Religious Affections*, p. 96.
33 *Religious Affections*, p. 97.
34 Locke's *Essay*, first published in 1689, went through five editions in Locke's lifetime. Edwards is reckoned to have first read the book around 1717 (George M. Marsden, *Jonathan Edwards: A Life* [New Haven, CT: Yale University Press, 2005], p. 62). The fourth edition of the *Essay* (1700) contained, among other new material, the chapter 'Of Enthusiasm', which was retained in the fifth (1706) and subsequent editions. Locke died in 1704. A question is, was the version of the *Essay*

that Edwards read the one that lacked the chapter 'Of Enthusiasm', or did he read the fourth or the fifth edition? As a student Edwards had access at Yale to the 1690 London edition of Locke's *Essay*, and to a later edition in his later life.

35 *Religious Affections*, p. 96.
36 *Religious Affections*, p. 132.
37 *Religious Affections*, pp. 205–6.
38 *Religious Affections*, pp. 205–6.
39 *Religious Affections*, p. 101.
40 *Religious Affections*, p. 193.
41 *Charnock*, p. 98.
42 *Charnock*, pp. 110–11.

PART 4

The Body, the Mind and Salvation

17

Two Visions of Being Saved as Deiform Perfectibility[1]

CARL MOSSER

To be saved is, ultimately, to be perfected. From the earliest literary works to the present, human beings have attempted to describe the deficiencies of our common nature and speculate about its potential perfectibility.[2] There are at least five ways in which human nature has been commonly thought perfectible, by:

1. correcting or healing our moral corruption;
2. actualizing our inherent physical and cognitive potentialities;
3. perfectly discharging the duties or roles to which we are called;
4. attaining the natural *telos* or end for which the human race exists, both individually and corporately;
5. overcoming death, attaining immortality.

Some have additionally identified human perfection with (6) becoming like God or the gods, what John Passmore refers to as 'deiform perfectibility'.[3]

Competing accounts of deiform perfectibility vary widely in their vision of ultimate salvation. This chapter will sketch and compare two of them. The first is transhumanism, a secular account rooted in technological naturalism. The second is the ecumenical Christian doctrine of deification, a theological account of union with God grounded in the resurrection of Jesus of Nazareth.[4] Observing similarities and differences between these visions provides proponents of each opportunity to think more deeply and expansively about humanity's potential. Christian biblical scholars and theologians may be inclined to view transhumanism as a heresy to simply denounce or a secular eschatological fantasy that does not merit serious consideration. That would be a mistake. Every heresy is an occasion to plumb the depths of orthodoxy for treasures old and new; every fanciful myth inadvertently bears witness to the true myth.[5] Consideration of transhumanism's most transgressive claims presents Christian theologians opportunity to reflect anew on the scriptural witness about what it ultimately means to 'be saved'.

The first part of this chapter will describe transhumanist aspirations. All versions of transhumanism focus on utilizing technology to correct human deficiencies and extend human capabilities. The boldest transhumanist aspirations, however, envision the conjoining of humanity and technology such that technological devices are not utilized in a merely instrumental sense, but become constituent parts of our nature. By means of this union, humans may eventually achieve a god-like status. The second part of this chapter will argue that the Christian Scriptures also support a bold vision of the transformation of human nature by means of instrumental union. In this vision, however, human beings attain deiformity because they are united to God as instruments of his reign and rule. They become by grace what the Son of God is by nature. In contrast with this vision of instrumental union, even the boldest transhumanist aspirations pale in comparison.

Transhumanist Aspirations for Immortality and God-likeness

The term *transhumanism* is still unfamiliar to some theologians. However, many people in the culture at large unfamiliar with the term have nonetheless been introduced to its core ideas. For example, several recent movies incorporate transhumanist themes. These include Scarlett Johansson in *Lucy* (2014), Matthew McConaughey in *Interstellar* (2014), and, most explicitly, Johnny Depp in *Transcendence* (2014). The April 2017 cover story for *National Geographic* was a lengthy descriptive advertisement for transhumanism even though the term itself appeared but once in passing.[6] Transhumanism can be described as a naturalistic philosophy, cultural movement, and interdisciplinary field of study that seeks to improve the human condition by enhancing human intellectual, physical and psychological capacities through technological advancement. The ultimate goal is to overcome death itself. As a programme for perfecting human nature in the five ways mentioned above, transhumanism appears to be the best naturalistic bet on offer.

Anders Sandberg identifies three strands of transhumanist thought: the individual, terrestrial and cosmic.[7] While some proponents focus on only one strand, most see transhumanism as a comprehensive world view in which all three are interwoven. Aspirations for immortality and god-like status are expressed in relation to each strand.

Individual transhumanism is concerned with improving one's life through technological enhancements in order to experience better health, refined emotions, new abilities and extended longevity. Transhumanists 'differ on whether this endeavor is merely about overcoming everyday limitations, becoming something akin to a Greek god, or totally escaping the human condition'.[8] But many agree with Max More's call for humans to 'strive for posthuman status, which entails modifications to human genetics, physiology, neurophysiology and neurochemistry and achieving a different motivational structure'.[9] In an essay titled 'Why I Want to be Posthuman When I Grow Up', Oxford philosopher Nick Bostrum defines a *posthuman* as a being that has at least one general central capacity 'that greatly exceeds the maximum attainable by any current human beings without recourse to new technological means'.[10] The three central capacities Bostrum focuses on are healthspan, cognition and emotion. Transhumanists like Bostrum aspire for such noble things as:[11]

- Much longer, healthier lives;
- Greater subjective well-being;
- Enhanced cognitive capacities; more knowledge and understanding;
- Unlimited opportunity for personal growth, beyond our current biological limits;
- Better relationships;
- Unbounded potential for spiritual/moral/intellectual development.

Stated thusly, there is nothing objectionable about these desires. However, achieving them requires more than changing the world around us or how we think about the world. Transhumanists are clear: *Human nature itself has to change.* Some transhumanists (e.g. Aubrey de Grey) are convinced scientists will soon 'cure' the aging process. Others place their money on the ability to replace nearly any part of our bodies with bionic prosthetics superior to the originals, updating them when they are damaged or wear out. Ray Kurzweil is convinced that the full realization of posthumanity will require abandonment of biological bodies altogether in favour of computer substrates onto which our minds are uploaded. In these ways transhumanists are on a quest for biological immortality, bionic immortality and virtual immortality.[12]

Terrestrial transhumanism focuses on the betterment of humanity through efforts to develop 'human condition-changing technologies' such as radical life extension, cryogenics, nanotechnology, cognitive enhancement, brain-computer symbiosis, whole brain emulation and space colonization.[13] Many transhumanists talk about taking control of the evolutionary process in order to expedite and direct the evolution of *Homo sapiens* into a new posthuman species. Efforts to create super-intelligent computers also fall under terrestrial transhumanism. These computers could control many aspects of society more efficiently than human beings can and perhaps even be used to control the weather and other aspects of the environment. Some transhumanists even favour 'some form of world government which, in one scenario, might be controlled by a machine super-intelligence'.[14] Transhumanists acknowledge the possibility that such an artificial intelligence (AI) might show little interest in preserving the biological environment or could even choose to exterminate human beings as a nuisance. But transhumanists assure us that such dystopian scenarios can be avoided by careful programming to ensure a friendly AI, building in safeguards, and carefully anticipating the likely consequences of each new technology that is implemented.

Cosmist transhumanism envisions a future in which technological developments permit super-enhanced human intelligence and super-intelligent AI – possibly conjoined – to colonize space. Some speculate that this could lead to the 'awakening' of the universe. If intelligence is seen as simply a function of highly organized matter, then creating super-intelligent, genuine AI, could lead to the spread of intelligence throughout the cosmos. Sandberg summarizes this view with an analogy: 'Just as supercooled water freezes outward from a seed ice crystal, so if intelligent life emerges anywhere it is likely to nucleate a "technosphere" bubble where matter is reorganized according to the dictates of mind.'[15]

Undergirding posthuman aspirations are a set of convictions about the limitations and malleability of human nature. The first of these is one that any Christian should readily endorse: 'humanity's potential is still mostly unrealized' (Transhumanist Manifesto, section 2).[16] But transhumanists typically go well beyond this simple claim. For example, Max More states:

> Transhumanists regard human nature not as an end in itself, not as perfect, and not as having any claim on our allegiance. Rather, it is just one point along an evolutionary pathway and we can learn to reshape our own nature in ways we deem desirable and valuable. By thoughtfully, carefully, and yet boldly applying technology to ourselves, we can become something no longer accurately described as human – we can become posthuman.[17]

According to transhumanist ideology, there is a moral imperative to fund technological research in areas that will hasten the transition from humanity to posthumanity. Evangelists of the transhumanist gospel announce that fantastic technological advances are just around the corner while also warning that *Homo sapiens* is on the brink of extinction through nuclear war, global pandemic, anthropogenic environmental destruction, or asteroid impact. The only way to ensure survival of the species is for governments and corporations to more generously fund research on aging, artificial intelligence, cryonics, nanotechnology, and other technologies with the potential to make breakthroughs resulting in superlongevity, super-intelligence and super well-being. Paradoxically, success may lead to *Homo sapiens* being supplanted by a posthuman species that benefits from the intelligently directed evolution and artificial enhancements humans introduce. *Homo sapiens* will be remembered for facilitating the emergence of this god-like species. Humanity may no longer exist, but the human race will have made a lasting name for itself.

The editors of the *Transhumanism Reader* recognize that these aspirations derive from 'an ancient drive for self-creation through self-definition'.[18] Many transhumanists readily express their hopes in divinizing terms and 'consider the possibility of God or gods emerging through naturalistic processes'.[19] For example:

intelligence could become god-like.[20]

science may someday develop the capability to resurrect the dead and build (and/or become) God(s).[21]

The friendly 'AI' project can be seen as an attempt to figure out how to design a 'god' that has positive properties. It turns theist assumptions around: not only would god be created in the image of humans, but the values it embodies would be defined by humans.[22]

Once we saturate the matter and energy in the universe with intelligence, it will 'wake up', be conscious, and sublimely intelligent. That's about as close to God as I can imagine . . . [W]e're going to transcend biological intelligence. We'll merge with it first, but ultimately the nonbiological portion of our intelligence will predominate.[23]

Through technology and cooperation, transhumanists predict a future in which human beings take charge of their individual and collective destiny. Disease and aging will be cured, biological limitations transcended, human flourishing maximized, and the environment renewed. This is the eschatology of Isaiah 65.19–25 realized by technological means apart from God. While most transhumanists see their world view as an extension of secular humanism, many scholars observe that transhumanist ideology secularizes traditional religious themes, concerns and goals while endowing technology with religious significance. Theologians and secular critics alike note unwitting parallels with Christian eschatological expectations, especially with the doctrine of deification or theosis.[24]

At the beginning of the movie *Transcendence*, Johnny Depp's character, Dr Will Caster, delivers a lecture on the probability that research will soon make a breakthrough that leads to computer super-intelligence and mind uploading. During the Q&A he is asked, 'So, you want to create a God? Your own God?' Dr Caster replies, 'That's a very good question. Um, isn't that what man has always done?' In an anti-technology terrorist attack, Caster is wounded and poisoned, leaving him a month to live. This motivates him to hasten his work in order to upload his mind onto a supercomputer. The upload is successful and Caster uses his expanded cognitive powers to address some of humanity's endemic problems. He develops nanotechnologies that allow him to make the lame walk, blind sea, deaf hear, raise the dead, and renew the environment. By merging with a super-intelligent computer, Caster becomes, in effect, a 'God'. But this messianic age is short-lived and fears arise about the potential to use these enhanced abilities in ways that are destructive to others. Everything falls apart because in uploading his mind, Caster endows the super-intelligent AI with human shortcomings for which there is no conceivable technological fix – things like selfishness, pride and insecurity. The movie ends with mixed messages about the potential benefits of radical human enhancement.

While transhumanists are optimistic about a posthuman future and the ability to build in safeguards, one has to wonder if such optimism is warranted in light of our track record with technological advancements. Without a doubt, we have used new technologies for great good. But we also use them to become more adept at theft, manipulation of the masses, procrastination, warfare and genocide. After the Turkish genocide of Armenians during the First World War, the world said, 'Never again!' Twenty-five years later technological advancements enabled the Third Reich to murder at least 4.5 million more people than the Turks did a generation earlier. The world again insisted, 'Never again!' Yet the ensuing decades have seen genocide and ethnic cleansing in Cambodia, Uganda, Rwanda, the former Yugoslavia, Darfur and elsewhere.

When it comes to implementing effective safeguards against the misuse of technology, humanity's track record isn't very good, and transhumanist claims that we'll somehow do better are hardly reassuring. And the reason why is simple: we are a morally corrupt race. We are frequently motivated by personal gain, pride, a sense of superiority over others, bitterness, vengeance, and a host of other vices. It is difficult to even conceive of a technological advancement that could possibly cure these defects. We have every reason to believe super-enhanced human beings or posthumans would be like the gods of the ancient Greek, Roman, Egyptian and Near Eastern pantheons: sometimes good and benevolent but basically selfish, petty, capricious, deceptive and frequently at war with one another vying for power and prestige – much as we are now. The difference is that we would have enhanced abilities which permit us to commit greater atrocities against one another and the environment, whether deliberately or by accident.

From the viewpoint of Christian theology, transhumanism echoes the ancient Manichaean disdain of the corrupt material body from which the soul must be rescued and the Pelagian reiteration of the ability of humans to will themselves to perfection.[25] It is mythology in the future tense that aspires to a sophisticated form of idolatry and preaches a naïve gospel of technological Messianism. But, as Alexander Schmemann observed, heresy 'is always the distortion, the exaggeration, and therefore the mutilation of something true.'[26] In this light, transhumanism can also be seen as a corrupted expression of an innate yearning for humanity's true *telos*, a distorted approximation of what God intends for his human creatures. And when set in contrast to biblical teaching, the contrast helps us to see more clearly how utterly whelming and stupendous the biblical vision of humanity's end really is.

Deiform Perfectibility through Instrumental Union with God

Let's begin with the Fall narrative in Genesis 3. The serpent tells Eve that God commanded the man and woman not to eat of the tree of the knowledge of good and evil because doing so would make them 'like God' (3.5). The serpent intimates that God is stingy, withholding something that would be very beneficial to the man and woman. But the careful reader of Genesis knows humans were created with the express intention to be like God: 'Let us make man in our image, after our likeness' (1.26–27). Careful readers also know that *all* the trees of the garden, including this one, were good and made for human consumption (2.9). In the second century, Irenaeus observed that Adam and Eve were recently created and God's prohibition is akin to withholding a good thing from a child who is not sufficiently mature to use it responsibly.[27] In the Fall, the man and woman prematurely take what God intends to eventually give and damage themselves. Like feeding a juicy (puréed) sirloin steak to an infant, something wholly good becomes poisonous. As a result, the man and woman become like God knowing good and evil (3.22), but that likeness is corrupted and they are sent out of Eden to block access to the tree of life to prevent that corruption from becoming permanent. Death is both penalty for their immature disobedience and a mercy that permits eventual redemption from its consequences.

The knowledge of good and evil is not primarily moral knowledge, but the ability to discern, anticipate, and wisely plan in order to rule well (cf. 1 Kings 3.9). However, when likeness to God is corrupted, this ability is quickly used for perverse ends. Cain, rather than use his knowledge to control jealousy and anger arising from the rejection of his offering, murdered his brother and lied about it (3.8–9). The knowledge that makes Adam, Eve and their progeny 'like God' is perversely employed to make Cain more like the serpent who murdered his parents through a lie (cf. John 8.44).[28] The goal of likeness to God is achieved, but, paradoxically, so is its opposite. A kind of morally defective likeness is attained that gives human beings the ability to do greater evil. By the time we get to Genesis 6, things have escalated to the point that we're told 'the wickedness of man was great in the earth' and 'every intention of the thoughts of his heart was only evil continually' (Gen. 6.5).

On this view, human nature must be healed and humanity's likeness to God restored. Thus, God sent 'his own Son in the likeness of sinful flesh' (Rom. 8.3) who 'emptied himself, by taking the form of a servant, being born in the likeness of men' (Phil. 2.7). Those who are redeemed are called to 'put on the new self, created after the likeness of God in true righteousness and holiness' (Eph. 4.24). Ultimately this is accomplished through death and resurrection – Christ's and ours.

Resurrection first appears in the book of Daniel. There resurrection is not mere resuscitation to the kind of life previously enjoyed. Rather, 'those who are wise shall shine like the brightness of the sky above; and those who turn many to righteousness, like the stars for ever and ever' (Dan. 12.3). Some kind of transformation of their being has taken place. Scholars sometimes refer to this as celestial deification: they display the beauty and glory of heavenly beings. Likewise, in the New Testament, Paul describes the resurrection body as manifesting a cluster of properties that include at least divine immortality, incorruptibility and glory (1 Cor. 15.35–54; cf. Rom. 2.6–7).[29] The word Paul uses for 'incorruption' (ἄφθαρτος) suggests both metaphysical and moral stability, a state of being in which it is impossible to become defective. The redeemed cosmos will similarly manifest glory and properties analogous to incorruption and immortality (Isa. 65.17–25; Rom. 8.19–21; 2 Pet. 3.13; Rev. 21.4, 23–27; 22.1–5).

In his letter to the Colossians, Paul says Jesus 'is the beginning, the firstborn from the dead' (Col. 1.18; cf. Rev. 1.5), suggesting that many will follow Jesus' example. Paul tells the Corinthians, 'Christ has been raised from the dead, the firstfruits of those who have fallen asleep' (1 Cor. 15.20) and lays down this principle: 'Christ the firstfruits, then at his coming those who belong to Christ' (1 Cor. 15.23). So, from the perspective of Christian theology, if we want to catch a glimpse of what fully realized human nature looks like, then we must look to the resurrected and ascended Jesus. Paradoxically, Paul also says that God in his mercy has *already* 'made us alive with Christ' (Eph. 2.5) and *already* 'raised us up with Christ and seated us with him in the heavenly realms' (Eph. 2.6). Paul's theology presupposes an ontology in which Christ and those he redeems are joined together in such an intimate, organic manner that things which are true of Christ in his union with the Father become true of those he redeems – partially now, fully when he returns.

According to Gospel accounts, the resurrected Jesus appeared to wear dazzling apparel (Luke 24.4) as well as mundane, to be unrecognizable even to close friends until he allowed them to perceive who he was (Luke 24.16, 31; John 20.14–15; 21.4–14), and to simply 'show up' at various locations (Matt. 28.9, 17; Luke 24.15, 36; John 21.1–4) – including entering rooms whose doors were locked (John 20.19, 26). After 40 days he was carried up into heaven (Luke 24.51) on a cloud (Acts 1.9; cf. Dan. 7.13). As Stephen was about to be stoned he was filled with the Spirit, allowing him to gaze into heaven. He is recorded as saying, 'Behold, I see the heavens opened, and the Son of Man standing at the right hand of God' (Acts 7.56). More interesting is the narrator's summation: Stephen 'saw the glory of God and Jesus standing at the right hand of God' (7.55). The 'and' (καί) here could be epexegetical, in which case the sense is he 'saw the glory of God, that is, Jesus, standing at the right hand of God'. If so, the ascended Jesus is depicted as the embodiment of God's glory. Either way, something like that may be suggested when Paul refers to 'the glory of God in the face of Jesus Christ' (2 Cor. 4.6).

The book of Revelation depicts the ascended Jesus with symbolic language designed to depict fulfilment of Daniel's description: 'The hairs of his head were white like wool, as white as snow. His eyes were like a flame of fire, his feet were like burnished bronze, refined in a furnace, and his voice was like the roar of many waters' (Rev. 1.14–15). Resurrection narratives and glimpses of the ascended Jesus in Acts and Revelation supply provocative hints about how Jesus' humanity has been transformed. The author of 1 John says that although the redeemed have already become God's children, 'what we will be has not yet appeared' (1 John 3.2a). But, the author goes on to say, 'we know that when he appears we shall be like him' (3.2b). How far does this likeness go? Jesus' exhortations to the seven churches make some of the most astonishing claims in the entire canon. For example, those who overcome will be given authority over the nations to rule them with a rod of iron, just as Jesus was (Rev. 2.27; 12.5; 19.15). But the boldest claim is this: 'The one who conquers, I will grant him to sit with me on my throne, as I also conquered and sat down with my Father on his throne' (Rev. 3.21). As we will see, they are enthroned with Jesus and his Father because they have a very important role to exercise in the transformed cosmos.

When Genesis 1.26–27 says humanity was created as God's image and likeness, Hebrew terms are employed and usually used in reference to idols (צלם, דמות). At a minimum, to be an image of a deity is to be a physical representation of that deity. The perversity of idolatry lies in the fact that human beings who were created to physically represent God within creation bow down to other created things, things which they themselves have fashioned. The living God must be represented by a living image.

Humanity was also made to have dominion over all the other living things God created (Gen. 1.26; Ps. 8.6). The terminology suggests humanity was intended not merely to represent God within creation, but to rule over it as his agent. Humans were made as servants of God, but not menial slaves as Ancient Near Eastern mythologies presumed. Rather, humans were made for the purpose of serving a function akin to the viceroy or vizier of an ancient monarch. They are to exercise rule on behalf of the king. It is an exalted position of dignity and responsibility. This idea is found in descriptions of final redemption from both testaments.[30]

> And the kingdom and the dominion and the greatness of the kingdoms under the whole heaven shall be given to the people of the saints of the Most High; their kingdom shall be an everlasting kingdom, and all dominions shall serve and obey them. (Dan. 7.27)[31]

> You were slain, and by your blood you ransomed people for God from every tribe and language and people and nation, and you have made them a kingdom and priests to our God, and they shall reign on the earth. (Rev. 5.10)

The rule mentioned in these passages is not autonomous or self-serving. Redeemed humans and Christ are *both* described as being given 'a rod of iron' with which to rule the nations (Rev. 2.27; 12.5). They are enthroned *together* at God's right hand (Rev. 3.21; cf. Eph. 1.20; 2.6). Believers who endure will 'reign *with* him' (2 Tim. 2.12).

A closely related theme is that of judging. In monarchic governments the authority to judge is ultimately a royal prerogative that can be delegated to magistrates. Paul encourages the Corinthians to be mindful of the fact that 'we must all appear before the judgement seat of Christ, so that each one may receive what is due for what he has done in the body' (2 Cor. 5.10). Yet in a previous letter he asks rhetorical questions which indicate they will also participate in rendering eschatological judgement: 'Do you not know that the saints will judge the world?' (1 Cor. 6.2) and 'Do you not know that we are to judge angels?' (1 Cor. 6.3). A similar vision of joint-judgement is found in a dominical saying: 'Truly, I say to you, in the new world, when the Son of Man will sit on his glorious throne, you who have followed me will also sit on twelve thrones, judging the twelve tribes of Israel' (Matt. 19.28; cf. Luke 22.28–30). According to Acts, though, God 'has fixed a day on which *he will judge* the world in righteousness *by a man* (ἐν ἀνδρὶ) whom he has appointed; and of this he has given assurance to all by raising him from the dead' (Acts 17.31). The man Jesus is the instrument through or by means of which God exercises judgement. Though not stated explicitly like it is in this verse, the same idea seems to be presupposed in those texts which talk about the eschatological rule or reign of Jesus and the saints. They are the instruments through or by means of which God will exercise rule within the new heavens and earth.

There are at least two kinds of union at work here. First, there is co-regency in which royal prerogative is jointly exercised by Jesus and redeemed humanity. Second, there is instrumental union between Jesus and redeemed humanity on the one hand, and instrumental union between them and God on the other. God rules and judges material creation through the instrumental agency of a co-regency held by Jesus and redeemed humans.

A mundane co-regency or similar arrangement (e.g. co-presidency of a corporation, co-chairing a committee) is a union in which members share authority and power. It can work only to the degree that its members are also united in their purposes, ends and values. The canonical witness envisions redemption as including the fulfilment of God's original intention that humanity have dominion over creation. That dominion is exercised in the form of a co-regency between the natural and adopted sons of God. Unlike a mundane co-regency, however, the union experienced by its members presumably cannot be disrupted by competing agendas, conflicting values, or contradictory decrees. In the division of labour they may not all do the exact same thing, but whatever any one of them does will be consistent with everything the rest do. Everybody's actions will serve the same final ends and instantiate the same values. Members of the co-regency operate in harmony unadulterated by even the slightest discordant note.

Eschatological co-regency is a form of union with God because the cornerstone figure around which the co-regency is constituted is the God-man Jesus Christ. But it is also a form of union with God in an instrumental sense. Mundane examples of instrumental unity abound. Jessica can use a knife to slice tomatoes, a backhoe to dig a trench, scissors to trim her hair, currency to pay a debt, a flashlight to see inside a room, or a computer to send an email. In each case a specific type of union obtains between Jessica and the instrument she utilizes. This kind of union can also obtain between agents. The paradigm example is slavery. Pharaoh built his cities through the instrumental agency of Israelite slaves. But this needn't be a coercive arrangement. Jessica can use her daughter to convey a message to her husband in the other room and her daughter can be eager to comply because she wants to help her mother. In these illustrations the instrumental unity that obtains is temporary, but there is no reason why instrumental agency could not be permanent, especially if there are additional ways in which union obtains.[32]

Instrumental unity is a lovely explanation for how God can rule and judge not just through the human nature assumed by the Word, but also through and together with all redeemed human beings as his co-workers (cf. 1 Cor. 3.9). On this model, then, God is (efficiently) causally related to redeemed humanity such that he is capable of performing some action(s) that he couldn't otherwise perform. But what sorts of actions could an omnipotent God be incapable of performing without human instrumental agency? That there could be such actions is easy to demonstrate. For example, God could not create Elisabeth, my wife and the mother of our six children, *ex nihilo*. He could create a woman who exactly resembles her, perhaps, but she would not actually be *my* wife or the mother of *our* children. To create that woman necessarily requires she have a particular genealogy, undergo various experiences, and stand in certain relations with other people. If God wants to create *her*, necessarily he must do so through instrumental means that involve agents other than God.

What sorts of things does God want to do through a race of redeemed beings? Scripture does not say but recall that humanity was created to be God's physical representation to the material creation, the living image of the living God. In the glimpses of the eschaton we are provided, redeemed human beings are depicted as sitting on thrones, being crowned, judging and ruling. Now consider the fact that the universe is immense. It is hard to know what it will be like when in full blossom, but passages like Romans 8 and Revelation 21–22 indicate that there will be significant transformation. *That* renewed cosmos is the creation in which God has always intended humanity to rule and reign. Whatever exactly such rule involves or entails, the Joseph narratives in Genesis 37–50 provide an apt analogy.

Once Joseph is elevated by Pharaoh, he is clothed in fine linen like Pharaoh's and given Pharaoh's signet ring (41.42). He rides in Pharaoh's chariot and receives the obeisance people usually reserved for Pharaoh (41.43). Only with respect to the throne itself is Pharaoh greater than Joseph (41.40). Joseph rules Egypt in the name of Pharaoh as 'lord of the land' (42.30), issuing decrees that, by virtue of his office and the signet ring with which they are stamped, are *Pharaoh*'s decrees. Thus, when Joseph sends wagons to bring his father Jacob to Egypt (45.27), they are described as 'the wagons Pharaoh had sent to carry him' (46.5). In all matters Joseph represents Pharaoh to others and speaks on his behalf. But he is not Pharaoh. Rather, he is the instrumental agent through whom Pharaoh exercises wise rule over the people and land of Egypt. And Joseph participates in this relationship willingly, but not to advance his own ends or agenda. He was chosen by Pharaoh to use his wisdom to rule Egypt in a providential manner that ensures the well-being of Pharaoh's subjects. *Mutatis mutandis*, in the new heavens and earth, deified human beings will be to God what Joseph was to Pharaoh; they will be to the rest of creation what Joseph was to the land and people of Egypt.

The New Testament says very little about the eternal state after all things in heaven and earth have been united in Christ according to God's eternal plan (cf. Eph. 1.10). But as C. S. Lewis observed, the promises of Scripture can be roughly reduced to being with Christ, being like Christ, having glory, to be in some sense feasted or entertained, and 'that we shall have some sort of official position in the universe'.[33] God created a vast cosmos immensely larger than the biblical authors themselves could have imagined, one that 'waits with eager longing for the revealing of the sons of God' when it 'will be set free from its bondage to decay' and obtain freedom (Rom. 8.19,

21). In this renewed cosmos, redeemed humanity will have been fully transformed into the image of God (cf. 2 Cor. 3.18). As the author of 1 John states, 'what we will be has not yet appeared; but we know that when he appears we shall be like him' (1 John 3.2). While the New Testament gives few details about humanity's ultimate potential, it indicates that it is fulfilled in deiform perfection by means of union with God and the meaningful exercise of his authority. A grand vision, indeed.

Concluding Contrast

Transhumanist dissatisfaction with human nature as it is presently exemplified inadvertently bears witness to the truth of the Christian conception of sin as both moral wrongdoing and corruption of nature. Transhumanist eschatologies tap into humanity's deepest intuitions about our potential as creatures whose fundamental vocation is to reflect the divine image and exercise dominion within God's world as his stewards. Transhumanists insist that our biology must be modified and our bodies enhanced. Christians say as much every time they proclaim belief in 'the resurrection of the dead and the life of the age to come' (Nicene Creed). Disagreement comes when discussion turns to the means by which this is achieved and the ends pursued once it is.

Transhumanists envision a future in which humanity instrumentally employs technology to become god-like to pursue whatever projects it might contrive. If attained, human beings will unite themselves with technological devices of their own making in order to transcend inherited cognitive and physical limitations, including death. We will then become the lords and gods of our own destiny. If one understands the human *telos* in evolutionary terms to become the first species that self-directs its own evolution, then genetic and other technologies provide some warrant for optimism. But technology possesses few resources by which our moral corruption could be corrected or healed. Genetic or chemical therapies permit the alteration of human behaviour in various ways, e.g. less prone to anger or depression, increased or decreased libido, increased sense of elation or confidence, difficulty telling lies, and so on. But it is not clear that further developments in these areas are likely to eradicate greed, pride, hatred, vindictiveness, infidelity, cowardice, indifference and the other vices in order to create morally perfect humans or posthumans. And as long as we remain morally defective creatures, we will not perfectly discharge our duties or roles. Humanity might, nonetheless, attain a form of deiform perfection, but apart from moral healing that could be a nightmare scenario. We might become lords and gods of our own destinies, but the destinies we determine for ourselves will conflict with those of our fellow posthumans and compete for resources. We would have become a race of deities like those of the ancient pantheons. At best, we would be able to devise coping strategies but would have no real hope for vanquishing evil or achieving a permanent peaceful union with others. Rejecting the mercy death represents for a morally corrupt race, the struggles we now face would be writ large and made unending.

The Christian Scriptures point to a vision of being saved that involves deiform perfection of a very different sort. The biblical vision as I understand it promises the perfection of human nature in all six of the ways mentioned at the beginning of this chapter. If it is true, we will be transformed into morally perfect agents whose inherent physical and cognitive potentialities are fully manifest. We will fulfil significant roles in the governance of God's cosmos, thereby attaining the natural *telos* of our species as creatures who bear God's own image and likeness. As resurrected beings, we will experience immortality, but it will be more than immortality by virtue of union with Christ, indwelling of the Spirit, and reflection of the Father's glory. What is presently true of Jesus in his resurrected and ascended state will be made true of us. We will, by grace, become truly deiform beings and thereby finally *fully* human beings. In comparison, transhumanism's most radical aspirations appear pale, meagre and wholly undesirable.

Notes

1 An earlier version of this chapter under a different title was presented as the first annual Lyceum Project Lecture in Oklahoma City. The Academy of Christian Studies and Josh Spears were generous hosts and the paper is improved because of their helpful questions and comments. The research for this chapter was supported by The Immortality Project, funded by the John Templeton Foundation in partnership with the University of California, Riverside.

2 For surveys of global religious and philosophical accounts, see Keith Ward, *Religion and Human Nature* (Oxford: Clarendon, 1998); John Passmore, *The Perfectibility of Man*, 3rd edn (Indianapolis, IN: Liberty Fund, 2000); and Harold Coward, *Perfectibility of Human Nature in Eastern and Western Thought* (Albany, NY: SUNY Press, 2008).

3 Passmore, *Perfectibility of Man*, p. 23. 'Deiformity' as a theological term goes back at least to Aquinas (e.g. *Summa Theologica*, I, q. 12, a. 6).

4 Nineteenth-century Protestant theologians of the Ritschlian school portrayed the patristic doctrine of deification as a distinctively Eastern and Hellenistic notion incompatible with the Western theological tradition, especially its Protestant forms. Russian Émigré theologians appropriated this construct but inverted the value judgements attached to its alleged absence. The historical record, however, shows that the doctrine has always been affirmed in the West, including the Magisterial Reformation. See further Carl Mosser, 'Deification: A Truly Ecumenical Doctrine', *Perspectives: A Journal of Reformed Thought* 30, 4 (2015), pp. 8–14; Carl Mosser, 'An Exotic Flower? Calvin and the Patristic Doctrine of Deification', in *Reformation*

Faith: Exegesis and Theology in the Protestant Reformations, ed. Michael Parsons (Milton Keynes: Paternoster, 2014), pp. 40–7.

5 Cf. C. S. Lewis: 'Now the story of Christ is simply a true myth: a myth working on us the same way as the others, but with this tremendous difference that *it really happened*: and one must be content to accept it in the same way, remembering that it is God's myth where the others are men's myths: i.e. the Pagan stories are God expressing Himself through the minds of poets, using such images as He found there, while Christianity is God expressing Himself through what we call "real things".' *The Collected Letters of C. S. Lewis, Volume 1: Family Letters 1905–1931*, ed. Walter Hooper (New York: Harper Collins, 2004), p. 977. In this case, we are talking about 'myths' in the future tense.

6 D. T. Max, 'Beyond Human', *National Geographic* 231, 4 (2017), pp. 40–63.

7 Anders Sandberg, 'Transhumanism and the Meaning of Life', in Calvin Mercer and Tracy J. Trothen (eds), *Religion and Transhumanism: The Unknown Future of Human Enhancement* (Santa Barbara, CA: Praeger, 2015), p. 4.

8 Sandberg, 'Meaning of Life', p. 4.

9 Max More, 'On Becoming Posthuman', *Free Inquiry* 14, 4 (1994), p. 38.

10 Nick Bostrum, 'Why I Want to be Posthuman When I Grow Up', in Max More and Natasha Vita-More (eds), *The Transhumanist Reader* (Oxford: Wiley-Blackwell, 2013), pp. 28–9.

11 This list is taken from Nick Bostrum, 'A Philosophical Quest for Our Biggest Problems', presentation at TEDGlobal 2005. Online: <www.ted.com/talks/nick_bostrom_on_our_biggest_problems>.

12 Brent Waters, 'Whose Salvation? Which Eschatology? Transhumanism and Christianity as Contending Salvific Religions', in Ronald Cole-Turner (ed.), *Transhumanism and Transcendence: Christian Hope in an Age of Technological Enhancement* (Washington, DC: Georgetown University Press, 2011), pp. 166–7.

13 Cf. Sandberg, 'Meaning of Life', pp. 8–9.

14 More, 'The Philosophy of Transhumanism', in *The Transhumanist Reader*, p. 13.

15 Sandberg, 'Meaning of Life', p. 14.

16 The Manifesto can be found in various places online and on pp. 54–5 of *The Transhumanist Reader*.

17 More, 'Philosophy of Transhumanism', p. 4.

18 Max More and Natasha Vita More, 'Roots and Core Themes', in *The Transhumanist Reader*, p. 2.

19 Sandberg, 'Meaning of Life', p. 17.

20 James Hughes, 'Transhumanism and Personal Identity', in *The Transhumanist Reader*, p. 229.

21 Giulio Prisco, 'Transcendent Engineering', in *The Transhumanist Reader*, p. 234.

22 Sandberg, 'Meaning of Life', p. 10.

23 Ray Kurzweil, *The Singularity is Near: When Humans Transcend Biology* (New York: Viking, 2005), p. 375.

24 E.g. Michael E. Zimmerman, 'The Singularity: A Crucial Phase in Divine Self-actualization?', *Cosmos and History* 4, 1–2 (2008), pp. 347–70; Todd T. W. Daly, 'Chasing Methuselah: Transhumanism and Christian *Theosis* in Critical Perspective', in *Transhumanism and Transcendence: Christian Hope in an Age of Technological Enhancement*, ed. Ronald Cole-Turner (Washington, DC: Georgetown University Press, 2011), pp. 131–44; Eugene Clay, 'Transhumanism and the Orthodox Christian Tradition', in Hava Tirosh-Samuelson and Kenneth L. Mossma (eds), *Building Better*

Humans? Refocusing the Debate on Transhumanism (Frankfurt: Peter Lang, 2011), pp. 157–80; Ronald Cole-Turner, 'Going beyond the Human: Christians and Other Transhumanists', *Dialog* 54, 1 (2015), pp. 20–6; Ian Curran, 'Becoming Godlike? The Incarnation and the Challenge of Transhumanism', *Christian Century* 134, 24 (2017), pp. 22–5.

25 Waters, 'Whose Salvation?', p. 171.

26 Alexander Schmemann, *For the Life of the World* (Crestwood, NY: St Vladimir's Seminary Press, 2004), p. 127.

27 *Dem.* 12, 14; *AH* 4.38.1–2.

28 The fact that death was not immediate does not nullify the fact of murder any more than it does for the administration of slow-acting poisons or brutal assaults that do not immediately kill their victims but are nonetheless the cause of death.

29 Individually, these properties are also attested in Dan. 12.2; Matt. 13.43; John 5.21–29; 17.5, 22; 1 Thess. 2.12; 2 Thess. 2.14; Rom. 8.21; 1 Cor. 2.7; 2 Cor. 3.18; 4.4, 17; Col. 3.4, 10; 2 Tim. 1.10; 2.10; 1 Pet. 1.7; 4.13–14; 5.1, 4, 10; 2 Pet. 1.3.

30 Also see Rev. 2.27; 20.6; 22.5; and 1 Cor. 4.8 (where Paul corrects the Corinthians' over-realized eschatology).

31 Translators differ on whether to translate 'his kingdom' or 'their kingdom' and 'serve and obey him' or 'serve and obey them'. This is not the place to adjudicate that. As will become clear momentarily, the difference becomes moot within the canonical context.

32 I believe there may be, in fact, several additional ways in which eschatological union with God obtains. Candidates include an enriched indwelling by the Holy Spirit, union as shared extension, the mutual manifestation of powers, hypostatic inherence, and something analogous to an emergent superorganism or holobiont.

33 C. S. Lewis, *The Weight of Glory* (New York: Touchstone, 1996), p. 31.

18

Theological Musings on Mental Illness: Between Sin and Sanctification

HANS MADUEME

The reality of mental illness is impossible to ignore.[1] About one in every four adults in the United States has a psychiatric affliction – most likely an anxiety or mood disorder – and almost half the population will experience at least one psychiatric episode in their lifetime. Data from the World Health Organization indicate that mental illness, in developed nations, is more common than cancer and cardiac disease. The statistics are staggering. In the United States alone, the costs of mental illness in 2002 and 2003 were close to $300 billion annually; globally, for 2010, those costs were estimated at $2.5 trillion (projected to expand to $6.0 trillion by 2030). At the same time, mental illness has been a remarkably polarizing issue among Christians. North American evangelicals, specifically, have struggled fully to integrate these stark realities with their faith.

David Murray, a pastor and theologian, helpfully lays out the two main perspectives as 'mental illness maximizers' and 'sin maximizers'.[2] On the one hand, mental illness maximizers are Christians who believe that underlying disease can sometimes impede the brain's ability to process thoughts and emotions, a process which leads to a wide range of mental illnesses, some quite incapacitating. On the other hand, sin maximizers – who are usually biblical counsellors – are more reluctant to affirm the reality of mental illness.[3] Mindful of doctrinal realities like sin and salvation, they are mental illness sceptics with a tendency to polemicize others who think differently. As a result, Christians who need help often feel rejected by the Church and turn to more compassionate secular counsellors.

As much as we might regret the contested nature of psychology's relationship to Christianity, it did not arise out of thin air. The Christian faith itself prompts important questions, not least of which concerns the doctrine of sanctification. The experience of sanctification is at the heart of God's will for his people, the means by which believers grow in the grace and knowledge of Jesus Christ. Although our union with Christ implies that we are already fully holy, the Christian life amid indwelling sin is the pursuit of holiness in the power of the Spirit. But mental illness complicates this dynamic of sanctification – on the one hand, many believers in history who seem to have suffered from mental afflictions saw their struggles as part of God's sanctifying process (e.g. William Cowper, John Bunyan, Charles Spurgeon, David Brainerd and others).[4] On the other hand, in modern times especially, a mental illness diagnosis can make it more difficult or even counter-intuitive for people to construe their experiences in light of sin and sanctification.

In calling the evangelical Church back to the faithful care of souls, Jay Adams' rejection of secular and Christian psychology was motivated at least in part by questions surrounding sanctification and sin.[5] 'Nouthetic counseling', he announced, was 'simply *an application of the means of sanctification*'.[6] Adams argued that authentic biblical counselling requires the agency of the Holy Spirit and the supernatural resources of Scripture.

The Christian care of souls is an urgent task that the Church must address effectively and with integrity, a task that requires a rich and nuanced theology of mental illness.[7] This chapter aims to provide a starting point by exploring areas at the interface of theology and psychopathology. I revisit lingering questions between mental illness maximizers and sin maximizers. Drawing insights from both perspectives, I clarify what is at stake in evangelical debate surrounding the sufficiency of Scripture and the doctrine of sin. In the process, I hope to contribute toward an evangelical theology of mental illness.

The Sufficiency of Scripture

Large areas of life and society are under the sway of the medical gaze. In the eyes of many, psychiatrists and psychologists are too eager to medicalize normal behaviour. Christians who share this perspective are inclined to frame mental illness as partially, or even largely, a 'social construct', a fiction invented by misguided experts that has deformed the human self-understanding.[8] Religious people are not alone in this worry – some secular thinkers harbour similar fears.[9] For their part, believers who resist a realist view of mental illness are almost always driven by theological commitments. They rely instead on their own biblically informed intuitions on how best to understand the ebb and flow of human motivation.

Given these attitudes, it is no surprise that Christians diagnosed with depression, or schizophrenia, or any other mental disorder, have been marginalized as perhaps weak in faith, struggling with sin or even demonic oppression.[10] Many have been harmed in the process. As Amy Simpson puts it:

> Spiritualizing mental illness translates to blaming sick people for their illnesses. It also means that family members of people with mental illness

also get the message that their sin and lack of faith may be the problem. It traps people into working harder and harder to achieve a level of righteousness that will justify their freedom from illness. This is not the gospel message, and it is very effective in discouraging people from acknowledging their struggles and seeking help.[11]

Simpson is only one of a multitude who have rightly sounded the alarm against such mistakes.

From the seventeenth to the nineteenth centuries, it was common for Christians to blame insanity on religious factors like divine punishment, personal sin or demonic influence. Scientific perspectives on insanity were still relatively rare and, while there was some recognition of the role of biology, Puritans like Cotton Mather tended to appeal 'to the supernatural realm, whether spurred by sin, demonic possession, divine punishment, or a struggle of faith'.[12] Such attitudes reflected earlier medieval views on madness; and while it is difficult to generalize this complex period, medieval believers tended to view psychiatric illness as symptomatic of demon possession. As one historian observed: '[M]ental illness . . . was believed to be demonic possession.'[13] Turning away from God was thought to bring madness and irrationality, the divine sentence for unholy lust and sinful desire.[14]

By the nineteenth century, Protestantism was beginning to fragment into 'liberal' and 'fundamentalist' factions. Among liberal Protestants, mental disturbance was conceived as a *physical* illness best understood by the emerging field of psychiatry. Protestant fundamentalists, however, continued to defend a more premodern view of insanity. They saw the connection between sin and insanity as essential in preserving the biblical picture of the world. As the historian Norman Dain observes:

> It should be noted, however, that the central issue for those who saw insanity as sinful was not so much the nature of insanity but the preservation of the biblical view of the subject: to reject the role of sin in the etiology of madness was equivalent to rejecting the Bible as the ultimate and inerrant source for Christian beliefs. The concern of revivalists then, and subsequently, was usually not so much with insanity as with defending their conception of Christianity against modernist liberal religion, and, later, against the new higher criticism of the Bible and Darwin's theory of natural selection.[15]

According to Dain, religious people have been interested in insanity more for its theological implications than for the care of the mentally disturbed. Perhaps that was to their shame, but they were also motivated by a concern that only Scripture should provide the categories with which to interpret the world, rather than the other way round:

The persistence of stigmatizing mentally disturbed people as sinful and personally blameworthy for their disorder cannot be accounted for simply as a long-held Christian belief. It is perhaps more important that to many Protestant clergy a challenge to the biblical concept of insanity seems to be a challenge to Christianity itself. Conservative Christians seem to believe that to abandon the idea that sin and the devil are the origin of most psychoses would be to deny the clearly stated views of Christ as reported in the New Testament and thus to deny the Bible as an inerrant source of all valid Christian belief.[16]

This defensive stance captures the concerns of those who appeal to the sufficiency of Scripture against mental illness discourse. On this view, Scripture is fundamentally all we need for our knowledge of God and addressing all problems of living. Since secular psychologies are attempting to instruct us on how to live our day-to-day lives, they should be rejected as counterfeit models of sanctification – the Bible alone is sufficient for believers.[17] Psychological research and practice may have ancillary benefits, but they cannot help Christians order their lives faithfully before the Lord.

If that represents how sin maximizers apply the idea of biblical sufficiency to psychology, we should ask whether such a position is defensible today. Most Christian integrationists[18] – 'mental illness maximizers' – would say *No*. One can affirm the sufficiency of Scripture while also recognizing those same Scriptures call us to be diligent students of general revelation. We are made in God's image; common grace allows believers to receive true insights about our world from non-believers. Christians should therefore engage the best research on mental illness to aid in caring for souls, receiving such research with gratitude and discernment.[19]

To sum up, sin maximizers claim that the sufficiency of Scripture precludes a positive assessment of mental illness discourse; Scripture and the psychological disciplines offer competing explanations on how best to navigate problems of living in a fallen world. In reply, mental illness maximizers remind us that divine revelation is not limited to Scripture but incorporates general revelation as well, revelation that is embedded in a wide range of psychological and psychiatric research.[20] If we reject that witness, we are despising God's gifts. In my judgement, helpful insights from both sin maximizers and mental illness maximizers deserve further nuance and clarification.

Against Maximizing Sin

Sin maximizers tend to overstate their case when they appeal to the sufficiency of Scripture. Their implicit argument makes key assumptions about biblical anthropology. The consensus within the Christian tradition is a dualistic (or hylomorphic) conception of the human constitution. I agree with that dualistic tradition and its roots in a doctrine of the intermediate state.[21] Biblical anthropology also resists reductively medical or scientific conceptions of what motivates human beings. We are not merely brains and bodies all the way down. Scripture also recognizes the inner life that reflects an immaterial, spiritual dimension to humanity, the terrain on which much of the drama is played out between God and humanity.

However, the intellectual heirs of Jay Adams oversimplify the situation. They often imply that physicians address *physical* defects in the body and brain, whereas pastors and biblical counsellors address *spiritual* defects in the soul (or spirit). They complain that the disciplines of psychology and psychiatry trespass on a domain that is not their rightful jurisdiction. It is the Bible, not secular psychologies, that speaks authoritatively to disturbances of the soul. In the words of Adams:

> Biblically, there is no warrant for acknowledging the existence of a separate and distinct discipline called psychiatry. There are, in the Scriptures, only three specified sources of personal problems in living: demonic activity (principally possession), personal sin, and organic illness. These three are interrelated. All options are covered under these heads, leaving no room for a fourth: non-organic mental illness.[22]

For Adams the idea of 'non-organic mental illnesses' is a category mistake – our bodies become sick, but it is our souls that are guilty of sin, or oppressed by demons.[23] Two points should be made in response.

First, as Adams himself often affirmed, a dualistic anthropology should be defended holistically to reflect the intimate connection between body and soul. In principle, then, we can expect that the body affects the soul in ways that impact mental and spiritual functioning. Psychologists and psychiatrists are able to access those areas; the sufficiency of Scripture hardly undermines that claim.

Second, an implication of the Fall of Adam and Eve is that sin has affected every area of the creaturely realm, including the inner person, i.e. our souls or spirits. We enter life under the condition of original sin; we sin inevitably, and we sin culpably. Eric Johnson highlights another aspect of the Fall, which he dubs 'biopsychosocial damage'.[24] This damage catches all the ways in which our cognitive, emotional and psychological capacities can be broken, sometimes as a result of underlying neural defects. These broken capacities should be categorized as 'weaknesses', states or conditions we *suffer from* and thus are not culpable for before the Lord. Such realities are part of the collateral damage of inhabiting a fallen world.

Biblical sufficiency allows us to frame the issues theologically, but Scripture itself gives no details or an exhaustive account of biopsychosocial damage.

Arguably, the biblical story largely *assumes* biopsychosocial health when it speaks about human sinning and flourishing (though there are notable exceptions[25] – e.g. Nebuchadnezzar experienced temporary madness in Dan. 4.29–37). Scripture's relative silence on human liability to biopsychosocial damage does not imply that biblical Christianity precludes such realities. At their best, psychologists and psychiatrists illuminate the realm of biopsychosocial injury.[26] As we shall see, it is likely that in many instances of psychiatric illness people are both suffering from biopsychosocial weaknesses *and* also guilty of personal sinning (sin as a factor in the mental illness and/ or resulting from it). All of this should temper polemical appeals to biblical sufficiency.

Against Maximizing Mental Illness

For their part, mental illness maximizers should take the priority of Scripture very seriously. The Scripture principle – *sola scriptura* – remains vital to evangelical thinking about mental illness. Since Scripture is God's infallible revelation, it is an epistemic safeguard against the failings of human reason. That holds true especially in light of the noetic effects of sin, sin's negative effects on our intellectual capacities. The scientific enterprise is enmeshed inescapably in the noetic effects of sin, effects that vary widely across the scientific disciplines. As an example, the noetic effects of sin on physics and physiology are less striking than on psychology and psychiatry.[27] As one theologian writes, 'Every discipline presupposes some doctrine of the human. In some disciplines that doctrine is very much on the surface and potential conflict between the Christian and others will be more to the fore. One might suggest that there is a principle of proximity to the anthropological.'[28] The closer the discipline's focus lies to the human person, the greater likelihood of conflict with biblical themes. In short, psychological research testifies to God's common grace but also reflects the noetic effects of sin. Unravelling these two elements is not easy and remains a source of contention in the literature. Rightly understood, the sufficiency of Scripture can serve here as a guide and a protection. It provides a framework within which – and lenses through which – to interpret psychological research.

The priority of Scripture also matters at the level of plausibility structures. Christians using psychiatric insights into biopsychosocial damage are plundering the Egyptians, but that benefit comes with a temptation to rely increasingly on secular, naturalistic categories. Over time, and perhaps unwittingly, biblical categories of sin and salvation can become less existentially meaningful.[29] The situation is reminiscent of evangelical scientists who practise methodological naturalism in the laboratory. According to Christian methodological naturalists, genuine science should only appeal to naturalistic explanations – as a *believer*, you can believe in supernatural causes and supernatural agents; however, as a *scientist* you cannot appeal to such realities in your research. You must be agnostic. At its worst, methodological naturalism inclines towards *metaphysical* naturalism; functionally the scientist no longer believes such supernatural entities exist at all.[30] The parallel with the disciplines of psychology and psychiatry is this: as an approved professional, you cannot appeal to biblical realities like sin and sanctification. And yet, psychology and psychiatry attempt to speak comprehensively to what is wrong with people and how they can find relief. This seems like a conflict of interest.[31] Christians who draw freely from these disciplines should resist naturalism creep as the plausibility structures of the guild seep into instinctive patterns of thought, rendering notions of sin and sanctification marginal or merely epiphenomenal.

Doctrine of Sin

Although Christians have often blamed mental suffering on personal sin or demonic oppression, the early Church was hesitant in attributing all suffering to human sin. In the Old Testament, Job's friends were rebuked for making that presumption. Similarly, in the New Testament the disciples asked Jesus about the man who was born blind: Was it this man that had sinned, or his parents? 'Neither this man nor his parents sinned', said Jesus, 'but this happened so that the works of God might be displayed in him' (John 9.3). Scripture makes a clear distinction between ordinary sickness and sickness as a direct result of sin or demonic influence.[32] On these grounds, and others, we should dispute the tendency in some Christian circles to blame the mentally ill for their condition.[33] Not only do such prejudices lack care and compassion, but personal sin is given too much credit. As I argued already, the Fall and its complex, multi-layered effects on body and soul must also be taken seriously.

Psychiatric Disorders and Human Sinfulness

Nevertheless, I wish to explore a different kind of error, namely, failing to draw on the doctrine of sin when the human experience is inexplicable without it. The diagnosis of mental illness usually excludes the category of sin on the grounds of compassion and non-judgementalism towards the afflicted. That is because many Christians (and non-Christians) understand sin in a *voluntarist* sense. In this way of thinking, I am only culpable when I sin 'consciously' or 'intentionally', but when desires, thoughts, words, or actions arise from me involuntarily or unconsciously, when I cannot 'control' myself, *then* I am not culpable. I have not sinned. According to this voluntarist approach to moral agency, I am only culpable for thoughts and actions over which I have control.[34]

Modern psychiatry, implicitly, shares this libertarian hamartiology. Consider the paraphilic disorders listed in the latest edition of the Diagnostic and Statistical Manual of Mental Disorders (DSM-5). This class of diagnoses includes voyeuristic, exhibitionistic, frotteuristic, paedophilic, fetishistic and transvestic disorders, as well as sexual masochism and sexual sadism. Similarly, DSM-5 groups the following conditions under the heading of 'disruptive, impulse-control, and conduct disorders': oppositional defiant disorder, intermittent explosive disorder, conduct disorder, and kleptomania. Each one of these so-called mental disorders has its own set of diagnostic criteria. For instance, the criteria for voyeuristic disorder are as follows:

> Over a period of at least six months, recurrent and intense sexual arousal from observing an unsuspecting person who is naked, in the process of disrobing, or engaging in sexual activity, as manifested by fantasies, urges, or behaviors.
> The individual has acted on these sexual urges with a nonconsenting person, or the sexual urges or fantasies cause clinically significant distress or impairment in social, occupational, or other important areas of functioning.
> The individual experiencing the arousal and/or acting on the urges is at least 18 years of age.[35]

The psychiatric manual adopts a purely symptom-based nosology; none of these disorders have any biological or neurological markers.

From a Christian standpoint, these diagnoses are wrongheaded. Most believers that have ever lived would have taken these conditions to be clear cases of disobedience; in a word, *sin*. They would have been right to do so. Sin is central to what these conditions describe.[36] But by labelling these symptom clusters as 'disorders', within the naturalistic frame of secular psychiatry, DSM-5 gives the ineluctable impression that these are sicknesses, not instances of sin. People suffer from these states; they are not blameworthy. Even the clinical description of these so-called mental illnesses, with its itemizing of 'diagnostic features', 'prevalence', 'development and course', 'risk and prognostic factors', 'differential diagnosis', 'comorbidity', etc. – all of this has the accoutrements of a *medical* disease. The language throughout DSM-5 is consistent with a biological psychiatry.[37]

Sin maximizers have a point here. These psychiatric diagnoses are 'vice-laden'; non-moral concepts are foregrounded whereas the embedded *moral* concepts are ignored. The hamartiological context almost vanishes completely. As one philosopher of psychiatry remarks:

These vice-laden disorders pose puzzling historical questions. Why has one kind of vice become an official psychiatric condition while other forms of vice do not? Not just the presence of these official vice-laden disorders, but the *absence* of other potential vice-laden disorders, is puzzling: Why not classify other forms of vice (e.g., white-collar insider trading, sex work, drug dealing, serial murder), or for that matter, moral failings (e.g., racism . . . or lying) as mental disorders? Vice-ladenness poses problems of both commission and omission vis-à-vis mental disorder concepts.[38]

All fair questions. To claim that personal sin, which can be intentional or unintentional, has no bearing on these so-called disorders is implausible. In my view, these diagnoses need to be supplemented or, better, *re-described* by developing a more comprehensive discursive system that combines hamartiological and biopsychosocial conceptual frameworks. Invoking the biblical language of sin is not callous; rather it places the struggle within a potentially redemptive matrix. God's grace is available – the Holy Spirit can work mightily through regeneration and sanctification. This point is controversial enough to require a defence.

On the Metaphysics of Mental Illness

People tend to think that someone diagnosed with a psychiatric illness suffers from a pathological disease: other things being equal, I'm not morally responsible for accidentally spraining my ankle, or having a genetic disease, or suffering a stroke; likewise, I'm not morally responsible for having a psychiatric disorder like schizophrenia or bipolar disorder. The assumption is that mental illnesses preclude the label of sin, presumably because people with mental illnesses cannot 'control' themselves and therefore should not be further shamed by labelling their behaviour as sinful, or perhaps because psychiatric disorders are organic diseases and should therefore not be framed in moral terms. The problem with these intuitions is that some 'mental illnesses' are conceptually dissimilar from medical disease, and that fact opens up space for rethinking the role of sin.

One of the big questions relates to the metaphysics of mental illness. What *kind* of thing is a mental disorder? Anti-realist views interpret mental illnesses as socially constructed realities. By those lights, a mental illness diagnosis does not describe anything real, an entity that exists in the actual world. The diagnosis is a useful fiction produced by social forces that are artificially imposed on the person. This anti-realist move is not only deployed by some conservative evangelical thinkers; prominent secular theorists have levelled similar claims. For instance, Allan Horwitz argues that modern psychiatry has overextended itself, often misclassifying normal reactions to difficult circumstances as mental disorders.[39]

Anti-realist approaches to mental illness gain plausibility from the history of psychiatry, how past beliefs about psychiatric illness have sooner or later turned out to be false.[40] Previously accepted diagnostic categories have been discarded into the dustbins of history; why think any of our current diagnostic models are true? This is a pessimistic induction argument from the history of psychiatry.[41] Consider: 'hysteria', a popular diagnosis in the nineteenth and early twentieth century, is no longer accepted.[42] In his treatise on insanity, the French psychiatrist Jean-Étienne Esquirol gave meticulous descriptions of mental disorders like lypemania, demonomania, and monomania.[43] Carl Wernicke, the famous German neuropathologist and psychiatrist, believed that somatopsychosis and anxiety psychosis were real mental illnesses.[44] In his classification of endogenous psychoses, Karl Leonhard confidently invoked disorders like 'parakinetic catatonia', 'phonemic paraphrenia', and 'insipid hebephrenia'.[45]

These disorders merely scratch the surface of the vast collection of now discarded historical diagnoses, every one of them long forgotten. In light of this pattern, some interpret psychiatric disorders to be *socially constructed kinds*. Realists, however, interpret such disorders in terms of the medical model, a somatic psychiatry. On this view, mental illnesses are medical or *essentialist kinds*, real entities rooted in brain neuropathology. A third approach avoids the metaphysical questions and categorizes diagnoses in terms of their practical usefulness, i.e. *practical kinds*.[46]

I find it intellectually unconvincing, if not irresponsible, to dismiss all mental illnesses as socially constructed.[47] I am a realist about mental illnesses like bipolar disorder and schizophrenia, but I agree with Horwitz and others that psychiatry has expanded the category of mental illness in unhelpful ways. In light of history, it is unwise to deny *any* socially constructive elements to psychiatric diagnoses. As one psychiatrist advises, 'We should not get backed into a corner claiming that social processes play no role in the construction of our categories. That is not a defensible position.'[48] The recognition that mental disorders are not generally essentialist (or medical) kinds allows the doctrine of sin to illuminate or even correct some psychiatric diagnoses.

The problem is that non-specialists uncritically accept the essentialist model. It is the default perspective at the popular level and explains why people think sin cannot play a role in mental illness.[49] Among mainstream psychologists who are believers, there is also strong resistance to thinking about mental illness in relation to the doctrine of sin.[50] Some of that is doubtless a reaction to how fellow Christians in the past – and present – have harmed or marginalized people with mental illness. But it may also stem from assuming the medical model – if mental disorders are medical or quasi-medical diseases, then 'sin' is an illegitimate category. Even if the medical model is rejected in favour of a multi-causal, multi-level understanding of psychiatric illness, this scenario is typically framed in terms of the nature–nurture interplay, a reductive category that marginalizes the reality of sin.

In what sense, then, does the medical model misread mental illnesses? Ian Hacking's technical distinction between 'natural' and 'interactive' kinds may help.[51] Natural kinds are events in nature, things that function by the laws of nature – e.g. water, sodium, heat, a horse, the colour yellow. Natural kinds are 'indifferent'. Regardless of whether or not they are classified by human beings, they simply exist as is. Conversely, interactive kinds are classifications that can change the people classified. When such classifications are known 'by people or those around them, and put to work in institutions, [they] change the ways in which individuals experience themselves – and may lead people to evolve their feelings and behaviour in part because they are so classified'.[52] Interactive kinds interact with the things they classify.

Consider a rose bush. It is a natural flower, indifferent to whatever humans choose to label it. Roses are unaware that humans classify them as 'flowers', that they are used in gardens, weddings, and so on; the future of a rose is not affected by what humans think of them. But that's different for a child diagnosed with ADHD or a teenager struggling with anorexia. These diagnostic labels are *interactive* kinds – they interact with the people classified by them.

Hacking proposed the idea of looping effects, the complex process by which classifications in the human sciences (e.g. psychiatry) can 'make up' new kinds of people. His thesis seeks to carve out a middle ground between realism and social constructionism.[53] The classifications shape the people who are classified, and in turn those same classified people influence and change the classification systems.[54] Thus, interactive kinds can explain transient mental disorders, conditions which seem to appear for a period and then vanish completely.[55] There is debate about the validity of aspects of Hacking's thesis[56] – but for present purposes, my interest lies in a basic point that Hacking brings to light: some psychological and psychiatric diagnoses are not caused by any neuropathology but are generated by social, cultural and other forces bound up with the very process of classifying them *as* disorders.

Let us return to the DSM-5 paraphilic and conduct disorders. I suspect that in most, if not all, cases these are not essentialist or medical kinds[57] with underlying neurobiological causes. Instead, they are best understood as *interactive* kinds. They are clinical diagnoses that have interacted in complex ways with the people so classified; those diagnostic labels have also influenced wider social and cultural practices and assumptions, including our understanding of human behaviour. Cluster B Personality Disorders show a similar pattern. Antisocial personality disorder, for example, is a failure 'to conform to social norms with respect to lawful behaviors', 'deceitfulness, as indicated by repeated lying, use of aliases, or conning others for personal profit or pleasure', 'impulsivity', 'lack of remorse', and the like.[58] Or consider narcissistic personality disorder, which describes someone who likely has 'a grandiose sense of self-importance', 'requires excessive admiration', 'is interpersonally exploitative', 'lacks empathy', and 'shows arrogant, haughty behaviors or attitudes'.[59] There is at present no definitive evidence that these are medical kinds – these are likely interactive, *moral* kinds.

Granted, paraphilic and conduct disorders are low-hanging fruit; disputing their validity will start no revolution.[60] But the same substantive concerns I have raised apply to other less colourful mental disorders (though perhaps to a lesser extent). Psychiatric classifications shape the conception of the self, both individually and communally.[61] More precisely, such classifications invariably shape the *moral* conception of the self. Is it possible that some of our current psychiatric diagnostic categories have developed in contingent ways that do not reflect the sober truth about people? Are there better, more reliable accounts of human motivation and patterns of behaviour?

If any affirmative answers are forthcoming, they should include the role of sin. In the biblical story, human life is oriented around God and our relationship to him. Sin has fractured that relationship and lies at the heart of the human predicament and what we can do about it. As broader ranges of human behaviour are medicalized by mental health professionals, the looping effects transform mental illness into an all-encompassing horizon by which people understand themselves. As one recent commentary suggests:

> According to research on moral typecasting, people tend to be perceived either as moral patients, who are viewed in terms of their capacity to suffer and as being acted upon in moral or immoral ways, or as moral agents, who are capable of acting morally or immorally. Where harm occurs, people are therefore typecast either as victims who suffer harm but lack responsibility and the capacity to act intentionally, or as perpetrators who are blameworthy, but lack the capacity to suffer. If people experiencing mental disorders are understood as harmed and suffering, moral typecasting implies they will see themselves, and will be seen by others, as lacking agency. The spreading concept of mental disorder would therefore have the looping effect of expanding the sense of passivity and victimhood... [A]s more and more people qualify for psychiatric diagnoses, they will increasingly understand themselves as patients rather than agents.[62]

This 'concept creep'[63] effectively closes people off from the dogmatic realities of sin and sanctification.

Some may worry that I'm committing the 'encyclopedic fallacy'[64] – the idea that Scripture speaks infallibly on every conceivable subject matter – since my argument entails that hamartiology can rightly delegitimize aspects of psychology and psychiatry.[65] The Word of God, after all, does not speak exhaustively on most spheres of knowledge. Scripture says nothing about cardiology, pulmonology, degenerative cases, and countless other areas of medicine; and yet, these diagnoses cover a wide range of physical ailments that affect millions of people daily. These remarkable medical insights are fruits of God's common grace; benefitting from them aligns fully with the great things of the gospel. As Herman Bavinck reminds us: 'Holy Scripture has a purpose that is religious-ethical through and through. *It is not designed to be a manual for the various sciences.* . . . In all the disciplines that are grouped around Scripture, our aim must be the saving knowledge of God.'[66] Medical disease and its many permutations in no way overturn the doctrine of sin and its role in the fabric of faith. At times the Lord heals our sicknesses through medicine, or miraculously without medicine; he even allows us to suffer through our afflictions – such experiences are divinely ordained, the means by which we draw near to God, sinners yearning to be made more holy.

But mental illness is not a medical disease. While I claimed earlier that mental illness discourse need not conflict with the Christian understanding of sin, the problem arises when the concept of mental illness overreaches, swallowing up large swathes of life, so that the very idea of sin loses existential traction. There *is* no encyclopedic fallacy. Sinful habits, prompted by the vicissitudes of life, are *moral* kinds; they become interactive kinds when they are given psychiatric classifications. The notion of sin obviously collapses if we wrongly treat these experiences as if they are natural kinds.[67] Evidently, we need to disentangle theological and conceptual ambiguities surrounding the concept of mental illness.

In the first place, each of us, with or without mental illness, suffers from a far deeper problem of original sin. The Fall of Adam and Eve puts us in the single family of condemned humanity (cf. Gen. 3); everyone is morally corrupt from birth (Ps. 51.5; Rom. 5.12–21; 1 Cor. 15.21–22).[68] Original sin is our core affliction, it conditions our existence, and it is why we need Jesus for salvation. In the Augustinian hamartiology, all humanity somehow participated in Adam's first sin and, from birth, are thus guilty and morally vitiated.[69]

In the second place, clear-cut mental illnesses are either genuine instances of biopsychosocial damage and/or symptoms of (as yet) unrecognized brain disease. Mental illnesses of this kind are sometimes associated with what *appear to be* sinful thoughts and behaviours. To the degree that those thoughts and behaviours no longer rightly disclose one's moral agency, *weakness* rather than sin is a more apt category. However, given how original sin conditions *all* of human existence, the reality is usually more grey than black-and-white, so that the experiences of the psychiatrically ill represent a complex blend of weakness and sin.

It is not that people afflicted with mental illness are sinning intentionally, that they are always in 'control' of their actions. Such a voluntarist conception of sin, while popular, is too narrow and experientially unconvincing. Scripture doesn't define sin primarily as those thoughts or actions I choose to do, or refrain from doing. Sin includes such items but is not limited to them. Rather sin should be understood *compatibilistically*, as those acts or desires that truly disclose my sinful heart. As Jesse Couenhoven notes: 'Emphasizing control has distracted us from noticing that we have very little control . . . over a wide range of beliefs, cares, desires, inattentions, and even volitions that we commonly consider persons responsible for.'[70] By 'compatibilism', then, I mean that genuine responsibility speaks more to 'self-disclosure' than 'self-making'.[71] People are responsible for what they personally own, i.e. 'we are responsible not only for what we choose to do but also for who we are'.[72] Jesus remarked that evil thoughts, murder, adultery, and other such sins flow 'out of the heart' (Matt. 15.19); our sins arise from 'the overflow of the heart' (Matt. 12.34). Persons are therefore morally responsible for internal desires or external actions that truly disclose their hearts.

In the third place, several 'mental illnesses' are likely nothing of the kind. They are social constructions that pathologize aspects of life, including variously ingrained habits of sin and dysfunction. Paraphilic disorders are a plausible example of such socially constructed mental illnesses. If the behaviours of these men and women truly disclose their hearts, then they are responsible – it is *morally* irrelevant whether these 'symptoms' are recurrent, intense, distressing, and so on.[73] It *would* be morally relevant if there was an underlying biological or neurophysiological defect causing these symptoms. In that case, the symptoms would not be genuinely disclosing the heart but would be indicative of a medical, not moral kind; or, perhaps, paraphilic disorders are a composite medical *and* moral kind, i.e. sin *and* weakness.[74] However, without any convincing evidence of a biogenetic basis to paraphilic disorders, this latter possibility is only speculative.[75]

Conclusion

This chapter was an exercise in theological ground-clearing in the hope of advancing the dialogue between mental illness maximizers and sin maximizers.

Clarifying the points of consensus and tension is vital toward developing a viable Christian approach to mental illness. Of course, much more than these reflections is needed to build a robust theology of mental illness, but whatever that grand edifice might look like once completed, this chapter seeks to start laying the foundation.

For many individuals with a diagnosis of mental illness, moral agency and the Christian categories of sin, regeneration and sanctification remain operative (*sin*, that is, in a compatibilist rather than a voluntarist sense). As long as their desires and behaviours are disclosing the states of their hearts, moral agency is alive and well. Caring for their souls requires explicitly theological resources and not merely medical or psychiatric ones. For those who suffer from mental illness, this is immensely good news. Far from being merely notional concepts, sin and sanctification turn out to be indispensable companions on the long journey to true healing.

The debates between mental illness maximizers and sin maximizers remain an important component of evangelical thinking about psychology. They raise enduring questions about sin and sanctification, the importance of biblical authority, and the need to recognize common grace in the secular disciplines. But they also point, regrettably, to the perennial tendency to privilege one of those legitimate concerns over the others. Confessional evangelicals can, and must, do better. We need to raise the level of the conversation. We need more balance, more theological consistency, and surely we need more courage to ask the hard questions – lest a faithful theology of mental illness remain ever elusive, a will-o'-the-wisp.[76]

Notes

1 This paragraph relies on D. E. Bloom, E. T. Cafiero, E. Jané-Llopis et al., *The Global Economic Burden of Non-Communicable Diseases* (Geneva: World Economic Forum, 2011); William Reeves, Tara Strine, Laura Pratt et al., 'Mental Illness Surveillance Among Adults in the United States', *Mortality and Morbidity Weekly Report* 60, 3 (2011), pp. 1–32.

2 The paragraph draws on David Murray's blog post, 'Double Dangers: Maximizing and Minimizing Mental Illness' (16 April 2016), http://headhearthand.org/blog/2013/04/16/maximizing-and-minimizing-mental-illness/. For a useful entry into the broader debate, see Eric Johnson (ed.), *Psychology and Christianity: Five Views*, 2nd edn (Downers Grove, IL: InterVarsity Press, 2010).

3 The 'biblical counselling' movement is not monolithic; e.g. the Christian Counseling and Education Foundation (CCEF), the Association of Biblical Counselors (ABC), and the Association of Certified Biblical Counselors (ACBC, formerly known as NANC [National Association of Nouthetic Counselors]), all three groups with different distinctives and emphases. For a helpful introduction, see David Powlison, *The Biblical Counseling Movement: History and Context* (Greensboro, NC: New Growth Press, 2010). See also Heath Lambert, *The Biblical Counseling Movement after Adams* (Wheaton, IL: Crossway, 2012).

4 E.g. see John Piper, *Tested by Fire: The Fruit of Suffering in the Lives of John Bunyan, William Cowper and David Brainerd* (Downers Grove, IL: InterVarsity Press, 2001); Zack Erswine, *Spurgeon's Sorrows: Realistic Hope for those who Suffer from Depression* (Fearn, Ross-shire: Christian Focus, 2014).

5 Jay Adams, *Competent to Counsel: Introduction to Nouthetic Counseling* (Phillipsburg, NJ: Presbyterian and Reformed, 1970). See also Jay Adams, *A Theology of Christian Counseling: More than Redemption* (Phillipsburg, NJ: Presbyterian and Reformed, 1979), esp. pp. 233–75.

6 Adams, *Competent to Counsel*, p. 73.

7 For a recent attempt, see Eric Johnson, *God and Soul Care: The Therapeutic Resources of the Christian Faith* (Downers Grove, IL: IVP Academic, 2017).

8 For this orientation, see Heath Lambert, *A Theology of Biblical Counseling: The Doctrinal Foundations of Counseling Ministry* (Grand Rapids, MI: Zondervan, 2016); Stuart Scott and Heath Lambert (eds), *Counseling the Hard Cases: True Stories Illustrating the Sufficiency of God's Resources in Scripture* (Nashville, TN: B&H, 2012). Cf. Heath Lambert, *The Gospel and Mental Illness* (Louisville, KY: Association of Certified Biblical Counselors, 2014), pp. 40–1, 45.

9 The literature is extensive – e.g. see Thomas Szasz, *The Myth of Mental Illness: Foundations of a Theory of Personal Conduct* (New York: Hoeber-Harper, 1961); R. D. Laing, *The Politics of Experience* (New York: Ballantine Books, 1967); E. Fuller Torrey, *The Death of Psychiatry* (Radnor, PA: Chilton Books, 1974). Cf. Norman Dain, 'Psychiatry and Anti-Psychiatry in the United States', in Mark Micale and Roy Porter (eds), *Discovering the History of Psychiatry* (New York: Oxford University Press, 1994), pp. 415–44; Gerald Grob, 'The Attack of Psychiatric Legitimacy in the 1960s: Rhetoric and Reality', *Journal of the History of the Behavioral Sciences* 47, 4 (2011), pp. 398–416.

10 For different perspectives on this issue, see Anastasia Philippa Scrutton, 'Is Depression a Sin or a Disease? A Critique of Moralizing and Medicalizing Models of Mental Illness', *Journal of Disability and Religion* 19 (2015), pp. 285–311; Marcia Webb, 'Toward a Theology of Mental Illness', *Journal of Religion, Disability and Health* 16 (2012), pp. 49–73.

11 Amy Simpson, *Troubled Minds: Mental Illness and the Church's Mission* (Downers Grove, IL: InterVarsity Press 2013), p. 107.

12 Heather Vacek, *Madness: American Protestant Responses to Mental Illness* (Waco, TX: Baylor University Press, 2015), p. 19. In fact, Mather often appealed to both natural and supernatural explanations of madness, apparently seeing them as complementary points of view – cf. Mary Ann Jimenez, *Changing Faces of Madness: Early American Attitudes and Treatment of the Insane* (Hanover, NH: University Press of New England, 1987), pp. 12–30. It is also noteworthy that the Puritans, influenced by English views on madness, recognized 'melancholia' as a kind of mental disease. On this point, see Stanley Jackson, 'Melancholia and Mechanical Explanation in Eighteenth Century Medicine', *Journal of the History of Medicine and Allied Sciences* 38 (1983), pp. 298–319.

13 Michael Dols, 'Insanity in Byzantine and Islamic Medicine', in John Scarborough, *Symposium on Byzantine Medicine* (Washington, DC: Dumbarton Oaks Papers, 1984), p. 143. I was alerted to this source by Horacio Fabrega, 'Psychiatric Stigma in the Classical and Medieval Period: A Review of the Literature', *Comprehensive Psychiatry* 31, 4 (1990), pp. 289–306.

14 Cf. Neaman, Judith, *Suggestion of the Devil: The Origins of Madness* (New York: Doubleday Anchor Books, 1975). However, these observations should be

counterbalanced by historical evidence that – even in the medieval period – lay and clerical physicians also drew on rational, more naturalistic explanations in their understanding of mental disorders. E.g. see Jerome Kroll, 'A Reappraisal of Psychiatry in the Middle Ages', *Archives of General Psychiatry* 29, 2 (1973), pp. 276–83; Richard Neugebauer, 'Medieval and Early Modern Theories of Mental Illness', *Archives of General Psychiatry* 36, 4 (1979), pp. 477–83; Jerome Kroll and Bernard Bachrach, 'Sin and Mental Illness in the Middle Ages', *Psychological Medicine* 14, 3 (1984), pp. 507–14.

15 Norman Dain, 'Madness and the Stigma of Sin in American Christianity', in Paul Jay Fink, and Allan Tasman (eds), *Stigma and Mental Illness* (Washington, DC: American Psychiatric, 1992), pp. 74–5.

16 Dain, 'Madness and the Stigma of Sin', p. 80. Such Christians also failed to distinguish between mental illness as a form of suffering that is a distal consequence of the fall vs mental illness associated proximally with personal sin.

17 This approach is clearly represented in Heath Lambert, 2017, '95 Theses for an Authentically Christian Commitment to Counseling', https://biblicalcounseling.com/ninety-five/. For example, see Thesis no. 31 – 'Because the Bible is the authority for every situation in life, whenever secular therapists write, teach, or counsel about matters of human living, they address matters that God covers authoritatively in his Word.'

18 For classic examples of the integrationist approach, see Daryl Stevenson, Brian Eck and Peter Hill (eds), *Psychology and Christianity Integration: Seminal Works That Shaped the Movement* (Batavia, IL: Christian Association for Psychological Studies, 2007); Stanton Jones, 'An Integration View', in *Psychology and Christianity*, pp. 101–28.

19 For an enthusiastic defence of this approach, see James Hurley and James Berry, 'The Relation of Scripture and Psychology in Counseling from a Pro-Integration Position', *Journal of Psychology and Christianity* 16, 4 (1997), pp. 323–45.

20 Despite this popular stance, 'general revelation' properly refers to the attributes of God, not the physical data of creation, much less the verdicts of natural science. E.g. see Nicolaas Gootjes, 'General Revelation and Science: Reflections on a Remark in Report 28', *Calvin Theological Journal* 30 (1995), pp. 94–107. The real claim, then, is that aspects of secular psychological research can be the fruit of God's common grace.

21 See John Cooper, *Body, Soul and Life Everlasting: Biblical Anthropology and the Monism-Dualism Debate*, 2nd edn (Grand Rapids, MI: Eerdmans, 2001). For a historical overview of monist and dualist options, see Stewart Goetz and Charles Taliaferro, *A Brief History of the Soul* (Malden, MA: Blackwell, 2011).

22 Jay Adams, *The Christian Counselor's Manual: The Practice of Nouthetic Counseling* (Grand Rapids, MI: Zondervan, 1973), pp. 9–10. For a similar perspective, see Heath Lambert, 'Introduction: The Sufficiency of Scripture, the Biblical Counseling Movement, and the Purpose of This Book', in *Counseling the Hard Cases*, pp. 1–24.

23 Adams is insisting on a proper division of labour; as a dualist, he clearly recognizes the holistic dimension to human persons. E.g. see Adams, *Christian Counselor's Manual*, p. 437.

24 Johnson, *God and Soul Care*, pp. 273–88.

25 For further discussion, see Johnson, *God and Soul Care*, p. 276.

26 A weakness in Edward Welch's otherwise helpful analysis of the relationship between brain disorders and sinful behaviour is that the phenomenon of

biopsychosocial damage is left undeveloped – see Edward Welch, *Blame It on the Brain?: Distinguishing Chemical Imbalances, Brain Disorders, and Disobedience* (Phillipsburg, NJ: Presbyterian and Reformed, 1998). For a helpful perspective, see Michael Emlet, *Descriptions and Prescriptions: A Biblical Perspective on Psychiatric Diagnoses and Medications* (Greensboro, NC: New Growth Press, 2017).

27 Cf. Stephen Moroney, *The Noetic Effects of Sin: A Historical and Contemporary Exploration of How Sin Affects Our Thinking* (Lanham, MD: Lexington, 2000). See also Alvin Plantinga, 'Sin and Its Cognitive Consequences', ch. 7 in *Warranted Christian Belief* (New York: Oxford University Press, 2000), pp. 199–240.

28 Graham Cole, 'Scripture and the Disciplines: The Question of Expectations', *Zadok Papers* 142 (2005), p. 5.

29 We should note that publications affiliated with the major evangelical psychological organizations are regularly trying to resist those secularizing forces (e.g. Christian Association for Psychological Studies; Society for Christian Psychology; American Association of Christian Counselors). For an example from the UK, see Christopher C. H. Cook (ed.), *Spirituality, Theology and Mental Health: Multidisciplinary Perspectives* (London: SCM Press, 2013).

30 Cf. Alvin Plantinga, 'Methodological Naturalism?' in Jitse M. van der Meer (ed.), *Facets of Faith and Science* (Lanham, MD: University Press of America, 1996), pp. 177–221.

31 There are often problematic economic and political motivations to expand the number of mental illness diagnoses. Some of these factors are charted in Allen Frances, *Saving Normal: An Insider's Revolt Against Out-of-control Psychiatric Diagnosis, DSM-5, Big Pharma, and the Medicalization of Ordinary Life* (New York: William Morrow, 2013).

32 Darrel Amundsen and Gary Ferngren, 'The Early Christian Tradition', in Ronald Numbers, and Darrel Amundsen (eds), *Caring and Curing: Health and Medicine in the Western Religious Traditions* (Baltimore, MD: Johns Hopkins University Press, 1986), pp. 45–6.

33 For analysis of North American lay attitudes to the mentally ill, see Matthew Stanford, 'Demon or Disorder: A Survey of Attitudes Toward Mental Illness in the Christian Church', *Mental Health, Religion and Culture* 10, 5 (2007), pp. 445–9.

34 These libertarian (or incompatibilist) instincts are common among Christian lay people and academics. In his otherwise brilliant analysis of sin, Cornelius Plantinga represents this view when he writes: 'I am supposing that incompatibilism is true – i.e. that an agent's freedom, and hence his moral responsibility, with respect to some act (or, in this case, the acquisition of some evil state of mind) is incompatible with that act's being determined by causes other than the agent' (Plantinga, Cornelius, *Not the Way It's Supposed to Be: A Breviary of Sin* [Grand Rapids, MI: Eerdmans, 1995], p. 24, n. 29). I disagree; what ultimately counts for the attribution of sin is not the presence or absence of control but, rather, whether the act or desire truly discloses our hearts.

35 American Psychiatric Association, *Diagnostic and Statistical Manual of Mental Disorders*, 5th edn (Washington, DC: American Psychiatric Publishing, 2013), p. 686 (henceforth *DSM-5*).

36 Interestingly, voyeurism and many of the paraphilic disorders are considered crimes in most American jurisdictions.

37 However, the DSM-5 explicitly says in its preface that its diagnostic criteria do not presuppose any specific etiology (biological or otherwise). I thank Mike Emlet for this reminder.

38 John Sadler, 'Vice and Mental Disorders', in K. W. M. Fulford, Martin Davies, Richard Gipps, George Graham, John Zadler, Giovanni Stanghellini and Tim Thornton (eds), *The Oxford Handbook of Philosophy and Psychiatry* (New York: Oxford University Press, 2015), p. 459.

39 Allan Horwitz, *Creating Mental Illness* (Chicago, IL: University of Chicago Press, 2001). Horwitz adopts a realist approach to major mental illnesses like bipolar disorder and schizophrenia, but he is very sceptical about many other current mental disorders.

40 I am paraphrasing Thomas Kuhn: 'All past beliefs about nature have sooner or later turned out to be false' (Thomas Kuhn, *The Road Since Structure: Philosophical Essays, 1970–1993*, James Conant and John Haugeland (eds) [Chicago, IL: University of Chicago Press, 2000], p. 115). Kuhn went on to say that: 'On the record, therefore, the probability that any currently proposed belief will fare better must be close to zero.' For this reference and the historical examples, I am indebted to Kenneth Kendler, 'The Nature of Psychiatric Disorders', *World Psychiatry* 15, 1 (2016), pp. 7–8.

41 For the classic pessimistic induction argument against scientific realism, see Larry Laudan, 'A Confutation of Convergent Realism', *Philosophy of Science* 48 (1981), pp. 19–49.

42 E.g. see Andrew Scull, *Hysteria: The Disturbing History* (Oxford: Oxford University Press, 2011).

43 See Jean-Étienne Esquirol, *Mental Maladies: A Treatise on Insanity*, trans. E. K. Hunt (Philadelphia, PA: Lea and Blanchard, 1845).

44 Cf. Wernicke, Carl, 1894, *Grundriss der Psychiatrie in Klinischen Vorlesungen* (Leipzig: Thieme, 1894).

45 Karl Leonhard, *The Classification of Endogenous Psychoses*, E. Robins (ed.), R. Berman (trans.), 5th edn (New York: Irvington, 1979). In Leonhard's defence, however, while 'insipid hebephrenia' is no longer a diagnosis, hebephrenic schizophrenia *is* a recognized subtype in the 10th revision of the International Statistical Classification of Diseases and Related Health Problems (ICD-10), a classification list by the World Health Organization.

46 For these three approaches – socially constructed kinds; essentialist kinds; practical kinds – see Kenneth Kendlar, Peter Zachar and Carl Craver, 'What Kinds of Things are Psychiatric Disorders?' *Psychological Medicine* 41 (2011), pp. 1143–50. The authors end up defending a fourth option: mechanistic property cluster kinds.

47 This conclusion is based on my encounters with people who struggle with mental illness (including patients I met during my medical training) – many of them had genuine disorders that were not socially constructed.

48 Kendler, 'Nature of Psychiatric Disorders', p. 11. He continues: 'There is no shame here. All scientific enterprises have social components. To suggest that we could keep psychiatry immune from social processes is unrealistic.'

49 However, most philosophers of psychiatry reject the essentialist model of mental illness: 'Few researchers and theorists explicitly endorse a full-blown [essentialist] kinds view of mental disorders, but those with a biomedical orientation are more inclined to do so than others, conceptualizing disorders as discrete entities and emphasizing biogenetic etiologies for them' (Erlend Kvaale and Nick Haslam, 'Essentialism versus Nominalism', in Robin Cautin and Scott Lilienfeld (eds), *The Encyclopedia of Clinical Psychology*, vol. 2 [Chichester: John Wiley and Sons, 2015], p. 1114.

50 Of course there are exceptions, e.g. see Mark McMinn, *Sin and Grace in Christian Counseling: An Integrative Paradigm* (Downers Grove, IL: IVP Academic, 2008).

51 E.g. see Ian Hacking, *The Social Construction of What?* (Cambridge, MA: Harvard University Press, 1999). Hacking's notion of 'natural kinds' was inspired by theories of reference developed by Hilary Putnam and Saul Kripke. Cf. Hilary Putnam, *Mind, Language, and Reality* (Cambridge: Cambridge University Press, 1975); Saul Kripke, *Naming and Necessity* (Cambridge, MA: Harvard University Press, 1980).

52 Hacking, *Social Construction of What*, p. 104.

53 He has defended 'dynamic nominalism' as the metaphysical underpinning of looping effects. E.g. see Ian Hacking, 'Making Up People', in Thomas Heller, Morton Sosna and David Wellbery (eds), *Reconstructing Individualism: Autonomy, Individuality, and the Self in Western Thought* (Stanford, CA: Stanford University Press, 1986), pp. 222–36.

54 Looping effects are not limited to classification systems and the people being classified but also extend to institutions (e.g. clinics, universities, talk shows); a knowledge base (disseminated by institutions); and the experts (e.g. psychiatrists, psychologists). For this expansion of Hacking's notion of interactive kinds, see Ian Hacking, 'Kinds of People: Moving Targets', *Proceedings of the British Academy* 151 (2007), pp. 285–318.

55 For a stimulating account, see Ian Hacking, *Mad Travelers: Reflections on the Reality of Transient Mental Illness* (Charlottesville, VA: University of Virginia Press, 1998).

56 E.g. see Jonathan Tsou, 'Hacking on the Looping Effects of Psychiatric Classifications: What is an Interactive and Indifferent Kind?' *International Studies in the Philosophy of Science* 21, 3 (2007), pp. 329–44. For critique of Hacking's earlier work on human vs natural kinds, see Rachel Cooper, 'Why Hacking is Wrong about Human Kinds', *British Journal for the Philosophy of Science* 55 (2004), pp. 73–85. For an interesting augmentation of Hacking's looping effects theory, with a rich account of a 'multitudinous' self, see Şerife Tekin, 'The Missing Self in Hacking's Looping Effects', in Harold Kincaid and Jacqueline Sullivan (eds), *Classifying Psychopathology: Mental Kinds and Natural Kinds* (Cambridge, MA: MIT Press, 2014), pp. 227–56. Even Hacking himself, in later work, has abandoned the concepts of 'natural kinds' and 'human kinds' because of interminable debates in the literature – cf. Hacking, 'Kinds of People'.

57 I'm using 'medical kind', 'essentialist kind' and 'natural kind' synonymously.

58 *DSM-5*, p. 659.

59 *DSM-5*, pp. 669–70.

60 Even secular scholarship has questioned whether paraphilias and other sexual deviances are genuine pathological diseases. E.g. see Andreas De Block and Pieter Adriaens, 'Pathologizing Sexual Deviance: A History', *Journal of Sex Research* 50 (2013), pp. 276–98. In DSM-5, 'paraphilia' was renamed to 'paraphilic disorder' in an attempt to reduce stigma.

61 Cf. Tekin, 'The Missing Self'.

62 Nick Haslam, 'Looping Effects and the Expanding Concept of Mental Disorder', *Journal of Psychopathology* 22 (2016), pp. 8–9. For the record, Haslam does not share my theological concerns.

63 Cf. Nick Haslam, 'Concept Creep: Psychology's Expanding Concepts of Harm and Pathology', *Psychology Inquiry* 27, 1 (2016), pp. 1–17. This article, the lead essay in a symposium, was followed by nine responses and a surrejoinder by Haslam.

64 See Roy Clouser, *The Myth of Religious Neutrality: An Essay on the Hidden Role of Religious Belief in Theories*, rev. edn (Notre Dame, IL: University of Notre Dame Press, 2005), pp. 111–21, where he describes this tendency as the 'encyclopedic assumption'.

65 As Alan Torrance remarks, 'the most challenging questions that haunt interdisciplinary analysis concern the "scope" of the respective academic disciplines present at the table. Might it be the case that one discipline is in a position to "trump" another or displace the explanations offered by another?' Alan Torrance, 'Retrieving the Person: Theism, Empirical Science, and the Question of Scope', in Malcolm Jeeves (ed.), *The Emergence of Personhood: A Quantum Leap?* (Grand Rapids, MI: Eerdmans, 2015), p. 203.

66 Herman Bavinck, *Reformed Dogmatics*, John Bolt (ed.), John Vriend (trans.), vol. 1 (Grand Rapids, MI: Baker Academic, 2003), p. 444, my emphasis.

67 A burgeoning literature supports these worries – e.g. see Allan Horwitz and Jerome Wakefield, *The Loss of Sadness: How Psychiatry Transformed Normal Sorrow into Depressive Disorder* (New York: Oxford University Press, 2007); Christopher Lane, *Shyness: How Normal Behavior Became a Sickness* (New Haven, CT: Yale University Press, 2007); Charles Barber, *Comfortably Numb: How Psychiatry is Medicating a Nation* (New York: Pantheon Books, 2008); Robert Whittaker, *Anatomy of an Epidemic: Magic Bullets, Psychiatric Drugs, and the Astonishing Rise of Mental Illness in America* (New York: Broadway Books, 2010); David Herzberg, *Happy Pills in America: From Miltown to Prozac* (Baltimore, MD: Johns Hopkins University Press, 2009); Ronald Bayer, *Homosexuality and American Psychiatry: The Politics of Diagnosis* (Princeton, NJ: Princeton University Press, 1987).

68 For a range of perspectives, see Hans Madueme and Michael Reeves (eds), *Adam, the Fall, and Original Sin: Theological, Biblical, and Scientific Perspectives* (Grand Rapids, MI: Baker Academic, 2014).

69 For a defence of original guilt and corruption, without Augustinian realism, see Hans Madueme, forthcoming, 'An Augustinian-Reformed Perspective', in Chad Meister and James Stump (eds), *Five Views on the Fall and Original Sin* (Downers Grove, IL: InterVarsity).

70 Jesse Couenhoven, *Stricken by Sin, Cured by Christ: Agency, Necessity, and Culpability in Augustinian Theology* (New York: Oxford University Press, 2013), p. 127.

71 Jesse Couenhoven, 'What Sin Is: A Differential Analysis', *Modern Theology* 25, 4 (2009), p. 577.

72 Couenhoven, *Stricken by Sin*, p. 129.

73 Although the *distress* often reported by those who suffer from paraphilia-related disorders can be striking and cause shame, alienating them from others, I am not convinced that this factor removes their struggle from the arena of sin. However, it does invite us to extend much patience, compassion and pastoral sensitivity.

74 Eric Johnson labels such dual conditions of sin *and* biopsychosocial damage as 'faults' – e.g. see Johnson, *God and Soul Care*, pp. 283–7. For a secular account of how problems like pathological gambling, alcoholism, sociopathy, unjustified violence and visceral bigotry should be construed as vice *and* sickness, see Mike Martin, *From Morality to Mental Health: Virtue and Vice in a Therapeutic Culture* (New York: Oxford University Press, 2006). Martin advocates for the integration of mental health and morality.

75 Cf. Martin Kafka, 'The Monoamine Hypothesis for the Pathophysiology of Paraphilic Disorders: An Update', *Annals of the New York Academy of Sciences*

989 (2003), pp. 86–94. While one can question Kafka's metaphysical assumptions about neurotransmitter causation, his conclusion is still noteworthy: 'it is certainly premature to conclude that monoaminergic neuro-regulatory perturbations are definitively involved in the pathophysiology of paraphilic sexual aggression . . . a specific role for these neuro-modulators in the paraphilic conditions remains neither proven nor rejected' (Kafka, 'Monoamine Hypothesis', p. 91). For a similarly inconclusive theory, see Jennifer Wong and Jason Gravel, 'Do Sex Offenders Have Higher Levels of Testosterone? Results from a Meta-Analysis', *Sexual Abuse* 30, 2 (2018), pp. 147–68.

76 I am very grateful to Robert Erle Barham, Kevin Eames, Mike Emlet, Stephen Greggo, Eric Johnson, David Murray, Keith Plummer and John Wingard for helpful comments on an earlier draft.

19

Saving Panpsychism: A Panpsychist Ontology and Christian Soteriology

JOANNA LEIDENHAG

The question of human ontology, and in particular the mind–body debate, has direct implications for Christian articulations of human salvation. As Murray A. Rae writes, God 'offers no salvation other than that which is worked out in and through the conditions God has established for creaturely existence'.[1] An important question for Christian theology and philosophy then becomes, What are these conditions? Christian philosophers have often been among the most ardent defenders of the reality of consciousness and the irreducibility of the mind or the soul for the very reason that these aspects of ontology have direct repercussions for soteriology. As such, this chapter explores some of the implications that the view of panpsychism may have for articulations of Christian salvation. Panpsychism has been neglected by theologians historically, yet given the attention it has received among philosophers it is timely for a theological assessment of it.

Panpsychism refers to groups of theories within the philosophy of mind which all hold that mental phenomena or phenomenal properties are fundamental to reality. This view, although counter-intuitive to contemporary Western ways of thinking, has a rich historical pedigree. Panpsychism was the philosophy of mind favoured by pre-Socratic philosophers such as Thales of Miletus, by Indian (Vedanta/Shankra) philosophy, by Renaissance polymaths such as Giordano Bruno and Tommaso Campenella, and by influential figures in Western modern philosophy such as William James and Alfred North Whitehead.[2] Though not with the same degree of frequency, theologians from across the Christian tradition – such as Wilhelm Gottfried von Leibniz (Protestant), Vladimir Lossky (Eastern Orthodox) and Pierre Teilhard de Chardin (Roman Catholic) – have adopted panpsychism. Among contemporary analytic philosophers, notable figures such as Thomas Nagel, David Chalmers, Galen Strawson and many others have come to defend the idea that consciousness is part of the basic fabric of the universe. The historical prevalence and increasing contemporary popularity of panpsychism among philosophers point to the fact that this ontology is worth serious consideration from Christian theologians.

It is not my intent to convince Christian theologians or philosophers to adopt panpsychism. Rather, my intent is to explore how the doctrine of salvation might be formulated if one were a panpsychist and, in so doing, test the fecundity of panpsychism for Christian theology with regard to this most central cluster of doctrines. As such, there is no argument here for the truth of panpsychism, merely an exploration of the consequences for Christian views of salvation *if* panpsychism were true. This seems a worthwhile hypothetical to consider for two reasons. First, imagining different ontological backdrops for theology can help uncover hidden assumptions within Christian theology and can bring to the foreground elements of soteriology which have been historically under-emphasized. Second, if panpsychism continues to grow in popularity among philosophers then this preliminary exploration of a panpsychist view of salvation could aid further interdisciplinary dialogue.

First, I give panpsychism a clear and sympathetic exposition in order to show that it is a position that a Christian theologian should seriously consider and could respectably adopt. Panpsychists are largely concerned with how to explain and situate the mental properties that allow for real experience, feeling or the comprehension of phenomena within the universe. Second, I explore the role of these properties or capacities for soteriology. It is argued that subjectivity is central to Christian views of salvation, and this implies that panpsychism presents an ontology that is at least compatible with Christian views of salvation. Third, I move beyond questions of compatibility to explore what constructive advantages panpsychism might have for articulations of systematic portraits of Christian salvation. The main advantage, to my mind, is that panpsychism equips Christian theologians to emphasize the cosmic scope of salvation that is communicated or perfected by the Holy Spirit.

Introducing Contemporary Panpsychism

'Contemporary panpsychism' refers to a range of positions held by philosophers of mind, cohering especially within the last 15 years. They all share the core assertion that mentality is fundamental. This differentiates panpsychism from various types of physicalism and emergentism. To further demarcate panpsychism from substance dualism, it is important (but often overlooked) to state that panpsychism does not posit individual human minds as fundamental. Instead, for most panpsychists whatever is taken as fundamental for the physical is also taken as fundamental for mentality.

Fundamentality can be parsed out in a number of ways, but in this context it is largely intended to mean that mental phenomena can neither be explained in terms of, nor reduced into, anything non-mental. Timothy Sprigge described panpsychism as the position that 'physical nature is composed of individuals, each of which is to some degree sentient ... [They may be said to have] sentience, experience, or in a broad sense, consciousness.'[3] Karl Popper and John Eccles prefer more theological language when they define (and criticize) panpsychism as the view that 'everything has a soul ... or a rudiment of a soul'.[4] We can take as the broad working definition that panpsychism is the view that *consciousness is a fundamental property of enough fundamental objects to account for human minds*. This definition leaves open the differences within panpsychism as to whether consciousness is an external/relational property (like other physical properties such as mass, spin and charge) or an intrinsic property which could account for the *quiddity* of things. This working definition also leaves open which objects are considered to be fundamental (such as protons, quarks, electrons, or the universe as a single whole), and how many fundamental objects need to have the property of consciousness in order to account for human minds, which is the panpsychists' ultimate explanatory goal.

The question immediately arises over how consciousness is being defined in this context. Most panpsychists seem content to adopt Thomas Nagel's definition, whereby an entity is conscious if 'there is something that it is like to *be* that organism – something that it is like *for* the organism'.[5] In this context, the basic ability to experience the world is the definition of consciousness. The complexity and quality of experience largely depends on the entity or organism in consideration; the more complex and unified the entity, the more complex the quality of experiencing and given an evolutionary developmental framework, higher-level cognitive capacities can subsequently develop. Therefore, a panpsychist might say that electrons are minimal subjects, but cannot think reflectively or act intentionally.[6] Rocks do not have a unified consciousness and can only be considered conscious as an aggregate of separate minimal subjects. However, animals (and one could argue, plants) do seem to have a unified consciousness with varying degrees of additional mental capacities.[7] It is only basic subjectivity or the ability to experience the world that is posited as fundamental. This definition of consciousness can be construed as a necessary but not a sufficient condition for the possible development of rationality, intentionality, complex awareness, self-consciousness, which is enjoyed by more mentally complex and integrated organisms.

The recent history of panpsychism is a story of how three widely respected, if provocative, philosophers made a counter-intuitive and theoretical underdog into a respectable and now increasingly popular position within philosophy of mind. These three philosophers are Thomas Nagel,

David Chalmers and Galen Strawson. Throughout most of the nineteenth and twentieth century panpsychism was a small component within larger metaphysical schemes, such as (Absolute) idealism (in the work of Gustav Fechner, Rudolf Lotze and more recently Timothy Sprigge) and Process philosophy (where it's often called *panexperientialism*). It wasn't until Thomas Nagel published an essay simply entitled 'Panpsychism' in 1979 that this position was concerned as an independent theory within philosophy of mind.[8] In this 're-igniting' essay, Nagel defined panpsychism as 'the view that the basic physical constituents of the universe have mental properties'.[9] This still popular definition captures the fact that many panpsychists wish to talk of mental properties, rather than pure mental entities, and that most seek to distance panpsychism from its previous association with idealism and process metaphysics. This disassociation of contemporary panpsychism from larger metaphysical and theological ideologies should embolden contemporary theologians to see panpsychism as a fairly theologically neutral and versatile ontology. A Christian theologian can adopt or reject contemporary panpsychism without inadvertently committing herself to these former philosophical and theological frameworks.

Nagel's 1979 essay defended two premises: (a) the realistic and irreducible status of (human) consciousness, and (b) the inadequacy of emergence theory to account for the relationship between mind and matter. The argument commonly runs that if mental properties are real (not illusionary as per materialism, epiphenomenalism, functionalism, etc.) and cannot be reduced to or arise in any way from the organizational complexity of material parts (as per strong emergence theory), then the only remaining option (aside from employing divine action) is to posit consciousness as fundamental (panpsychism or substance dualism). It is further argued that panpsychism is to be preferred over substance dualism. As a dual-aspect monism (often of the Russellian variety), the place of consciousness in the world within panpsychism is the same as the place of materiality, giving hope for scientific understanding of consciousness and avoiding the interaction problem. Nagel's logic here might be regarded as the mixture of two popular arguments for panpsychism: (a) the *argument from origination*, which states that, since the effect cannot be greater or wholly other than the cause, the mind must either pre-exist or be a brute nature of the universe from the beginning; and (b) *the last man standing argument*, that no other explanation for consciousness seems possible. Despite giving clear expression to these arguments, Nagel concluded:

> It [panpsychism] appears to follow from a few simple premises, each of which is more plausible than its denial, though not perhaps more plausible than the denial of panpsychism.[10]

Nagel memorably summarized that panpsychism 'has the faintly sickening odour of something put together in the metaphysical laboratory'.[11] And yet, if one accepts Nagel's two premises, and doesn't wish to invoke supernatural agency as an explanation for each individual consciousness, then it is difficult not to find this presentation of panpsychism compelling in some way.

It is also worth noting that in his more recent controversial book *Mind and Cosmos*, Nagel reiterates his support for panpsychism.[12] Nagel's affirmation of panpsychism is on the basis of (c) *the argument from continuity*. This argument for panpsychism is clearly summarized by Nagel as follows:

> But since conscious organisms are not composed of a special kind of stuff, but can be constructed, apparently, from any of the matter in the universe, suitably arranged, it follows that this *monism* will be universal. Everything, living or not, is *constituted from elements* having a nature that is both physical and non-physical – that is, capable of combining into mental wholes. So this reductive account can also be described as a form of panpsychism: all the elements of the physical world are also mental.[13]

This argument for panpsychism based on ontological continuity within the universe has been made not only by contemporary panpsychists, but is found in the biological work of Ernst Haeckel, William Kingdon Clifford, Sir Charles Scott Sherrington and Sir Julian Huxley.[14] The monist argument is one of the oldest arguments for panpsychism, along with the (d) *argument from indwelling powers*, which suggests that motion and dynamism, which undergirds causation, is best explained by mentality. Given that motion and causation are fundamental, grounding motion in mentality results in an argument for panpsychism.[15] It is worth noting here that both arguments (c) and (d) give epistemic priority to the human experience and apply interiorly known properties analogically to the wider creation. These are both part of a wider (e) *argument from analogy*, the idea that whatever can be said about humanity can be applied analogically throughout creation. Therefore, panpsychism denies the conception of humanity as radically and ontologically unique, although human mentality is seen to have unique properties or higher-level capacities.[16]

Following Nagel's 1979 essay, panpsychism remained an intriguing but unattractive position for most philosophers of mind. In 1994 David Chalmers altered the playing field and added considerable support to the panpsychist position. With his exposition of the 'hard' problem of consciousness and his zombie-thought experiments, Chalmers provided a vivid defence of the first of Nagel's two premises, the realism and irreducibility of the mental. David Chalmers' 1996 monograph supporting panpsychism expresses the position as 'a variety of dualism'. He argues that:

> To bring consciousness within the scope of a fundamental theory, we need to introduce *new* fundamental properties and laws.... There is nothing especially transcendental about consciousness; it is just another natural phenomenon ... to embrace dualism is not necessarily to embrace mystery.[17]

Chalmers' commitment to naturalism keeps any notion of spirituality, transcendence or mystery at arm's length. In so doing, however, he provides an important example of how to buffer against pantheism. By arguing for fundamental consciousness as 'just another natural phenomenon', Chalmers shows how panpsychism can posit creaturely or created minds throughout the universe as fundamental and possibly ubiquitous, without implying that these minds are identical to God or in any way constitute God.

We now turn to the third major figure in the recent history of panpsychism. Whereas Nagel's essay had returned panpsychism to the philosophical map, and David Chalmers had made panpsychism a serious option, it was Galen Strawson who threw down the gauntlet and made panpsychism impossible to ignore for contemporary philosophers of mind. In 2006, Strawson published an article entitled, 'Realistic Monism: Why Physicalism Entails Panpsychism'.[18] Strawson argued that the only metaphysically conceivable form of physicalism (the reigning ontology of the last century) is in fact panpsychism. Strawson took panpsychism on the offensive and argued in such a way that his physicalist and emergentist colleagues found themselves having to justify how their positions managed to avoid or deny panpsychism. This publication has since been referred to as 'something of a watershed event in recent analytic philosophy of mind',[19] which brought 'panpsychism to the attention, and critical scrutiny, of mainstream philosophers of mind, thereby making a new generation aware of its appeal'.[20]

The Combination Problem

Although panpsychism seems to be growing in popularity, it possesses something of an Achilles heel: the so-called *combination problem*. This refers to a group of problems regarding how the fundamental micro-phenomena (feelings) or micro-subjects combine in such a way as to constitute a macro-phenomena or macro-subject, such as human beings experience.[21] Without such an account panpsychism loses much of its explanatory appeal. The 'combination problem' was a phrase coined by William Seager, but the problem was famously articulated by William James a century earlier:

> Take a hundred [feelings], shuffle them and pack them as close together as you can (whatever that may mean) till each remains the same feeling it

always was, shut in its own skin, windowless, ignorant of what the other feelings are and mean.[22]

The upshot of this monadic view of fundamental consciousness is that 'private minds do not agglomerate into a higher compound mind'.[23] The idea that minds are just not the sort of things that can combine boils down to an intuition that many philosophers find highly compelling. The panpsychist needs to tell a story of combination to alleviate this intuitive problem.

In addition, the story of combination must account for mid-level subjects (animal minds), without entailing that larger entities – such as cities, planets, solar systems, and perhaps even the universe as a whole – are also individual consciousnesses. This is *the boundary problem*.[24] This is particularly relevant for Christian theologians, since panpsychism can too easily become a form of pantheism, where a universal and perhaps divine mind is built from smaller minds, if the boundary problem cannot be suitably answered.

There are various proposals to solve the combination and boundary problems. Models such as Leibniz's view of a *dominant monad* and Philip Goff's concept of *phenomenal bonding* represent *constitutive* panpsychism.[25] This means that there is a constitutive relationship between the micro-subjects and the resulting macro-subjects, so that truths at the micro-level determine truths at the macro-level in such a way as to maintain the notion of causal closure. The alternative is *non-constitutive* panpsychism such as Godehard Brüntrup's *emergent panpsychism* or William Seager's notion of *fusion*, which posit that the macro-subject is more than the sum of the combined/infused micro-subjects.[26] Although these models seem promising solutions, no one model has been widely adopted by panpsychists. In lieu of a consensus regarding a solution to the combination problem, panpsychists are prone to defend the version of panpsychism that they deem is best suited to minimizing the force of the combination problem. There are two main routes taken by contemporary panpsychists to adapt panpsychism in response to the combination problem.

The first route taken by panpsychists maintains *atomistic panpsychism*, whereby micro-entities combine to account for human consciousness. However, this model reduces the level or type of mentality at the micro-level. For example, David Chalmers and Sam Coleman suggest that *panprotopsychism* may be one way around the combination problem.[27] This position means that, 'there is some *other* class of novel fundamental properties from which phenomenal properties are derived . . . *protophenomenal* properties, [which] are not themselves phenomenal but together they can yield the phenomenal'.[28] Panprotopsychism provides the additional mystery as to the nature of experiences that do not have experiences (subjects to experience them). Given the mysterious nature of this third class of properties (not phenomenal and not purely material), panprotopsychism is not in a better position to give a positive account of combination. If the first-perspective perspective is what is irreducible to the material, then it could also be irreducible to the non-phenomenal. This is why Strawson and Nagel both maintain subject-panpsychism whereby even electrons have 'a standpoint on the world'.[29] Although very difficult to imagine, an attempt is made below to try and make sense of the claim for such extremely minimal subjects. Subject-panpsychism is referred to as simply 'panpsychism' in subsequent sections unless otherwise stated.

The second route for the panpsychist to answer the combination problem is to abandon atomistic panpsychism altogether so that the combination of micro-consciousnesses no longer has to be accounted for. The alternative is *holistic* panpsychism, sometimes referred to as *priority cosmopsychism*; the panpsychist version of priority monism.[30] On this view, 'exactly one basic consciousness, the cosmic consciousness exists'.[31] Accordingly, the universe as a single entity is fundamental (rather than the smallest building blocks of the universe), and animal mid-level minds are grounded not by combination, but by being subsumed within the whole single cosmic-consciousness.[32]

Contemporary cosmopsychists, such as Yujin Nagasawa, Khai Weger, Itay Shani, Freya Mathews and Philip Goff each argue that the nature or type of consciousness attributed to the cosmos is probably a very different and simpler subjectivity than that which neurologically complex and evolved humans enjoy.[33] It is clear that for most cosmopsychists, this absolute consciousness is not akin to the personal God of monotheistic faiths.[34] However, it is also clear that this position can easily be used to posit pantheism or panentheism, where the cosmic consciousness is referred to as 'God'.[35] If priority cosmopsychism successfully avoids the combination problem, it has certainly not yet accounted for the boundary problem, or how mid-level minds are not lost in 'an engulfing oceanic consciousness'.[36] Just as atomistic versions of panpsychism must account for combination in order to explain human minds, holistic panpsychism must account for the individuation of subjects. Without such an account, holistic panpsychism holds no advantage over atomistic panpsychism and has the added disadvantage of being further estranged from the natural/physical sciences.[37]

If the panpsychist cannot account for either the constitutive combination or cosmic individuation of human consciousness, then it might seem that the panpsychist is in the same mystery-laden position as the emergentist,[38] only worse off due to the greater counter-intuitive character of panpsychism. Panpsychists, however, argue that even though the combination/boundary problem is yet to receive a satisfactory solution, their position is still a better option than strong emergence theory. This is because the concept of emergence and the concept of combination are not equally difficult problems. It is argued that whereas strong emergence theory cannot (or in some cases, does not) hope for a reductive explanation from macro-consciousness to micro- or macro-physical complexity, panpsychism can still at least search for an explanation of macro-consciousness from micro-consciousness. The choice between panpsychism and strong emergence currently comes down to what type of mystery you are willing to accept and what kinds of explanation for mind you hope to find.

As a view of finite minds and the ontology of nature, there is no a priori reason to suppose that panpsychism rules out Christian theism. In fact, many of the arguments for panpsychism are also arguments in favour of theism. For example, (a) *the argument from origination* can be seen to 'buttress the cosmological argument, making it hard to avoid some kind of necessary entity'.[39] J. P. Moreland argues that seven of Skribina's 11 arguments for panpsychism[40] lend support to classical theism and overlap with his own defence of consciousness originating directly from God through divine 'injection' in each new living organism.[41] If one does not presuppose metaphysical naturalism, then there does not seem to be any compelling philosophical reason why divine action could not provide a sufficient account of consciousness. God could simply inject souls or minds into certain organisms alongside the necessary laws and means of mental–physical interaction.[42] The purpose of this chapter, however, is to explore the possible theological advantages of combining panpsychism and Christian theism. The story here would be that God creates human and animal minds by creating consciousness in the beginning, either within the fundamental constituents of the universe or by gifting the universe as a single whole consciousness, and also creating some principle and means of combination or individuation. As Christian philosopher Charles Taliaferro suggests: 'a theistic-dualistic-panpsychist metaphysics is more cogent than its popular counterparts', and thereby an 'eminently challenging' position which Christian philosophers should seriously consider.[43]

Salvation and Minimal Subjectivity

We have seen that panpsychists posit minimally experiential subjects or properties as fundamental to the universe. What difference can this ontology make for our understanding of salvation? In order to answer this question, a brief account of the role of subjectivity within soteriology is required. If creaturely ontology is irrelevant to salvation, or if the ability for experience plays no role within soteriology, then panpsychism will make little to no difference to Christian articulations of salvation. Contrary to this view, however, the argument that follows is that minimal subjectivity is a necessary (but not sufficient) condition for a creature to receive salvation.[44]

There are numerous ways to understand what is entailed by 'salvation' within Christianity. An almost trivial version claims that salvation constitutes a change in the recipient from 'unsaved' to 'saved'. What this basic definition already implies is that salvation is clearly distinguished from annihilation and re-creation, but it involves the saved creatures' endurance through time and change.[45] I argue that such a change requires the capacity for subjective experience. Below I examine five elements of salvation. While each of these five elements are not shared by all Christian traditions, each has strong historical precedence and together they encapsulate something of the breadth of Christian soteriology. I will argue that each element entails that the saved or transformed recipient must be a *subject*. In no particular order, the five elements of salvation are: (1) revelation or knowledge of God; (2) moral transformation; (3) relational transformation, justification and atonement; (4) the liberation from sin, evil, suffering and death; and finally (5) deification.

Revelation, or Knowledge of God

Revelation, or knowledge of God, is one facet of salvation that most clearly requires a mental subject as its recipient. One aspect of the saving work of Jesus Christ's incarnation and the sending of the 'Spirit of Truth' is to reveal God to humanity; to give creatures *knowledge* of that which we could never obtain otherwise (see John 14.17; 15.26; 16.13; 1 John 4.6; cf. 1 Cor. 12.3; Eph. 1.13). There is an eschatological expectation that 'the earth will be full of the knowledge of the Lord as the waters cover the sea' (Isa. 11.9). Although this phrase has often been interpreted as poetic hyperbole, it could be read to support the view that some basic knowledge of God will be ubiquitous throughout creation. This realist interpretation then also allows for a robust notion of the worship and testimony of creation (Ps. 19.1-4; Job 12.7-9).

Although a computer or a non-conscious entity can carry information, that entity cannot be said to have knowledge. Plato famously defined knowledge as 'justified true belief'. Although much ink has been spilled debating this definition, the idea that knowledge as belief must be held by a subject and cannot float free of a knower, is probably the least controversial aspect of this definition. Knowledge can only be a property of knowing subjects; entities with at least minimal subjectivity. The higher-level ability to know what one knows requires self-consciousness, and the ability to discern, judge, analyse and evaluate one's beliefs requires rationality. In material creatures, these higher-level cognitive capacities seem intrinsically linked with the function of a neurological network (a brain). However, the panpsychist might claim that if other non-neurologically endowed entities have a receptive experience and unique perspective of the world, then these entities can be said to have very basic beliefs. If one were to adopt an externalist epistemology, then the redeemed minimal subjects (who as redeemed would presumably be functioning in the correct manner) may even be justified in their beliefs, such as to have knowledge. That is, salvation as a transformation of knowledge might be considered a viable concept when the knowledge in question is a basic awareness and experience of the world or of God from an individual viewpoint, even without the ability to reflect upon these experiences.

Moral Transformation

The aspect of salvation pertaining to morality refers to the infusion, elevation, healing or cultivation of virtues and affections and is sometimes referred to as 'habitual grace' and enables the recipient to 'work deeds meritorious of eternal life, which exceed the capability of nature'.[46] It seems a straightforward intuition that moral responsibility requires moral agency, which further requires subjectivity. To be a moral agent there must be a self that is able to act intentionally and, to at least some extent, act freely. Therefore, objects with no subjective self, intentionality or free will (such as rocks) cannot undergo moral transformation. Is it coherent, then, to speak of moral transformations within minds of only minimal subjectivity, which although conscious, do not have the attributes of will or affections?

It seems that moral transformation is a change that occurs only at the higher level of cognitive and affective mental attributes. Although higher-level attributes must be undergirded by a self or minimal subjectivity that will also be transformed, a moral transformation is neither necessary nor meaningful without these higher-level cognitive and affective attributes. Perhaps the only way in which moral transformation might be deemed meaningful for these minimal subjects is if it is subsumed within the previous category of knowledge or revelation. If a correct experience of God for a minimal subject is an experience with both truth value and moral value, then minimal subjects may stand in need of moral transformation in this very limited sense.

Relational Transformation, Justification and Atonement

Perhaps the most central facet of salvation, which distinguishes it from other non-religious articulations of moral or epistemological improvement, is that recipients of salvation are placed in a right relationship with God. Restoration of the divine–creature relationship is often seen as the goal of God's forgiveness and is at the root of the concepts of 'justification' and 'atonement'. Not all relationships, such as spatial relationships or some forms of legal relations, require mental properties or subjective capacities. For example, the books on my bookshelf stand in both a spatial relation to me (for which neither party needs consciousness), and in the legal relationship of ownership (for which only one party needs consciousness). Theologians often employ these non-personal relations in a metaphorical manner. For example, a person may be said to be found 'in Christ' or 'indwelt by the Spirit' which are spatial metaphors. Some theologians use legal metaphors, such as 'ransom' to express how the death and resurrection of Christ saves human persons. Although these are non-personal metaphors, they are intended to say something about distinctly personal relationships; the type of reciprocal relationship that is possible only between two persons. The need for a personal relationship has been one prevalent reason why Christian theologians often limit salvation to human persons.

Personhood includes conscious subjectivity as well as other higher cognitive powers. For example, a good personal relationship is often parsed out in the language of love whereby persons desire the good of and union with the other. To receive and give love entails the more basic capacity of experiencing the actions of the other from a particular subjective viewpoint as being *for you* or directed at you, as well as being able to respond in an intentional way. Of course, personal relationships can be asymmetrical, such as when a recipient of love does not reciprocate the affections. A relationship of unreciprocated love would be a more limited, but still a *personal* relationship. This is what a personal relationship with God might mean for minimal subjects. Minimal subjectivity is a passive capacity that enables the entity to receive the love of another, in this case God. The relational transformation for minimal subjects may entail that this love of God is received in the correct manner, as God intends the creature to receive it.

The Liberation from Sin, Evil, Suffering and Death

What creatures move *away from* in the transformation of being saved is often referred to as sin, suffering or death. Of these three, suffering is the clearest experiential category. Pain, as a particular type of suffering, is often a paramount example of *qualia* or a phenomenal experience. There can be no question that salvation from suffering requires subject recipients. It is not as clear that sin and death pertain only to conscious subjects. Sin is often articulated through the language of privation, as a lack of something.[47] There are good reasons to suppose that privation *as a normative category* is best understood as experiential. For instance, hunger is the experience of a lack of food in a different way from how half a plate of food might be described as a lack of food. Hunger, by virtue of being a negative experience, has a normative quality about it, in the way that half a glass of water (without additional experiential categories added into the context) does not. Sin, although notoriously difficult to define, seems more like the kind of lack that is normative and so requires a subject of experience. Therefore, it is not possible for an object without the capacity for subjective experiences to be considered sinful, even if it is considered broken or deficient in some way. However, if minimal subjects are fallen and are experiencing their environment in a way that is not intended by God, then concepts of privation seem viable for minimal subjects; what it is like to be a minimal subject would change if this was a universe without sin or privation.

Although no one can know whether death is experienced by the disembodied soul, it seems justified to suggest that the liberation from death or the resurrection of the person *is* an experience. This is largely because of the link between life and consciousness; and the intuition for the human subject that there is something it is like to be alive which is plausibly shared by all living organisms. However, can the same be said for non-living subjects as in the case of minimal subjects as posited in panpsychism? It seems reasonable to suppose that if there is something-it-is-like-to-be a non-living conscious entity, then the annihilation or re-creation of that entity constitutes a subjective change in a way that is analogous to the death and resurrection of a living subject.

Deification

Theosis or deification pertains to a 'change in terms of ontology' that is 'fundamental, radical, a rebuilding of what it is to be human from the roots up'[48] so that human beings become 'partakers of the divine nature' (2 Peter 1.4).[49] This transformation expresses not only the 'ultimate goal of human existence'[50] but is 'a way of summing up the purpose of creation' as a whole.[51] Without giving a more thorough description of deification, the concept of *theosis* tends to have a subject of experience in mind when describing how humanity participates in the divine energies as a microcosm of the deification of the whole of creation whereby God will become 'all in all' (1 Cor. 15.28).[52] The energies of God, as the outgoing actions and attributes of God, seem to be ways in which the creature *experiences* the divine. This suggests that some minimal subjectivity is necessary in order to even passively participate in the divine energies. Understood as such, *theosis* might refer to the holistic change that occurs when a creaturely subject experiences God at the root of their being or undergoes a constitutive union with God.

The above goes some way to providing an argument for two large claims:

1. A necessary creaturely condition for the possibility of salvation is to be created with subjectivity.
2. That it is meaningful to speak of the salvation of minimal subjects.

For a creature to receive (or require) salvation it must have the ability to endure the transformation from 'unsaved' to 'saved' and experience reality from a particular viewpoint. The need for subjectivity in the context of soteriology should not be a very controversial statement. The idea that minimal subjectivity is sufficient for some limited notion of salvation is a more controversial proposal. As such, my argument stands in continuity with, but extends beyond, much of the historic Christian tradition, according to which salvation entails the possession of a *human* soul due to specific higher-level mental properties, chief among which is rationality.[53] This brings us to the third section of this chapter. To this point I have outlined a contemporary view of panpsychism and I have argued that a recipient of salvation must at least be a minimal subject. In what follows, I offer up a constructive proposal for what salvation might look like if a Christian theologian were to adopt a panpsychist ontology.

A Panpsychist View of Salvation

The main consequence of what has been said so far is that Christian panpsychism can hope and speak of the salvation of the entire cosmos. Christian theology depicts a post-mortem future that is not solely a disembodied habitation of a heavenly realm, but includes a new physical universe (and specifically a new earth). Revelation 5 is a good example of the cosmic scope of biblical eschatology which can be interpreted as consistent with panpsychism.[54] In Revelation 5.13 there is a clear vision of the end with the cosmic scope of redemption as happening 'in heaven, on earth, under the earth'. The voices of created subjects that praise God come from heaven, earth and the sea and are described as 'all creatures' or 'all creation' and they are described as worshiping God with 'all that is in them'. Such an understanding of creation as a subject of both worship and frustration is not only found in the apocalyptic symbolism of Revelation.[55] Romans 8.18–23 also describes the 'eager longing' and 'groaning' of the creation and 'the hope that the creation itself will be set free from its bondage to decay and will obtain the freedom of the glory of the children of God'.[56] The same freedom and glory that pertains to human salvation (as children of God) is here spoken of as hoped for by all creation (see also Col. 1.16 and Eph. 1.22).

The (c) *argument from continuity* for panpsychism is based on the idea that evolutionary continuity between species and the presupposition of ontological monism implies that what is said of humanity must also be said for the rest of the universe in some corresponding sense. Panpsychist soteriology facilitates a view of salvation where humans are not treated as radical differently from the rest of creation. Instead, the same continuity and discontinuity would apply to the *whole* of creation. Just as the human subject who exists now must in some way be the same human who receives a perfecting transformation and resurrection on the last day, so the same fundamental subjects of the cosmos might be found perfected in the new creation. Although there remains a level of discontinuity in the noetic, moral, relational and ontological transformation from 'unsaved' to 'saved', panpsychism offers a picture of a capacity that spells out how this creation is fundamentally transformed, and not replaced.[57]

As well as extending the scope of salvation to the whole cosmos, it is worth considering how a Christian panpsychism may constrain the theological articulation of human salvation and resurrection. This also addresses the question of whether Christian panpsychism entails extending salvation to the whole of cosmos, or merely allows for it. Panpsychists who hold that micro-subjects constitute the macro-subject (constitutive panpsychism) would need to say that if even one micro-subject is changed or replaced, then the macro-subject changes, albeit a very small change. This view implies that at the final resurrection, for the same human to be resurrected that has died, the same micro-subjects, that is the same body, needs to be resurrected (leaving aside for the moment the problem of personal endurance through the intermediate state). For constitutive panpsychism, micro-subjects cannot be annihilated and replaced without annihilating and replacing the human subject that depends on them. A constitutive Christian panpsychist could still limit the salvation of micro-subjects to those who constitute a human macro-subject at the point of death. Micro-subjects, on this model, would participate in salvation by virtue of their relationship to the macro-subject.[58] However, limiting salvation to human persons and their constituent micro-subjects seems to go out of its way to deny the cosmic scope of soteriology.

A panpsychist who holds that there is an emergent (non-constitutive) relation between the human macro-subject and the micro-subjects of the human body could hold that the human macro-subject is multiply realizable. On this view, different micro-subjects (a different body) could realize an identical human macro-subject. Therefore, although God has the option of transforming micro-subjects, God could still annihilate all non-human subjects and create new ones at the general resurrection without annihilating and re-creating humanity as well. A Christian panpsychism, then, does not *entail* the extension of soteriology to the entire cosmos, but it provides a clear ontological basis for this extension, were it deemed theologically desirable.

The concept of subjectivity implies (but, as above, does not entail) that every aspect of the cosmos is irreplaceable.[59] Although electrons may be identical under the measurements of the natural sciences, if each one is a minimal subject, with a distinct point of view on the world, they are not identical to God. This endurance of subjects is neither by virtue of the impact that subjects have on God,[60] nor solely because of their value to or impact on human beings,[61] but due to their own intrinsic value. A panpsychist ontology gives Christian theology both the tools and added incentive to articulate a model of salvation which includes the whole of this creation as being transformed, and not annihilated and then replaced as many have understood the promise of a *new* creation.[62]

This model does require theologians to use the concept of salvation in a more flexible or differentiated sense than on a view of exclusively human salvation. The substantial difference between types of subjects that panpsychism posits means that salvation cannot be identical in every case. That is, while all creation may be said to be saved, transformed, perfected, and to experience the fullness of God according to its created capacity, this does not mean (for example) that all saved subjects have the propositional knowledge that 'Jesus is Lord', since not all subjects on this view have the capacity of propositional knowledge. Jay McDaniel, in his discussion of theodicy and animal suffering, writes that Christianity's

> hope is not that all creatures share in the same kind of fulfilment beyond death. Rather it is that all creatures share in the kind of fulfilment appropriate to their own interests and needs. What a pelican chick might know as a fulfilment of needs would have its own kind of harmony and intensity, one quite different from what humans might know.[63]

If Christian soteriology can differentiate between the experience of fulfilment for pelican chicks and human beings, I see no reason why minimal subjects, even electrons or other fundamental particles, could not be included under the same extended logic. As argued above, as long as there is at least a minimal subjectivity, then the concept of salvation is viable in some form. Salvation on this panpsychist model is, therefore, both a once-and-for-all change for the entire cosmos *and* comes in degrees according to the mode or type of salvation being discussed, which depends on the subjectivity of recipient creature. This means that salvation is both universal in scope and intimately particular in application.

A different advantage which panpsychism may bring to soteriology is that, in highlighting the importance of subjectivity within soteriology, a Christian panpsychism could give fresh emphasis to the role of the Holy

Spirit in communicating salvation to creatures. That is, because panpsychism posits mentality throughout the universe it can facilitate a unique harmonization between the work of the Spirit as Creator and as Perfecter or Sanctifier. Taken from passages in the Psalms which describe the breath of God throughout creation, and Genesis 1.2 which describes the *ruach elohim* (breath of God) as 'hovering over the face of the waters', the Holy Spirit is also the *Creator Spiritus*. The other chief aspect of the Holy Spirit's work is soteriological and pertains to communicating the justification by Jesus Christ to the believer and sanctifying them.[64] As Christaan Mostert summarizes it, the role of the Spirit is to make 'our justification a reality for *us in our concrete experience*'.[65] Although there is no necessary tension between these two aspects of the Spirit's activity within Christian theology, panpsychism can be seen to more closely harmonize these two distinct works of the Spirit; as immanent creator throughout the cosmos and intimate sanctifier to creaturely subjects.

What I am suggesting is a view of the indwelling of the Holy Spirit as part of a soteriology which is not limited to human beings, because all of creation can experience and encounter the Spirit of God (according to their own limited subjective capacity). Therefore, the indwelling of the Holy Spirit is not exclusive to the temple or to humanity, but both of these function as a microcosm for the hope of Spirit's presence throughout creation.[66] As Frank Macchia writes: 'Pneumatology implies that we need to expand the narrative of justification beyond the Christian's conversion and development, even beyond the explicit details of the Christ event, *to involve creation and its calling*.'[67] The ontology of panpsychism may aid theologians in articulating the cosmic scope of the Spirit's saving presence.

Finally, a word of caution: it is possible yet inadvisable to conflate a vision of salvation and the panpsychist vision of combination or the unification of consciousness.[68] Such an appropriation of panpsychism would be a mistake for Christian thought in two ways. First of all, panpsychist unification does not seem to offer the type of transformation that salvation requires. Panpsychist combination does not, in and of itself, seem to correct faulty aspects of the two subjects which are unified. As such, salvation through unification with other minds may eradicate alienation, but it cannot erase the problems of sin, suffering, death and evil. The only form of unification which incorporates the necessary element of transformation of the creature is unification with God, of *theosis*. This, as we saw above, means that *theosis* is one important element of Christian salvation.

This brings us to the second reason I do not think a Christian panpsychism should use the panpsychist combination as a model for *theosis*. Although the various models of mental combination are still a controversial and incomplete area of debate within panpsychist philosophy, it is safe to say that any resulting panpsychist model of mental combination should remain solely between creaturely minds, and not include the Divine. Not only is it always a problematic idea to articulate the nature of God within a created ontology, but also panpsychists are searching for a very strong notion of combination where the two subjects merge or fuse or are phenomenally bonded into *one single complex subjectivity*. In some sense, the two constituent subjects cease to exist in a distinct manner. Some theologians may be content for creaturely assimilation into the divine life, but not vice versa. My concern is that such total unification between creaturely and divine minds would invite either a pantheistic notion of God, whereby the final end is a single God/Universe Subject, or a view whereby unification with creation is necessary for a finite and contingent God to flourish or be complete. As such, I urge theologians only to consider panpsychism as the ontological structure of creation, and not to seek to employ panpsychism as a totalizing philosophy.

Conclusion

Historically, panpsychism has not been considered an ontology that is amenable, or even compatible, with Christian theology. However, panpsychism is undergoing a revival of serious attention by mainstream philosophers of mind, and as such has become disentangled from previous associations with absolute idealism and process philosophy/theology. As such, contemporary discussions of panpsychism deserve new and serious attention from Christian theologians and philosophers.

This chapter explored what potential advantages and risks panpsychism would entail for soteriology, were it to be adopted by Christian theologians. After outlining contemporary panpsychism, I argued that for a creature to be saved or be a recipient of God's salvation, the only necessary creaturely condition is to be a subject. That is, to endure over time as the recipient of experiences. This is the description of a minimal subject, which (some) panpsychists posit as fundamental throughout creation. More complex subjects, such as human beings and other complex living organisms, have additional mental capacities such as rationality, volition, desires and self-consciousness. Although these additional capacities give greater depth and meaning to recipients of salvation, I argued that minimal subjectivity was sufficient to be saved in some equally minimal sense.

On the base of this understanding of the relationship between salvation and subjectivity, this chapter imagined a constructive articulation of salvation for a Christian panpsychism. Panpsychism strongly emphasizes the cosmic scope of salvation, because each minimal fundamental subject could be meaningfully saved and transformed, rather than be annihilated and re-created in the new creation. The second potential advantage to soteriology was the emphasis which panpsychism, by virtue of highlighting the subjective receiving of soteriology, gives to the work of the Holy Spirit in salvation. It was suggested that panpsychism could bring harmony to the work of the Spirit as Creator and as Perfecter. Although the cosmic scope and the role of the Holy Spirit are aspects of salvation which an increasing number of theologians wish to affirm, few other ontologies allow for such a robust expression of these ideas as panpsychism does. Finally, one risk was outlined in that any employment of a panpsychist theory of combination or unification as a possible model for salvation was refuted. It was concluded that if Christian theologians adopt panpsychism, and there are some good reasons for doing so, then this should be an ontology regarding God's creation, and should not be used as a totalizing philosophy which answers all of theology's concerns or from which theology might build a doctrine of God.

Notes

1 Murray A. Rae, 'Salvation and History', in Ivor J. Davidson and Murray A. Rae (eds), *God of Salvation: Soteriology in Theological Perspective* (Farnham: Ashgate 2011), p. 89.

2 See David Skrbina, *Panpsychism in the West* (Cambridge, MA: MIT Press, 2007).

3 Timothy L. S. Sprigge, 'Panpsychism', 1998, *Routledge Encyclopedia of Philosophy*, www.rep.routledge.com/articles/thematic/panpsychism/v-1.

4 Karl Popper and John Eccles, *The Self and the Brain* (New York: Springer, 1977), p. 15.

5 Thomas Nagel, 'What Is it Like To Be a Bat?', *The Philosophical Review* 83, 4 (October 1974), p. 436; David Chalmers, *Facing Up to the Problem of Consciousness* (Oxford: Oxford University Press, 2011), p. 5; Chalmers, 'Panpsychism and Panprotopsychism', in Godehard Brüntrup and Ludwig Jaskolla (eds), *Panpsychism: Contemporary Perspectives* (Oxford: Oxford University Press, 2017), p. 19; Galen Strawson, 'Mind and Being', in *Panpsychism: Contemporary Perspectives*, p. 80. Timothy L. S. Sprigge independently gave the same definition of consciousness in Sprigge, 'Final Causes', *The Aristotelian Society Supplementary Volume* XLV (1971), p. 166.

6 As will be seen below, panprotopsychists and cosmopsychists do not make this first claim.

7 Debate over plant consciousness and extrasensory perception continues. Much depends on the type of capacities that are considered signs of consciousness. If reaction to external stimuli, communication between organisms within physical proximity is sufficient then one may be justified in considering advocates for some minimal plant consciousness. For a survey of the literature, see A. H. M. Nagel, 'Are Plants Conscious?', *Journal of Consciousness Studies* 4, 3 (March 1997), pp. 215–30. For internationally bestselling advocates, see Peter Tompkins and Christopher Bird, *The Secret Life of Plants: A Fascinating Account of the Physical, Emotional, and Spiritual Relations Between Plants and Man* (London: Harper and Row, 1989); Daniel Chamovitz, *What a Plant Knows: A Field Guide to the Sense* (Scientific American/Farrar, Straus and Giroux, 2013).

8 Thomas Nagel, 'Panpsychism', in *Mortal Questions* (Cambridge: Cambridge University Press, 1979).
9 Sam Coleman 'The Real Combination Problem: Panpsychism, Micro-Subjects, and Emergence', *Erkenn* 79 (2014), 22; Nagel, 'Panpsychism', p. 181.
10 Nagel, 'Panpsychism', p. 181.
11 Quoted in William E. Seager, 'Consciousness, Information, and Panpsychism', *Journal of Consciousness Studies* 2, 3 (1995), pp. 283-4.
12 Thomas Nagel, *Mind and Cosmos: Why the Materialist Neo-Darwinian Conception of Nature is Almost Certainly False* (Oxford: Oxford University Press, 2012).
13 Nagel, *Mind and Cosmos*, p. 57.
14 Skrbina, *Panpsychism in the West*, pp. 131-3, 141-4, 191-2.
15 Skrbina, *Panpsychism in the West*, pp. 26-33. Skrbina's nine main arguments for panpsychism are listed on pp. 250-1.
16 D. S. Clarke, *Panpsychism: Past and Recent Selected Readings* (Albany, NY: State University of New York Press, 2004), pp. 11-17.
17 David J. Chalmers, *The Conscious Mind* (Oxford: Oxford University Press, 1996), pp. 126, 128.
18 Galen Strawson, 'Realistic Monism: Why Physicalism entails Panpsychism', *Journal of Consciousness Studies* 13 (10-11) (2006), pp. 30-1.
19 Leemon B. McHenry and George W. Shields, 'Analytic Critiques of Whitehead's Metaphysics', *Journal of the American Philosophical Association* 2, 3 (2016), p. 492.
20 Coleman, 'The Real Combination Problem', p. 22.
21 David Chalmers outlines seven combination problems. Cf. Chalmers, 'The Combination Problem in Panpsychism', in *Panpsychism: Contemporary Perspectives*, p. 183.
22 William James, *Principles of Psychology* (New York: Dover, [1890] 1950), p. 160. Importantly, James also denied the combination of material particles or forces, so that water 'exists only for the bystander' (pp. 158-9).
23 James, *Principles of Psychology*, p. 160.
24 Gregg Rosenberg, *A Place for Consciousness: Probing the Deep Structure of the Natural World* (Oxford: Oxford University Press, 2004), pp. 77-90.
25 G. Leibniz, *Principles of Nature and of Grace*, part 3 in R. Ariew and D. Garber (eds), *Philosophical Essays* (Cambridge, MA: Hackett, [1714] 1989); Philip Goff, 'The Phenomenal Bonding Solution to the Combination Problem', in *Panpsychism: Contemporary Perspectives*, pp. 283-302.
26 Godehard Brüntrup, 'Emergent Panpsychism', in *Panpsychism: Contemporary Perspectives*, pp. 48-70; William Seager, 'Panpsychism, Aggregation and Combinatorial Infusion', *Mind and Matter* 8, 2, pp. 167-84.
27 Chalmers, 'Panpsychism and Panprotopsychism'; Coleman, 'The Real Combination Problem'.
28 Chalmers, *The Conscious Mind*, pp. 126-7.
29 Nagel, *Mind and Cosmos*, pp. 57-8, n.16.
30 Jonathan Schaffer, 'Monism: The Priority of the Whole', *Philosophical Review* 199, 1 (2010), pp. 31-76; Philip Goff, *Consciousness and Fundamental Reality* (Oxford: Oxford University Press, 2017), pp. 227-8, 236-41.
31 Yujin Nagasawa and Khai Wager, 'Panpsychism and Priority Cosmopsychism', in *Panpsychism: Contemporary Perspectives*, p. 116.
32 Goff, *Consciousness and Fundamental Reality*, p. 237.

33 Nagasawa and Wager, 'Panpsychism and Priority Cosmospsychism', p. 117; Goff, *Consciousness and Fundamental Reality*, pp. 245–6; Freya Mathews, *For Love of Matter: A Contemporary Panpsychism* (New York: State University New York Press, 2003), pp. 62–4.

34 Goff, *Consciousness and Fundamental Reality*, pp. 245–6.

35 Nagasawa and Wager, 'Panpsychism and Priority Cosmopsychism', p. 117. Timothy Sprigge accepts the pantheistic interpretation; T. L. S. Sprigge, 'Pantheism', *Monist* 80, 2 (April 1997). Others propose that panpsychism is the closest ontological companion of panentheism: Skrbina, *Panpsychism in the West*, p. 21; J. P. Moreland, *Consciousness and the Existence of God: A Theistic Argument* (New York: Routledge, 2008), pp. 115–16; U. Meixner 'Panpsychism and Idealism', in *Panpsychism: Contemporary Perspectives*, p. 399.

36 Italy Shani, 'Cosmopsychism: A Holistic Approach to the Metaphysics of Experience', *Philosophical Papers* 44, 3 (2015), p. 390.

37 Weger and Nagasawa admit to the tension between holistic panpsychism and the natural sciences, 'Panpsychism and Priority Cosmopsychism', pp. 126–7. This is in contrast to atomistic panpsychism which seems to be deeply compatible with the methodology and reigning principles (i.e. reductionism, causal closure, natural/physical sciences).

38 Philip Goff previously argued this in 'Why Panpsychism Doesn't Help Explain Consciousness', *Dialectica* 63, 3.

39 Pat Lewtas, 'Panpsychism, Emergentism, and The Metaphysics of Causation', *Pacific Philosophical Quarterly* 97, 2 (2016), p. 14.

40 Moreland, *Consciousness and the Existence of God*, pp. 118–26.

41 For more on this 'creationist' view, see Joshua R. Farris, *The Soul of Theological Anthropology: A Cartesian Exploration* (Abingdon: Routledge, 2017).

42 In this way, (b) *the last-man standing argument* will not be an appealing argument for panpsychism for most theists.

43 Charles Taliaferro, 'Dualism and Panpsychism', in *Panpsychism: Contemporary Perspectives*, pp. 369–70.

44 This chapter only offers comment on the importance of subjectivity on the side of creature and does not enter into the various debates surrounding divine subjectivity.

45 See in the present volume, Ryan Mullins, 'Identity through Time and Personal Salvation'.

46 Aquinas, *Treatise on Grace*, Q. 109, art. 9, 993, in *Basic Writings of St Thomas Aquinas*, ed. and trans. Aton C. Pegis (New York: Random House, 1945).

47 E.g. Augustine, *Confessions*, 7.12.18; Anselm of Canterbury, 'On the Fall of the Devil', trans. Ralph McInerny, in B. Davies and G. R. Evans (eds), *Anselm of Canterbury: The Major Works* (Oxford: Oxford University Press, pp. 193–232); Thomas Aquinas, *Summa theologiae*, trans. Fathers of the English Dominican Province (New York: Benziger Bros, 1948), Part I, Q.49, Art. 1, 3.

48 Andrew Louth, 'The Place of Theosis in Orthodox Theology', in M. J. Christensen and J. A. Wittung (eds), *Partakers of the Divine Nature* (Grand Rapids, MI: Baker Academic, 2007), pp. 39–40.

49 For summaries of *theosis* in Western and Eastern theology, see Carl Mosser, 'The Greatest Possible Blessing: Calvin and Deification', *Scottish Journal of Theology* 55, 1 (2002), pp. 36–57; Jonathan D. Jacobs, 'An Eastern orthodox Conception of Theosis and Human Nature', *Faith and Philosophy* 26, 5 (Special Issue 2009), pp. 615–27.

50 G. I. Mantzaridis, *The Deification of Man* (Crestwood, NY: St Vladimir's Seminary Press, 1984), p. 12.

51 Louth, 'The Place of Theosis in Orthodox Theology', p. 36.

52 See in the present volume, Carl Mosser, 'Two Visions of Being Saved as Deform Perfectibility'.

53 Thomas Aquinas is often the example of the view that a rational soul is required for salvation because rationality directly 'apprehends the universal notion of good and being, is immediately related to the universal principle of being'. This allows the rational soul to survive the unnatural separation from the body in a manner which animal or vegetable souls cannot. Aquinas, *Summa Theologiae*, II-II, 2, 3, co.; cf. III 91.5.

54 Thanks to Kris Huiser for pointing this out. Cf. Kris Huiser, 'Animals and Universal Redemption: All Dogs Go to Heaven', in Hannah Bacon, Wendy Dossett and Stephen Knowles (eds), *Alternative Salvations: Engaging the Sacred and the Secular* (London: Bloomsbury Academic, 2015), pp. 141–50.

55 See Psalm 66; 69; 98; 104; 108.7; Isaiah 43.20.

56 Both ἡ κτίσις ('creation') and τά πάντα ('all things') in the New Testament have been interpreted in a variety of ways. However, most modern commentators understand this phrase to include everything in the created universe which is non-human. For 'creation', see D. Moo, *The Epistle to the Romans* (Grand Rapids, MI: Eerdmans, 1996), p. 514; C. E. B Cranfield, *Romans* (London: T&T Clark, 1975), pp. 411–12; For 'all things', see J. D. G. Dunn, *The Epistles to the Colossians and to Philemon* (Grand Rapids, MI: Eerdmans, 1996), p. 104; P. Grabe, 'Salvation in Colossians and Ephesians', in J. G. van der Watt (ed.), *Salvation in the New Testament: Perspectives on Soteriology* (Leiden: Brill, 2005), pp. 290–3. For 'all things' in the context of a cosmic soteriology, see Colossians 1.15–20; Ephesians 1.10; Ephesians 4.10; Revelation 21.5.

57 A non-panpsychist example of this view of salvation is John Wesley's 1811 sermon 'The General Deliverance'. He states that: 'The whole brute creation will then, undoubtedly, be restored, not only to the vigour, strength and swiftness which they had at their creation, but to a far higher degree of each than they ever enjoyed.' Wesley implies the endurance of the same subjects, the same 'they' which undergo significant transformation, rather than the creation of new creatures of the same species. See John Wesley, 'Sermon 60 – The General Deliverance', http://wesley.nnu.edu/john-wesley/thesermons-of-john-wesley-1872-edition/sermon-60-the-general-deliverance/.

58 This seems to be Aquinas' answer within his hylomorphism for how the human intellectual soul contains the sensitive and nutritive souls. Aquinas, *Summa Theologiae*, III 91.5.

59 This was one of Leibniz's main reasons for adopting panpsychism, since it gave God's creation both maximum value (best of all possible worlds) and God sufficient reason for creating this specific universe (principle of sufficient reason). See G. Leibniz, *On Nature Itself*, p. 820, section 12 and *Principles of Nature and of Grace*, section 3, in R. Ariew and D. Garber (eds), *Philosophical Essays* (Indianapolis, IN: Hackett, 1714/1989).

60 A. N. Whitehead, *Process and Reality: An Essay in Cosmology*, ed. David Ray Griffin and Donald W. Sherburne (New York: Free Press, 1978), pp. 347–51.

61 C. S. Lewis, *The Problem of Pain* (New York: HarperCollins, 1940, 1966), pp. 143–4; John Polkinghorne, *The God of Hope and the End of the World* (New Haven, CT: Yale University Press, 2002), p. 123.

62 This panpsychist view can be seen to be an extension of animal theologians who speak of animal subjects not being replaced by new animals of the same species, but the redemption of the self-same individual animals. Jürgen Moltmann, *The Coming of God: Christian Eschatology*, trans. Margaret Kohl (Minneapolis, MN: Fortress, 2004), p. 132; David L. Clough, *On Animals: Volume One, Systematic Theology* (London: T&T Clark, 2012), pp. 133–53. Christopher Southgate distinguishes this between 'objective immortality' where a creature continues to exist in the memory of God and 'subjective immortality' where the creature's own subjectivity continues to exist. Christopher Southgate, *The Groaning of Creation: God, Evolution and the Problem of Evil* (Louisville, KY; London: Westminster John Knox Press, 2008), pp. 86–7.

63 Jay B. McDaniel, *Of God and Pelicans: A Theology of Reverence for Life* (Louisville, KY: Westminster John Knox Press, 1989), p. 45.

64 See Frank D. Macchia, *Justified in the Spirit: Creation, Redemption, and the Triune God* (Grand Rapids, MI: Eerdmans, 2010).

65 Christaan Mostert, 'Salvation's Setting: Election, Justification and the Church', in Ivor J. Davidson (ed.), *God of Salvation* (Farnham: Ashgate, 2011), p. 131. Italics added.

66 This idea is argued by N. T. Wright extensively. See *Paul and The Faithfulness of God* (London: SPCK, 2013), pp. 475–516; 1074–95.

67 Frank D. Macchia, *Justified in the Spirit: Creation, Redemption and the Triune God* (Grand Rapids, MI: Eerdmans, 2010), p. 30.

68 Such as in Pierre Teilhard de Chardin's discussion of the inevitable unification of complexity-consciousness into the Christogenesis, which he calls the Omega point. For example, Teilhard wrote: 'I can be saved only by becoming one with the universe', *Christianity and Evolution*, trans. René Hague (London: Collins, 1971), p. 128. See also *Science and Christ*, trans. René Hague (London: Collins, 1968), pp. 45–58; Pierre Teilhard de Chardin, *The Phenomenon of Man*, trans. Bernard Wall (New York: Harper and Row, 1959).

20

The Body and the Beatific Vision

MARC CORTEZ

A number of passages promise that the eschatological state will involve seeing God 'face to face' (1 Cor. 13.12) so that we come to know him 'as he is' (1 John 3.2). Historically, then, the *visio Dei* has played a prominent role in Christian accounts of salvation. Indeed, for many, the beatific vision just is the highest *telos* of the human person. At the same time, though, we also celebrate the central significance of the resurrection, which declares the centrality of transformed embodiment as fundamental to the eschatological state. However, as Isaac Morales points out, it has not always been easy to see how these two eschatological convictions 'fit together'.[1]

Traditionally, the beatific vision has been understood as a direct intellectual apprehension of the divine essence that is not mediated through any creaturely reality. After all, if I have to see God 'through' some creaturely reality, then I am not really seeing him 'face to face'. Thus, to the extent that we emphasize the beatific vision, we seem to downplay the importance of the resurrection. Although such a view might affirm the reality of the resurrection body, it does not 'seem to give bodies anything to do'.[2]

In light of this difficulty, we have two options. We could eliminate or significantly de-emphasize the *visio Dei* in our accounts of salvation despite the theological prominence of the beatific vision throughout history, or we could seek to revise traditional accounts of the beatific vision so that it no longer seems to minimize the significance of the resurrection body. Several scholars have recently pursued the latter course, specifically arguing that we should follow the example of people like John Owen and Jonathan Edwards, who contend that the resurrection body is central to the beatific vision itself.[3] They maintain that this offers a way of uniting these two central truths into a more adequate vision of eschatological salvation.

In this chapter, we will explore this argument further. To provide some shape to the argument, we will focus specifically on a recent argument offering three reasons why Jonathan Edwards depicts the beatific vision as embodied in ways that make it substantially preferable to the classic account offered by Thomas Aquinas. As Hans Boersma neatly summarizes:

Edwards's account is one that treats the resurrection of the body as significant, even indispensable for the deifying vision of God. It is also an account that regards Christ – the 'grand medium' of the *visio dei* – as the consummate theophanic appearance of God. And it is, finally, an account that takes seriously the infinite progress of the vision of God, beginning in this life, continuing in the intermediate state, and on into the eternity of the resurrection.[4]

According to Boersma, then, we have three reasons for thinking that the Thomistic approach needs to be corrected by a more Edwardsian understanding of the beatific vision: (1) the Thomistic view makes the body extraneous to the beatific vision; (2) it offers a view of humanity's *telos* that is not adequately Christocentric; and (3) it portrays the eschatological state as overly static. After considering each of these arguments more closely, I will suggest that: (a) the Thomistic view has at least some resources for addressing these concerns; and (b) the Edwardsian account faces a number of significant challenges of its own. I will then bring the chapter to a close by proposing ways in which we might revise both accounts further to offer a more satisfying way of understanding the relationship between the resurrection body and the beatific vision.

Unpacking the Three Worries

We need to begin by establishing the precise nature of the three worries people have raised about the classic understanding of the beatific vision as it relates to the resurrection body.[5]

The Extraneous Worry

The first worry stems from Aquinas' conviction that the beatific vision is the highest end of the human person, that we experience the beatific vision in the intermediate state, and that being reunited with the body in the resurrection does not change anything with respect to the quality or intensity of the beatific vision.[6] Taken together, these convictions seem to entail that the resurrection body does not play any intrinsic role in the beatific vision and, consequently, in achieving humanity's highest end. If that is so, the fact that Aquinas emphasizes that we do in fact have resurrection bodies seems to make them no more than the fancy ribbon wrapped around an expensive present. It might be attractive, but it is largely irrelevant for our enjoyment of the gift itself.

Aquinas' argument largely depends on his understanding of human cognition in general. According to him, the body is necessary for cognition in this life because it is the means by which the intellectual soul receives 'phantasms' – i.e. the sensory impressions from which it abstracts knowledge of the universal forms.[7] When it comes to the *visio Dei*, however, the situation is far different since the invisible divine essence 'cannot be seen by means of phantasms'.[8] As McCord Adams explains, 'For, on Aquinas's analysis, vision requires a *perfect* likeness of the object seen. No finite created likeness can mediate a *vision* of the infinite being! If any created intellect is to see God, the divine essence itself must be united to the cognitive power.'[9] She goes on to point out that this means Aquinas thinks that it is at least possible to experience the beatific vision even in this life, though here the beatific vision would come *in spite of* the body rather than being mediated through it. This also allows Aquinas to maintain that redeemed humans experience beatific vision in the intermediate state, completely independently of the resurrection body.[10] On both accounts, embodiment is unnecessary for receiving the *visio Dei*.

However, this does not mean that Aquinas thinks the beatific vision is completely unrelated to the resurrection body. Instead, Aquinas maintains that the resurrection does result in a kind of increase with respect to the beatific vision. For Aquinas, only the body/soul composite is a metaphysically complete human person. Consequently, although the disembodied soul was already experiencing beatific vision in the intermediate state, the resurrection brings the body into that experience as well, allowing the whole human person to receive the *visio Dei*. However, Aquinas rejects the idea that this involves an increase in the quality or intensity of the beatific state. Instead, he argues that the resurrection involves an increase in the *extent* or *scope* of the beatific vision since it now includes the body as well.[11] This conclusion follows from Aquinas' argument that the beatific vision cannot be mediated through bodily realities. If that is the case, although Aquinas can allow that embodiment might *detract* from one's ability to experience beatific vision, primarily as a source of corruption and distraction, it becomes difficult to imagine how possession of a body could *increase* that experience in any qualitative way.

Before moving on, we should note that this is the position Aquinas articulated in *Summa Theologiae*, which includes his latest writings on the subject. Earlier in his career, Aquinas had argued that the resurrection led to both an intensive and an extensive increase in the beatific vision,[12] a position that had a number of influential supporters in the thirteenth and fourteenth centuries.[13] By the time of the *Summa*, though, his thinking had shifted, probably as a result of his continued engagement with Aristotle's cognitive psychology.[14] As Aquinas came to realize, to claim that the resurrection body affects the intensity of the beatific vision itself suggests that even in the eschaton humans will only know God through intellectual abstraction, never reaching the point where we will see him 'face to face'.

In the end, then, although Aquinas emphasizes the truth of the resurrection, he does not think that the resurrection body plays any intrinsic role in the beatific vision itself. And since Aquinas also views the beatific vision as the highest end of the human person, his view also suggests that the body is not intrinsic to humanity's own highest end. Thus, it still sounds as though the body is merely an *accidental* addendum to a state in which the human soul has already achieved perfect happiness.

The Christological Worry

The second issue also stems from Aquinas' conviction that beatific vision involves direct, intellectual contemplation of the divine essence. Suzanne McDonald raises this concern with particular clarity in an article focusing on the differences between Aquinas and John Owen.[15] McDonald recognizes that Aquinas presents the beatific vision as clearly grounded in Christology given that a person cannot be saved, and thus able to experience the beatific vision, apart from Christ. However, McDonald contends that solution is not entirely satisfying since it makes Jesus merely the instrumental means through which we arrive at the state of being able to experience the beatific vision. What it does not do is make Christ 'intrinsic to the essence of the beatific vision itself'.[16]

Here McDonald has two specific concerns in mind. First, she worries that Aquinas' account makes Christ's embodied humanity extrinsic to the *means* of the beatific vision. Remember that for Aquinas, knowledge of God's essence cannot be mediated by the 'phantasms' we receive through the sensory capacities of the material body. However, if the perfect vision of God's essence cannot be mediated by embodied realities, then it follows that even Christ's own resurrected body cannot be the means by which we see God's essence in the eschatological state. Instead, we have a direct vision of God's essence, which entails, according to McDonald, that Christ's humanity plays no direct role in mediating the beatific vision.

Similarly, McDonald contends that Aquinas' view of the beatific vision is inadequately Christological with respect to its *content*. For Thomas, the beatific vision involves knowledge of the undifferentiated divine essence, which certainly includes a vision of the Son in his eternal relationships with the Father and the Spirit. However, this means, according to McDonald, that Aquinas does not focus on the incarnate Christ as being central to the content of the beatific vision. Instead, she argues that once Aquinas begins to talk about the vision itself, 'Christ seems to fade from view'.[17]

On both points, means and content, McDonald contends that Aquinas' approach runs contrary to those biblical texts that clearly emphasize the incarnate Christ as the necessary and perfect revelation of God (e.g. John

14.9; Heb. 1.1–4), a reality that she maintains will last into the eschaton. Thus, 'Christ the incarnate Son will always be the mediator between us in our humanity and the Triune God, even in glory.'[18]

The Static Worry

The third concern has to do with the way Aquinas presents the beatific vision as a settled state of perfection. As Boersma explains: '[A]n eternal restful gazing at God may appear so static and bereft of movement or activity that it seems hard to imagine that such a vision of God actually brings delight.'[19] To understand this concern, it is important to see that it too is related to the idea that the beatific vision is an unmediated, intellectual apprehension of the divine essence. As Matthew Levering explains:

> The vision of God cannot be a finite concept or judgment of the mind about God, nor can it be based upon knowing a likeness of God. Rather, it must be intimate knowing that locates us within the divine life itself. Only in this way could we 'see him as he is' in his divinity (1 John 3.2).[20]

However, this entails that the *visio Dei* 'will be an all-at-once, participatory "seeing" of the Father, Son and Holy Spirit'.[21] As Aquinas maintains, 'what is seen in the Word is not seen successively, but at the same time.'[22]

Quite a number of Protestant scholars have argued that such a static-state view of humanity's eschatological condition is contrary to the Bible's own emphasis on embodied activity as central to humanity's *telos*.[23] Although Thomists often appeal to the idea that any such continued creational activity necessarily involves the kind of unending temporality that they find incredibly unsatisfying, it seems at least somewhat reasonable to contend that embodied life, even if it involves the kinds of bodies that are radically transformed by the resurrection, will involve at least some kind of temporality. The biblical vision of the eschaton indicates both that we have bodies and that we do things with our bodies, yet both of these suggest at the very least that the eschatological state will involve whatever kinds of temporal transitions are necessary to support such bodily motions. This in turn raises questions about whether the apparently static reality of the beatific vision is entirely adequate to what we know about the embodied nature of resurrected life.

The Edwardsian Revision

With these three worries in mind, we can now move on to consider why some might think that the approach to the beatific vision offered by Jonathan

Edwards is clearly superior with respect to its account of the resurrection body. At first glance, though, Edwards' understanding of the beatific vision seems rather similar to that of Aquinas. Both affirm that disembodied souls can experience beatific vision in the intermediate state,[24] and each also maintains that the beatific vision is an intellectual apprehension of the divine being.[25] Thus, although Edwards routinely describes the intermediate state using the language of embodiment, he clearly affirms that the human soul continues to exist in a conscious state between death and resurrection, which Edwards describes as 'a blissful abode' and 'a very happy state',[26] during which the human person experiences a vision of God's beauty and glory. And, as Boersma points out, Edwards also describes the beatific vision as an intellectual apprehension in ways that sound notably Thomist. Edwards thus denies that bodily sight can ever see the essence of the invisible God.[27] Although we can and do see the glory of God through material objects now, that is merely God's condescension to the limitations of our 'infant state'.[28] Edwards contrasts this with the 'intellectual view' in which God 'is beheld with the understanding'.[29]

Boersma begins to differentiate the two views by noting the important role that embodied sight plays in Edwards' understanding of the eschatological state. As Boersma explains: 'Edwards complements the intellectual vision of God not only by highlighting the affective aspect of the beatific vision, but also by insisting that the eyes of the body will have a role to play.'[30] Most important, for Boersma, is the central role that is played by our vision of Christ's glorified body. Although he recognizes that Aquinas also affirms the importance of Christ's own resurrected body, he contends that Christ's human body plays no significant role in Aquinas' understanding of the beatific vision. In contrast, Edwards declares that, 'there will doubtless be appearances of a divine and inimitable glory and beauty in Christ's gloried body, which it will indeed be a ravishing and blessed sight to see.'[31] This could be interpreted merely as offering a second way of experiencing beatific vision. In other words, maybe Edwards thinks we experience beatific vision *both* through a direct intellectual vision of God's being that comes without any embodied mediation *and* through an indirect vision of God's beauty that we see in the redeemed world around us and pre-eminently in Christ's human body. However, Boersma argues that Edwards has something else in mind. Rather than suggesting merely that the embodied vision is a supplement to beatific vision, Boersma contends that Edwards thinks our embodied vision of Christ's body is the necessary means through which we experience the beatific vision. According to Boersma, then, 'Edwards goes out of his way . . . to emphasize that in eternity the saints will have the ability to see bodily sights and that the very vision of the Godhead comes through the physical sight of the body of Christ. It is the union of the two natures that allows the saint to move from a bodily vision of Christ's humanity to an acknowledgement also of his divinity.

Thus, the bodily vision of Christ's human nature will, in turn, put the saints in touch with the Godhead.'[32]

To support this account, Boersma draws on Edwards' discussion of happiness in heaven, in which Edwards raises concerns about the idea of having an 'immediate and intuitive view' of someone else's mind.[33] According to Edwards, this would mean experiencing things in precisely the same manner that God experiences them, which would result in a 'union of personality' and a violation of the creator/creature distinction. Instead, Edwards contends that Christ is the only one who can have this kind of *immediate* vision of the divine essence in virtue of the hypostatic union. Even in the resurrected state, all other humans must see God by means of 'manifestations or signs' and pre-eminently through the humanity of Jesus Christ as the 'grand medium' of the knowledge of God. Boersma thus concludes: 'Mediation is not just a this-worldly phenomenon. It also characterizes our relation to God in the hereafter.'[34]

The obvious problem for such an account is that it seems to cut God's people off from ever having a true vision of God's essence, requiring the continuation of both the sacramental mediation of God's presence and the necessity of faith. Yet Boersma rejects this conclusion, arguing instead that because of our perfect union with Christ, who himself is the perfect union of deity and humanity, we will have a true vision of God's essence in and through our vision of Christ's humanity. Thus, 'Edwards's vision of Christ is truly a *visio dei*: the believer really does see God, but he sees him in Christ. Christ may be the "grand medium" of the vision of God, but in the eschaton, this medium is no longer a sacrament.'[35]

According to Boersma, this account offers resources for addressing all three of the worries we previously discussed. First, it avoids the extraneous worry by maintaining that embodiment is intrinsic to experiencing the beatific vision since we cannot have any such experience apart from having bodily sight of the glorified body of Jesus Christ. Second, Edwards' account makes Jesus central to the beatific vision not only in being the one who makes the *visio Dei* possible, but also as the necessary and eternal mediator of the beatific vision to God's people. And third, Boersma maintains that the mediated nature of the beatific vision allows Edwards 'to posit a never-ending progression in the vision of God to ever-greater intimacy'.[36] Since the *visio Dei* is mediated through Christ's humanity, Edwards can present the beatific vision itself (i.e. not just its comprehension) as something that can increase throughout eternity.[37]

A Response to the Edwardsian Revision

We have now seen at least some of the reasons why people think Edwards' approach to the beatific vision is superior to that of Aquinas with respect to three specific concerns. In this final section, I will take a closer look at this Edwardsian argument and suggest that this revision runs into some important difficulties of its own.

The Extraneous Worry

I will focus much of my response here because this concern motivates some of the issues raised by the other two worries. And here we need to be clear about the specific nature of the concern. As I mentioned earlier, Aquinas clearly affirms the importance of the resurrection body and its necessity for the full flourishing of the redeemed human person. Although we might legitimately critique Thomas for not saying enough about the nature of this embodied existence, it simply would not be accurate to suggest that the body is eschatologically extraneous in any absolute sense.

Consequently, the real focus of the worry must be on the idea that Aquinas makes the body extraneous to the beatific vision itself. Yet why exactly would this constitute a significant objection? Anyone who affirms even the possibility of an intermediate state in which human persons exist in conscious relationship with God and other humans must maintain that the body is non-essential for performing at least some fundamentally important human activities. Even if we contend that disembodiment results in some significant limitation of these activities, we are still claiming that at least *this* state and at least *these* activities can be performed without a body, which would seem to entail that the body bears only an accidental relationship to some human conditions and activities. Of course, we could avoid that implication by denying even the possibility of an intermediate state. Since both of the views we are considering here maintain the intermediate state, however, we can set that option aside for now. It must be, then, that the worry arises from the fact that Aquinas presents the body as extraneous not just to some human activities but to the one activity that he defines as humanity's *highest* activity. Yet this would entail that the body is extraneous to humanity's ultimate end. Yet the Edwardsian approach seems to encounter a similar difficulty. Let us grant for a moment Edwards' argument that the beatific vision must be mediated in some way through Christ's resurrected body. This makes it necessary for there to be at least one resurrected body in the eschaton – that of Christ. But what exactly makes it necessary for there to be others? Here again the problem arises with respect to the intermediate state. Edwards maintains that the saints experience beatific vision in the intermediate state, which must mean that the saints have some kind of disembodied vision of Christ's resurrected humanity, through which God mediates the intellectual *visio Dei*. However, this suggests that only *Christ's* resurrected body is essential to beatific vision, raising the question of whether our own resurrected bodies are extraneous in much the same way as in Thomas' account.

Much of Boersma's argument focuses on the extent to which Edwards emphasizes the importance of embodiment, even envisioning the intermediate state in highly somatic ways. Yet this alone will not suffice to establish that the body is more essential to the beatific vision in Edwards' account than it is in that of Aquinas. Merely stating repeatedly that the body is important for beatific vision will not make it so. What we need is some account of why an *embodied* vision of Christ's resurrected humanity is somehow superior to a *disembodied* vision despite the fact that the vision itself is inherently intellectual. In one sermon, Edwards offers seven reasons why we should affirm the significance of the resurrection. Interestingly, though, most of them focus on the resurrection as the completion of God's redemptive purposes for creation, all of which Aquinas would be happy to acknowledge.[38] Only the first focuses directly on the beatific vision: 'the reunification of body and soul means that the saints will be "happy in the whole man".'[39] Yet this is precisely what Aquinas affirms with his argument that the resurrection involves an *extensive* increase in the beatific vision rather than an *intensive* one. The same could be said for Edwards' consistent affirmation that resurrected bodily sight allows us to see and experience God's glory throughout the new creation, preeminently in the resurrected bodies of the other saints. Yet this too could easily be understood as an extension of an already existing and perfectly realized *visio Dei* received through disembodied sight of Christ's resurrected humanity.

For Boersma's argument to work, we would need to maintain that bodily sight makes a qualitative difference in such a way that bodily sight is somehow intrinsic to the full experience of the beatific vision. And this might seem relatively easy to do given that Edwards clearly affirms the progressive nature of the beatific vision, contending that it is only with the resurrection that we arrive at the full beatific state.[40] For Edwards, then, the intermediate state is only a penultimate realization of the beatific vision, a state that is clearly surpassed by the true *visio Dei* we experience in the resurrection. However, although this means that Edwards clearly *affirms* the necessity of embodiment for the beatific vision, it is something else to say that his view offers a meaningful *explanation* for why this is so. Given how Edwards defines the beatific vision, it is not entirely clear why *embodied* sight would make such a difference in the quality of the *visio Dei*.

The primary reason offered by Edwards for affirming the superiority of the beatific vision of the resurrected state involves the progress of redemption. For Edwards, the saints primarily see God's beauty and glory through his redemptive works. This is one of the fundamental reasons he maintains the progressive nature of the beatific vision: the more the saints see of God's redemptive works, the more they can relish the beauty and glory displayed through them. Since the full outworking of God's redemptive purposes only comes in the new creation with the resurrection of the saints, we cannot have a full experience of beatific vision before the resurrection.[41] As important as this affirmation might be for Edwards, however, it falls short of explaining why we should view embodiment as *integral* to the vision itself. The saints in the intermediate state seem perfectly capable of seeing and celebrating God's beauty through the redemptive works thus far accomplished. So it does not appear that embodiment is an absolute requirement for the kind of beatific vision Edwards has in mind. Thus, although some might approve of the more progressive nature of Edwards' view of the beatific vision, it is difficult to see that as a sufficient reason to think that he has thereby made embodiment more central to the beatific vision itself.

Alternatively, we could try to address this challenge by arguing that bodily sight offers a fundamentally different way of seeing God's glory, and that seeing God's glory in this way, rather than through spiritual sight alone, offers some kind of improvement on the beatific vision of the intermediate state. As Boersma has rightly argued, though, Edwards is better understood as saying that bodily sight is the *means* of receiving beatific vision rather a qualitatively different *kind* of beatific vision. If that is the case, though, it becomes unclear why a difference in *means* (bodily vs spiritual) would result in a qualitative difference with respect to the *visio Dei* itself.

A third option might try to draw from Edwards' concern that affirming an unmediated (i.e. disembodied) *visio Dei* would collapse the creator/creature distinction. Here again, though, this seems to make only Christ's resurrected body necessary, thus establishing the mediated nature of beatific vision, rather than our own resurrected bodies.[42] In the end, it is hard to avoid the impression that Edwards should certainly be credited with emphasizing the centrality of the resurrection body for eschatological flourishing, but that lacking some account of how *bodily* sight is intrinsic to the *visio Dei*, his view also struggles with the extraneous concern, at least insofar as it involves our own resurrected bodies.

The Christological Worry

Regarding the Christological concern, Edwards' account would seem to be on much surer footing. After all, he clearly affirms the centrality of Christ's humanity throughout his discussion of the beatific vision. However, here as well we can ask: (1) whether Aquinas' account has resources for maintaining a robustly Christological view of the beatific vision; and (2) whether Edwards' account runs into its own difficulties.

Regarding the first, Simon Gaine has criticized the idea that Thomas thinks of Christ's humanity as something that is only necessary for getting us into the eschatological state and is not essential to the beatific vision itself. Instead, he contends that Thomas affirms the centrality of Christ's humanity with respect to both the means and the content of the beatific vision. Regarding content, Gaine points to the fact that a beatific vision of the divine essence would necessarily include knowledge of all God's works, preeminent among which would be the incarnation. Consequently, the humanity of Christ is integral to the beatific vision.[43] Regarding means, Gaine rejects the notion that Aquinas presents Christ as only necessary for the possibility of beatific vision. Instead, he contends that union with Christ is the continuing ground for the *visio Dei*. He uses the analogy of someone viewing a panoramic landscape that can only be seen from the top of a particular hill:

> The view can be seen without any instrument acting as a medium, that is, without binoculars or a telescope or any such thing. In that sense the view is unmediated . . . However, it is impossible for any sightseer to take in a panoramic view without being in the right spot, in the right place. The heavenly Body of Christ is then the 'place' from which the divine essence is viewed.[44]

Such an account would seem to be thoroughly Christological in the sense that Christ's body is absolutely central both for the possibility of the beatific vision and for its ongoing reality, even though it would continue to maintain that the body of Christ is not itself the medium through which we receive the *visio Dei*.

Interestingly, though, we can also raise a Christological concern about the Edwardsian account. Here again Gaine is helpful. According to him, the Thomist has the advantage of being able to maintain 'the solidarity of Christ the Head and his members in a single Body by their sharing of the same beatifying knowledge'.[45] In other words, on this reading of Thomas we can maintain that in virtue of his human nature, Christ receives the same beatific vision as that of the saints. Edwards' account, on the other hand, seems to suggest either that Christ does not experience beatific vision or that he receives beatific vision in a fundamentally different way from the rest of us, unless, of course, we want to envision that Christ experiences beatific vision by gazing at his own resurrected body. Yet theologians have long maintained that Christ is fully human in such a way that his humanity serves as an exemplar of true humanity. It would thus seem at least odd to posit a fundamental difference precisely at the point where humanity reaches its highest end.

The Static Worry

We have already addressed one of the key issues related to this concern when discussing the fact that Edwards' emphasis on the progressive nature of the beatific vision cannot by itself establish that the resurrection body is itself integral to his understanding of the beatific vision. Consequently, we can deal with this worry more succinctly, focusing primarily on identifying a few ways in which the Thomist account might be able to address this concern as well.

Here it is important to see that this worry stems from the conviction that so-called 'static' states of the eschaton are inherently flawed. Consequently, if Thomas' beatific vision results in a static view of the eschaton, it must be abandoned or corrected. Addressing the relative pros and cons of the debate between static and dynamic views of the eschaton would take us too far afield at this point. But it is at least worth recognizing that the logic of this third worry depends entirely on the validity of the argument that static-state views of the eschaton are inherently flawed. I am sympathetic to that argument, but it is a position that cannot merely be assumed in this discussion.

Setting aside those broader considerations regarding the nature of the eschatological state, I want to focus on the question of whether Aquinas' understanding of the beatific vision necessarily results in a static view of the eschaton. We could try to respond to this worry by making a distinction between vision and comprehension. In other words, affirming that beatific vision involves a perfect vision of God does not require us to affirm as well that the saints will have immediate and perfect comprehension of that vision. Indeed, given God's infinity and incomprehensibility, it seems entirely possible to maintain instead something like Gregory of Nyssa's view in which comprehension of the divine essence will involve the infinite and eternal expansion of our finite, cognitive capacities such that we continually comprehend more of the incomprehensible divine essence.[46] Such a move would allow us to affirm that the beatific vision involves both static and dynamic elements. It is static insofar as the *visio Dei* itself is perfect and complete, yet it remains dynamic insofar as humans will continue to grow in their comprehension of the divine essence for all eternity. Although I think such an account is worth exploring, it does not seem available to Thomas given his insistence that perfect happiness in heaven requires whatever kind of perfect comprehension human minds can handle.[47] Consequently, even eternal growth in comprehension would result, for Thomas, in the eternal dissatisfaction of the human person.

A likelier response will focus on the fact that Aquinas affirms eschatological embodiment. Although Thomas spends comparatively little time discussing what exactly we will be doing with our bodies in the eschaton, what he does say about the resurrected body suggests that we will in fact be doing *something* with them.[48] Otherwise, why would Aquinas bother detailing the attributes of the eschatological body and how it is more suited to resurrected life than our current bodies? And, as Gaine explains, 'While he [Aquinas] takes the human desire to know the essence of God as fulfilled, that is, brought to rest, by the act of beatific vision, the wider beatitude of the saints beyond this formal core involves in the dynamism of a whole set of further acts which give diverse expression to the beatitude already attained.'[49] Thus, although we might critique Aquinas for neglecting to discuss the embodied nature of the eschaton more thoroughly, we should at least recognize that nothing about his view of the beatific vision itself generates this concern.

Expanding the Ultimate Telos *of the Human Person*

In the end, I find myself unconvinced by the three reasons offered for thinking that Edwards' account of the beatific vision is superior to that of Aquinas. I agree that any adequate account of the eschatological *telos* of the human person should be able to maintain that the body is intrinsic to humanity's highest end, that Christ is both instrumentally and materially integral to that end, and that we should construe this end in such a way as to allow at least some kind of movement and development. However, we have at least some reasons for thinking that (1) Aquinas' approach to the beatific vision has the resources to affirm all three of these principles coherently and (2) Edwards' approach runs into difficulties that would need to be addressed before declaring it the clear victor. In other words, both have problems and neither has a significant advantage in how it deals with these continuing difficulties.

Before concluding this discussion, though, we should explore (all too briefly) a few of the options we have for addressing the continuing question of the relationship between the resurrection body and the beatific vision. We could, of course, deal with the issue by rejecting either of the presenting problems. To anyone who denies the resurrection or the beatific vision, there is no problem here to resolve. However, assuming that we prefer less drastic solutions, four possibilities suggest themselves.

The first two focus on the intermediate state. As we have seen, many of the worries addressed above derive from the idea that human persons exist in a disembodied state between death and resurrection, along with the corresponding implications this has for the significance of the body, particularly if these disembodied human persons continue to participate in activities typically understood as central to human identity and purpose. Consequently, it would be easy to conclude that if we eliminated the intermediate state from our understanding of the beatific vision, the above worries would dissipate rather quickly. We could do this by (1) eliminating the intermediate state itself or (2) denying that human persons experience the beatific vision during the intermediate state. Both utilize the same logic: if we contend that human persons never experience beatific vision apart from embodiment, we can more easily maintain that embodiment is essential to the beatific vision. While some might well find either of these options attractive for various reasons, we should be careful about drawing such a conclusion too hastily. The fact that one reality never occurs without another does not demonstrate that the latter is an intrinsic feature of the former. For example, as many philosophers have pointed out, the fact that all humans who have ever existed have been born on planet Earth does not entail the conclusion that being born on planet Earth is necessary to being human. Consequently, even those who opt for one of these two intermediate state solutions would still need to provide some account of *why* the body is integral to the beatific vision if they want to avoid the concerns raised above.

A third option would focus instead on the nature of the beatific vision itself. Both Edwards and Aquinas deny that the beatific vision can be directly equated with anything we receive through bodily sight, maintaining that it involves a purely intellectual apprehension. If we argued instead that the beatific vision was a fully embodied reality, thus maintaining that the *visio Dei* is somehow identical to some embodied experience (e.g. bodily sight of Christ's resurrected body), it would inevitably follow that the resurrection body is integral to the beatific vision. To do so, however, would seem to require us to pay a rather high price by surrendering some long-standing theological commitments. On the one hand, we could maintain this position by affirming that material realities can provide direct access to God's essence. Thus, for resurrected eyes to see Christ's resurrected body just is to see the divine essence. However, such a move would at least raise questions about how to maintain this without collapsing the creator/creature distinction and seriously revising widely held beliefs about divine transcendence. The more likely way of maintaining this view would be to continue denying that material realities provide direct access to the divine essence and accept the conclusion that this entails not having direct knowledge of God even in our resurrected state. Instead, we would need to affirm that human knowledge of God is eternally mediated, sacramental, and faith-based. In light of the biblical claim that we will ultimately come to know God 'face to face', however, many will find this too high a price to pay as well.

The final option, and the one that seems the likeliest candidate for further exploration, is simply to accept that it does not appear to be the case that the body is essential to the beatific vision and find some other way of establishing the fundamental significance of the body for human purpose and identity in the eschaton. To do this, we could reject the idea that beatific vision alone comprises the highest *telos* of the human person, arguing instead that the true end of the human person is multifaceted and includes not only the beatific vision but also things like living in embodied community with other believers, serving as God's image bearers in the new creation, and so on. On this account, even those who maintain that human persons experience beatific vision in the intermediate state would not run into difficulties with also affirming that the resurrection is necessary for achieving humanity's highest end since the former would only be a partial realization of the latter. And, as long as we made it clear how the body was essential for realizing at least some aspects of this ultimate *telos* (e.g. by maintaining the impossibility of serving as God's image bearers in the new creation apart from possessing a resurrected body), then we will have adequately grounded the essentiality of the resurrection irrespective of its particular role with regard to the beatific vision.[50] Admittedly, such a position would be easier to affirm for those inclined toward Edwards' vision of our eschatological state with his robust account of embodied human activity in the new creation. Thomas's theology, on the other hand, seems to affirm rather explicitly that the ultimate end of the human person is singular and unified (i.e. not multifaceted in the sense intended above).[51]

In this discussion, then, we have seen two different ways theologians have sought to relate the beatific vision to the resurrection body, along with some reasons people have offered for suggesting that the approach represented by Jonathan Edwards offers a significant advancement on the more traditional account represented by Thomas Aquinas. I have argued instead, though, that neither account has a significant advantage over the other with respect to making the body intrinsic to the beatific vision itself. Additionally, we took a brief look at some other ways of addressing the issue, the first three of which also sought to find a way of establishing the essentiality of the resurrection body for the beatific vision. Yet the first two ultimately fail to offer any real explanation for the body's significance and the third comes at a rather steep price. Consequently, I have suggested that the likeliest way of reconciling these two fundamental truths about the eschatological state is to affirm that the ultimate *telos* of the human person is a complex reality that includes both the beatific vision and the resurrection as essential aspects but in which the latter is not an intrinsic feature of the former. This allows us to retain the most widely held ways of understanding the nature of the beatific vision along with the fundamental significance of the resurrection for human purpose and identity.

Notes

1 Isaac Augustine Morales, '"With My Body I Thee Worship": New Creation, Beatific Vision, and the Liturgical Consummation of All Things', *Pro Ecclesia* 25, 3 (2016), p. 337.

2 Marilyn McCord Adams, 'Why Bodies as Well as Souls in the Life to Come?', in *The Science of Being as Being: Metaphysical Investigations* (Washington, DC: Catholic University of America Press, 2012), p. 264.

3 E.g. Suzanne McDonald, 'Beholding the Glory of God in the Face of Jesus Christ: John Owen and the "Reforming" of the Beatific Vision', in Kelly M. Kapic and Mark Jones (eds), *The Ashgate Research Companion to John Owen's Theology* (Abingdon: Ashgate, 2012), pp. 141–58; Kyle C. Strobel, *Jonathan Edwards's Theology: A Reinterpretation* (New York: Bloomsbury, 2014); Hans Boersma, 'The "Grand Medium": An Edwardsean Modification of Thomas Aquinas on the Beatific Vision', *Modern Theology* 33, 2 (2017), pp. 187–212. For a distinct article with some overlapping themes, see also Joshua R. Farris and Ryan A. Brandt, 'Ensouling Beatific Vision: Motivating the Reformed Impulse', *Perichoresis* 15, 1 (2017), pp. 67–84.

4 Boersma, 'The "Grand Medium"', p. 188.

5 It will be important to keep in mind throughout this chapter that we are not dealing with different approaches to the beatific vision as a whole. Instead, we are focusing more narrowly on the soteriological and anthropological implications of different ways of understanding the relationship between the resurrection body and the beatific vision.

6 For good summaries of Aquinas on the beatific vision, see Phillip Blond, 'The Beatific Vision of St Thomas Aquinas', in *Encounter between Eastern Orthodoxy and Radical Orthodoxy: Transfiguring the World through the Word* (Farnham: Ashgate, 2009), pp. 185–212; Peter S. Dillard, 'Keeping the Vision: Aquinas and the Problem of Disembodied Beatitude', *New Blackfriars* 93, 1046 (2012), pp. 397–411; Matthew Levering, *Jesus and the Demise of Death: Resurrection, Afterlife, and the Fate of the Christian* (Waco, TX: Baylor University Press, 2012); Simon Gaine, 'Thomas Aquinas and John Owen on the Beatific Vision: A Reply to Suzanne McDonald', *New Blackfriars* 97, 1070 (2016), pp. 432–46; Morales, 'With My Body I Thee Worship'.

7 *ST* I, Q84, A7.

8 Adams, 'Why Bodies as Well as Souls in the Life to Come?', pp. 274–75.

9 *ST* I-II, Q4, A5.

10 See esp. Dillard, 'Keeping the Vision'.

11 *ST* I–II, Q4, A5, ad. 5.

12 Blond, 'The Beatific Vision of St Thomas Aquinas', p. 196.

13 See esp. Caroline Walker Bynum, *The Resurrection of the Body in Western Christianity, 200–1336* (New York: Columbia University Press, 1995), pp. 279–317; and Dillard, 'Keeping the Vision'.

14 Blond, 'The Beatific Vision of St Thomas Aquinas', p. 198.

15 Gaine, 'Thomas Aquinas and John Owen on the Beatific Vision'.

16 McDonald, 'Beholding the Glory of God', p. 150.

17 McDonald, 'Beholding the Glory of God', p. 154. She goes on to point out, however, the importance of remembering that Aquinas never gave an extended treatment of the beatific vision in its own right. 'Had he done so the person of Christ might well have been central to it, but the fact remains that he did not, and the Thomas tradition did not develop the doctrine along these lines either' (ibid.).

18 McDonald, 'Beholding the Glory of God', p. 153.

19 Boersma, 'The "Grand Medium"', p. 187.

20 Levering, *Jesus and the Demise of Death*, p. 111.

21 Levering, *Jesus and the Demise of Death*, p. 113.

22 *ST* I, Q12, A10.

23 E.g. N. T. Wright, *Surprised by Hope: Rethinking Heaven, the Resurrection, and the Mission of the Church* (New York: HarperOne, 2008); J. Richard Middleton, *A New Heaven and a New Earth: Reclaiming Biblical Eschatology* (Grand Rapids, MI: Baker Academic, 2014).

24 Boersma, 'The "Grand Medium"', p. 193.

25 Edwards thus explicitly denies that God's essence can be viewed through bodily sight: 'Tis not any sight with the bodily eyes. [True] blessedness of the soul don't enter in at that door; [this] would be to make the blessedness of the soul depend [on] the body, or the happiness of men's superior [parts] be dependent on the inferior' ('The Pure in Heart Blessed', *WJE* 17:61).

26 *WJE* 18:93; 13:540. For a nice summary of Edwards' writings about heaven, see Robert W. Caldwell III, 'A Brief History of Heaven in the Writings of Jonathan Edwards', *Calvin Theological Journal* 46, 1 (2011), pp. 48–71.

27 *WJE* 17:59.

28 *WJE* 17:59.

29 *WJE* 17:63.

30 Boersma, 'The "Grand Medium"', p. 198. Boersma notes that the two differ with respect to the role of the affections in the beatific vision. For Aquinas, the affections follow the intellectual vision, while Edwards maintains their inseparable unity. Yet even if this interpretation is correct, it does not seem to generate any significant differences with respect to their understanding of the role the body plays in beatific vision. Either way, both seem to be maintaining, both in their account of the intermediate state and the idea of a purely intellectual vision of God, that embodiment is not essential to the beatific vision.

31 *WJE* 17:62.

32 Boersma, 'The "Grand Medium"', p. 199.

33 *WJE* 18:427–8.

34 Boersma, 'The "Grand Medium"', p. 201.

35 Boersma, 'The "Grand Medium"', p. 203.

36 Boersma, 'The "Grand Medium"', p. 205.

37 As Caldwell explains, 'Edwards . . . argued that perfection is not a static state but admits degrees. One who is perfected merely has no sin or natural defect; she still retains the potentiality for growth and increase in holiness' (Caldwell, 'A Brief History of Heaven in the Writings of Jonathan Edwards', p. 62). See also Amy Plantinga Pauw, '"Heaven Is a World of Love": Edwards on Heaven and the Trinity', *Calvin Theological Journal* 30, 2 (1995), pp. 392–400.

38 Boersma, 'The "Grand Medium"', p. 193.

39 Boersma, 'The "Grand Medium"', p. 195. The other six reasons all involve the resurrection as the completion of God's redemptive purposes for creation, all of which are things that Aquinas would affirm as well.

40 For an excellent discussion of the progressive nature of the beatific vision in Edwards' theology, see Strobel, *Jonathan Edwards's Theology*, pp. 107–24.

41 See esp. *WJE* 18:427–34.

42 Additionally, it is not clear to me that Aquinas' understanding of beatific vision as a direct intellectual apprehension necessarily runs afoul of Edwards' objection anyway. Nothing about Aquinas' position suggests that the beatific vision involves us having *precisely the same* experience that God himself has when knowing his own divine essence. At the very least, there would always be the difference that I receive beatific vision as a gift through participation in the divine life rather than experiencing it as something that is properly my own.

43 Gaine, 'Thomas Aquinas and John Owen on the Beatific Vision', p. 436. It is worth keeping in mind here, though, that Aquinas can only maintain that Christ's resurrected humanity is integral to the beatific vision as a consequence of the Fall and Redemption given that he thinks it wisest to maintain that the Son would not have become incarnate had there been no Fall. Given that beatific vision is humanity's highest end irrespective of the Fall, then, it must be the case that Aquinas thinks it at least hypothetically possible for humanity to have arrived at the state of beatific vision apart from Christ's resurrected body.

44 Gaine, 'Thomas Aquinas and John Owen on the Beatific Vision', p. 439.

45 Gaine, 'Thomas Aquinas and John Owen on the Beatific Vision', p. 445.

46 For more on Gregory of Nyssa's account, see Paul M. Blowers, 'Maximus the Confessor, Gregory of Nyssa, and the Concept of "Perpetual Progress"', *Vigiliae Christianae* 46, 2 (1992), pp. 151–71; Krishna Robb-Dover, 'Gregory of Nyssa's "Perpetual Progress"', *Theology Today* 65, 2 (2008).

47 *ST* I, Q12, A7.

48 *ST Supplementum Tertiæ Partis*, Q75–86.

49 Gaine, 'Thomas Aquinas and John Owen on the Beatific Vision', p. 444.

50 For a good discussion of this in relation to Aquinas' theology, see Germain Gabriel Grisez, 'The True Ultimate End of Human Beings: The Kingdom, Not God Alone', *Theological Studies* 69, 1 (2008), pp. 38–61. For an excellent description of Edwards' view of heaven, along with the likelihood that his theology is amenable to a more complex understanding of humanity's ultimate *telos*, see Caldwell, 'A Brief History of Heaven in the Writings of Jonathan Edwards'.

51 See, for example, Peter F. Ryan, 'Must the Acting Person Have a Single Ultimate End?', *Gregorianum* 82, 2 (2001), pp. 325–56.

Index of Names

Abelard, Peter xviii, 54, 55, 56, 57, 58, 59, 60, 61, 62, 63, 64, 65, 66, 67, 70, 73
Abraham 130, 152, 178
Adam 46, 47, 54, 55, 56, 57, 58, 61, 62, 63, 65, 66, 67, 77, 147, 152, 177, 178, 189, 223, 227, 271, 282, 293, 301
Adams, Jay 282, 285, 295, 296, 297, 328, 341
Adams, Marilyn McCord 328, 341
Adriaens, Pieter 300
Alain of Lille 58
Alciphron 29, 30, 31, 33, 38, 39
Allen, Michael 199
Allen, Mike 197
Allison, Dale C. 53
Alston, William 91, 92, 100
Ambrose 127, 132, 139
Ames, William 197
Anderson, Ray S. 155
Anselm xviii, 20, 21, 22, 68, 69, 72, 73, 74, 75, 76, 77, 78, 79, 80, 216, 323
Aquinas, Thomas xix, xxiii, 22, 58, 66, 67, 73, 103, 105, 106, 107, 108, 109, 110, 111, 116, 117, 121, 217, 247, 250, 324, 326, 329, 333, 334, 336, 337, 340, 341, 343
Arbour, Benjamin xx, 36, 39, 157
Arcadi, James M. xxi, 101, 233
Ariew, R. 322, 324
Aristotle 125, 127, 137, 139, 141, 158, 161, 169, 184, 210, 212, 217, 247, 328
Armstrong, D.M. 21
Athanasius 71, 86, 148, 155
Audi, Robert 160, 170
Augustine xix, 20, 22, 54, 56, 59, 60, 61, 64, 67, 103, 105, 106, 107, 109, 116, 117, 121, 124, 125, 126, 127, 128, 129, 130, 131, 132, 133, 134, 135, 136, 137, 138, 139, 140, 141, 142, 165, 178, 323, 340
Aulen, Gustaf 70, 80

Baber, Harriett 233, 237, 238, 239, 244
Bachrach, Bernard 297
Bacon, Hannah 324
Baker, Lynne Rudder 183
Baker, Mark C. 21
Barham, Erle 301
Barnes, Timothy 141
Barrett, C.K. 198, 199, 200
Barth, Karl xxi, 148, 153, 155, 156, 201, 202, 203, 204, 205, 206, 207, 208, 209, 211, 213, 214, 215, 216, 217
Basil of Caesarea 149, 150, 156
Basinger, David 36, 171
Bauckham, Richard 23
Bavinck, Herman 79, 293, 301
Bayer, Ronald 301
Bealer, George 183
Beardslee, John W. 197
Beilby, James K. 22, 51, 182
Bennett, Tony 6, 7
Bergmann, Michael 37
Berkeley, George xviii, 24, 25, 27, 28, 29, 30, 31, 32, 33, 37, 38, 39
Berkhof, Louis 71, 72, 200
Bernard of Clairvaux 58, 59
Berry, James 297
Best, Isabel 231, 232
Bethge, Eberhard 231
Bettenson, Henry 142
Beveridge, Henry 171, 198
Bigelow, John 23
Bird, Christopher 321
Blackburn, Simon 183
Blatti, Stephan 20
Blond, Phillip 341
Bloom, D.E. 295
Blowers, Paul M. 216, 217, 343
Bock, Darrell L. 198, 199
Bockmuehl, Markus 145, 155
Boersma, Hans 326, 327, 330, 331, 332, 334, 335, 341, 342

344

INDEX OF NAMES

Boethius xxi, 22, 201, 202, 209, 210, 211, 213, 215, 217
Bolt, John 79, 301
Bonhoeffer, Dietrich xxi, 218, 219, 220, 221, 222, 223, 224, 225, 226, 227, 228, 229, 230, 231, 232
Bostrum, Nick 267, 279
Brainerd, David 282, 296
Brandt, Ryan A. 341
Bray, Dennis 101
Bray, Gerald 148, 155
Brower, Jeffrey 65
Brown, W.S. 155
Bruce, F.F. 199
Brunner, Emil 171
Bruno, Giordano 303
Brüntrup, Godehard 309, 321, 322
Bunyan, John 282
Burleigh, J.H.S. 141
Burns, J. Patout 141
Buytaert, E.M. 64, 65, 66, 67
Bynum, Caroline Walker 341

Cafiero, E.T. 295
Cairns, David 155
Caldwell III, Robert W. 99, 342, 343
Callender, Craig 21
Calvin, John 39, 71, 72, 99, 104, 121, 165, 171, 187, 188, 197, 198, 199, 200, 278, 323
Campenella, Tommaso 303
Capes, Justin 178, 179, 182, 183
Cartwright, Stephen R. 55, 64, 65, 66, 67
Cary, Philip 141
Caster, Will 269, 270
Cautin, Robin 299
Chadwick, Henry 139
Chalmers, David John 139, 303, 306, 307, 308, 309, 321, 322
Charnock, Stephen xxi, 246, 247, 248, 249, 250, 251, 252, 257, 258, 259, 260, 261
Childs, Brevard 52
Christ xv, xx, xxi, 14, 15, 16, 17, 18, 22, 24, 34, 35, 38, 45, 46, 47, 48, 50, 51, 52, 53, 57, 65, 66, 70, 71, 72, 73, 74, 75, 76, 77, 79, 80, 81, 85, 86, 87, 88, 89, 90, 91, 92, 93, 95, 96, 97, 98, 100, 102, 103, 104, 105, 108, 109, 110, 111, 113, 114, 115, 116, 117, 118, 119, 120, 121, 123, 130, 133, 134, 135, 136, 141, 143, 144, 145, 146, 147, 150, 151, 152, 153, 154, 155, 164, 168, 183, 185, 186, 187, 188, 189, 190, 191, 192, 193, 194, 195, 196, 197, 198, 199, 200, 201, 202, 203, 204, 205, 207, 208, 209, 211, 212, 214, 215, 216, 217, 218, 219, 220, 221, 223, 224, 225, 226, 227, 228, 229, 230, 231, 233, 234, 235, 236, 238, 239, 240, 241, 242, 243, 244, 245, 248, 249, 250, 251, 257, 272, 273, 274, 275, 276, 278, 279, 281, 284, 301, 312, 314, 319, 325, 327, 329, 330, 331, 332, 333, 334, 335, 336, 338, 339, 343
Christiansen, Michael J. 99, 323
Chrysostom, John 103, 121
Cicero 126, 137, 141
Clark, Mary 138, 142
Clarke, D.S. 322
Clarke, Randolph 178, 179, 182, 183
Clay, Eugene 279
Clifford, William Kingdon 166, 167, 171, 307
Clough, David L. 325
Clouser, Roy 301
Code, Lorraine 170
Coleman, Sam 309
Cole-Turner, Ronald 279, 280
Colish, Marcia L. 55, 64
Colson, F.H. 52
Comes, Alain 21
Congar, Yves 109, 122, 123
Cooper, John 297
Cooper, Rachel 300
Cortez, Marc xv, xxii, xxiii, 101, 326
Cotnair, Aaron 101
Cottingham, John 51
Couenhoven, Jesse 294, 301
Courtenay, William J. 66
Coward, Harold 278
Cowper, William 282, 296
Craig, William Lane 14, 22, 37
Cranfield, C.E.B. 199, 200, 324
Craver, Carl 299
Crisp, Oliver xix, 9, 21, 54, 64, 80, 85, 94, 95, 96, 99, 100, 101, 154, 178, 181, 183, 184
Crisp, Thomas M. 19
Crocker, James 142
Cross, Richard 100
Curran, Ian 280
Cyprian 218, 231

Dabney, D. Lyle 143, 154, 156
Dahill, Lisa E. 231

INDEX OF NAMES

Dain, Norman 283, 296, 297
Daly, Todd T.W. 279
Dancy, Jonathan 169, 170
Danker, Frederick William 198
David 180
Davies, Brian 80, 323
Davies, Martin 299
Davis, S.T. 183
Dawkins, Richard 171
De Block, Andrea 300
De Chardin, Pierre Teilhard 303, 325
De Lubac, Henri 121
De Molina, Luis xx, 175, 176, 182
DeGrey, Aubrey 267
Denzinger, Heinrich 66
DePaul, Michael 170
Deweese-Boyd, Ian 37
Dicker, Georges 29, 37, 38
Dillard, Peter S. 341
Dols, Michael 296
Donaldson, J. 184
Donne, John 246, 258
Dosset, Wendy 324
Dougherty, Trent 37
Dummett, Michael 233, 236, 237, 238, 239, 244
Dunn, James D.G. 200, 324
Duns Scotus 73, 183, 184

Eames, Kevin 301
Eberhart, Christian 52
Eccles, John 305, 321
Eck, Bryan 297
Eddy, Paul R. 51, 182
Edwards, Jonathan xxi, xxii, xxiii, 34, 39, 89, 99, 100, 246, 247, 251, 252, 253, 254, 255, 256, 257, 258, 259, 260, 261, 326, 327, 330, 331, 332, 333, 334, 335, 336, 337, 338, 339, 340, 341, 342, 343
Ehrenberg, Alain 202, 211, 212, 217
Elizabeth 116
Emery, Gilles 121
Emlet, Michael 298
Erickson, Millard J. 170, 171
Ernst, Cornelius 121
Erswine, Zack 296
Esau 178
Euphranor 29, 30, 31, 33
Eusden, John Dykstra 197
Evans, C. Stephen 183
Evans, G.R. 80, 323
Eve 65, 177, 271, 285, 293

Fabrega, Horacio 296
Fahey, Michael 141
Fales, Evan 25, 36
Farris, Joshua xv, 68, 79, 101, 171, 183, 323, 341
Farrow, Douglas 122
Fechner, Gustav 306
Feinberg, John S. 22
Fesko, John V. xx, xxi, 185, 197, 200
Fields, Keota 29, 30, 37, 38
Fitzgerald, Allen D. 139, 141, 142
Fitzmyer, Joseph A. 199, 200
Flint, Thomas P. xix, 21, 37, 85, 86, 93, 94, 95, 96, 97, 98, 100, 101, 171, 182
Floyd Jr., Wayne Whitson 232
Foley, Richard 161, 170
Fox, Robin Lane 140
Franks, Robert S. 80, 81
Fraser, Donald 121
Freddoso, Alfred 182
Freud, Sigmund 166
Fulford, K.W.M. 299

Gaffin Jr., Richard B. 200
Gaine, Simon 336, 338, 341, 343
Gale, Richard M. 20
Ganssle, Gregory 22, 39
Garber, D. 322, 324
Gasser, George 20
Gavrilyuk, Paul L. 99
Gelber, Hester Goodenough 197
Gentile, Jesse 101
Gilbert de la Porree 109
Gilhooly, John R. 36
Gilligan, T.F. 141
Gilmore, Cody 21
Gockel, Matthias 216
Godsey, John D. 232
Goetz, Stewart 21, 37, 297
Goff, Philip 310, 322, 323
Goggin, Sister Thomas Aquinas 121
Gomes, Alan W. 80
Goodwin, Thomas 197
Gootjes, Albert 260
Gootjes, Nicolaas 297
Grabe, P. 324
Grace, Madison xxi, 218, 231
Graham, George 299
Graham, Jeannine M. 216
Gravel, Jason 301
Greco, John 37, 159, 170, 172
Green, Adam 36, 37, 172
Green, Barbara 232

INDEX OF NAMES

Green, Clifford 231, 232
Green, Joel B. 155
Greggo, Stephen 301
Gregory of Nyssa 21, 337, 343
Griffiths, Paul J. 9, 21
Grisez, Germain Gabriel 343
Grob, Gerald 296
Gross, Julius 55, 64
Groves, J. Alan 52
Grow, Bobby 156
Grummett, David 244
Guilfoy, Kevin 65
Gupta, Bina 20

Habets, Myk xix, xx, 99, 143, 154, 155, 156
Hacking, Ian 291, 300
Haeckel, Ernst 307
Haldane, Robert 193
Hall, David W. 100
Hallonsten, Gösta 99
Hamilton, S. Mark xv, xviii, 36, 39, 68, 79, 101
Hampton, Jean 51
Hanby, Michael 138, 142
Hasker, William 171
Haslam, Nick 299, 300
Haslanger, Sally 20
Hawley, Katherine 5, 6, 20
Hawthorne, John 20, 21
Haynes, Stephen R. 231
Hays, Richard B. 44, 52
Hecker, Bryan 197
Heidegger, Martin 125, 139
Heller, Mark 20
Heller, Michael 21
Heller, Thomas 300
Helm, Paul xxi, 22, 33, 39, 246, 260
Heppe, Heinrich 79
Hershenov, David B. 20
Herzberg, David 301
Hick, John 22
Hieb, Nathan G. 216
Hildebrand, Stephen 156
Hill, Charles E. 52, 216
Hill, Craig C. 23
Hill, Edmund 121, 140
Hill, Jonathan 100
Hill, Peter 297
Hodge, Charles 191, 198, 199, 200
Hooper, Walter 279
Horton, Michael xiii
Horwitz, Allan 289, 290, 299, 301

Hotchkiss, Valerie 197
Houck, Daniel xviii, 54, 67
Howard-Snyder, Daniel 36, 37, 39
Hudson, Hud 20, 22
Huemer, Michael 51
Hughes, James 279
Huiser, Kris 324
Hünermann, Peter 66
Hunt, David P. 36
Hunt, E.K. 299
Hurley, James 297
Huxley, Sir Julian 307
Hylas 32, 38

Irenaeus 71, 225, 232, 271
Isham, C.J. 21

Jacob 178, 276, 323
Jacobs, Jonathan D. 323
James III, Frank A. 52, 216
James, William 303, 308, 322
Jané-Llopis, E. 295
Janko, Richard 141
Jaskolla, Ludwig 321, 322
Jeffery, Steve 80
Jerome 193
Jesus 10, 11, 14, 15, 18, 24, 34, 35, 47, 48, 50, 66, 87, 88, 89, 93, 94, 95, 101, 102, 104, 106, 108, 109, 110, 111, 114, 115, 116, 117, 118, 120, 121, 122, 133, 134, 144, 146, 147, 150, 151, 152, 153, 164, 177, 178, 179, 190, 192, 199, 201, 202, 203, 204, 205, 206, 207, 208, 209, 211, 212, 213, 214, 215, 216, 218, 226, 233, 235, 265, 272, 273, 274, 275, 278, 281, 287, 293, 394, 312, 318, 319, 329, 332, 341
Jewett, Robert 199, 200
Jimenez, Mary Ann 296
Job 287
John 179, 181
Johnson, Adam J. xxi, 141, 201, 215, 216, 217
Johnson, Dru 101
Johnson, Eric 285, 295, 296, 297, 301, 302
Johnson, Glen 215
Johnson, Keith L. 215
Johnson, Marcus 186, 187, 188, 195, 197, 198, 200
Johnston, William B. 99
Jones, Mark 341

INDEX OF NAMES

Jones, Paul Dafydd 216
Joseph 276
Josephus 52
Judas 177, 178, 179, 181, 183
Julian of Eclanum 140

Kafka, Martin 301, 302
Kapic, Kell M. 341
Kasemann, Ernst 200
Katzoff, Charlotte 38
Kaye, B.N. 52
Keener, Craig 178, 183
Keller, James 25, 37
Kelly, Geffrey B. 232
Kemeny, Paul C. 55, 64
Kendal, D 183
Kendlar, Kenneth 299
Kenny, Anthony 139
Kincaid, Harold 300
King, Peter 65
Kinghorn, Kevin 34, 39
Kirkpatrick, Katherine xix, 124
Kirkpatrick, Matthew D. 142
Kisel, Theodore 139
Kittel, Gerhard 198
Knowles, Stephen 324
Kohl, Margaret 325
Koons, Robert 183
Kraay, Klaas J. 22
Krauss, Reinhard 231, 232
Kripke, Saul 183, 300
Kroll, Jerome 297
Kuhn, Thomas 299
Kurzweil, Ray 267, 279
Kvaale, Erlend 299
Kvanvig, Jonathan L. 21, 157, 159, 162, 163, 164, 169, 170, 171

Laing, R.D. 296
Lambert, Heath 295, 296, 297
Lane, Christopher 301
Lang, Peter 216, 280
LaPorte, Joseph 183
Lavere, George J. 141
Le Poidevin, Robin 21
Legge, Dominic 109, 110, 121
Leidenhag, Joanna xxii, 303
Levering, Matthew 330, 341
Levi 178
Lewis, C.S. 153, 156, 276, 279, 280, 324
Lewtas, Pat 323
Lilienfeld, Scott 299
Lim, Daniel 183

Lincoln, Abraham 8, 9
Locke, John 252, 253, 254, 256, 258, 260, 261
Loke, Andrew xx, 175, 182, 183, 184
Lombard, Peter 66, 71
Lonergan, Bernard 112, 113, 122
Lossky, Vladimir 303
Lottin, Dom 58, 66
Lotze, Rudolf 306
Louth, Andrew 323, 324
Loux, Michael J. 19, 20, 22
Lowe, E.J. 22
Lucas, J.R. 22
Lukens, Nancy 231
Luscombe, D.E. 66
Luther, Martin 103, 121, 151, 243

Macchia, Frank 319, 325
Madueme, Hans xxii, 281, 301
Majid, Shahn 21
Malony, H.N. 155
Mangabeira Unger, Roberto 21
Manley, David 139
Manley Hopkins, Gerard 37
Manson, William 145
Mantzaridis, G.I. 324
Marenbon, John 64, 65
Marmadoro, Anna 100
Marshall, Christopher D. 52
Martin, Mike 301
Marx, Karl 166
Mathews, Freya 310, 323
Mawson, T.J. 9, 21
Max, D.T. 279
Maximus 216, 217, 343
May, James M. 141
May, Theresa 8
Mays, John Bentley 217
McBrayer, Justin P. 37
McCall, Thomas H. 80
McCord Adams, Marilyn 22, 328, 341
McCormack, Bruce L. 89, 90, 99, 100, 216
McDaniel, Brannon 140
McDaniel, Jay B. 318, 325
McDaniel, Kris 125, 137, 139, 141
McDonald, Suzanne 329
McHenry, Leemon B. 322
McInerny, Ralph 323
McKim, Robert 25, 36, 37
McKirland, Christa 100, 101
McMinn, Mark 300
McWilliam, Joanne 136, 141

Meconi, David Vincent 134, 135, 141
Meister, Chad 301
Melissus 124, 125
Merricks, Trenton 4, 20, 21
Micale, Mark 296
Middleton, J. Richard 342
Migne, J.P. 123
Milgrom, Jacob 53
Milton, John 44, 52
Moltmann, Jürgen 325
Montmarquet, James A. 159, 161, 169, 170
Monton, Bradley 21
Moo, Douglas 199, 200, 324
Morales, Isaac Augustine 326, 340, 341
More, Max 266, 268, 279
More, Natasha Vita 279
Moreland, J.P. 37, 184, 311, 323
Moroney, Stephen 298
Moroney, Stephen K. 39, 298
Morris, Leon 51
Morris, Thomas V. 25, 36, 92, 100
Moser, Paul K. 25, 36, 37, 39, 170
Moses 32, 33, 34, 46, 130, 190, 191
Mosser, Carl xxii, 87, 88, 91, 100, 101, 265, 278, 323, 324
Mossma, Kenneth L. 279
Mostert, Christaan 319, 325
Muller, Richard A 198
Mullins, Ryan T. xvii, 3, 22, 23, 94, 95, 96, 101, 323
Murphy, Gannon 99
Murphy, Jeffrie G. 41, 51
Murphy, Nancey 21, 155
Murray, C.D. 240, 244
Murray, David 281, 302
Murray, John 199
Myers, Ben 80

Nagasawa, Yujin 310, 322, 323
Nagel, Thomas 303, 305, 307, 308, 310, 321, 322
Neaman, Judith 296
Nebridius 126
Nelkin, Dana K. 38
Nero 14
Neugebauer, Richard 297
Nicole, Roger R. 216
Noah 218
Nozick, Robert 51

Odo of Tournai 179, 183
Olson, Eric T. 21

Olson, Roger E. 99
Origen 148
Oswald, Hilton 121
Ovey, Michael 80
Owen, John 326, 341, 343
O'Collins, G. 183

Packer, J.I. 51, 165, 171
Pajon, Claude 260
Palamas 123
Pannenberg, Wolfhart 21, 113, 156
Pappas, George S. 37
Parfit, Derek 22
Parmenides 124, 125, 136
Parsons, Michael 279
Pasnau, Robert 21
Passmore, John 265, 278
Paul, the Apostle 15, 16, 17, 27, 44, 45, 46, 51, 52, 56, 65, 105, 145, 146, 147, 151, 152, 165, 186, 187, 188, 189, 190, 191, 192, 193, 195, 196, 197, 199, 200, 206, 242, 243, 245, 274, 280, 325
Peels, Rik 36, 39
Pelikan, Jaroslav 197
Penrose, Roger 21
Perszyk, Ken 100, 183
Peter 91, 147, 179, 181
Peters, Ted 156
Peterson, Michael 171
Peter the Venerable 58
Philipps, Richard D. 80
Philo 52
Pickard, Stephen 154
Piper, John 296
Placher, William C. 155
Plantinga, Alvin 34, 39, 161, 171, 298
Plantinga, Cornelius 298
Plantinga Pauw, Amy 342
Plato 125, 139, 312
Plotinus 127, 139
Plummer, Keith 301
Polanyi, Michael 155
Polkinghorne, John 21, 324
Pope Innocent II 58
Pope Innocent III 235
Popper, Karl 305, 321
Porphyry 127
Porter, Joy 296
Powlison, David 295
Pratt, Laura 295
Preece, Gordon 154
Pritchard, Duncan 170

INDEX OF NAMES

Pugh, Ben 143, 154
Putnam, Hilary 300

Radcliff, Alexandra S. 216
Rae, Murray 303, 321
Rahner, Karl 111, 113, 114, 121, 122
Rai, Scott B. 184
Ramsey, Boniface 140
Ramsey, Paul 100
Ray, David 324
Rea, Michael 9, 20, 21, 26, 37
Reeves, William 295, 301
Reichenbach, Bruce 171
Resnick, Irven M. 183
Reta, José Ortez 141
Rickless, Samuel C. 37, 38
Robert of Melvin 109
Roberts, A. 184
Roberts, John Russell 29, 31, 37, 38
Roberts, Robert C. 159, 162, 170
Roberts, T.A. 155
Robson, Mark Ian Thomas 22
Rogers, Katherin A. 9, 21, 22
Rosenberg, Gregg 322
Rotelle, John E. 140
Rudavsky, Tamar 66
Rumscheidt, Martin 232
Runggaldier, Edmund 21
Russell, Robert John 21, 22
Russell, Robert P. 140
Rutledge, Jonathan xviii, 40
Ryan, Peter F. 343

Sach, Andrew 80
Sadler, John 299
Sandberg, Anders 266, 268, 270
Sanders, Fred 80, 154
Satan 206, 229
Schaffer, Jonathan 322
Schaff, Philip 139
Scheeben, Matthias Joseph 121
Schellenberg, J.L. 25, 30, 34, 36, 38
Schillebeeckx, Edward xix, xxi, 111, 112, 113, 114, 115, 116, 120, 122, 233, 234, 235, 236, 239, 244
Schleiermacher, Friedrich 114, 122
Schmemann, Alexander 270, 280
Schreiner, Thomas R. 51, 199, 200
Schrenk, Gottlob 198, 199
Scott, Stuart 206
Scroggs, Robin 199

Scrutton, Anastasia Phillipa 296
Seager, William 308
Shani, Italy 310, 323
Shedd, William G.T. 80
Sherrington, Sir Charles Scott 307
Shields, George W. 322
Shults, F. Leron 155
Sider, Theodore 20, 21
Simon of Tournai 58
Simpson, Amy 296
Skrbina, David 321
Slater, Peter 141
Smart, J.J.C. 20, 21, 51
Smeaton, George 104, 121
Smith, J.K.A. 139
Smith, John E. 259
Smolin, Lee 21
Smythe, Shannon Nicole 217
Snowdon, Paul F. 20
Socrates 180
Solle, Dorothee 216
Sorabji, Richard 22
Sosa, Ernest 158, 159, 169, 170
Sosna, Morton 300
Southgate, Christopher 325
Spiegel, James 39
Sprigge, Timothy 305, 306, 321, 323
Spurgeon, Charles 282
Stanghellini, Giovanni 299
Staniloae, Dumitru 123
Stanton, Jones 297
Stefan, Matthias 20
Steinhart, Eric 12, 22
Stephen 273
Stevenson, Daryl 297
Stewart, Melville Y. 23
Stothert, Richard 139
Stott, Douglas W. 232
Stott, John R.W. 52
Strawson, Galen 303, 306, 308, 310, 321, 322
Strine, Tara 295
Strobel, Kyle C. 99, 101, 215, 341, 342
Studebaker, Steven M. 144, 153, 154, 156
Stump, Eleonore 25, 36, 37, 90, 100
Stump, James 301
Sullivan, Jacqueline 300
Sutherland, S.R. 155
Swarley, W.M. 52
Swenson, Philip 37

INDEX OF NAMES

Swinburne, Richard 20, 21, 22, 179, 180, 183, 184
Szasz, Thomas 296

Taber, Tyler xviii, 24, 36, 37
Taliaferro, Charles 21, 297, 311, 323
Tanner, Kathryn xix, 23, 70, 80, 114, 115, 116, 117, 118, 120, 122, 152, 153, 155, 156
Tanner, Norman 244
Tapp, Christian 21
Taylor, Andrew 21, 23
Taylor, Charles 211, 217
Tredennick, Hugh 139
Tekin, Serife 300
Tertullian 136, 184
Thales of Miletus 303
Thiselton, Anthony 198
Thomson, G.T. 79
Thornton, Tim 299
Timpe, Kevin 22
Tompkins, Peter 321
Torrance, Alan 301
Torrance, David W. 99, 198, 199, 200
Torrance, Ian 23
Torrance, J.B. 216
Torrance, Thomas F. 99, 145, 147, 148, 149, 150, 151, 152, 155, 156, 198, 199, 200, 216
Torrey, E. Fuller 296
Treier, Daniel J. 171
Trickett, Greg xviii, 24
Tsou, Jonathan 300
Turner, J.T. 101
Turner, Jason 141

Ursinus, Zacharias 198

Vacek, Heather 296
Van den Brink, Gijsbert 39
Van der Kooi, Cornelis 143, 154
Van Inwagen, Peter 20, 21, 37
VanDrunen, David 197, 200
Vidu, Adonis xix, 71, 72, 73, 74, 80, 102, 121
Vlachos, Christ 198
Von Leibniz, Wilhelm Gottfried 303, 309, 322, 324
Von Soosten, Joachim 231
Vos, Geerhardus 195, 200
Vriend, John 79, 301

Wahlberg, Tobias Hansson 22
Wainwright, William J. 34, 39, 183
Walker, Nigel 51
Walton, Kendall L. 141
Ward, Keith 278
Ware, Timothy Kallistos 86, 99
Wasserman, Ryan 139, 180, 183
Waters, Brent 279, 280
Weaver, Denny J. 52
Webb, Marcia 296
Webster, John 23, 155
Weger, Khai 310, 323
Weingart, Richard E. 66
Welch, Edward 297, 298
Welker, Michael 216
Wellbery, David 300
Wenger, Thomas L 198
Wenham, G.J. 52
Wernicke, Carl 290, 299
Wessling, Jordan 101
West, Charles C 232
Westphal, Merold 165, 166, 171
Wetzel, James 141
Whitehead, A.N. 324
Whittaker, Robert 301
Williams, Bernard 51
Williams, Garry J. 216
Williams, Rowan 132, 140, 141
Williams, Thomas 65
Williamson, Hannah 215
Willis-Watkins, David 216
Wingard, John 301
Winkler, Kenneth 37
Wisse, Jakob 141
Witherington, Ben, III 23
Witsius, Herman 103, 104, 121
Witting, Jeffrey A. 99
Wittung, J.A. 323
Wollebius, Johannes 197
Wong, Jennifer 301
Wood, W. Jay 159, 162, 170
Woznicki, Christopher 101
Wright, Elizabeth 244
Wright, G.N. 37, 38, 39
Wright, N.T. 141, 199, 200, 325, 342
Wundt, M. 140
Wyclif, John 234, 234

Yandell, Keith 22
YHWH 44, 46
Young, Frances 139, 216

INDEX OF NAMES

Zachar, Peter 299
Zadler, John 299
Zagzebski, Linda Trainkaus 38, 158, 159, 160, 161, 164, 169, 170
Zalta, Edward N. 38, 65, 182, 183, 184
Zimmerman, Dean W. 19, 20, 21, 23
Zimmerman, Michael E. 279
Zum Brunn, Emilie 129, 130, 133, 138, 140, 142
Zwingli, Ulrich 64

Index of Subjects

Absence 138, 140, 234, 240, 241, 244, 278, 289, 298
Action xvi, 41, 43, 44, 50, 54, 60, 68, 92, 98, 104, 108, 109, 110, 111, 113, 117, 119, 120, 121, 123, 132, 133, 138, 158, 166, 167, 175, 176, 179, 204, 210, 212, 227, 228, 238, 250, 253, 256, 275, 306, 311
Adoption 16, 105, 186, 188
Adoptionism, adoptionist 96, 97, 111
Affection 246, 248, 251, 252, 253, 254, 255, 256, 257, 258, 259, 260, 261, 313, 314, 342
Agency xvi, xxii, 100, 104, 113, 151, 215, 275, 282, 288, 292, 294, 295, 301, 307, 313
Anhypostatic 95
Antecedent/constitutive condition vs. consequent condition 111, 112, 113, 120
Anthropology, anthropological xv, xvi, 9, 59, 125, 126, 144, 147, 148, 149, 150, 155, 163, 165, 183, 201, 202, 206, 208, 252, 258, 284, 285, 297, 323
Ascension xix, 102, 103, 105, 108, 110, 111, 112, 113, 114, 115, 118, 119
Aseity 113
Assumption of human nature 85, 92, 93, 94, 95, 96, 97, 98, 101, 135, 152
Atonement xviii, xx, xxi, 9, 10, 40, 47, 68, 69, 70, 71, 72, 73, 74, 75, 76, 77, 78, 79, 80, 99, 104, 121, 134, 135, 138, 175, 177, 201, 203, 204, 208, 209, 215, 216, 217, 234, 312, 313, 314
 At. Model vs. At. Theory 69
Attribute, attributes 87, 95, 106, 313, 315, 338
 Communicable At. 87
Autonomy 212, 213, 214, 215, 259, 300
Aversio 133, 135

Baptism 56, 62, 63, 116, 117, 118, 122, 154, 185, 229, 230, 249
Beatific Vision xxii, xxiii, 13, 18, 19, 93, 326, 327, 328, 329, 330, 331, 332, 333, 334, 335, 336, 337, 338, 339, 340, 342, 343
Being xix, 33, 93, 124, 125, 126, 127, 128, 129, 130, 131, 132, 133, 134, 135, 136, 137, 138, 139, 180, 181, 184, 202, 203, 204, 205, 207, 209, 211, 212, 214, 216, 219, 221, 222, 224, 228, 232, 243, 250, 267, 321, 324, 328, 329, 331, 341
Belgic Confession 185, 197
Belief 3, 23, 36, 37, 39, 56, 63, 65, 155, 157, 158, 163, 166, 168, 169, 170, 171, 229, 235, 238, 244, 277, 284, 298, 299, 301, 312
 Based Be. 160, 161
 Basic Be. 161, 167, 313
Beneficence 149, 152, 153
Berkeleyan Idealism BI 24, 25, 27, 28, 30, 32, 33, 34, 35, 37, 38
Bible 32, 134, 164, 169, 256, 283, 284, 285, 287, 330
Biblical Studies xiii, 87, 89, 169
Body xvi, xx, xxi, xxii, xxiii, 5, 10, 17, 18, 91, 94, 123, 131, 132, 136, 141, 148, 149, 151, 178, 180, 184, 191, 192, 193, 195, 209, 223, 225, 226, 229, 230, 233, 234, 235, 236, 238, 239, 240, 241, 242, 243, 244, 245, 250, 253, 254, 263, 270, 272, 274, 285, 287, 297, 303, 317, 324, 326, 327, 328, 329, 331, 332, 333, 334, 335, 336, 337, 338, 339, 340, 341, 342, 343
 Bo. of Christ 17, 18, 141, 151, 191, 225, 230, 234, 235, 236, 238, 239, 240, 241, 242, 243, 245, 331, 336

INDEX OF SUBJECTS

Canon, canonical 144, 145, 146, 235, 273, 275, 280
Cartesianism, Cartesian xx, 162, 163, 183, 323
Catholic xiv, xix, xxi, 104, 111, 185, 218, 231, 233, 234, 235, 236, 241, 244, 247, 249, 303, 341
Causality xvi, 109, 121, 140, 194
Chalcedon, Chalcedonian 105, 113, 114
Character 191, 196, 200, 211, 227, 230, 254, 259, 310
Christo-ecclesiology xxi, 218, 219
Christology, christological 88, 92, 96, 97, 100, 102, 104, 105, 111, 112, 113, 114, 117, 118, 130, 134, 144, 148, 150, 153, 180, 181, 183, 184, 187, 208, 211, 213, 216, 219, 224, 227, 228, 230, 329, 335, 336
  Ch. from below 117
  Krypsis Ch. 88, 100
  Spirit Ch. 117
  Substance Ch. 111
Christus Victor 10, 70, 80
Church xxi, 17, 19, 48, 71, 86, 91, 120, 136, 143, 144, 146, 150, 151, 168, 169, 177, 201, 205, 216, 217, 218, 219, 220, 221, 223, 224, 225, 226, 227, 228, 230, 231, 233, 235, 243, 245, 246, 260, 281, 282, 287, 296, 298, 325, 342
Command 49, 57, 60
  Divine Co. 60
Communicatio idiomatum, communication of attributes 94, 95
Community 220, 221, 222, 223, 224, 225, 226, 227, 228, 229, 230, 237, 238, 239, 242, 340
Concupiscence 59, 62, 63, 67, 131
Condemnation 189, 191, 192, 206
Consciousness xxii, 10, 30, 111, 114, 221, 223, 258, 303, 305, 306, 307, 308, 309, 310, 311, 312, 314, 315, 319, 320, 321, 322, 323, 325
Consequence xviii, 19, 29, 43, 51, 61, 70, 72, 74, 75, 90, 97, 135, 191, 205, 259, 297, 316, 343
Constance, Council of 235
Consummation 185, 192, 340
Conversio 133, 134, 135, 136, 137, 138
Corruption xx, 16, 34, 94, 133, 178, 182, 248, 265, 271, 277, 301, 328
Counseling 257, 282, 295, 296, 297, 300
Covenant 44, 46, 47, 76, 77, 116, 152, 200, 203, 204, 205

Creation 176, 202, 203, 208, 209, 210, 215, 243, 250, 259, 273, 275, 276, 297, 307, 312, 315, 316, 37, 318, 319, 320, 321, 324, 325, 334, 335, 340, 342
  New Creation 14, 15, 16, 18, 19, 41, 77, 243, 250, 321, 334, 335, 340
Creationism xx, 177, 178, 182
Creator 87, 88, 131, 132, 136, 141, 147, 149, 153, 202, 213, 214, 259, 319, 321, 332, 335, 339
Creator/Creature distinction xix, 88, 89, 259, 332, 335, 339
Creature xv, xix, 60, 61, 66, 86, 87, 88, 89, 90, 91, 92, 98, 105, 106, 107, 117, 128, 129, 133, 135, 136, 141, 148, 149, 150, 151, 155, 164, 176, 202, 204, 213, 214, 248, 249, 250, 251, 258, 259, 311, 313, 314, 315, 316, 318, 319, 320, 323, 325, 332, 335, 339
Culture 211, 213, 215, 244, 251, 266, 298, 301

Death 183, 187, 189, 190, 191, 192, 193, 201, 205, 207, 208, 209, 212, 216, 219, 228, 230, 265, 266, 271, 272, 277, 278, 280, 296, 312, 314, 315, 317, 318, 319, 331, 338, 341
  De. of Christ 17, 46, 47, 51, 70, 71, 72, 73, 74, 75, 76, 77, 190, 209, 228
Debt 55, 57, 58, 61, 62, 63, 64, 66, 71, 72, 73, 74, 75, 76, 77, 78, 140, 153, 275
Defence 21, 22, 26, 27, 30, 37, 44, 54, 63, 165, 205, 289, 297, 299, 301, 307, 311
Degrees xix, 124, 125, 132, 133, 135, 137, 138, 196, 212, 219, 255, 275, 293, 303, 305, 324
Deification xxii, 85, 86, 113, 114, 115, 116, 119, 141, 156, 216, 265, 269, 272, 278, 312, 315, 323, 324
Determining condition xxi, 185
Dichotomy, dichotomous 148
Dikaiosune 44, 193, 200
Discipleship 219, 229, 231, 232
Divine Language Argument DLA 27, 29, 30
Divinization xix, 85, 86, 156
Docetism 111
Dogmatics xv, xvii, 68, 71, 102, 105, 109, 116, 143, 145, 146, 197, 200, 201, 205, 216, 301

354

INDEX OF SUBJECTS

Dominican xix, 121, 197, 217, 233, 323
Dort, Synod of 175, 177, 182
Doxastic control, voluntreerism, etc. 157, 160, 161, 167, 168
Dualism, duality, dualist xx, xxii, 9, 12, 21, 128, 129, 132, 138, 144, 148, 149, 177, 178, 183, 184, 297, 304, 306, 307, 308, 323

Ecclesiology xxi, 218, 219, 220, 228, 230
Economy, economic 72, 77, 107, 115, 130, 136, 144
Efficacy xviii, 68, 69, 71, 73, 75, 77, 78, 79
Efficiency 69, 71, 73, 77, 79, 109
Election, elect 75, 76, 77, 79, 177, 186, 188, 202, 208, 213, 214, 217, 225, 325
Embodiment xxii, 21, 273, 326, 328, 331, 332, 334, 335, 337, 339, 342
Emergentism 304, 323
End, telos xxii, 94, 135, 150, 151, 162, 191, 210, 265, 271, 277, 278, 326, 327, 338, 339, 340, 343
Endurantism 4, 5, 10, 11, 14, 16, 19, 20
Energies 100, 113, 315
  Divine En. 100, 315
Enhypostatic 95, 96
Enlightenment 194
Epistemology xx, 51, 157, 158, 160, 162, 163, 164, 165, 166, 167, 168, 169, 170, 171, 313
Eschaton, eschatology, eschatological xvi, xvii, xxiii, 3, 9, 10, 11, 12, 15, 16, 17, 18, 19, 22, 40, 85, 86, 89, 93, 94, 95, 96, 97, 98, 100, 144, 147, 149, 152, 186, 189, 192, 193, 196, 221, 265, 269, 274, 275, 276, 277, 279, 280, 312, 316, 325, 326, 327, 328, 329, 330, 332, 333, 335, 336, 337, 338, 339, 340
Essence 86, 87, 89, 119, 129, 130, 148, 175, 180, 181, 183, 225, 227, 247, 251, 326, 328, 329, 330, 331, 332, 336, 337, 338, 339, 342
  Divine Es. 86, 89, 100, 175, 251, 327, 328, 329, 342
Eternalism, eternalist xviii, 3, 4, 5, 8, 9, 11, 12, 13, 14, 15, 16, 17, 18, 19, 20
Ethics xx, 145, 151, 166, 167, 168, 184, 217, 227, 231, 232, 247
Eucharist xxi, 17, 141, 233, 234, 235, 236, 237, 238, 239, 240, 241, 242, 243, 244, 245
Eutychianism 113

Evil xvii, xviii, 3, 9, 10, 11, 12, 13, 14, 15, 16, 19, 24, 25, 26, 27, 35, 41, 44, 45, 50, 60, 66, 67, 127, 128, 129, 131, 176, 183, 198, 206, 271, 272, 278, 294, 298, 312, 314, 319, 325
Ex nihilo 125, 149, 275

Faith xv, 25, 34, 35, 38, 44, 45, 47, 57, 66, 67, 74, 76, 77, 80, 81, 107, 119, 122, 134, 138, 145, 147, 151, 164, 167, 168, 172, 185, 186, 188, 190, 191, 193, 194, 195, 196, 197, 200, 212, 214, 215, 218, 224, 226, 229, 230, 231, 247, 279, 281, 282, 283, 293, 296, 298, 323, 332, 339
Fall 70, 80, 86, 88, 90, 98, 104, 111, 112, 126, 129, 130, 131, 133, 135, 137, 165, 186, 223, 225, 227, 267, 271, 285, 287, 293, 301, 343
Fallenness 112, 128, 221
Federalism 187
Figural reading 144
Filiation 106, 108, 120
Filioque 103, 120
Foreknowledge 182
Forensic 48, 119, 185, 187, 190, 191, 193, 199, 217, 242
Forgiveness 18, 40, 51, 57, 63, 81, 114, 119, 153, 187, 190, 314
Foundationalism xx, 160, 161, 166
  Weak Found. xx, 160, 161
Four-dimensional eternalism 3, 8, 9, 11, 12, 13, 14, 15, 16, 17, 18, 19
Four-dimensionalism 3, 4, 5, 6, 8, 11, 12, 14, 19, 20, 23
Fourth Lateran Council 235
Freedom xvi, xx, 16, 148, 175, 176, 177, 179, 182, 190, 191, 192, 204, 213, 214, 215, 235, 253, 258, 260, 276, 283, 298, 316
Free Will 26, 57, 58, 65, 127, 128, 132, 133, 175, 177, 182, 183, 313
Functionalism 157, 169, 306

Gallican Confession 185
Gentile, Gentiles 44, 45, 46
Gift 47, 64, 77, 103, 104, 106, 107, 110, 112, 119, 132, 144, 152, 153, 250, 251, 252, 256, 327, 342
Glorification xv, 94, 113, 114, 118, 186
Glory 16, 17, 34, 43, 44, 45, 77, 103, 118, 146, 150, 151, 153, 210, 216, 249, 272, 273, 276, 278, 280, 316, 330, 331, 334, 335, 341

355

INDEX OF SUBJECTS

Gnostic xiii, 128
Grace 34, 47, 60, 61, 67, 81, 89, 99, 103, 104, 109, 110, 117, 118, 120, 129, 138, 141, 144, 146, 149, 150, 152, 153, 164, 176, 177, 182, 183, 185, 188, 192, 195, 197, 202, 203, 213, 229, 248, 250, 251, 252, 255, 259, 266, 278, 281, 284, 286, 289, 293, 295, 297, 313, 322, 324
Guilt xvi, xviii, 42, 54, 55, 57, 58, 59, 63, 64, 65, 66, 67, 167, 192, 206, 209, 212, 301
  Original Gu. 54, 55, 58, 59, 63, 64, 301

Habit *habitus*, habituation 133, 135, 138, 162, 247, 248, 249, 250, 251, 258
Haecceity 183
Harmatiology, hamartiological 58, 59, 129, 157, 288
Healing xvii, 3, 10, 11, 12, 13, 14, 15, 18, 23, 152, 168, 265, 277, 295, 313
Hell 16, 18, 19, 60, 61, 62, 63, 66, 67, 216
Heresy 235, 265, 270
Hermeneutic 137, 144, 145, 146, 154, 155, 171
Hiddenness xviii, 24, 25, 26, 30, 31, 34, 36
Holiness xx, 187, 196, 199, 217, 224, 272, 281
Holy Spirit see "Spirit"
Honour 43, 44, 72, 73, 74, 75, 76, 77, 78
Hope 211, 256, 278, 279, 282, 294, 296, 306, 311, 316, 318, 319, 324, 342
Humankind 202, 203, 210
Humean supervenience 5
Humility 134, 135, 159, 160, 162
Hylomorphic Theory 175, 178, 179, 180, 181, 182, 183, 184, 285
Hylomorphism, hylomorphic xx, 9, 175, 178, 179, 180, 181, 182, 183, 184, 285, 324
Hypertime 22
Hypostasis 113
Hypostatic union xix, 88, 98, 104, 113, 114, 122, 145, 332

Idealism, idealist, idealistic xviii, xxii, 24, 25, 27, 28, 29, 30, 32, 33, 35, 37, 38, 162, 163, 164, 306, 320, 323
Identity 178, 181, 201, 202, 208, 209, 211, 213, 215, 217, 224, 226, 240, 244, 253, 279, 323, 323, 338, 339, 340
  Id. Through Time 3, 10, 12
Ignorance 164, 247, 248

Illness 209, 229, 281, 282, 283, 284, 285, 286, 287, 289, 290, 291, 292, 293, 294, 295, 296, 297, 298, 299, 300, 301
Imago Dei, image of God xx, 88, 100, 146, 149, 151, 163, 164, 165, 167, 168, 171, 213, 221, 271, 273, 276, 277, 278, 284, 340
Imitatio Christi 151, 227
Immanent causal relation 7
Immaterialism, immaterial 10, 12, 27, 131, 132, 171, 178, 179, 180, 181, 183, 184, 285
Immensity, immense 106, 117
Immortality 265, 266, 267, 272, 278, 325
Immutability 107, 127
Imputation 48, 75, 187, 193, 195
Incarnation 48, 70, 74, 76, 80, 90, 93, 95, 96, 97, 98, 100, 101, 110, 111, 112, 115, 144, 150, 153, 154, 178, 180, 181, 183, 227, 228, 238, 280, 312, 336
  In. as Atonement Theory 70
Individualism 212, 215, 300
Infant, infants 54, 55, 56, 57, 58, 59, 60, 61, 62, 63, 64, 66, 67, 271, 331
Interdisciplinary xiii, xiv, xv, xvi, 169, 183, 304
Intertextuality 144

Jew, Jews 27, 44, 45, 178, 183
Judgement xviii, 206, 274, 330
Justice 40, 41, 42, 43, 44, 45, 46, 51, 56, 59, 60, 63, 66, 71, 72, 73, 74, 75, 76, 77, 78, 79, 103, 135, 208, 210, 252
Justification xv, xx, xxi, 42, 51, 70, 75, 81, 134, 138, 158, 160, 163, 164, 165, 167, 168, 176, 185, 186, 187, 188, 189, 190, 191, 192, 193, 194, 195, 196, 197, 198, 199, 200, 217, 231, 234, 239, 242, 243, 244, 312, 313, 314, 319, 325

Kenoticism, kenotic 88, 183
Kingdom xiii, 11, 13, 14, 15, 17, 19, 56, 151, 168, 213, 218, 274, 280, 343
Knowledge xx, 25, 34, 92, 121, 122, 149, 151, 157, 158, 159, 160, 161, 162, 163, 164, 165, 166, 168, 169, 170, 175, 176, 177, 182, 189, 198, 201, 251, 267, 271, 281, 284, 293, 300, 312, 313, 318, 329, 332, 336, 339
  Animal Kn. vs. Reflective Kn. 158, 165, 170

INDEX OF SUBJECTS

Law 43, 49, 50, 56, 60, 65, 70, 72, 74, 75, 76, 77, 80, 105, 127, 188, 189, 190, 191, 192, 193, 196, 197, 198, 200, 208, 212, 213, 218, 256
Lex talionis 42, 48, 49, 50, 53
Liberation 212, 216, 312, 314, 315
Life 187, 189, 192, 193, 195, 201, 202, 204, 209, 210, 212, 213, 214, 215, 216, 219, 220, 223, 227, 228, 230, 231, 247, 248, 249, 250, 256, 257, 258, 260, 261, 266, 267, 271, 272, 277, 279, 281, 282, 285, 293, 294, 297, 298, 313, 315, 320, 327, 328, 330, 338, 341, 342
Lightest Punishment *mitissima poena* 60, 62, 67
Lord's Supper 17, 18, 230, 238
Love 18, 50, 64, 72, 75, 76, 87, 90, 107, 108, 112, 115, 116, 117, 118, 119, 120, 121, 122, 126, 127, 129, 131, 133, 135, 136, 138, 147, 150, 151, 152, 153, 164, 168, 175, 177, 183, 185, 202, 206, 208, 213, 221, 246, 249, 253, 256, 314, 323, 342

Magis esse 129
Manicheanism, Manichean 126, 127, 128, 131, 140
Mechanism 46, 47, 68, 69, 70, 71, 72, 73, 74, 75, 76, 78, 181
Mental disorders xxii, 281, 282, 284, 285, 286, 287, 288, 289, 290, 291, 292, 293, 294, 295, 296, 297, 298, 299, 300, 301
Mental illness maximizers xxii, 281, 282, 284, 286, 294, 295
Mercy 45, 46, 50, 52, 55, 56, 61, 62, 74, 130, 134, 271, 272, 278
Merit 42, 57, 63, 65, 72, 74, 75, 76, 77, 79, 81, 103, 109, 110, 111, 119, 127, 137, 153, 215, 265
Metaphor 136, 137, 138, 141, 145, 225
Metaphysical universalism 5, 7
Metaphysics, metaphysical xvii, xviii, 4, 5, 6, 7, 9, 24, 27, 48, 58, 86, 87, 90, 91, 93, 94, 95, 96, 98, 99, 100, 124, 125, 126, 130, 133, 134, 136, 137, 138, 182, 233, 234, 235, 239, 244, 272, 287, 289, 290, 300, 302, 306, 307, 311, 322, 323, 341
Methodology, methodological xvi, 26, 124, 136, 286, 287, 298, 323
Middle Knowledge xx, 175, 176, 177, 182

Mind xviii, xxii, 10, 11, 24, 27, 28, 29, 30, 31, 32, 33, 34, 42, 92, 98, 127, 136, 146, 163, 164, 167, 168, 169, 249, 253, 254, 255, 263, 268, 270, 298, 300, 303, 304, 305, 306, 307, 308, 309, 311, 320, 321, 322, 330
  Mi.-Body Relationship xxii, 303
Minus esse 129, 130, 138
Mission, missional xiii, xix, 79, 102, 103, 104, 105, 106, 107, 108, 109, 110, 112, 113, 114, 115, 116, 117, 118, 119, 120, 122, 151, 152, 296, 342
  Divine Mi. xix, 102, 103, 105, 106, 107, 108, 112, 113, 116, 117, 119
Molinism xx, 175, 178, 179, 183
Monism, monist 124, 125, 127, 138, 297, 306, 307, 308, 317, 322
Monophysitism 113
Moral Exemplar 70
Multiple incarnations simpliciter objection 101
Mutability 104

Naturalism 248, 258, 286, 287, 298, 308, 311
Nature vii, xv, xvi, xvii, xx, xxi, xxii, 3, 10, 21, 29, 32, 33, 51, 55, 56, 61, 62, 67, 75, 76, 77, 83, 85, 86, 87, 88, 89, 90, 91, 92, 93, 94, 95, 96, 97, 98, 99, 100, 101, 102, 104, 107, 108, 109, 110, 111, 112, 113, 114, 115, 117, 119, 120, 121, 123, 128, 131, 136, 149, 151, 155, 156, 157, 158, 163, 169, 170, 176, 178, 180, 181, 182, 183, 184, 186, 197, 200, 201, 202, 203, 209, 210, 211, 212, 213, 214, 215, 220, 221, 224, 228, 229, 230, 236, 237, 240, 242, 246, 247, 248, 250, 251, 255, 256, 258, 259, 266, 267, 268, 272, 275, 277, 278, 281, 283, 291, 299, 305, 306, 307, 309, 310, 311, 313, 315, 320, 322, 323, 324, 327, 330, 332, 333, 334, 335, 336, 337, 338, 339, 340, 342
  Christ's Human Na. 88, 90, 93, 94, 95, 96, 97, 98, 104, 109, 111, 113, 114, 118, 120, 135, 332
  Divine nature xix, 76, 85, 86, 87, 88, 91, 93, 97, 98, 99, 108, 118, 163, 170, 180, 183, 251, 315, 323
  Human nature 58, 67, 76, 87, 88, 89, 90, 92, 93, 94, 95, 96, 97, 98, 100, 101, 104, 108, 109, 110, 111, 113,

114, 115, 117, 118, 119, 120, 121, 135
Na./Essence Distinction 87
Nestorianism, Nestorian 97, 111
New Testament 10, 15, 87, 102, 122, 145, 146, 178, 198, 199, 224, 272, 276, 277, 284, 287, 324
Nothingness 124, 125, 128, 129, 130, 131, 140, 208
Numerical identity 7, 12

Obedience xxii, 65, 72, 76, 81, 103, 104, 109, 110, 111, 112, 113, 114, 116, 117, 118, 119, 120, 123, 151, 154, 186, 192, 193, 197, 205, 208, 212, 213, 250
Old Testament 46, 47, 114, 117, 127, 145, 287
Omnipotence, omnipotent 104, 150, 177
Omnipresence, omnipresent 106, 107, 117
Omniscience, omniscient 9
Ontology, ontological xv, xvii, xviii, xix, xxi, 3, 4, 8, 9, 16, 18, 22, 87, 88, 107, 122, 124, 125, 127, 128, 129, 130, 132, 133, 135, 136, 137, 138, 148, 162, 163, 170, 189, 192, 207, 216, 220, 221, 222, 232, 233, 234, 235, 236, 237, 239, 240, 241, 242, 243, 246, 272, 303, 304, 306, 307, 308, 311, 315, 316, 318, 320, 321
Ontological hunger, *wanting-to-be* 130, 131, 132, 133, 135, 137
On. of time 3, 4, 8, 9, 22
Ontological pluralism 124, 125, 136, 137, 138
Social On. xxi, 221, 236, 239, 241
Open theism 9
Operation 31, 104, 117, 118, 122, 198, 207, 249, 254, 256
Ordo salutis xiv, 186, 188, 194, 197, 200

Pain xviii, 16, 48, 113, 253, 256, 314, 324
Panpsychism xiii, xxii, 303, 304, 305, 306, 307, 308, 309, 310, 311, 315, 316, 317, 318, 319, 320, 321, 322, 323, 324, 325
Participation 85, 87, 88, 89, 90, 91, 92, 93, 97, 98, 121, 129, 132, 135, 144, 148, 149, 210, 211, 212, 213, 215, 224, 225, 226, 228, 239, 251, 342
Participatio Christi 151
Pa. in the divine nature xix, 85, 98, 210, 211, 212, 215, 228, 229, 251, 342

Pelagianism, Pelagian 58, 59, 63, 64, 132, 139, 140, 141, 270
Pentecost xix, 102, 103, 108, 111, 112, 114, 115, 116, 119, 120, 144, 153, 154
Perdurantism 20
Perfectibility xxii, 265, 271, 278
Perfection 152, 167, 265, 277, 278, 330, 342
Persistence through time 3, 4, 6, 7, 9, 10, 22
Personal identity xvi, 3, 6, 7, 12, 178, 251
Personhood xxi, 86, 94, 95, 96, 97, 98, 179, 182, 201, 203, 205, 207, 209, 211, 213, 215, 217, 219, 220, 223, 224, 225, 226, 301, 314
Phenomenology, phenomenological 124, 125, 137, 138, 235, 236
Philosophy, philosophical xv, xvi, xvii, xviii, xxi, 3, 8, 9, 10, 11, 19, 24, 40, 41, 42, 51, 58, 73, 93, 126, 127, 140, 148, 157, 169, 182, 194, 235, 257, 258, 278, 283, 284, 202, 209, 210, 211, 217, 232, 244, 251, 266, 279, 299, 300, 303, 306, 308, 311, 319, 320, 321, 323
Analytic Ph. xvii, 24, 87, 169, 233, 236, 303, 308
Ph. of Religion xiii, 24, 183, 244
Physicalism, physicalist xxii, 10, 12, 304, 308, 322
Pneumatology, pneumatological xix, 143, 144, 145, 153, 225, 319
Powers-metaphysics 91, 100
Predestination xx, 175, 177, 179, 181, 182, 183
Pre-existence 177, 178
Presence 11, 25, 33, 34, 55, 102, 103, 106, 107, 111, 116, 117, 120, 137, 138, 146, 148, 149, 187, 188, 192, 195, 200, 216, 217, 225, 226, 227, 233, 234, 235, 236, 238, 239, 241, 244, 289, 319, 332
Presentism, presentist xvii, 4, 5, 8, 9, 10, 11, 13, 14, 15, 16, 19, 20
Priest, priestly, priesthood 120, 149, 152, 153, 217, 235
Problem of divine hiddenness PDH xviii, 24, 25, 26, 27, 28, 30, 31, 32, 34, 35, 36
Problem of evil, general POE 9, 12, 19, 25, 26, 27, 35, 36, 183, 325
Processions xix, 103, 105, 106, 107, 110, 112, 118, 123, 251

358

INDEX OF SUBJECTS

Prolepsis, proleptic 3, 15, 16, 17, 18, 19
Promise 11, 12, 14, 15, 16, 17, 18, 44, 45, 52, 102, 103, 141, 145, 214, 318, 326
Protestant xviii, xix, xxi, 68, 69, 71, 78, 79, 103, 104, 134, 138, 185, 194, 229, 231, 243, 247, 257, 278, 283, 284, 296, 303, 330
Protos xx, 144
Providence 182
Psychiatry 283, 285, 286, 287, 288, 290, 291, 293, 296, 297, 299, 301
Psychology, psychological xxii, 7, 12, 13, 203, 206, 209, 214, 233, 238, 240, 251, 253, 266, 281, 282, 284, 285, 286, 287, 291, 293, 295, 297, 298, 299, 300, 322, 328
Punishment xviii, 40, 41, 42, 43, 46, 47, 48, 49, 50, 51, 55, 56, 57, 58, 60, 61, 62, 63, 65, 66, 67, 71, 72, 73, 74, 75, 76, 133, 205, 208, 283

Realism 187, 291, 299, 301, 307
Redemption 16, 17, 47, 48, 66, 86, 87, 89, 111, 115, 147, 152, 187, 188, 193, 194, 242, 243, 244, 271, 274, 275, 296, 316, 324, 325, 343
Reformation xx, 71, 134, 185, 194, 247, 278
Regeneration xv, xx, xxi, 34, 246, 247, 248, 249, 250, 251, 252, 253, 254, 255, 257, 258, 259, 260, 261, 289, 295
Relativity 8
Religion 183, 198, 218, 224, 244, 252, 256, 257, 278, 279, 283, 296, 298
Religious Diversity 26, 35
Repentance 43, 46, 51, 119, 223, 229
Representation 205, 207, 208, 211, 215, 216, 217, 230, 234, 276
Representative xxi, 30, 73, 75, 76, 186, 189, 201, 205, 206, 207, 208, 212, 215, 217, 227
Responsibility xxii, 71, 157, 169, 175, 204, 212, 220, 227, 259, 274, 292, 294, 298, 313
Restitution 49, 69, 71
Restoration xviii, 11, 41, 42, 46, 76, 78, 103, 259, 313
Resurrection xv, xvii, xxiii, 3, 9, 10, 12, 14, 15, 16, 17, 23, 70, 76, 77, 88, 89, 112, 113, 114, 115, 122, 123, 144, 147, 149, 153, 187, 192, 201, 209, 212, 228, 265, 272, 273, 314, 315, 317, 326, 327, 328, 329, 330, 331, 333, 334, 335, 337, 338, 339, 340, 341, 342
Retribution, retributive xviii, 40, 41, 42, 43, 44, 45, 46, 47, 48, 49, 50, 51, 71, 72, 77, 78
Retributivism xviii, 40, 41, 42, 43, 45, 47, 48, 49, 50, 51
Retrieval xvii, 137, 149
Revelation 214, 220, 221, 224, 225, 226, 227, 228, 230, 251, 252, 273, 276, 284, 286, 297, 312, 313, 316, 324, 329
Reward 11, 14, 65, 103, 104, 108, 109, 110, 118
Righteous, Righteousness xxi, 11, 14, 15, 16, 43, 44, 75, 78, 117, 134, 165, 166, 167, 186, 187, 188, 189, 190, 192, 193, 195, 196, 199, 200, 206, 208, 242, 243, 251, 272, 274, 283

Sacrament, sacraments xxi, 58, 151, 228, 229, 230, 233, 235, 236, 244, 332, 339
Sacrifice 12, 47, 52, 57, 65, 72, 74, 77, 112, 113, 114, 135, 208
Salmurianism 73
Salvation xv, xvi, xvii, xviii, xix, xx, xxi, xxii, 3, 9, 10, 11, 12, 14, 15, 19, 24, 25, 26, 27, 35, 44, 45, 46, 52, 62, 65, 68, 72, 74, 75, 78, 79, 80, 86, 94, 96, 102, 107, 110, 111, 112, 119, 120, 122, 124, 125, 126, 127, 130, 133, 134, 135, 136, 137, 138, 143, 144, 145, 146, 147, 149, 152, 153, 157, 168, 175, 186, 187, 188, 190, 192, 194, 195, 196, 197, 198, 208, 216, 218, 219, 226, 227, 228, 229, 230, 233, 246, 263, 265, 279, 280, 281, 286, 293, 303, 304, 311, 312, 313, 314, 316, 317, 318, 319, 320, 321, 323, 324, 325, 326
Sanctification xv, xx, xxi, xxii, 85, 119, 124, 134, 154, 168, 185, 186, 187, 188, 189, 191, 192, 193, 194, 195, 196, 197, 199, 216, 230
Saint, saints xx, 14, 22, 77, 89, 134, 231, 255, 274, 331, 332, 333, 334, 336, 337, 338
Satisfaction xv, xviii, 10, 68, 69, 71, 72, 73, 74, 75, 76, 78, 80, 81, 126, 127, 135, 186, 189, 193, 199, 234, 240
  Anselmian Sa. xviii, 68, 73, 78
Scholasticism, scholastic xxi, xxii, 246, 247, 249, 251, 253, 258

INDEX OF SUBJECTS

Scripture xx, 32, 33, 40, 41, 42, 43, 47, 51, 56, 60, 65, 70, 75, 78, 79, 127, 144, 145, 146, 147, 148, 152, 154, 164, 189, 195, 197, 198, 217, 255, 256, 258, 276, 282, 283, 284, 285, 286, 287, 293, 294, 296, 297, 298
Second Helvetic Confession 185, 197
Self, selfhood 146, 147, 153
Simplicity 211
Sin xvi, xvii, xviii, xxii, 9, 10, 19, 26, 33, 34, 35, 40, 41, 46, 47, 48, 51, 54, 55, 56, 57, 58, 59, 60, 61, 62, 63, 64, 65, 66, 67, 71, 72, 74, 75, 76, 79, 88, 91, 103, 119, 125, 129, 134, 135, 138, 141, 151, 157, 165, 166, 167, 168, 169, 171, 186, 189, 190, 191, 192, 193, 194, 196, 199, 205, 206, 207, 208, 209, 211, 220, 223, 229, 248, 277, 281, 282, 283, 284, 285, 286, 287, 288, 289, 290, 291, 293, 294, 295, 296, 297, 301, 312, 314, 315, 319, 342
  Noetic Effects of Si. 33, 157, 165, 166, 167, 169, 171, 286
  Original Si. xviii, 9, 54, 55, 56, 57, 58, 59, 61, 62, 63, 64, 65, 66, 67, 103, 178, 182, 183, 285, 293, 301
  Si. Maximizers xxii, 281, 282, 284, 288, 294, 295
Society xxi, 42, 198, 212, 267, 282, 298, 321
Soteriological problem of evil SPE 24, 25, 26, 27, 30, 31, 32, 35, 38, 39
Soteriology, soteriological xiv, xv, xvi, xvii, xviii, xix, xxi, xxii, 10, 12, 24, 25, 31, 35, 36, 71, 75, 77, 79, 102, 103, 119, 124, 125, 129, 132, 135, 136, 137, 138, 144, 147, 148, 149, 150, 153, 168, 186, 187, 194, 197, 218, 219, 226, 230, 241, 242, 303, 304, 311, 312, 316, 319, 320, 321, 324
Soul xvi, xx, 10, 19, 57, 65, 94, 126, 127, 128, 129, 130, 131, 132, 135, 136, 138, 148, 149, 164, 169, 175, 179, 179, 180, 181, 182, 183, 184, 209, 212, 247, 248, 249, 250, 253, 254, 255, 256, 257, 258, 259, 270, 282, 284, 285, 287, 295, 296, 297, 301, 303, 305, 311, 315, 316, 323, 324, 328, 329, 331, 334, 341, 342
Sovereignty 177, 213
Spacetime 4, 5, 8, 13, 149
Spiration 106, 108, 115, 119

Spirit, Holy Spirit xiii, xix, xx, xxi, 3, 11, 15, 16, 85, 89, 90, 91, 92, 98, 102, 103, 104, 105, 106, 107, 108, 109, 110, 111, 112, 113, 114, 115, 116, 117, 118, 119, 120, 121, 122, 123, 143, 144, 145, 146, 148, 149, 150, 151, 152, 153, 154, 186, 189, 191, 192, 193, 196, 197, 200, 215, 217, 222, 223, 224, 225, 226, 228, 229, 236, 241, 245, 246, 247, 248, 249, 250, 251, 253, 254, 255, 256, 257, 259, 260, 261, 273, 278, 280, 281, 282, 285, 289, 304, 312, 314, 319, 321, 325, 329, 330
  Manichean Sp. 128
Stage theory 20
State of ultimate pneumatization 123
Stellvertretung 201, 204, 205, 207, 208, 209, 216, 217, 227
Substance 9, 10, 12, 20, 21, 27, 28, 32, 33, 93, 96, 97, 106, 107, 108, 111, 125, 127, 128, 131, 132, 138, 148, 171, 177, 178, 181, 183, 184, 209, 233, 234, 235, 239, 247, 248, 250, 251, 304, 306
  Divine Su. 106
  Su. Dualism 9, 12, 21, 138, 177, 178, 183, 184, 304, 306
Substitution xxi, 47, 52, 71, 135, 187, 201, 204, 205, 206, 207, 208, 215, 216, 217
  Penal Su. xviii, 10, 40, 51, 65, 68, 69, 71, 72, 73, 74, 75, 76, 78, 79, 80, 187, 207, 208, 217, 234
  Reparative Su. xviii, 68, 69, 71, 75, 76, 77, 78, 79
Suffering xvii, xviii, 10, 11, 13, 14, 15, 16, 19, 23, 25, 26, 47, 48, 52, 57, 59, 79, 120, 121, 193, 205, 216, 217, 286, 287, 289, 292, 296, 297, 312, 314, 318, 319
Sufficiency 68, 69, 71, 73, 74, 77, 210, 282, 284, 285, 286, 296, 297
Suicide 130
Supererogation 74, 75

Technology 266, 267, 268, 269, 270, 277
Teleology, teleological xxi, 51, 164, 167, 202
Telos xx, 144, 147, 149, 150, 210, 265, 271, 277, 278, 326, 327, 338, 339, 340, 343
Theism, theist 19, 25, 26, 34, 35, 167, 172, 259, 269, 311
Theodicy xiii, 26, 44, 45, 318

INDEX OF SUBJECTS

Theology 182, 183, 187, 194, 197, 199, 200, 208, 209, 213, 216, 217, 218, 219, 220, 228, 230, 231, 232, 244, 246, 247, 251, 257, 270, 272, 279, 282, 295, 296, 298, 301, 303, 304, 316, 318, 319, 320, 321, 323, 324, 325, 340, 341, 342, 343
  Analytic Th. 157, 220, 226
  Broken-Trinity Th. 73
  Systematic Th. xiii, xv, xvi, xxi, 40, 54, 89, 200, 216, 232, 325
Theopoeisis 85
Theopoetic transformation, transformative theopoetic journey xx, 144, 149, 150, 153
Theory of Final Assumptions TFA 85, 92, 93, 94, 95, 96, 97, 100
Theosis xiii, xix, 85, 86, 87, 88, 89, 90, 91, 92, 93, 97, 98, 99, 149, 150, 156, 234, 251, 279, 315, 319, 323, 324
Third Article Theology xx, 143, 144, 149
Time xiii, xvii, xviii, 3, 4, 5, 6, 7, 8, 9, 10, 11, 12, 13, 14, 15, 16, 17, 18, 19, 22, 29, 103, 105, 107, 112, 115, 116, 135, 136, 149, 163, 176, 177, 178, 180, 181, 182, 203, 225, 237, 256, 312, 320, 323
Timelessness, timeless 9, 135
Time slices 5, 17, 163
Traducianism xx, 177, 178, 179, 182, 183
Transformation xx, xxii, 86, 98, 115, 118, 119, 120, 135, 137, 141, 149, 188, 192, 211, 266, 272, 276, 312, 313, 314, 316, 317, 319, 324
Transgression 47, 48, 65, 67, 186, 189
Transhumanism xxii, 265, 266, 267, 268, 269, 270, 271, 278, 279, 280
Transignification 233, 234, 236, 237, 238, 240, 241, 242
Trent, Council of 185, 197, 234
Trichotomy, trichotomous 148
Trinity, triune, trinitarian xv, 73, 86, 90, 93, 103, 104, 105, 106, 107, 108, 112, 113, 114, 115, 116, 117, 118, 120, 143, 144, 146, 149, 150, 151, 153, 154, 164, 167, 171, 180, 202, 204, 325, 330, 342
Truth-maker theory 8
Two-minds Christology 92

Union 180, 181, 185, 186, 187, 188, 192, 193, 194, 195, 197, 198, 200, 265, 266, 271, 272, 274, 275, 277, 278, 280, 281, 314, 315, 331, 332, 336
  Instrumental Un. 91, 92, 100, 266, 271, 274, 275

Un. with Christ xv, xx, xxi, 77, 85, 87, 88, 89, 119, 152, 185, 186, 187, 188, 192, 193, 194, 195, 197, 198, 200, 281, 322, 336
Universalism 5, 7, 73

Vicarious 47, 52, 72, 150, 151, 227, 230
Vice 157, 159, 160, 164, 288, 289, 299, 301, 320
  Intellectual Vi. 157, 159, 160
Virtue xx, 11, 15, 135, 136, 138, 157, 158, 159, 160, 161, 162, 163, 164, 165, 166, 167, 168, 169, 170, 172, 175, 176, 180, 183, 187, 222, 243, 276, 278, 301, 315, 317, 318, 321, 332, 336
  Epistemic Vi. 158
  Intellectual Vi. 157, 158, 159, 160, 161, 163, 164, 167, 168, 170, 172
  Vi. Epistemology xx, 157, 158, 160, 162, 165, 166, 168
Visio Dei 265, 266, 268, 271, 273, 277, 278, 326, 327, 328, 330, 332, 333, 334, 335, 336, 337, 339

Weight of Glory 153, 280
Westminster Confession of Faith 200, 218
Westminster Longer Catechism 186, 197
Westminster Shorter Catechism xxi, 185, 197
Will for Happiness *voluntas beatitudinus* 132
Work xiii, xv, xvii, xviii, xx, xxi, 3, 10, 15, 16, 25, 29, 36, 58, 64, 66, 67, 70, 71, 72, 73, 74, 75, 76, 77, 78, 80, 81, 86, 90, 91, 98, 99, 100, 101, 102, 107, 109, 111, 112, 114, 117, 118, 120, 128, 135, 139, 144, 147, 149, 150, 151, 153, 154, 155, 157, 161, 185, 186, 191, 192, 193, 194, 195, 196, 198, 201, 202, 204, 205, 207, 208, 214, 215, 216, 217, 219, 220, 222, 223, 225, 226, 227, 228, 229, 230, 231, 234, 237, 246, 247, 248, 252, 255, 256, 257, 258, 259, 260, 269, 274, 275, 289, 292, 300, 306, 307, 312, 313, 319, 321, 334
  Christ's Wo. xvii, xviii, 15, 72, 73, 76, 77, 78, 98, 135, 147, 186, 191, 193, 194, 195, 196, 198, 201, 202, 207, 214, 217, 219, 226, 227, 228
Wrath 43, 44, 45, 46, 63, 72, 73, 76, 77, 78, 208

www.ingramcontent.com/pod-product-compliance
Lightning Source LLC
Chambersburg PA
CBHW021930290426
44108CB00012B/789